QUEER DICKENS

QUEER DICKENS: EROTICS, FAMILIES, MASCULINITIES

HOLLY FURNEAUX

OXFORD

UNIVERSITY PRESS

OXFORD
UNIVERSITY PRESS

Great Clarendon Street, Oxford OX2 6DP

Oxford University Press is a department of the University of Oxford.
It furthers the University's objective of excellence in research, scholarship,
and education by publishing worldwide in

Oxford New York

Auckland Cape Town Dar es Salaam Hong Kong Karachi
Kuala Lumpur Madrid Melbourne Mexico City Nairobi
New Delhi Shanghai Taipei Toronto

With offices in

Argentina Austria Brazil Chile Czech Republic France Greece
Guatemala Hungary Italy Japan Poland Portugal Singapore
South Korea Switzerland Thailand Turkey Ukraine Vietnam

Oxford is a registered trade mark of Oxford University Press
in the UK and in certain other countries

Published in the United States
by Oxford University Press Inc., New York

British Library Cataloguing in Publication Data

Data available

Library of Congress Cataloging in Publication Data

Data available

Typeset by SPI Publisher Services, Pondicherry, India
Printed in Great Britain
on acid-free paper by the
MPG Books Group, Bodmin and King's Lynn

ISBN 978-0-19-956609-9

1 3 5 7 9 10 8 6 4 2

For Sally Ledger
In loving memory

Contents

Illustrations

All illustrations are reproduced courtesy of the Charles Dickens Museum, London.

Acknowledgements

I am grateful to my families and friends, and for the enabling academic environments that made this book possible. My deepest thankfulness is to Sally Ledger, exceptionally cherishing mentor and friend, who supported and guided this work from the beginning. I also feel particularly grateful to Ben Winyard, who read and commented on various drafts and shared his great wisdom unstintingly.

The staff and student communities at Birkbeck and, later, Leicester, have been wonderfully conducive to this research, and I was fortunate to receive time at Leicester that allowed me to develop and complete the project in the ways I wished to. It has been a privilege to work with students at both institutions, whose thoughtful responses continue to help me to rethink. The community at the Charles Dickens Museum in London also supported my work, and staff there were generous in assisting with the illustrations. Particular thanks are due to Florian Schweizer, curator of the Charles Dickens Museum, for his advice and friendship. My thanks to everyone who discussed these ideas with me at various stages of their gestation, particularly Marie Banfield, David Clark, Harry Cocks, Laura Coffey, Vybarr Cregan-Reid, Gowan Dawson, Eli Dryden, Jenny Hartley, Andrew Mangham, Robert Maidens, Anne Schwan, Michael Slater, and Susan Zieger. Bill Cohen and Mark Turner provided incisive criticism at a particularly formative stage, for which I am most appreciative. Special thanks to Adam Broughton, always 'theguidingstarofmyexistence'.

Various parts of this book have previously been published in other forms, and I am grateful to their editors for permission to reprint.

An early kernel of Chapter 2 was printed in *Wilkie Collins: Interdisciplinary Essays*, ed. Andrew Mangham (Cambridge: Cambridge Scholars Press, 2007), pp. 22–36.

A shorter version of Chapter 3 was published as 'Charles Dickens' Families of Choice: Elective Affinities, Sibling Substitution, and Homoerotic Desire', in *Nineteenth Century Literature*, 62.2 (2007), 153–92. I am thankful to Joe Bristow and the anonymous readers of *NCL* for detailed feedback that was instrumental to the development of this project.

Preliminary ideas for Chapter 5 appeared in 'Dickens and Sex', special issue of *Critical Survey*, co-ed. by Holly Furneaux and Anne Schwan, 17.2 (2005), 34–47.

Introduction
Telling it Straight: Dickens
in a Queer Context

In November 1835 Charles Dickens visited Newgate's condemned cell, coming face to face with James Pratt and John Smith, who were convicted under a sodomy law only fully repealed in England in 1967.[1] Dickens recounted this encounter in a short sketch, 'A Visit to Newgate', which he published in *Sketches by Boz* in 1836: 'In the press-room below were three men, the nature of whose offence rendered it necessary to separate them, even from their companions in guilt.'[2] The third prisoner, a guardsman committed on robbery with menaces, awaited a reprieve with some confidence; the other two men, Pratt and Smith, stood dejectedly at the far end of the room: '[These] two had nothing to expect from the mercy of the crown; their doom was

---

[1] Under a Tudor act of 1533 all acts of sodomy were punishable by death in England until 1861, when sentences were reduced to penal servitude of between ten years and life. The death penalty for sodomy was abandoned in practice after 1835, but convictions continued throughout the period of Dickens's career. H. G. Cocks calculates that in the period 1806–1900 an average of 'eighty-nine committals took place every year. However, in some years, especially during the 1840s, more than one hundred and fifty men were committed.' *Nameless Offences: Homosexual Desire in the Nineteenth Century* (London and New York: Tauris, 2003), p. 25. For further details of the anti-sodomy laws of Dickens's period see H. Montgomery Hyde, *The Other Love: A Historical and Contemporary Survey of Homosexuality in Britain* (London: Mayflower, 1972), pp. 106–9; and Jeffrey Weeks, *Coming Out: Homosexual Politics in Britain from the Nineteenth Century to the Present* (London: Quartet, 1977), pp. 11–14.

[2] Charles Dickens, 'A Visit to Newgate', *Sketches by Boz* (London: Penguin 1995), pp. 234–48, p. 244. Here, and in all further quotations from Dickens's work, the first reference is given in a footnote; thereafter references are given in the text. W. J. Carlton identifies these inmates in 'The Third Man at Newgate', *Review of English Studies* 8 (1957), 402–7.

sealed; no plea could be urged in extenuation of their crime, and they well knew that for them there was no hope in this world. "The two short ones", the turnkey whispered, "were dead men'" (p. 244–5). The turnkey's prediction, as Dickens indicated in a footnote, was dead right. Pratt and Smith became the last men to receive the death penalty for what was legally termed the 'detestable and abominable vice of buggery'; they were hanged in front of the prison on 27 November 1835. As *The Times* reports, every other capital convict of the September and October sessions was reprieved except these two men.[3] *The Times* reportage infers the justness of this treatment by repeatedly invoking the derogatory euphemisms 'abominable offence' and 'unnatural crime' for Smith and Pratt's infringement.[4] A similarly pejorative attitude is expressed by Magistrate Hesney Wedgwood, who described the accused in a private letter as 'degraded creatures'.[5] Despite this rhetoric of aberrance, sex between men in Newgate in the 1830s was, as Sarah Wise has documented, a familiar occurrence.[6] Dickens's account of Pratt and Smith is notably free of the condemnatory language found in other reports of the time, avoiding depreciatory descriptions in favour of the neutral term 'crime'. Indeed Dickens extends to Pratt and Smith the sympathy that at this point in his life he felt particularly strongly for all victims of capital punishment. In the carefully phrased observation that 'for them there was no hope in this world', Dickens even implies the possibility of salvation for sodomites, a controversial public move given the dominant discourse of abomination at this time.

Dickens visited Newgate with the publisher of his sketches, John Macrone, and an American journalist Nathaniel Parker Willis. Willis's account of the day excises Pratt and Smith, recounting one capital convict rather than three: 'We were there an hour or two and were

---

[3] Pratt and Smith were two of 13 people to be executed, not for murder (for which there were a further 21 executions) in England and Wales in 1835. For these statistics see Keith Hollingsworth, *The Newgate Novel: 1830–1847*, (Michigan: Wayne State University Press, 1963), p. 231.

[4] *The Times*, 28 September 1835, 23 November 1835.

[5] Magistrate Hesney Wedgwood to Lord Russell, November 1835, quoted by Cocks, p. 38.

[6] As Sarah Wise puts it: 'if two men were kept in the same cell, the wardens had noted that crimes have been committed of a nature not to be more particularly described', *The Italian Boy: Murder and Grave-Robbery in 1830s London* (London: Jonathan Cape, 2004), p. 215.

shown some of the celebrated murderers confined for life, and one young soldier waiting for execution.'[7] This range of responses to the convicts – censure, silence, and sympathy – demonstrates the divergence of attitudes in the period even towards outlawed sexual acts. As this book shows, the debate around less easily defined relationships and forms of eroticism was even broader, encompassing wide-ranging support for emotional and erotic bonds between men and for ways of being that eschewed marriage and reproduction. Dickens's participation in public debates on the punishment of sodomy (albeit in a fairly inexplicit register, only fully discernable to those who remembered the details of the recent trial), and his compassionate treatment of Pratt and Smith, may seem surprising, especially to those who regard Dickens as an icon of Victorian respectability and of, in particular, so-called Victorian family values. In this book I argue that Dickens's early sympathy with Pratt and Smith was to develop into a career long dedication to the positive representation of same-sex desire and other non-heterosexual life choices. This book contributes to the ongoing revision of conceptions about Dickens and his age (neither so prudish or punitive as we once imagined), arguing that this eminent Victorian can direct us to the ways in which his culture could, and did, comfortably accommodate homo-eroticism and forms of family founded on neither marriage nor blood. Long seen as the foremost proponent of an emotionally freighted brand of Victorian domesticity, the Dickensian domestic can also be seen as influential in its accommodation of surrogate and adoptive parenting, same-sex desire in homo-affirmative families of choice and intimate treatments of the body. There are, as the opening vignette of Pratt and Smith's execution registers, limits to the cultural accommodation of such diversity. This book also scrutinizes those figures and plots that cannot be integrated into the social fabric and register a resistance to that society, looking at, for instance, Dickens's incurable bachelors and emigrations to more permissive exotic and culturally eroticized locales.

Dickens, through his favourite reading, institutional visits, and friendships, was immersed in a distinctly queer historical and literary milieu. Many of the favourite reads that he publicly championed, especially

---

[7] Nathaniel Parker Willis, *Dashes at Life With a Free Pencil*, ephemera section (New York: 1845), quoted in *The Letters of Charles Dickens*, vol. I:1820–1839, Pilgrim Edition, ed. Madeline House and Graham Storey (Oxford: Clarendon Press, 1965), p. 88.

those eighteenth-century picaresques of which he was so openly fond, contain explicit scenes of same-sex erotics. The picaresque tradition also provided a wealth of foundling narratives, which, as I discuss in Chapter 1, Dickens was to build upon as he developed personal and literary interests in non-marital and non-reproductive forms of kinship. In his journalism and correspondence and through the ventriloquized reading habits of David Copperfield, Dickens recounted a personal literary heritage that includes works by Daniel Defoe, who produced the notoriously Sapphic *Roxana* (1724) and the 1701 poem 'The True Born Englishman', which includes explicit reference to sodomy as a foreign vice. Dickens was similarly fond of Tobias Smollett, whose novels *The Adventures of Roderick Random* (1748) and *The Adventures of Peregrine Pickle* (1751) discuss male correspondences 'not fit to be named'.[8] Notably, *Roderick Random*, which imaginatively sustained David Copperfield 'for a month at a stretch', presents one of the most extended, open defences of sodomy in Western literary history.[9] Earl Strutwell's vindication elucidates the advantages to health and other practical benefits, such as reduced bastardy, of such a practice. He triumphantly concludes with an appeal to erotic hedonism: 'I have been told there is another motive perhaps more powerful than all these, that induces people to cultivate this inclination; namely the exquisite pleasure attending its success.'[10] The careful caveat in *David Copperfield* that 'whatever harm was in some of' these tales 'was not there' for the young David (p. 60), demonstrates Dickens's appreciation that his somewhat risqué favourites might not be considered ideal reading material for a child.

Sexual knowledge acquired from a relatively respectable literary tradition was most probably supplemented for Dickens by his reading of libertine

---

[8] Tobias Smollett, *The Adventures of Roderick Random* (Oxford: Oxford University Press, 1979), p. 199. Such suspicion explicitly attaches to the gorgeously attired Captain Whiffle and his surgeon, Mr Simper. In *The Adventures of Peregrine Pickle*, a German Baron and Italian Marquis are chastized for their 'abominable practices'. The hero's 'indignation' fails to mask the jubilance of the portrayal of the desiring count's approaches to the baron, 'whom he viewed with rapture', 'then boldly ravished a kiss and began to tickle him under the ribs, with such expressions of tenderness'. The Baron does not share Peregrine's 'just detestation for all such abominable practices', his enthusiastic response declaring him 'not averse to the addresses of the count' (Oxford: Oxford University Press, 1969), p. 242.
[9] Charles Dickens, *David Copperfield* (London: Penguin, 1996), p. 60.
[10] Smollett, *Roderick Random*, p. 310.

material such as John Cleland's pornographic eighteenth-century classic, *Fanny Hill, or Memoirs of a Woman of Pleasure* (1750). Joss Lutz Marsh makes a convincing case for Dickens's transposition of the central elements of Cleland's novella to tell a parallel story of female desires in *Dombey and Son* (1846–8). Dickens could have obtained this text, which includes graphic same-sex bed scenes featuring both women and men, from friends. As Marsh argues, such texts would have been readily available in Dickens's social circle, which included *Household Words* contributor and freelance pornographer George Augustus Sala and Richard Monckton Milnes, a close friend who was known to be a 'generous' owner of an expanding library of erotic materials.[11] Colette Colligan has argued that Dickens also put news coverage to queer use in his fiction, using his knowledge of recent scandalous prosecutions to express the 'not-so-covert homosexual proclivities' of particular characters, such as Major Bagstock in *Dombey and Son*. She reads the major's army nickname, Flower, as a thinly veiled allusion to an 1833 incident in which an MP, William John Bankes, was found after hours 'in company with a soldier named Flower [...] having been surprised with his breeches and braces unbuttoned at ten at night, his companion's dress being in similar disorder'.[12] Bankes's trial attracted considerable public attention, not least because of the testimony to his good character provided by such well known figures as the Duke of Wellington.[13] Dickens was also a reader of contemporary French fiction, a corpus in which many of the nineteenth century's most overt homoerotic articulations can be found. He read French proficiently, reading Victor Hugo and George Sand, and stocking books by Paul de Kock and Balzac, whom 'he particularly admired', in his library.[14]

---

[11] Joss Lutz Marsh, 'Good Mrs Brown's Connections: Sexuality and Story Telling in Dealings with the Firm of Dombey and Son', *ELH* 58 (1991), 405–26, p. 411. For details of Sala's pornographic writings see Marsh and Matthew Sweet, *Inventing the Victorians* (London: Faber, 2001), pp. 194–5.

[12] Colette Colligan, 'Raising the House Tops: Sexual Surveillance in Charles Dickens's *Dombey and Son* (1846–8)', *Dickens Studies Annual* 29 (2000), 99–123, p. 116.

[13] See Hyde, p. 110 and Neil Bartlett, *Who Was That Man? A Present for Mr Oscar Wilde* (London: Serpent's Tail, 1988), pp. 58–9.

[14] Philip Collins, 'Dickens's Reading', *Dickensian* 60 (1964), 136–51, p. 142. The catalogue of Dickens's final library collection includes entries for Balzac and de Kock. *Catalogue of the Library of Charles Dickens from Gad's Hill*, ed. J. H. Stonehouse (London: 1935).

Dickens had a personal affection for friends whose most intense, perhaps physical, relationships were same-sex. Fred Kaplan has argued for Dickens's appreciation of a spectrum of male intimacy, including the sexual, as enjoyed by some of by some of his friends, such as Chauncey Hare Townsend.[15] Though Dickens was especially immersed in a variety of male homosocial communities, which gave him a particular understanding of the range of relationships between men and the diversity of masculinities, he also appreciated queer women and intense female bonds. He patronized Ada Issacs Menken, who dedicated her somewhat Sapphic book of poetry, *Infelicia* (1868), to him, and made an effort to meet George Sand.[16] Geraldine Jewsbury and Jane Carlyle's friendship was well known to Dickens, who met both women socially through a network of shared friends.[17] Jewsbury expressed her erotic regard for Jane Carlyle in letters that frequently cast one or other of them in the role of male lover: 'I feel to love you more and more every day, and you will laugh, but I feel towards you much more like a lover than a female friend.'[18] Dickens also had some insight to the relationship between Angela Burdett Coutts and Hannah Meredith, Coutts's

[15] Fred Kaplan, *Dickens and Mesmerism: The Hidden Springs of Fiction* (Princeton: Princeton University Press, 1975), p. 198.

[16] The *Dictionary of National Biography* identifies Dickens as one of the men of letters with whom Menken 'contracted intimacies' (*DNB*, 'Ada Isaacs Menken'), and Jeanette Foster analyses the homoerotic content of Menken's *Infelicia in Sex Variant Women in Literature* (London: Frederick Muller, 1958), p. 140; recounting his meeting with Sand, Dickens described her as 'chubby, matronly, swarthy, black-eyed', with 'nothing of the bluestocking about her, though absolutely self-confident in all her opinions' (Kaplan, *Dickens*, Baltimore and London: John Hopkins University Press, 1988, p. 341).

[17] He respected their individual talents: he particularly wanted Jane Carlyle to attend his reading of *The Chimes*, feeling that her judgment 'would be invaluable' (Kaplan, *Dickens*, p. 177). He placed a similar value on Geraldine Jewsbury's writing, as his 1850 letter scouting her for *Household Words* demonstrates. Charles Dickens to Geraldine Jewsbury, February 1850, repr. in *Selections from the Letters of Geraldine Endsor Jewsbury to Jane Welsh Carlyle*, ed. Mrs Alexander Ireland (London: Longmans, 1892), p. 363. They continued to correspond about Geraldine's submissions to the periodical throughout the early 1850s.

[18] Jewsbury to Jane Carlyle, 29 Oct 1841, *Letters*, p. 39. Writing again some months later about her feelings for her new suitor, Jewsbury assures Carlyle that: 'This last year has been the best I ever had [...] I have found you, and now I wonder how I ever lived without you, and it is strange, but you are of infinitely more worth and importance in my eyes than "my new friend." You come nearer to me; I don't feel towards you as if you were a woman' (1 Jan 1842, *Letters*, p. 43).

governess and closest friend and live-in companion throughout her life. He commented, somewhat unsympathetically, on Hannah Meredith's extreme attachment, suggesting that she 'would do anything conceivable or inconceivable to make herself interesting to Miss Coutts'.[19]

Dickens's somewhat sardonic appraisal of this female friendship is at variance with his own enthusiastic pursuits and portrayals of male intimacy. Rosemarie Bodenheimer relates Dickens's own homosocial immersions to his literary interest in male bonds: 'Both his professional and leisure hours were centred on friendships or working relationships with other men. It is not altogether surprising that relationships between men in his fiction are more fully charged with erotic energy and conflict than those between men and women.'[20] This book is predominantly concerned with queer masculinities, tracing the repercussions of, for example, Dickens's particular admiration of figures who exhibited particularly tender and nurturing styles of masculinity such as Captain Thomas Coram, who established the London Foundling Hospital, and Doctor Charles West, who opened the Great Ormond Street Children's Hospital and pioneered English paediatrics.[21] As I'll explore, queer figures such as the bachelor dad and the male nurse recur in Dickens's writings on these personal heroes and in fictional treatments of a range of tender masculinities, some of which were co-authored with his close friend Wilkie Collins. I am interested in the ways in which Dickens's portrayals of nurturing masculinity and his concern with touch and affect between men challenge what we have been used to thinking about Victorian ideals of maleness. At the same time, tender male touching calls into question current understandings of the sexual, suggesting the difficulty of firmly demarcating the erotic.

Chapter 1 examines Dickens's fascination with families bonded neither by blood nor marriage, focusing on bachelor adoptions to discuss some neglected aspects of masculinity, the desire not to reproduce but to nurture. The bachelor continues to be the key figure for

---

[19] Kaplan, *Dickens*, p. 337.

[20] Rosemarie Bodenheimer, *Knowing Dickens* (Ithaca and London: Cornell University Press, 2007), pp. 91–2.

[21] Coram is discussed in Chapter 1. On Dickens's admiration for West see Jules Kosky, *Mutual Friends: Charles Dickens and the Great Ormond Street Children's Hospital* (London: Weidenfeld and Nicholson, 1989).

Chapter 2, which explores the interplay between the repeated celebration of the unmarried male and serial publication, arguing for the queer possibilities of serialization to make a case against the heterosexually friendly shape often attributed to the Victorian novel. In Chapter 3 my attention shifts to the erotic, in an exploration of the homoerotic motives for marriage and attention to Dickens's queer use of contemporary ideas about the parity of sibling bodies. Chapter 4 offers a detailed look at the limitations to the domestic accommodation of queer desires, investigating the homoerotic possibilities of overseas locales. Dickens's gentle men are the heroes of Chapters 5 and 6, which explore the erotic context for understanding his repeated depictions of male nursing, and look beyond the sexual to the wider implications of the celebration of restorative male touch.

This book endeavours to chart a two-directional literary genealogy, through which Dickens gained his understanding of, and access to, methods of representation of queer desire and adapted these, often compulsively and repeatedly, across his work to develop influential modes of queer expression. I suggest that Dickens made use of both the explicitly sexual materials discussed here and of less overt explorations of queer intimacy presented by some of his favourite authors including Edward Bulwer Lytton and Alfred Tennyson. As I will argue, the serialization of Dickens's novels, Dickens's own control (as periodical editor) over juxtapositions of material, and his careful management of his relationship with regular readers and encouragement of particular modes of reading, were all important aspects in the early reception of Dickens's fiction and journalism. These aspects disrupted the traditional marital trajectory attributed to the Victorian novel, allowing Dickens's regular readers to develop a competence in queer interpretation. Such readers, whose queer debt to Dickens is demonstrable, included Thomas Hughes and Mary Elizabeth Braddon, Walt Whitman, and many of the writers who first attempted to treat homosexuality with candour, such as Edward Clarke and E. M. Forster. In a final brief postscript dedicated to the aftertexts of recent film and television versions of Dickens's work I explore the ways in which Dickens's queer legacy is variously extended, revised and disavowed.

This book claims a central position for Dickens in queer literary history. This would not have surprised early twentieth-century homosexual novelist and theorist Edward Prime-Stevenson. In 1908, Prime-Stevenson, alias

Xavier Mayne, included Dickens's fiction within his survey of 'The Uranian in Belles-Lettres':

There is some interest in noticing how frequently certain British novelists have made 'passional friendship' a vehement factor in their stories, even to its being the most vital trait of a book. Thus Dickens, in a series of his stories and their characters: David Copperfield and the handsome Steerforth – Eugene Wrayburn and Mortimer Lightwood in *Our Mutual Friend* – and Sydney Carton in the tragic *A Tale of Two Cities*.[22]

In Prime-Stevenson's 1913 short story 'Out of the Sun', the protagonist, Dayneford, assembles a queer library in which *David Copperfield* is placed among a 'special group of volumes – mostly small ones […] crowded into a few lower shelves, as if they sought to avoid other literary society, to keep themselves to themselves, to shun all unsympathetic observation'.[23] In Dayneford's library Dickens's novel is placed alongside, amongst others, Tennyson's *In Memoriam*, Walt Whitman's work, a translation of 'The Thousand Nights and a Night', sexological writings, and Prime-Stevenson's own explicitly homosexual writing under the name of Mayne. This book, in part, re-energises and endeavours to explicate this queer context, exploring the connections between Dickens's writing and these works.

QUEER DICKENS, AND OTHER (APPARENT) OXYMORONS

In reading nineteenth-century materials I define queer as that which demonstrates that marriage and reproduction are not the only, or indeed the dominant or preferred, modes of being, and, in doing so, undoes an unhelpfully narrow model of identity as determined by a fixed point of sexual orientation. This book rejects a false logic that places marriage and

[22] Xavier Mayne, *The Intersexes* (privately printed, 1908), p. 279, 369.
[23] Edward Prime-Stevenson, 'Out of the Sun', from Prime-Stevenson's collection *Her Enemy, Some Friends and Other Personages: Stories and Studies of Human Hearts* (Florence: Obsner, 1913). Reprinted in *Pages Passed from Hand to Hand: The Hidden Tradition of Homosexual Literature in English from 1748–1914*, ed. Mark Mitchell and David Leavitt (London: Chatto, 1998), pp. 394–403, p. 396. For a sustained exploration of Dayneford as bibliographer and Prime-Stevenson's work under his various writerly names see James Gifford, *Dayneford's Library: American Homosexual Writing, 1900–13* (Amherst: University of Massachusetts Press, 1995).

the biological family as central to thinking about the Victorian and the
Dickensian, in favour of an exploration of other forms of intimacy,
affinity, and family formation. My interest in the inadequacy of the
binaries that oppose heterosexuality and homosexuality, the familial and
the anti-domestic, draws upon the work of gender and queer theorists,
notably Eve Kosofsky Sedgwick, Judith Butler, and, most recently Sharon
Marcus, all of whom expose the culturally ascribed primacy of heterosexuality to be a myth, and reveal the commensurability of queer and straight
desire.[24] Marcus's inspiring *Between Women* examines the comfortable
continuities between female bonds (erotic and otherwise) and Victorian
marital and familial relations. She takes up a recent turn in queer studies
away from an abject reliance on the mutually reinforcing matrix of
supposed normativity and transgression.[25] Instead, she suggests that the
Victorian period offers a critically liberating terrain in which such binaries
have not yet been conceptually fixed. By moving away from the pervasive
assumptions of recent scholarship in which 'gender and sexuality as
defined by marriage and the family have been opposed to gender and
sexuality as defined by same-sex bonds', Marcus 'proposes that we try to
understand how they were intertwined in ways that make homosexuality
and heterosexuality less than useful categories for dividing up the Victorian world'.[26]

Queer, in what I find its most enabling incarnations, moves us
beyond the constricting binary of homo *or* hetero, which as theorists
of sexuality have shown us, has come to be an obsession since the
creation of homosexuality – closely followed by heterosexuality – as

[24] See especially Judith Butler, *Gender Trouble: Feminism and the Subversion of
Identity* (London: Routledge, 1990) and *Undoing Gender* (New York: Routledge,
2004); Eve Kosofsky Sedgwick, *Epistemology of the Closet* (Berkely: University of California Press, 1990) and *Tendencies* (Durham: Duke University Press, 1993); Sharon
Marcus, *Between Women: Friendship, Desire, and Marriage in Victorian England* (Princeton: Princeton University Press, 2007).
[25] Laura Doan's recent discussion of the methodologies of historians of sexuality
similarly identified the problematic critical investment in the normative and the maintaining of queer alterity ('Queer Trouble: On the Limits of Lesbian History', paper
presented to the Queer at King's London Seminar, January 2007). A similar critical
position is charted in relation to earlier historical period by Karma Lochrie in *Heterosynchrasies: Female Sexuality When Normal Wasn't* (Minneapolis: University of Minnesota Press, 2005).
[26] Marcus, p. 22.

concepts and identities in the late nineteenth century.[27] As Michel Foucault momentously described the effect of the 1870s sexological invention of homosexuality: 'The psychological, psychiatric, medical category of homosexuality was constituted from the moment it was categorized – Westphal's famous article of 1870 on "contrary sexual sensations" can stand as its date of birth [...] The sodomite had been a temporary aberration; the homosexual was now a species.'[28] Though, as various theorists have noted, Foucault's argument does not preclude investigation of the different styles, experiences and understandings of sexuality prior to the Victorian fin de siècle, the originary narrative (that Foucault traces through the appropriately epochal ideas of 'species' formation and 'date of birth') has changed the ways we think about sexuality, as the variety of 'perversions' coined by sexology were quickly whittled down into one key conceptual binary.[29] As Sedgwick puts it:

It is a rather amazing fact that, of the very many dimensions along which the genital activity of one person can be differentiated from that of another (dimensions that include preference for certain acts, certain zones or sensations, certain physical types, a certain frequency, certain symbolic investments, certain relations of age or power, a certain species, a certain number of participants, etc. etc. etc.), precisely one, the gender of object choice, emerged from the turn of the century and has remained as *the* dimension denoted by the now ubiquitous category of 'sexual orientation'.[30]

In the period just before the sexologists' categorizations, I argue, there was a greater flexibility in the thinking of the erotic, less focused on object choice, and better able to articulate desires that expand and expose the limits of what now registers as the sexual. These desires, as they are

[27] In her preface to the 2008 edition of a foundational text for queer theory, *Epistemology of the Closet*, Eve Kosofsky Sedgwick describes that book's queerness as its 'resistance to treating homo/heterosexual categorisation – still so volatile an act – as done deal, a transparently empirical fact about any person' (2008, Berkeley and Los Angeles: University of California Press, 1990), p. xvi.
[28] Michel Foucault, *The History of Sexuality: Volume 1*, trans. Robert Hurley (1976, repr. London: Penguin, 1998), p. 43.
[29] See David Halperin, 'Forgetting Foucault: Acts, Identities and the History of Sexuality', *Representations* 63 (1998), 93–120. For Foucault's own critique of the seductive lure of moments of apparent origin see Michel Foucault, 'Nietzsche, Genealogy, History' (1971), repr. in *The Foucault Reader*, ed. Paul Rabinow (London: Penguin, 1991), pp. 76–100.
[30] Sedgwick, *Epistemology*, p. 8.

expressed in Dickens's work, include the yearning not to reproduce but to
parent, a longing to restore and heal damaged bodies, and a range of non-
(or not necessarily) genital physical intimacies and tendernesses.
I am indebted to the methods of rethinking offered in queer projects –
such as Judith Halberstam's *Female Masculinity* in which she uses this
collision of terms to explore how in current European and North American cultures 'masculinity and maleness are profoundly difficult to pry
apart'[31] – that have made me want to scrutinize such apparent oxymorons
as queer Dickens, bachelor dads, and tender masculinity. This book,
however, makes a case for the validity and importance of a variety of
conjunctions outside, and indeed, antithetical to, a central domain of
queer theory as it is currently constituted: queer parenting, queer family,
queer domesticity, queer tenderness, and queer happiness. This is a
different project to those which take as their focus 'those queer bodies
and knowledges that exist outside the boundaries of sanctioned time and
space, legal status, citizen-subjecthood, and liberal humanism', and thus
view queer as outside of community, kinship, and domesticity.[32] This
book departs from Halberstam's vision of 'ravers, club-kids, HIV-positive
barebackers, rent boys, sex workers, homeless people, drug dealers, and the
unemployed' as exemplary 'queer subjects' by virtue of their rejection of,
and/or working relationship to, 'the domains that other people assign
to privacy and family'.[33] By presenting the historical case that (to answer
Judith Butler's question) kinship has not always been heterosexual,
I suggest that a queer theory that rejects domestic and familial possibilities
impoverishes the field of enquiry by, albeit knowingly and archly, siding
with conservative twentieth and twenty-first-century presumptions that
those who deviate from a heteronormative life script are in opposition to
'the' family. Lee Edelman, for example, in a resistance to the ideology of
'reproductive futurism' that constantly affirms the value of the child to
endorse heterosexual relations and foreclose queer possibilities said to
threaten the child, argues for an 'embrace of queer negativity' that 'can
have no justification if justification requires it to reinforce some positive

[31] Judith Halberstam, *Female Masculinity* (Durham and London: Duke University Press, 1998), p. 2.
[32] 'What's Queer about Queer Studies Now', David Eng with Judith Halberstam and José Muñoz, *Social Text* 23 (2005), 1–18, p. 13.
[33] Judith Halberstam, *In a Queer Time and Place: Transgender Bodies, Subcultural Lives* (New York: New York University Press, 2005), p. 10.

social value, its value, instead resides in its challenge to value as defined by the social, and thus in its radical challenge to the very value of the social itself'.[34] I appreciate the righteous anger that wishes to reject the social and the family as these forms of community are currently so narrowly and exclusively defined in much of Europe and North America; the frustration generated by what David Eng describes as 'the relentless moralising that characterises much of our contemporary debate on the erosion of "family values"', where such values are perceived, exclusively, as the preserve 'of traditional white, middle-class parenthood and the nuclear family'.[35]

As Lauren Berlant has argued, 'a staged crisis in the legitimacy of the most traditional, apolitical, sentimental, patriarchal family values' in Regan-era America worked to conflate good citizenship with 'heterosexual, reproductive family values', creating a 'intimate public sphere', drained of political activism and agency.[36] Conservatives such as Gertrude Himmelfarb and Margaret Thatcher famously blurred the distinction between 'Victorian values' and 'family values', using these terms interchangeably to refer to the so-called morality of a mythologized nuclear unit, free from such transgressions as illegitimacy.[37] This anachronistic use of the term Victorian insidiously erased the much richer historical understandings of family available in that period, erroneously asserting that a particularly narrowly conceived model of nuclear kin was a natural form of long duration. Those queer theorists whose objection to the culturally engrained form of heterosexual nuclear family leads them to

[34] Lee Edelman, *No Future: Queer Theory and the Death Drive* (Durham and London: Duke University Press, 2004), p. 21. For an earlier theorization of the opposition between homosexuality and community see Leo Bersani, *Homos* (Cambridge, MA: Harvard University Press, 1995). Both books are discussed in 'The Antisocial Thesis in Queer Theory', Robert Caserio, Lee Edelman, Judith Halberstam, Jose Esteban Munoz, Tim Dean, *PMLA*, 121.3 (2006), 819–27, in which Caserio makes a compelling case for the value of Edelman's project as a response to the 'idea that gays have a vocation to redeem their erotic pleasures for everyone's future benefit' (p. 825).

[35] David Eng. 'Transnational Adoption and Queer Diasporas', *Social Text* 21.3 (2003), 1–37, p. 3.

[36] Lauren Berlant, *The Queen of America Goes to Washington City: Essay on Sex and Citizenship* (Durham and London: Duke University Press, 1997), pp. 178, 179.

[37] See Gertrude Himmelfarb, *The Demoralisation of Society: From Victorian Values to Modern Values* (London: Institute of Economic Affairs, 1995), for a summary of the recent use of these terms in the UK and US, and repeated assertions that nuclear 'family values [...] were so much a part of Victorian values' (p. 55). For a recent example of the persistence of this rhetoric see Gaby Hinsliff's report, 'Bring Back Victorian Values, says Key Tory', *Observer*, 10 December 2006.

reject kinship and domesticity as varieties of queer experience, act to strengthen, rather than contest, the conservative appropriation. This project, through attention to the expandability of Victorian kin in, for example, widespread practices of non-biological adoption, seeks to broaden modern understandings of familial bonds, demonstrating that 'families of choice' and 'elective affinities' have a long and emotionally rich history. The minor significance of marriage and reproduction as motivators of kinship formation in the Victorian period exposes the artifice at work in the modern belief that family is a heterosexual institution. As relatively recent history shows, there is nothing natural in the near synonymy now attributed to the familial and heteronormativity.

I propose, then, that a historicist approach to Dickens's work can open up new ways of conceptualizing queer in relation to the domestic. By looking at the various literary and actual accommodations and experiences of queer desires and lives in the period of Dickens's career and in queer-affirmative twentieth and twenty-first-century after-texts, I explore queer spaces that can be inhabitable and even enjoyable. It is my hope that this book will present some directions for the development of queer optimism, an affect sadly under-represented in a field laden with shame and fascinated by the death drive. This emphasis presents a particularly acute example of a wider trend in literary and theoretical work, in which darker readings are associated with critical sophistication – indeed a recognition of a darker Dickens has invigorated Dickens studies for the past fifty years – whilst sunnier, more optimistic interpretations appear to be naïve and wilfully, perhaps dangerously, partial. This is certainly the case in queer theory, itself an intellectual trajectory that developed in part as a response to the AIDS crisis; here optimism has seemed an insensitive mode that fails to register the suffering of queer subjects while buying into ideologies – the happy ending, the happy family – too firmly associated with reproductive heterosexuality. As Michael Snediker, a rare advocate of queer optimism, has pointed out: 'queer theory, for all its contributions to our thinking about affect, has had far more to say about negative affects than positive ones'.[38] Sedgwick has made a similar argument in her retrospective on the prevalence of paranoid, rather than reparative, reading practices, endemic in queer work including her own foundational *Between Men*. She argues that

---

[38] Michael Snediker, 'Queer Optimism', *Postmodern Culture* 16.3 (2006), 1–48, p. 5.

'queer studies in particular has had a distinctive history of intimacy with the paranoid imperative'.[39] This mode particularly attends to, amongst other acts of unveiling, 'the detection of hidden patterns of violence and their exposure' and takes, as Snediker identifies, 'melancholy and aggression' as its key terms.[40]

Though hugely enabled by the wealth of Sedgwick's queer insight, this book works counter to existing readings of same-sex desire in Dickens's fiction that assert that Dickensian homoeroticism is most, or only, legible in acts of violence. Sedgwick's only extended readings of Dickens's work, in *Between Men*, inaugurated this tradition. In her interpretations of *Our Mutual Friend* and *The Mystery of Edwin Drood* Sedgwick conflates male-male desire with brutal attacks, perceiving positive representations of intimacy between men as 'much less tinged with the sexual' than the male-male bonds expressed through persecution and murder.[41] The anxiety and brutality bound up in such attachments is consonant with Sedgwick's influential theory of the violent break that modern culture imposes onto the homosocial continuum, so that male bonding is prescribed at the expense of male homosexuality, which must be aggressively repudiated. My readings of, for example, homoerotically motivated intermarriage and tender same-sex nursing

[39] Eve Kosofsky Sedgwick, *Touching Feeling: Affect, Pedagogy, Performativity* (Durham: Duke University Press, 2003), p. 126.

[40] Sedgwick, *Touching Feeling*, p. 143, Snediker, p. 24.

[41] Sedgwick, *Between Men: English Literature and Male Homosocial Desire* (New York: Columbia UP, 1985), p. 5. Examples of the homoerotic violence thesis at work include William Cohen's reading of *Great Expectations in Sex Scandal: The Private Parts of Victorian Fiction* (Durham: Duke University Press, 1996), which will be fully discussed in Chapter 5; J. M. Léger's, 'The Scrooge in the Closet: Homoerotic Tropes in the Novels of Charles Dickens' (doctoral thesis, University of Notre Dame, 1991); Vybarr Cregan-Reid's, 'Drowning in Early Dickens', *Textual Practice* 19.1 (2005), 71–91, p. 82, and Cregan-Reid's, 'Bodies, Boundaries and Queer Waters: Drowning and Prosopopœia in Later Dickens', *Critical Survey* 17.2 (2005), 20–33. In his final chapter, Léger moves to a brief exploration of 'homocentric domestic spaces', but spends the four earlier chapters detailing forms 'of homophobia in Dickens' (p. 224), through a methodology that combines Sedgwick's model of male murderous rivalry with Steven Marcus's quasi-psychoanalytic speculation in *The Other Victorians: A Study of Sexuality and Pornography in Mid-Nineteenth-Century England* (London: Weidenfield and Nicolson, 1966) that homosexuality and flagellation were inextricably linked in the Victorian imagination. In essays on drowning and queer waters in Dickens, Vybarr Cregan-Reid uses a Sedgwick-ian model to suggest that Dickens deployed images of 'carefully encoded male rape' to enact vicious retribution on his nastiest characters ('Drowning in Early Dickens' p. 82).

challenge Sedgwick's belief in the 'radically discontinuous relation of male homosocial and homosexual bonds', which has been foundational to the discipline of queer theory.[42] While offering a necessary corrective of existing histories of sexuality, this book is strongly committed to demonstrating the fallacy of the influential paradigm that the homoerotic emerges most strongly in Dickens's work through violence. Instead, the book traces an abundance of gentler, but no less eroticized, same-sex encounters.

In its emphasis on the life preserving rather than the life threatening, this book also departs from a thriving tradition of queer tragedy, in which queer lives are inevitably cut short and/or marked predominantly by loss and suffering than by any more positive affect. For evidence of the dominance of a long tragic tradition in culture and criticism we could look to E. M. Forster's resistance to a terminal end to his novel *Maurice* (written 1913–14, published 1971): 'A happy ending was imperative. I shouldn't have bothered to write otherwise. I was determined that in fiction anyway two men should fall in love and remain in it for the ever and ever that fiction allows.' Forster felt that the 'keynote' of happiness made it impossible, and indeed at the time of composition illegal, to publish, whereas 'if it ended unhappily, with a lad dangling from a noose or with a suicide pact, all would be well'.[43] Forster's appreciation of the way that fatal endings allow homosexual narratives to be told is borne out by a wealth of critical work on the close literary historical connections between queer desire and elegy, a form that allows the expression of such desire at the moment that it becomes unrealizable with the death of the beloved.[44] As Jeff Nunokawa has put it with regard to the way AIDS is widely interpreted as a terminal gay disease, this assumption confirms a 'deep cultural idea about the lethal character of male homosexuality'.[45]

[42] Sedgwick, *Between Men*, p. 5.

[43] E. M. Forster, *Maurice* (London: Penguin, 2005), p. 220.

[44] See, for example, George Haggerty, 'Love and Loss: An Elegy', *GLQ* 10.3 (2004), 385–405; Haggerty 'Desire and Mourning: The Ideology of the Elegy' in *Ideology and Form in Eighteenth Century Literature*, ed. David Richter (Texas: Texas Tech University Press, 1999), pp. 185–206; Jeff Nunokawa, '*In Memoriam* and the Extinction of the Homosexual', *ELH* 58, (1991), 427–38.

[45] Jeff Nunokawa, 'All the Sad Young Men: AIDS and the Work of Mourning' in *Inside/Out: Lesbian Theories, Gay Theories*, ed. Diana Fuss (New York and London: Routledge, 1991), pp. 311–23, p. 311. For further interrogations of the cultural association between homosexuality and fatality see Ellis Hanson, 'Undead', in *Inside/Out*,

More recently Heather Love and Sara Ahmed have each made a case that tragedy is a valued and historically integral component of queer, in order to argue against culturally prescribed happiness. As Love puts it: 'In this brave new world one can be gay without being tragic; however, one may only belong by erasing all traces of the grief, that, by definition must remain sealed off in the past of homosexual abjection.'[46] Love's lament for a recent embrace of gay happiness in the media and by gay people, seems untimely in the aftermath of blockbusting queer tragedy, Ang Lee's 2005 film based on the short story by Annie Proulx, *Brokeback Mountain*. While Love considers the film to be 'one of the most satisfying representations of homosexual suffering in years', I am more inclined to agree with Love's own awareness of the dominance of terminal representations of gay and lesbian life as the near ubiquitous mode throughout the twentieth century, and with those critics who observed that there was nothing new or surprising about the tragic framing of male/male desire in *Brokeback Mountain*, which through melodramatic punishment is made palatable to a wide audience.[47] This debate echoes Vito Russo's groundbreaking early 1980s discussion of Hollywood portrayals of homosexuality, in which he asserts that without the death of one buddy (here he is discussing Ratso Rizzo in John Schlesinger's *Midnight Cowboy*, 1969), the two male friends 'would

---

pp. 324–40, and Elaine Showalter, *Sexual Anarchy: Gender and Culture at the Fin de Siècle* (London: Bloomsbury, 1991).

[46] Heather Love, 'Compulsory Happiness and Queer Existence', *New Formations* 63 (2008), 52–64. See also Love, *Feeling Backward: Loss and the Politics of Queer History* (Massachusetts: Harvard University Press, 2007), which explores and affirms 'the emphasis on injury in queer studies', a field in which critics are 'more willing to investigate the darker aspects of queer representation and experience and to attend to the social, psychic, and corporeal effects of homophobia' (p. 2). Sara Ahmed has argued that 'happiness for some involves persecution for others [...] The unhappiness of the deviant performs its own claim for justice. While we should take care not create a romance out of such unhappiness, we can note that not only does it expose injustice, but it can also allow those who deviate to find each other, as bodies who do not or cannot follow the lines that are assumed to lead to happy endings.' *Queer Phenomenology: Orientations, Objects, Others* (Durham: Duke University Press, 2006), p. 105.

[47] Love, 'Compulsory Happiness', p. 55. See, for example, contributions to the special issue of *Film Quarterly on Brokeback Mountain* 60.3 (2007), especially Joshua Clover and Christopher Nealon, 'Don't Ask, Don't Tell', pp. 62–7, which identifies the recurrence in this film of a 'discomfortingly familiar trope, wherein queer love must be punished by fatal violence', Ara Osterweil, 'Ang Lee's Lonesome Cowboys', pp. 38–42, and D. A. Miller, 'On the Universality of Brokeback Mountain', pp. 50–60.

have lived happily ever after – and who would stand for that?'[48] Nearly three decades after Russo attempted to open *The Celluloid Closet*, the same question stands.

I do not want to deny the continuing importance of tragic queer narratives, of a kind that Love deems to be essential in 'allow[ing] that being gay can make you unhappy and even give you a sense of what it is like to live with such feelings'; to do so at a time of ongoing, in places deepening, anti-queer prejudice, violence, and various forms of legislative and social exclusion, in what Sedgwick calls 'a world full of loss, pain and oppression', would be daft and politically irresponsible.[49] I do, however, want to risk telling a new story. I will propose, and demonstrate the historical validity of, an alternative narrative line of queer nurture, tenderness, possibility, and survival. In this other narrative, even contagion plots – as I argue by tracing the infectiousness of nursing, as an aptitude for tender touch and affect is passed from carer to patient – can also hold more optimistic possibilities.

Though not the focus of this book, important existing queer work on Dickens has explored intimate female relationships. In an earlier incarnation of this project, which only focused on same-sex desire, I aimed for an equally detailed treatment of both male and female homoerotics. I discovered, for example, the completely different historical contexts for Dickens's very different portrayals of female and male marital resistance, exploring the distinct affects and narratives of spinsterhood and women's pain at marital separation from their intimate female friend.[50] Given Dickens's complex gendered divergence of these treatments and my more extended research on masculinities, a detailed exploration of Dickens's queer women is beyond the scope of this book. However, I do make space for the iconic queer figure of Miss Wade (*Little Dorrit*, 1855–7), who has been variously identified (and disavowed) as Dickens's proto-lesbian. The inclusion of Miss

[48] Vito Russo, *The Celluloid Closet: Homosexuality in the Movies* (New York: Harper and Row, 1981), p. 86.
[49] Love, 'Compulsory Happiness', p. 59. Sedgwick, *Touching*, p. 138.
[50] Holly Furneaux, 'Homoeroticism in the novels of Charles Dickens' (doctoral thesis, University of London, 2005). Important recent accounts of relationships between women in the period include Marcus, *Between Women*, and Martha Vicinus, *Intimate Friends: Women who Loved Women 1778–1928* (Chicago: University of Chicago Press, 2004).

Wade in this book is not to reassert her female masculinity, indeed
I argue against the general application of a gender inversion model
which is particularly inapplicable to this figure; rather I use her as a
case study for how my thinking differs from existing queer work on
Dickens. Miss Wade becomes legible as proto-lesbian through a familiar
twist of the queer tragedy trope in which the homosexual, if not fatal, is
bad, mad, and dangerous to know.[51] Mary Armstrong suggests that the
lesbian label is so often appended to Miss Wade, in sharp distinction to
the absence of corresponding analysis of any other female figure in
Dickens, because 'she simply fits most agreeably into a larger, long-
established perception within which women who desire other women
are evil and diseased'. Armstrong boldly holds open 'the possibility that
Miss Wade exhibits no more intensity of female-female desire than, say,
Esther Summerson, but is labelled a lesbian by Dickensians because she
alone is negative enough [...] evil enough, to deserve the title'.[52] Reviews of the 2008 BBC serialization of *Little Dorrit* directed by prolific
adaptor of eighteenth and nineteenth-century works and neo-Victorian

[51] For a classic homophobic account of Miss Wade see Arthur Adrian: 'Dickens again
demonstrates his awareness of the dark undercurrents in the human psyche. There can be
no doubt that Meagles is dealing with a lesbian [...] It could be argued that Dickens
introduces Miss Wade as another example of how the victim of neglect may fall under
sinister influences. Having had no parental guidance during her formative years, she has
been moulded by unnatural forces in her environment'. *Dickens and the Parent-Child
Relationship* (Ohio: Ohio University Press, 1984), p. 94. More recently feminist and
queer theorists have offered anti-homophobic readings of this figure, see Annamarie
Jagose, 'Remembering Miss Wade: *Little Dorrit* and the Historicizing of Female Perversity', *GLQ* 4.3 (1998), 423–51; and Anna Wilson, 'On History, Case History, and
Deviance: Miss Wade's Symptoms and Their Interpretation', *Dickens Studies Annual* 26
(1998), 187–201. For a characteristic refutation of such sustained, informed work on
Miss Wade and sexuality see Janet Retseck, 'Sexing Miss Wade', *Dickens Quarterly*, 15
(1998), 216–25.
[52] Mary Armstrong, '"What Can You Two Be Together?": Charles Dickens, Female
Homoerotic Desire and the Work of Heterosexual Recovery' (doctoral thesis, Duke
University, 1995), p. 227. Armstong's thesis presents another important account of
inter-female desire in Dickens. See also the published section of this, 'Pursuing Perfection: Dombey and Son, Female Homoerotic Desire, and the Sentimental Heroine',
Studies in the Novel, 28.3 (1996), 281–302. Though I am otherwise indebted to Marcus's
Between Women, her work on Dickens in that book, which explores the power imbal-
anced sadomasochistic relationship between Miss Havisham and Estella in *Great Expectations*, and its consonance with contemporary tales of the erotic and abusive
treatment of dolls, unhelpfully passes forward the widespread belief that same-sex desire
is most legible as violence and pathology in Dickens's work.

novels, Andrew Davies, suggest the continuation of the link between Miss Wade's shadiness and the legibility of her desires for women. Serena Davies describes 'the sinister Miss Wade' (played by Maxine Peak) as 'a character whom Andrew Davies has turned into a lesbian.' As Davies clarifies 'Dickens didn't write her as a lesbian – but she just is.' 'There are all sorts of things Dickens didn't realise about his characters.'[53] This odd disavowal of Dickens's sexual knowledge suggests the continuation of the powerful stereotypes of Victorian and Dickensian prudery, despite the energetic work of thinkers such as Michael Mason and Matthew Sweet.[54] Davies, who had recently directed an adaptation of Cleland's *Fanny Hill* (BBC4, 2007), could be expected to be aware of at least one historically available model for the understanding of desire between women.

As well having read Cleland's novella and other pornographic materials, Dickens had a direct model for Miss Wade's relationship with Tattycoram in Maria Edgeworth's *Belinda* (1801), which was one of the first things that he borrowed on joining the London Library.[55] *Belinda* has received recent scrutiny from lesbian historians, due to Edgeworth's portrayal of a cross-dressing mannish woman whose deviance from social codes is marked by her name, Harriot Freke. As I've argued in more detail elsewhere, Edgeworth's presentation of this character's captivation of a younger woman, Miss Moreton, who 'ran away from her friends to live with this Mrs Freke', has many points of resemblance with Dickens's portrayal of Miss Wade's relationship to Harriet Beadle, who leaves her employers/adoptive family to cohabit with her.[56] An important point of difference, though, between these portrayals is Dickens's insistence on Miss Wade's accordance with ideals of feminine beauty. Dickens's non-masculine rendering of Miss Wade suggests the greater range of conceptual possibilities in a period before sexological accounts yoked homosexuality to gender inversion.[57] Though

[53] Serena Davies, *Telegraph Review*, 18 October 2008, p. 2.

[54] See Michael Mason, *The Making of Victorian Sexuality* (Oxford and New York: Oxford University Press, 1994), and Sweet, *Inventing*.

[55] Both volumes of *Belinda* were issued to Dickens on 18 October 1841, 'Records from the London Library', repr. in Collins, 'Dickens's Reading', p. 146.

[56] Maria Edgeworth, *Belinda* (London and New York: Pandora, 1987), p. 229. Furneaux, 'Homoeroticism'.

[57] Judith Butler has critiqued the legacy of sexological accounts of inversion as 'the most reductive' 'heterosexual logic that requires that identification and desire be mutually exclusive', *Bodies that Matter: On the Discursive Limits of Sex* (New York and London: Routledge, 1993), p. 239.

existing queer readings of Miss Wade have focused on the way in which Dickens's representation anticipates late nineteenth- and early twentieth-century classifications of female invert and lesbian,[58] I propose, in this brief example and through my methodology throughout, that late nineteenth-century concepts are less useful for understanding Dickens's characters than the queer literary and social contexts which were already available to Dickens, and in which, as we have briefly seen, he was immersed. Miss Wade makes her more detailed appearance in this book, then, not as proto-lesbian, but as one of Dickens's queer travellers, who operate in an already well established mid-nineteenth-century literary and cultural nexus of understandings and representations of queer spaces, geographies, and emigrations.

Whilst recognizing the limitations to queer possibility in Dickens's work, this book strives towards a genealogy of more positive queer affect and experience, a history overwritten by the doomed life-stories popularly attributed to twentieth-century homosexuals, but which can, I hope, be made available anew. Looking at the ways in which non-marital, non-reproductive agendas and same-sex erotics were consonant with mid-Victorian society, this book only rarely uses queer in its predominant nineteenth-century sense (the OED dates the first explicit use of the term to denote homosexuality to 1894) of 'strange, odd, peculiar, eccentric', 'of questionable character, suspicious dubious'. Dickens uses the term in this way in, for example, the presentation of Master Humphrey, as discussed in Chapter 2, and in his autobiographical fragment when he describes himself, aged nine, as 'the very queer small boy'.[59] Though some of the relationships, spaces, and practices considered here are eccentric – such as the unconventional architectures of the boathouses and shooting gallery turned hospital inhabited, respectively, by bachelor dads and nursing men – the emphasis of the book is on the diversity of families, erotics, and masculinities that Dickens's society and work could comfortably accommodate.

---

[58] Despite her concern about anachronistic reading, Jagose examines Miss Wade's sexuality through the 'medical discourses of disease and contamination', identifying 'sites upon which later sexual orders and later sexual identities can batten' (pp. 429, 427). Similarly Armstrong suggests that we can 'detect in Miss Wade's pathology an early glimpse of what will evolve, some twenty or thirty years later, into a burgeoning, heavily medicalized "understanding" of female homoerotic desire. Miss Wade is [...] a kind of half-invert' ('What can you two be together?', pp. 264–66).

[59] John Forster, *The Life of Charles Dickens*, I, (London: Chapman and Hall, 1872), p. 5.

1

Reconfiguring the Domestic:
Bachelor Dads

Domestic units bonded through neither blood nor marriage are so
numerous in Dickens's work, they outweigh depictions of what we
have come to describe as the 'nuclear' family of married parents and
offspring. The alternative presentations of kinship that proliferate in
Victorian fiction displace the biological family as a natural given and
demand a further debunking of the fantasy that the Victorian era
enshrined a narrowly conceived form of family. In an important corrective to the belief in a monolithic Victorian family model, George
Behlmer has argued that 'this reputed golden age of domesticity saw
intense if inconclusive combat over the meaning of family and home';
Leonore Davidoff et al. suggest similarly that 'the meanings and values
attached to family even within the same group could be varied and often
contradictory. The model of family harmony was in tension with more
radical ideas about familial relations such as the beliefs of Owenite
socialists'; while John Gillis posits that 'the early nineteenth century
saw the most sustained period of experimenting with family and marriage prior to the 1960s and 70s'.[1] As these theorists have recognized, in
periods of rapid social change an imagined domestic space of stability
and continuity becomes particularly appealing, so that – both then and
now – there is some cultural investment in the idea of a contented
grouping of parents and children. This kind of imaginative thinking

---

[1] George Behlmer, *Friends of the Family: The English Home and its Guardians, 1850–
1940* (Stanford: Stanford University Press, 1998), p. 3; Leonore Davidoff, Megan
Doolittle, Janet Fink, Katherine Holden, *The Family Story: Blood, Contract and Intimacy
1830–1860* (London and New York: Longman, 1999), p. 101; John Gillis, *A World of
their own Making: Myth, Ritual and the Quest for Family Values* (New York: Harper
Collins, 1996), p. 66.

informs the 1871 census definition: 'The natural family is founded by marriage and consists, in its complete state, of husband, wife, and children.'[2] There was, as Behlmer observes, a major disparity between this statement and the census's earlier findings: 'A household [...] frequently sheltered individuals beyond the nuclear family core – servants, apprentices and lodgers, not to mention distant kin. In 1851 just thirty-six percent of households contained a married couple, at least one child, and no one else.'[3] This gap between the definition of the family and the lived experience immediately calls into question the use of the term 'natural family', and points to the incoherence of conceptions of a 'complete' family as neither a statistical majority nor an unchallenged ideal.

Nonetheless, Dickens has been tenaciously associated with a selective vision of Victorian domesticity, which conflates the domestic with the marital and the procreative.[4] While domesticity is undoubtedly at the emotionally invested heart of Dickens's work, offering a fantasized panacea to wider social suffering, it is a rigorously defamiliarized domestic that Dickens persistently recommends. The composition of his family circles is diverse and capacious, encompassing relationships beyond those usually seen to structure and generate a narrowly conceived model of family based on heterosexuality and reproduction. As Helena Michie reminds us, Dickens's wide-ranging composition of

---

[2] Quoted by Behlmer, *Friends*, p. 26.

[3] Quoted by Behlmer, *Friends*, p. 26.

[4] See, for example, Michael Slater, *An Intelligent Person's Guide to Dickens* (London: Duckworth, 1999): 'Dickens was, in his idealisation of "hearth and home" and the family circle, very much a man of his age, an age when the British monarchy under Victoria and Albert was reconstituted as a highly domestic institution [...]. Through the very nature of his books, Dickens was in himself a remarkable intensifier of the cult of domesticity' (p. 93). Dickens's association with the ideal home has been attributed to his canny commercial exploitation of the 'twin teloi of domesticity and popularity'. Karen Chase and Michael Levenson, *The Spectacle of Intimacy: A Public Life for the Victorian Family* (Princeton: Princeton University Press, 2000), p. 95. Mary Poovey's exploration of Dickens's expert production and manipulation of 'an iconography of "Dickens"' suggests that he exploited a perceived commitment to domesticity to establish his popularity. Poovey quotes an 1850 review in *Fraser's Magazine* which cites the central reason for Dickens's popularity as 'his deep reverence for the household sanctities, his enthusiastic worship of the household gods' *Uneven Developments: The Ideological Work of Gender in Mid-Victorian England* (Chicago and London: University of Chicago Press, 1988), pp. 108–9. For a thorough listing of the critical positioning of family as 'a Dickensian speciality' from the nineteenth century on, see Catherine Waters, *Dickens and the Politics of the Family* (Cambridge: Cambridge University Press, 1997), p. 2, 15.

family 'is true, not only of his many lodging houses where characters connected only by physical proximity come to care for each other and to form contingent communities, but also of his more stable homes'.[5] The flexibility of Dickens's vision of what constitutes family is clear in his imagining of the 'fallen' women residents of Urania Cottage, the rehabilitation home he established with Angela Burdett Coutts, as 'an innocently cheerful family while they live together there'.[6] In a letter to Coutts, Dickens discusses the importance of 'promoting friendly and affectionate feeling among them' and presents these bonds in familial terms: 'she had thought they would become like sisters'.[7] Although once the home had been running for several years Dickens believed 'individual attachments' among the women there to be 'rare',[8] his idealized, early vision of this community as familial demonstrates his rejection of an ideological alignment of domesticity with a particular model of sexual morality, based strictly on marital monogamy and procreation. The exuberant diversity of Dickens's fictional families – which embrace such figures as unmarried foster fathers, heterosexually resistant bachelors and spinsters, same-sex couples, and endorse both single and multiple parenting – gives the lie to traditional formulations of the Dickensian domestic that identify a single, statically gendered model.[9]

    [5] Helena Michie 'From Blood to Law: The Embarrassments of Family in Dickens' in *Palgrave Advances in Charles Dickens Studies*, ed. John Bowen and Robert Pattern (Basingstoke: Palgrave, 2005), pp. 131–55, p. 134.
    [6] Charles Dickens to Angela Burdett Coutts, 28 October 1847, *Pilgrim*, V (1981), pp. 177–9, p. 177. For Dickens's description of the range of women admitted to the institution, which accommodated the destitute and petty criminals as well as 'young women from the streets', see 'Home for Homeless Women' *Household Words*, 23 April 1853; For more on Dickens's imaginative engagements with these women see Jenny Hartley, *Dickens and the House of Fallen Women* (London: Methuen, 2008).
    [7] Charles Dickens to Angela Burdett Coutts, 3 November 1847, *Pilgrim*, V, pp. 181–8, p. 186, p. 184.
    [8] 'Home for Homeless Women', p. 133.
    [9] See, in particular, Alexander Welsh, *The City of Dickens* (Oxford: Clarendon, 1971): 'Presiding over each hearth is a cheerful female eidolon' (p. 150); and Margaret Lane, 'Dickens on the Hearth' in *Dickens 1970: Centenary Essays*, ed. Michael Slater (London: Chapman and Hall, 1970), pp. 153–72. More recently various critics have flagged the disparity between a persistent cultural memory of Dickens's families and the textual evidence. See Richard Barickman, Susan MacDonald, and Myra Stark, *Corrupt Relations: Dickens, Thackeray, Trollope, Collins and the Victorian Sexual System* (New York: Columbia University Press, 1982), p. 61 and Waters, p. 15.

Dickens's work, as well as wider contemporary fiction by authors including George Eliot, Anthony Trollope, and Wilkie Collins, continually contests the idea of a 'natural' family, calling into question its gendered and erotic components. All use narratives that celebrate surrogate parenting, particularly foster fathering, to question the assumed moral superiority of the biological family unit and denaturalize the received family pattern of physically related kin. In this, and the following two chapters I explore the strategies of domestic representation, through which Dickens and his contemporaries challenge the assumed primacy of both heterosexuality and reproduction in the formation of family. In this chapter's focus on the plot of adoption, in which both marriage and reproduction are displaced as the only available or laudable means of family formation, I look broadly at the queer parameters of the Dickensian domestic.

THE QUEER ON THE HEARTH: QUEER KINSHIP?

Some queer theorists continue to reject the possibility that parenting can ever be a queer activity. Frustrated by what she sees as the 'new homonormativity of the recent lesbian baby boom', Judith Halberstam resists the 'assimilating [of] gays and lesbians into the mainstream of the life of the nation and the family'.[10] Similarly Lisa Duggan is frustrated by a 'homonormativity' that, through, for example, campaigns for gay marriage rights and entry to the military, 'does not contest dominant heteronormative assumptions and institutions, but upholds and sustains them, while promising the possibility of a demobilized gay constituency and a privatized, depoliticized gay culture anchored in domesticity and consumption'.[11] Lee

---

[10] Halberstam, *Queer Time and Place*, p. 180, p. 153.
[11] Lisa Duggan, *The Twilight of Equality? Neoliberalism, Cultural Politics and the Attack on Democracy* (Boston: Beacon Press, 2003), p. 50.

Edelman, who mounts an articulate refusal of the cultural dictate that gays and lesbians must be model citizens, perceives child rearing to be in the service of 'reproductive futurism', that values heterosexuality for its ability to reproduce and vilifies the single male:

> Not for nothing [. . .] does the historical construction of the homosexual as distinctive social type overlap with the appearance of such literary creations as Tiny Tim, David Balfour, and Peter Pan, who enact, in an imperative most evident today in the uncannily intimate connection between Harry Potter and Lord Voldemort, a Symbolic resistance to the unmarried men (Scrooge, Uncle Ebeneezer, Captain Hook) who embody, as Voldemort's name makes clear, a wish, a will, or a drive towards death that entails the destruction of the Child.[12]

Though, I am persuaded by Duggan's arguments for the political cost of a gay neo-liberalism that advocates domestic privacy at the expense of collective political action, arguments about 'heteronormativity' have too great a price, when they remove the domestic sphere and family life from the realm of queer possibility. For Edelman and Halberstam the family and reproduction are firmly aligned with heteronormativity, making the only queer option a wholesale rejection of all forms of family. As well as presenting an unpalatably prescriptive pattern for queer life (antisociality, antidomesticity, and regret for the increasing number of lesbian, gay, bisexual, transsexual, and transgendered parents who have been unable 'to resist the appeal of futurity, or refuse the temptation to reproduce') these accounts fail to distinguish between 'the institutions of family, heterosexuality and reproduction', placing queer in opposition to all these things, while failing to recognize the continuing contestation of what constitutes family and the increasing distance between sexual and reproductive agendas.[13] By defining family as a 'heterosexual institution', these accounts perpetuate the appropriation of the meaning of family by the far right, erasing wider, and historically discernable, formations of kinship.

The abundance of non-heterosexual and non-reproductive families in Victorian fiction based around the figure of a single male, who wants

---

[12] Edelman, *No Future*, p. 21.
[13] Edelman, p. 17, Halberstam, *Queer Time*, p. 1. On the 'defamiliarising impact of new technologies through which many of the most deeply taken-for-granted assumptions about the "naturalness" of reproduction are displaced' see *Reproducing Reproduction: Kinship, Power and Technological Innovation*, ed. Sarah Franklin and Helena Ragone (Philadelphia: University of Pennsylvania Press, 1998), p. 4.

not to annihilate children but to nurture them, suggests an alternative historical conception of kinship, along lines that do not automatically instate marriage or biology as the central determinant. Such a history suggests that modern Western preoccupation with the reproductive, nuclear family is an ideal of recent origin;[14] one which, in its currently much attacked, too inflexible and claustrophobic form, in itself does not have much of a future. Sara Ahmed has recently explored the dominant twenty-first-century arrangement of domesticity around compulsory heterosexuality, describing this as a form of repetitive strain injury. Building on the work of Judith Butler, she argues that bodies and families 'take the shape of norms that are repeated over time and with force'.[15] Ahmed examines the processes through which individuals are orientated towards a particular sexuality, critiquing the unrelenting straight lines of affiliation on the family tree and the schematic 'presumption that the child must inherit the life of the parent that requires the child to follow the heterosexual line'.[16] These straight lines and repeated family norms are not, however, the dominant mode across a wide range of Victorian literature. The many narratives from this period that feature a single adoptive parent resist the replication of the kind of straight biological model that Ahmed critiques. By examining these more devious and twisted lines of affiliation, I identify historical resistance to the idea of a single family model, perpetuated by an inflexible pattern of marital reproductive heterosexuality.

Through my examination of Dickens's work I propose a historical negative to Judith Butler's question, 'Is Kinship Always Already Heterosexual?' While Butler outlines the various factors that make

---

[14] Janet Carsten concludes that 'the stable nuclear family of mid-twentieth century Britain or North America was a rather minor historical blip in a much more dynamic and complex' history of kinship. *After Kinship?* (Cambridge: Cambridge University Press, 2004), p. 17. In *Like Our Very Own: Adoption and the Changing Culture of Motherhood* (Kansas: University Press of Kansas, 2000), Julie Berebitsky charts the hardening of US attitudes and policies towards the adoptive family from the 1920s–50s, so that adoption was most often denied to applicants, such as unmarried women who had been welcomed prior to the 1920s, who did not approximate a nuclear model of the opposite-sex companionately married, white, middle-class couple. Berebitsky includes interesting examples of the increasing prejudice against spinster or bachelor adoptions by the US Children's Bureau and documents that by the 1950s some states went so far as to legislate against single person adoptions (pp. 118–27).
[15] Ahmed, *Queer Phenomenology*, p. 91.
[16] Ahmed, *Queer Phenomenology*, p. 85.

twenty-first-century subjects too eager to answer in the affirmative
(the potency of particular renderings of Freud and Lacan, for example,
that, emphasizing heterosexual coitus as the origin of the child, give
that moment an overdetermined symbolic importance), Dickens's
writings demonstrate a much greater flexibility in the thinking and
modelling of family, offering elective, affective formations of a kind
that have been influentially described as 'families of choice'.[17] Kath
Weston's pioneering *Families We Choose: Lesbians, Gays, Kinship* first
used such terminology in order to complicate modern Western 'procreative assumptions' about kinship, resisting 'more conventional views
of family that locate gay people outside kinship's door'.[18] Weston,
together with those scholars who have built upon her work, break up
the imagined binary of straight=family/gay=no family, by examining
life-affirming elective kinship bonds.[19]

The wide range of domestic formations in Victorian literature participate in wider contemporary debates about what constitutes family, and
whether a distinction between real and fictive kin can ever be made. Such
discussions anticipate the arguments of many modern anthropologists and
literary scholars that all forms of kinship can be most accurately perceived
as fictive.[20] The controversial Bastardy Clauses of the New Poor Law
of 1834, for example, highlighted an anxiety about the knowability
of paternity. Changes in legislation to make mothers newly financially
responsible for their illegitimate children responded, in large part, to
anxieties that paternity functioned under the old system as a speech act.
Mothers could (falsely if they chose) name a father to make him so in more
concrete terms than mere generation; he would be publicly recognized as

[17] Judith Butler, 'Is Kinship Always Already Heterosexual?', *differences*, 13.1 (2002),
14–44.
   [18] Kath Weston, *Families We Choose: Lesbians, Gays, Kinship* (New York and Oxford:
Columbia University Press, 1991), p. 17.
   [19] See especially Jeffrey Weeks, Brian Heaphy and Catherine Donvan, *Families of
Choice and Other Life Experiments* (London and New York: Yale University Press, 2001)
and *Queer Families, Queer Politics*, ed. Mary Bernstein and Renate Reimann (New York:
Columbia University Press, 2001).
   [20] See Marc Shell, *Children of the Earth: Literature, Politics and Nationhood* (Oxford:
Oxford University Press, 1993); Sarah Franklin and Susan Mckinnon, *Relative Values:
Reconfiguring Kinship Studies* (Durham and London: Duke University Press, 2001);
Marianne Novy, *Reading Adoption: Family and Difference in Fiction and Drama* (Michi-
gan: University of Michigan Press, 2005).

such and made financially responsible for the child. Alternatively a single mother could erase the father by refusing to name him, thus forcing the parish to provide. Later in the century, as Jenny Bourne Taylor has noted, Henry Maine's *Ancient Law* (1861) emphasizes 'the historical variability of legal and social institutions, seeing the family itself as "complex, artificial, and strange", based on essentially fictional codes'.[21] Maine's recognition of the significance of non-blood kinship alliances continually undermines his effort to position the patriarchal family as the basis for society. He famously argued that the creation of family ties through the 'Fiction of Adoption' was central to civilization, urging his readers to 'look on the family as constantly enlarged by the absorption of strangers within its circle' and 'to regard the fiction of adoption as so closely stimulating the reality of kinship that neither law nor opinion makes the slightest difference between a real and an adoptive connection'.[22]

Throughout his career Dickens participated in these debates, emphasizing the constructed nature of family and endorsing nurtured ties over genealogy. In *Nicholas Nickleby* (1838–9), for example, he has the benevolent Charles Cheeryble offer an equivocal interpretation of the inevitability of familial feeling, in which nature is never wholly separable from nurture:

Parents who never showed their love, complain of want of natural affection in their children – children who never showed their duty, complain of want of natural feeling in their parents [. . .] Natural affections and instincts, my dear sir, are the most beautiful of the Almighty's works, but like other beautiful works of His, they must be reared and fostered, or it is as natural that they should be wholly obscured.[23]

Dickens's debunking of the affective corollary to biology is sustained throughout his work, from *Sketches by Boz* (1836) to his late Christmas

[21] Jenny Bourne Taylor, 'Representing Illegitimacy in Victorian Culture' in *Victorian Identities, Social and Cultural Formations in Nineteenth Century Literature*, ed. Ruth Robbins and Julian Wolfreys (Basingstoke: Macmillan, 1996), pp. 119–42, p. 129. Rosalind Coward also explores Maine's work, arguing that 'his was not a defence of the naturalness of this [patriarchal] family', in *Patriarchal Precedents: Sexuality and Social Relations* (London: Routledge, 1983), p. 21.

[22] Henry Summer Maine, *Ancient Law* (New Brunswick: Transaction, 2002), p. 133.

[23] Charles Dickens, *Nicholas Nickleby* (London: Penguin, 1999), p. 563–4.

writings of the 1860s.[24] In an early sketch about Astley's circus he presents natural affection between biological relatives as staged and clichéd:

Fathers are invariably great nuisances on the stage, and always have to give the hero or heroine a long explanation of what was done before the curtain rose [...] Or else they have to discover, all of a sudden, that somebody whom they have been in constant communication with, during three long acts, without the slightest suspicion, is their own child: in which case they exclaim, 'Ah! What do I see? This bracelet! That Smile! These Documents! Those Eyes! Can I believe my senses? – It must be! – Yes – it is, it is my child!' – 'My father!' exclaims the child; and they fall into each other's arms, and look over each other's shoulders; and the audience give three rounds of applause.[25]

Dickens's own work persistently rejects what he shows here to be the false logic of the biological mechanism for placing the foundling within a family.

Dickens famously had a longstanding interest in orphaned and dispossessed children, and in the principal English institution for their care, the London Foundling Hospital, established by Captain Thomas Coram in 1739. These subjects are revisited in the 1867 Christmas number of Dickens's periodical *All the Year Round*, 'No Thoroughfare', which he co-authored with Wilkie Collins.[26] This story is framed around the removal of a boy, Walter Wilding, aged twelve, from the Hospital by his supposed, and deeply loved, mother: 'the dear parent to whom my heart was mysteriously turned by Nature when she first spoke to me, a strange lady.'[27] When he discovers, after her death, that there is actually no biological relationship between them, Walter is distraught at the incoherency of his emotions, without a 'Natural' tie to rationalize them:

[24] In his study of Balzac's 'rambunctiously radical curiosity about all of the different ways in which "family" might be understood or enacted', Michael Lucey similarly explores the way in which a demystifying of 'the sentiments that are supposed to adhere in "natural" families' participates in the author's broader project to make 'finally untenable a reading of any family structure as presocial, natural, human, disinterested.' *The Misfit of the Family: Balzac and the Social Forms of Sexuality* (Durham and London: Duke University Press, 2003), pp. 4, 12, 19.

[25] 'Astleys', *Sketches by Boz*, pp. 128–35, p. 134.

[26] After the publication of 'No Thoroughfare' visitors and donations to the Foundling Hospital increased to the extent that the board invited Dickens to become a governor. See Dickens's letter to Mrs Fields, 25 May 1868, *Pilgrim*, XII, p. 120.

[27] Charles Dickens and Wilkie Collins, 'No Thoroughfare', collected in *The Christmas Stories*, ed. Ruth Glancy (London: Everyman, 1996), pp. 672–793, p. 680.

This dreadful discovery is something I can't realise even yet. We loved each other so dearly – I felt so fondly that I was her son. She died [. . .] in my arms – she died blessing me as only a mother *could* have blessed me. And now, after all these years, to be told she was *not* my mother! O me, O me! I don't know what I am saying' (p. 693).

Walter only partially recovers from the shock of being dispossessed of 'the treasured delusion' (p. 712), spending his short remaining time in the story searching for the other foundling registered under his name. In a turn to a strictly genealogical model of inheritance, which is questioned by other characters who place more weight on the 'thirteen years under [his] late dear mother's care [. . .] and eight of them her confidentially acknowledged son' (p. 679), Wilding insists that the natal child has a 'natural claim' to the maternal legacy of the wine-merchant's business (p. 698).

Wilding also expends his remaining energy in 'forming a kind of family' with the employees of his warehouse (p. 681): 'I can at least show that I am not ashamed to have been a Foundling, and that I who never knew a father of my own, wish to be a father to all in my employment' (p. 681). Wilding insistently celebrates his institutional upbringing, finding in it a pattern for alternative social organization: 'I was not used in my childhood to that sort of individual existence which most individuals have led, more or less in their childhood. After that time I became absorbed in my late dear mother. Having lost her, I find that I am more fit for being one of a body than one by myself one' (pp. 681–2). Despite reservations from some employees, Wilding succeeds in instituting a fairly 'united family' (p. 683), which follows the Hospital's nurturing of a successful concert and chapel choir, specializing in the works of one of the institution's founding 'fathers', Handel: 'The [choir] was led and chiefly taught, by Wilding himself: who had hopes of converting his dependents into so many Foundlings, in respect of their capacity to sing sacred choruses' (p. 717). The authorial reservations implicit in this somewhat whimsical and curtailed presentation of this large, communal family – Wilding dies before he has had an opportunity fully to develop his 'kind of family' (p. 681) – draw on wider concerns about the appropriateness of institutional care for children in this period, and perhaps an increased later nineteenth-century cynicism about the efficacy of eighteenth-century models of benevolent paternalism, on which the Foundling Hospital was founded. The inspiration, however, that the foundling narrative provides for the authors' remodelling of domesticity and for their interrogation of the constitution of 'natural' family ties is consonant with the long-term concerns of Dickens's and Collins's work.

FATHERS BEYOND BIOLOGY: MR BROWNLOW AND MR BROWNLOW

Mr Brownlow, the benevolent adoptive father of Dickens's most famous foundling narrative, *Oliver Twist* (1837–9), presents a good example of the way in which, in Dickens's fiction and beyond, the conjunction 'bachelor dad' need not be incoherent. Previously the best friend of Oliver's now deceased father, Brownlow has no biological connection to the boy, but adopts him as the child member of an all-male coterie, which also encompasses Grimwig and Mr Losberne. Given that there was no legal framework for adoption in Britain until the passing of the Adoption Act in 1926 this relationship is purely an elective affinity, entirely occasioned by Brownlow's willingness to take responsibility for the dispossessed child. Katrina Wegar has suggested that adoptive families can challenge 'narrow biocentric definitions' 'that presume a biological basis of kinship, parenthood and identity',[28] and Dickens's Brownlow queers the family in just such a way, separating kinship from questions of biology. As modern anthropological explorations of current adoption practices are beginning to recognize, adoptive families can challenge the ascribed naturalness of biological families, thereby calling into question the cultural primacy accorded to heterosexuality and reproduction.[29]

The term 'bachelor dad' reads as oxymoronic; it combines what is widely seen to be a reproductive identity – fatherhood – with an identity that resists reproduction and is often seen to be outside of, or somehow antithetical to the family – bachelorhood. In *Female Masculinity* Halberstam orchestrates a similar collision of terms to ask why it is 'that

---

[28] Katrina Wegar, 'Introduction' to *Adoptive Families in a Diverse Society*, ed. Katrina Wegar (New Brunswick: Rutgers, 2006), pp. 1–16, p. 4.
[29] See especially Mary Watkins, 'Adoption and Identity: Nomadic Possibilities for Reconceiving the Self', in *Adoptive Families in a Diverse Society*, pp. 259–74, p. 260.

masculinity and maleness are profoundly difficult to pry apart.'[30] The figure of the bachelor dad, so popular in the work of Dickens and his contemporaries, raises the question of why conceptions of fatherhood are so rigidly linked to biological paternity and to what, in considering the nineteenth century, we tend to think of as the unambivalently heterosexual institution of marriage. As Gillis puts it, increasingly through the nineteenth century 'husbandhood provided a man's link to his children to the extent that it now became difficult, if not impossible, to imagine a bachelor father'.[31] By exploring celebratory Victorian representations of the unmarried adoptive father, we see what has been occluded in culturally affirmed or, to use Halberstam's term, 'heroic' models of family and masculinity.

Dickens's naming of his Mr Brownlow may well have been inspired by his acquaintance with one John Brownlow, librarian of the Foundling Hospital, author of foundling fiction, and self-appointed authority on the physical and emotional care of institutionalized children. Once a child charge of the Hospital, Brownlow remained within the institution acquiring a long and personal perspective on the changing treatment of these children. Dickens was a near neighbour of the Foundling Hospital and had a family pew at its chapel whilst living at Doughty Street, where he wrote *Oliver Twist*. After the family moved in 1840, he wrote to John Brownlow about the pew.[32] Robert Colby, the first to speculate on the connection between these two Brownlows, points to the improvements in the quality of Foundling Hospital life that John Brownlow had effected through his reforms of the apprenticeship system (in response to cases of masters' cruelty) and diet, to argue that 'in naming Oliver's benefactor Mr Brownlow, Dickens seems to have been paying a tribute to one of the most dedicated social servants of his age'.[33] Certainly Dickens shared John Brownlow's concerns about the current handling and appropriate reform of both the bodily and emotional care of institutionalized children. In 1827 Brownlow felt compelled to write to the Foundling Hospital's Committee of Education with his 'Observations on the Education and General Treatment of the Children of the

---

[30] Halberstam, *Female Masculinity*, p. 2. [31] Gillis, *A World*, p. 190.
[32] 26 February 1840, *Pilgrim*, II, pp. 33–4.
[33] Robert Colby, *Fiction with a Purpose* (Bloomington: Indiana University Press, 1967), p. 129.

Foundling Hospital', including a plea for the governors' 'humane consideration'. He was concerned by changes in the educational system, which meant that the youngest children (aged from five to nine or ten) no longer received the more personal attention of mistresses in the lower school, but instead had to learn along the row from their peers, under the rigorous military discipline of a single master. The foundling child, Brownlow argues, 'requires the sympathy of some one capable of entering into his griefs, and if in the place of this kindly treatment, he is obliged to conform to a cold and unrelaxed discipline, what will be the result upon himself?'[34]

Dickens's famous attack on the Yorkshire schools in *Nicholas Nickleby* includes similar arguments, resonating with and participating in such wider discussions about the appropriate personal as well as practical care of children, both in institutions and in the family. This novel, as John Bowen has noted, is more widely concerned with the 'real and difficult emotional and economic demands' of childcare.[35] There are various discussions of the financial cost presented by family increases. Mrs Nickleby, for example, envisages becoming a paid foster mother to Smike, receiving 'something certain for his board and lodging, and some fair arrangement was come to, so that we undertook to have fish twice-a-week' (p. 561), and Mr Kenwigs memorably responds to a threat to his family's inheritance with a death-wish on his new-born: 'Let him die. He has no expectations, no property to come into. We want no babies here [. . .] Take 'em away, take 'em away to the Fondling' (p. 444).

Dickens's portrayal of the Yorkshire institutions to which many such surplus children were sent pays particular attention to an unmet hunger, not only for victuals, but for intimacy and affection:

There were little faces which should have been handsome, darkened with the scowl of *sullen* dogged suffering; there was childhood with the light of its eye quenched, its beauty gone, and its helplessness alone remaining; there were vicious-faced boys brooding, with leaden eyes, like malefactors in a jail; and there were young creatures on whom the sins of their frail parents had

[34] John Brownlow, 'Observations on the Education and General Treatment of the Children of the Foundling Hospital', unpublished pamphlet (1827), London Metropolitan Archives, A/FH/MO1/067, p. 9.
[35] John Bowen, *Other Dickens: Pickwick to Chuzzlewit* (Oxford: Oxford University Press, 2000), p. 121.

descended, weeping even for the mercenary nurses they had known, and lonesome even in their loneliness. With every kindly sympathy and affection blasted in its birth, with every young and healthy feeling flogged and starved down (p. 97, emphasis added).

The terms of this description are very similar to those used in Brownlow's 'Observations', in which he also speaks of the Foundling child's potential 'sullenness', as a result of such emotional neglect: 'He is chap-fallen, and his character becomes marked by a mixture of obstinacy and sullenness' (p. 17). While, as in 'No Thoroughfare', an institution could provide inspiration for a happily expansive conception of family, such an optimistic model is in tension with the socially reformist agenda, concerned to remove the potential for neglect and mistreatment of institutionalized children, that Dickens and Brownlow shared.

In his hybrid text, *Hans Sloane: A Tale Illustrating the History of the Foundling Hospital in London* (1831), part novella, part institutional history and mission statement, John Brownlow similarly explores the potential emotional deprivations of such an upbringing. His hero spends his childhood in the unreformed Hospital of the mid eighteenth century, an experience portrayed as fundamentally different to parental care:

In private life, the fond parent looks upon the little traits of character exhibited by his child, as so many pilot balloons, which mark the course it will take in after days. But these tokens, either of intellect or otherwise, were, in the case of Hans Sloane, unperceived or unheeded; for he had neither father nor mother to watch the progress of his youth, and enhance the value of his boyish deeds, or to attach a value where none belonged. To sum up the history of his early years: – he worked hard, and fared bad; behaved sometimes well and sometimes ill; was often punished, and seldom praised: possessed an aptitude of intellect, without the means of displaying it; and affections, without an object on which to bestow them; and was only distinguished from the rest of his tribe, by a miniature portrait around his neck.[36]

Such details as the miniature portrait of Hans's mother on which the discovery of the foundling boy's identity rests have led to discussions about the extent to which this text operated as a partial source for

[36] John Brownlow, *Hans Sloane: A Tale Illustrating the History of the Foundling Hospital in London* (London: F Warr, 1831), p. 103.

Dickens's *Oliver Twist*.[37] Given that Dickens later relied heavily on Brownlow's writing to construct an article about the Foundling Hospital for his periodical *Household Words*, it seems highly likely that such material not only informed his depiction of a particular foundling in *Oliver Twist*, but had an impact on his wider attention to the care of institutionalized children in his next novel, *Nicholas Nickleby*.

Nicholas Nickleby and *Hans Sloane* also share a concern with reproductive disequilibrium. Children, in these texts and throughout Dickens's oeuvre, are often surplus and unwanted, or longed for, but not possible. Both texts depict an awful surplus of unwanted children. Susan Zieger considers the abandoned boys at Squeers' establishment, Dotheboys Hall as 'the ruins of a reproductive heterosexuality reimagined as perverse, because it fails to nurture its own progeny.'[38] The night-time scenes at Dotheboys Hall, with the apparently surplus, half-starved boys piled together, seem uncomfortably to chime with Thomas Malthus's influential theory of population, in which increases in population will always outstrip increases in food production, resulting in starvation of the poorest. Dickens – who was determinedly anti-Malthusian throughout his career, celebrating large working-class families, like the Cratchits in *A Christmas Carol* (1843), more than any other form of biological family – critiques the supply and demand of children from a rather different angle. His work goes on to develop a counter-theme, which is given an unusually extended treatment in Brownlow's *Hans Sloane*; the affective repercussions of childlessness. Mr and Mrs Humphries, who adopt Hans Sloane, are unable to have children, a condition that severely tests their religious faith: 'The dispensation which deprived them of the endearments attached to the characters of father and mother was felt with more regret than, as Christians, they dared avow' (p. 110). For them, adoption offers a new family member as well as being a channel for religious reconciliation and social benevolence. In his 1852–3 novel, *Bleak House*, Dickens has the charismatic detective Mr Bucket

[37] Colby, *Fiction*; David Paroissien, *The Companion to Oliver Twist* (Edinburgh: Edinburgh University Press, 1992), p. 225; Laura Schattschneider, 'Mr Brownlow's Interest in *Oliver Twist*', *JVC* 6.1 (2001), 46–60; Jenny Bourne Taylor, '"Received, a Blank Child": John Brownlow, Charles Dickens and the London Foundling Hospital – Archives and Fictions', *Nineteenth Century Literature* 56.3 (2001), 293–363.
[38] Susan Zieger, 'Children, Class and Sexuality in Dickens's and McGrath's *Nicholas Nickleby*', paper given at Dickens Universe, UC Santa Cruz, August 2006.

articulate a similarly frank explanation of infertility and its emotional repercussions: 'My wife, and a lodger, constitute my family. Mrs Bucket is as fond of children as myself, and as wishful to have 'em; but no. So it is. Worldly goods are divided unequally, and man must not repine'.[39] In *Our Mutual Friend* (1864–5), Mr and Mrs Boffin's search for a child to adopt is, like that of Mr and Mrs Humphries, precipitated by their own inability to have a baby. As Mr Boffin puts it: 'Mrs Boffin and me had no child of our own, and had sometimes wished that how we had one.'[40] Wistful assertions of a reproductive insufficiency are set against examples of the over-sufficiency of reproduction, such as the surplus, unwanted child population at Dickens's Dotheboys Hall and Brownlow's Foundling Hospital. Highlighting the uneven surplus and scarcity of children across classes, these authors show reproduction to be awry – not a beautiful natural mechanism, but a chancy process that can have the perverse results of child neglect and abuse, at the same time as other adults long for children who are not forthcoming.

While these mutual concerns perhaps point to an intertextuality between Dickens's and Brownlow's writing, Dickens was to use Brownlow's work most explicitly in the 1853 article that he co-authored with William Henry Wills, 'Received, A Blank Child'. This piece recounts their visit to the Foundling Hospital, drawing heavily on Brownlow's 1847 *Memoranda; or Chronicles of the Foundling Hospital*, which, in part, recapitulates the historical sections of *Hans Sloane*. As Jenny Bourne Taylor has noted, Brownlow receives an unnamed 'walk on part' in this article as the secretary who is so affectionately greeted by the children; this effects a partial erasure of his identity which parallels Dickens's and Wills's unattributed use of Brownlow's *Memoranda*.[41] Nonetheless, Dickens and Wills depict the figures of secretary and matron as a beloved, organic part of this community: 'The young shoots started up with their shrill hooray! twining round and sprouting out from the legs and arms of the two officials with a very pleasant familiarity.'[42] This – albeit highly sentimental – flowery language is

[39] Charles Dickens, *Bleak House* (London: Penguin, 1996), p. 762.
[40] Charles Dickens, *Our Mutual Friend* (London: Penguin, 1997), p. 96.
[41] Jenny Bourne Taylor, 'Received', p. 305.
[42] Charles Dickens and W. H. Wills, 'Received, A Blank Child', *Household Words*, 19 March 1853, vol. 7, pp. 49–53, p. 50.

consonant with Dickens's project of naturalizing non-biological affinities while questioning the perceived naturalness and superiority of blood relations.

In his moving depictions of the plight of these vulnerable children and his personal interactions with young charges of the Foundling Hospital, Brownlow, perhaps quite self-consciously given his repeated documentations of the institution's history of male benevolent care, follows a venerable tradition of compassionate, child-orientated men. Captain Thomas Coram, whom Brownlow particularly revered, and two of the Hospital's principal early champions, George Frederick Handel and William Hogarth – both Guardians on the Institution's board – were all childless men who made their philanthropic interest personal, becoming intimately involved in the lives of these children. While Coram 'stood godfather to more than twenty foundlings', Hogarth – who famously drew new attention to the sufferings of street children in his portraits and engravings – along with his wife Jane, fostered numbers of foundlings at their home in Chiswick.[43] In 'Received, A Blank Child' Dickens variously commends Coram, describing him as 'the gentle sea-captain' and praising Coram's 'tender heart', unhardened by his military experiences and work in the American plantations.[44] This emphasis on the conjunction of militarism and tenderness echoes Dickens's portrayal of trooper George in *Bleak House* (a novel that he was completing at the time of this article).[45] The gentle military man is a figure that Dickens returned to in his delineations of the hands-on foster fathering provided by the likes of Corporal Théophile and Major Jemmy Jackman in the 1860s Christmas numbers.

In his journalism Dickens frequently commended the personal qualities of men who voluntarily took on the care of children. In another article co-authored with Wills for *Household Words*, for example, praise is bestowed on the 'frank' and 'free' relationship between the chaplain and the boys at the Philanthropic Farm School at Red Hill, which

---

[43] Kit Wedd, *The Foundling Museum Guidebook*, (London: The Foundling Museum, 2004), p. 13. Katherine Field, *Hogarth's Children*, exhibition catalogue, (London: The Foundling Museum, 2007), pp. 36, 43.

[44] Dickens and Wills, 'Received', p. 50.

[45] George's conjunction of militarism with a powerful healing ability receives full attention in Chapter 6.

Dickens and Wills visited in the summer of 1852.[46] The Farm School, a reformatory for boy criminals, about a third of whom were orphans 'either by death or transportation of their parents, or by being born like brutes, and bred in ignorance of any home', worked on a system of individual treatment like that earlier recommended by Brownlow.[47] Dickens and Wills were particularly impressed by the enlightened model of care that allowed these boys (in an organic rhetoric they would re-use in their account of the Foundling Hospital) to 'blossom':

It is obvious that boys differing so greatly in age, and working upon the farm under so many differing circumstances, cannot be managed by one rigid system. Military discipline does not suit children; the drill sergeant is an excellent man in his way, but they are not to be drilled into honesty and virtue [. . .] We are glad therefore to find at Redhill that the rules are few, the punishments still fewer. Boys are trained to think for themselves; each is judged on his own merits, and guided as far as possible with a strict view to the development of his own character. Good people are as multiform as blossoms in a summer hedge.[48]

In *Little Dorrit* Dickens has Mr Meagles eulogize Coram, as a figurehead for the appropriate care of dispossessed children. Meagles bestows Coram's name, instead of that of the contemporary parochial 'guardian', on Tattycoram, previously Harriet Beadle: 'The name Beadle being out of the question, and the originator of the Institution for these poor foundlings having been a blessed creature of the name of Coram, we gave that name to Pet's little maid'.[49] Though the Meagles's partial incorporation of 'Tattycoram' into their family in a servant role is not a happy one – she keenly feels the disparity between her domestic treatment and that of the Meagles's almost excessively beloved daughter Pet – it is motivated, at least in part, by the same concerns that were

[46] Charles Dickens and W. H. Wills, 'Boys to Mend', *Household Words*, 11 September 1852, vol. 5, pp. 597–602, p. 602. I am grateful to Wu Di for recommending this article to me.
[47] Dickens and Wills, 'Boys', p. 598.
[48] Dickens and Wills, 'Boys', p. 599.
[49] Charles Dickens, *Little Dorrit* (London: Penguin, 1998), p. 31. Jenny Bourne Taylor analyses the connotations of the Meagles's renaming of Harriet Beadle, through which they (in part) elide the similarity between her first given name and the family patronym in 'Received', p. 352, and Beryl Gray discusses the indeterminacy of Tattycoram's position within this family as conveyed by this name and the various descriptors applied to her, in 'Nobody's Daughters: Dickens's Tattycoram and George Eliot's Caterina Sarti', *George Eliot Review* 32 (2001), 51–62.

expressed by John Brownlow. Having observed 'all those children ranged tier above tier' at the Foundling Hospital, Mr and Mrs Meagles prepare for a character that has not experienced personal, individual care: 'We shall know what an immense deduction must be made from all the influences and experiences that have formed us – no parents, no child-brother or sister, no individuality of home, no Glass Slipper, or Fairy Godmother' (p. 31).

As the examples of Hogarth and the other Foundling 'fathers' suggest, such creations of new familial bonds did occur in Britain throughout the eighteenth and nineteenth centuries. Penny Kane identifies a variety of literary and actual examples in which more distant kin very often take in orphans or children of poorer relatives, such as the grandfather who became a permanent guardian to his grandchildren in the 1840s after the collapse of his son-in-law's business.[50] George Behlmer suggests that 'adoption was also undertaken as a neighbourly act' and was regarded in some working-class communities as the 'highest expression of hospitality'.[51] Behlmer documents the semi-formal adoptions organized by Poor Law authorities as well as private agencies and charities in the decades leading up to legalization. He observes the variety of motivations apparent in the adoption advertisements that proliferate in *Bazarre, Exchange and Mart* at the end of the nineteenth century, which ranged from those seeking a bright, attractive baby to those requesting a strong child able to do general domestic work.[52] Claudia Nelson's work on North America, where legalized adoption began in 1851 with the Massachusetts statute, identifies a similar range of motives. Nelson traces a general shift from an early emphasis on adopted children as a source of cheap domestic help or farm labour to a more affective attitude towards adoptees; she suggests that by the 1890s 'their proper "work" was presented as the spiritual and emotional uplift of adults'.[53]

[50] Penny Kane, *Victorian Families in Fact and Fiction* (Basingstoke: Macmillan, 1995), p. 11.
[51] Behlmer, *Friends*, p. 299. See also Behlmer, 'What's Love Got to Do With It? Adoption in Victorian and Edwardian England', in *Adoption in America: Historical Perspectives*, ed. Wayne Carp (Michigan: University of Michigan Press, 2002), pp. 82–100.
[52] Behlmer, *Friends*, p. 295.
[53] Claudia Nelson, *Little Strangers: Portrayals of Adoption and Foster Care in America, 1850–1929* (Bloomington and Indianapolis: Indiana University Press, 2003), p. 7.

The often complex combination of emotional, economic and practical impulses that came together in many actual cases of nineteenth-century adoption are expressed in Dickens's narratives of working adoptees. Miss Wade's perspective on Tattycoram's uncomfortable position in the Meagles household points to the more cynical affects potentially at work in adoptive guardianship:

Here is your patron, your master. He is willing to take you back, my dear, if you are sensible of the favour and choose to go. You can be, again, a foil to his pretty daughter, a slave to her pleasant wilfulness, and a toy in the house showing the goodness of the family. You can have your droll name again, playfully pointing you out and setting you apart, as it is right that you should be pointed out and set apart. (Your birth, you know; you must not forget your birth) (p. 319).

Although these sentiments enter the text through what is presented as Miss Wade's distorted, perverse vision, here, as elsewhere, the wider narrative events offer some support for Miss Wade's perspective. Just as her comments about the connections between governesses, wives and slaves are supported by wider Victorian debates and incidents within the narrative, Tattycoram has, indeed, been laughed at for the name appended to her, whilst Mr Meagles is preoccupied with the circumstances of her illegitimate birth, imagining 'what her mother's story must have been' (p. 315) and seeing 'in this unhappy girl, some reflection of what was raging in her mother's heart before ever such a creature as this poor thing was, in the world' (p. 313). Miss Wade's interpretation suggests a more circumspect reading of Tattycoram's position and that of other orphans partially incorporated into the middle-class family as domestic servants. The orphaned Charley who becomes personal maid, as well as nurse and pupil, to Esther in *Bleak House* as 'a present' 'with Mr Jarndyce's love' (p. 385) is another example. However, in Dickens's fiction and more broadly in Victorian literature, the emotional impetus and familial feeling towards non-related adoptees is most often the focus of such narratives.

Responses to *Oliver Twist* have been troubled by Brownlow's apparent lack of motive for adopting the boy. The closing portrayal of Brownlow's bachelor community denies the heterosexist and biocentric logic of a series of literary conventions and readerly expectations particularly associated with the Victorian novel, in which marriage is positioned as the ultimate narrative achievement. As Richard Dellamora points out, 'the one thing that Dickens does not offer at the end of the novel is a representation of a conventional

see also Rumsa

nuclear family. The fraternity of Brownlow, Mr Grimwig, Mr Losberne, and Oliver with which the novel ends is too obviously an inverse image of Fagin's fraternity not to have something odd about it.'[54] Oliver's previous experiences of surrogate parenting at Fagin's den, with the Sowerberrys, and in the workhouse, lead him to assume that his offering an economic use value is indispensable to his accommodation within a household. Fearful that Brownlow will send him away, Oliver pleads to be allowed to stay as a servant (p. 108), anticipating the historically realistic fate of Tattycoram and Charley. Although it is clear that the Brownlow and Maylie establishments prize the moral and educational development of children beyond their present economic productivity, Oliver remains possessed by a desire to be useful, zealously running errands and making endless nosegays; he feels 'so happy' if Rose or Mrs Maylie 'wanted a flower that he could climb to reach, or had forgotten anything he could run to fetch, that he could never be quick enough about it' (p. 263). The child's unshakeable conviction that some form of return for care will be expected operates as part of Dickens's critique of Poor Law provision as well as exposing the interestedness within adoptive bonds, which despite their elective quality are not necessarily any less (or more) exacting than biological connections.[55] Although Oliver expects to contribute to the domestic economy of Brownlow's household, appreciating the self-interest that (as Nelson's work on early American adoption law demonstrates) motivated many surrogate parents, his benefactor's benevolence confounds such expectations.

Brownlow's desire to parent Oliver is explicitly undermotivated: 'There is something in that boy's face [. . .] something that touches and interests me' (p. 80); 'I feel [. . .] more strongly interested in your behalf than I can well account for, even to myself' (p. 108). In both these moments Brownlow is ostensibly endeavouring to recollect the 'countenance of which Oliver's features bore a trace' (p. 80). As is so common in Dickens's novels, physical resemblance reveals blood-lines making Oliver a walking testimony to his maternity. However, Brownlow has only a connection of affinity to this family, having once been the dearest friend of Oliver's father. This friendship is, in itself, intensified

---

[54] Richard Dellamora, *Friendship's Bonds: Democracy and the Novel in Victorian England* (Philadelphia: University of Pennsylvania Press, 2004), p. 44.
[55] Schattschneider discusses Brownlow's and the Maylies' refusal to turn Oliver to their profit as a marker of their beneficence, pp. 50–2.

by the resemblance that Brownlow had perceived between his friend, Edwin Leeford, and Leeford's older sister, to whom Brownlow had been engaged. This sister, typically not named but described almost exclusively in terms of comparison with her surviving brother – 'that fair creature of his blood and kindred' (p. 408), 'he had his sister's soul and person' (p. 411) – dies on the day she is to marry Brownlow, thereby short-circuiting a plot that had the potential to render Brownlow, all other narrative strands remaining equal, Oliver's uncle by affinity.

By breaking the familial link, Dickens repudiates the long literary tradition that he satirizes in the sketch on 'Astleys'. As Nelson has suggested, the popularity of what she calls 'the lost heir motif' in nineteenth-century melodrama points to wider 'preoccupations of the day, including the frequent desire to see the well born as naturally, not merely environmentally, different from the poor' and concerns about lines of inheritance.[56] Brownlow's bachelor desire to parent offers a decided departure from melodramatic and picaresque conventions, diverging from eighteenth-century plots, such as those advanced in some of Dickens's favourite picaresque novels, Henry Fielding's *Tom Jones: A Foundling* (1749) and Tobias Smollett's *Humphrey Clinker* (1771), which revolve around a revelation of biological connection (Squire Allworthy is found to be Tom's maternal uncle, while Humphey discovers his natal father), and from earlier likely nineteenth-century models for *Oliver Twist*, such as *Hans Sloane*.[57] Here, as so often in foundling fictions, Hans's adoptive parents, the Humphries, eventually discover that they have a biological relationship to the boy and give thanks 'for the miraculous interposition, by which they had been restored to a relative of whom they had every reason to be proud' (p. 147). Mrs Humphries's 'sudden wish' (p. 112) to adopt Hans out of all the available Foundlings,

---

[56] Claudia Nelson, *Family Ties in Victorian England* (Connecticut: Praeger, 2007), pp. 165–6.

[57] Robert Colby discusses the preference for natal restoration in eighteenth and early nineteenth century foundling literature, such as Agnes Maria Bennett's *The Beggar Girl and Her Benefactors* (1797), in which the beggar girl is discovered to be the natural daughter of her wealthy benefactor (p. 120). Michele S. Ware has noted Dickens's rejection of such plot lines in *Bleak House*, in which Esther's 'discovery of her mother's identity does not bring a close to the narrative' and Esther is emphatically not restored as the daughter of a nobleman as Dickens 'creates a different kind of nobility for her, based on personal virtue rather than birth'. ' "True Legitimacy": The Myth of the Foundling in *Bleak House*', *Studies in the Novel* 22 (1990), 1–9, pp. 5–6.

is hereby given a retrospective biological rationale. Her particular desire to parent Hans is produced, John Brownlow suggests, by her true womanliness (child nurturing in this novella and in Brownlow's 'Observations' is predominantly the province of women) and by blood. Though Dickens and Brownlow have much in common in their attitudes towards childcare, Dickens markedly differs from Brownlow in rejecting a turn to biological family as a fantasized panacea to the sufferings of institutionalized children in this period.

David Lean's highly influential 1948 film inaugurates a long tradition in *Twist* adaptations of rendering coherent Brownlow's tangential attachment to Oliver by re-routing his bloodline. In Lean's film, as in many more recent productions including Lionel Bart's musical (which opened in 1960), Carol Reed's iconic 1968 film of this, Tim Greene's 2004 South African retelling of the novel, and the BBC's 2007 serial directed by Coky Giedroyc, Brownlow becomes Oliver's maternal grandfather.[58] This significant alteration speaks to twentieth and twenty-first-century investments in narrative 'logic' as bio-logic. The persistence of this particular form of plot simplification suggests that for modern audiences a non-biological motive for parenting simply won't make sense, and perhaps will also not provide the type of happy family ending apparently craved by the diverse range of consumers for these rather different productions. Dickens's novel, however, allows the initially tenuous connection between Oliver and Brownlow to form the basis for idyllic closure:

Mr Brownlow adopted Oliver as his own son, and removing with him and the old housekeeper to within a mile of the parsonage house, where his dear friends [the Maylies] resided, gratified the only remaining wish of Oliver's warm and earnest heart, and thus linked together a little society, whose condition approaches as nearly to one of perfect happiness as can ever be known in this changing world (p. 451).

---

[58] *Oliver Twist*, dir. David Lean, Independent Productions, 1948; *Oliver!*, dir. Carol Reed, Columbia Pictures, 1968; *Boy Called Twist*, dir. Tim Greene, Monkey Films and Twisted Pictures, 2004; *Oliver Twist*, dir. Coky Giedroyc, BBC, 2007. Notably Roman Polanski's *Oliver Twist*, Pathé, 2005 eschewed this popular manoeuvre, instead, through an excision of the Maylies and Oliver's mother's back-story, making a feature of Brownlow's social and familial disconnection from the boy.

Mrs Maylie's relationship to her adopted 'niece' Rose (who is discovered to be Oliver's maternal aunt) parallels that of Brownlow and Oliver. Like Brownlow, Mrs Maylie expands upon the pleasures of becoming family to an unrelated orphaned child: 'Not the less my niece [. . .] not the less my dearest child. I would not lose her now for all the treasures of the world. My sweet companion, my own dear girl –' (p. 438). While, through Oliver and Rose's relationship, there is a latterly discovered biological connection between these households, they are related just as firmly by their comparable accommodation of adopted children. Dickens's halcyon vision here offers a more flexible way of thinking about family than that endorsed by the majority of adaptations of the novel.

While paternity is no pre-requisite to fatherhood in Dickens's work, Oliver does manifest inherited characteristics which endear him to Brownlow. Dickens briefly narrates Brownlow's increasing attachment to his adopted child, emphasizing the appeal of Oliver's parity to his biological father: 'Even when I first saw him [..] there was a lingering expression in his face that came upon me like a glimpse of some old friend flashing on one in a vivid dream'(p. 413); '[Brownlow] traced in him new traits of his early friend, that awakened in his own bosom old remembrances, melancholy, and yet sweet and soothing' (p. 453). These traces, at two removes, might afford remembrance both of Leeford and the sister he resembles who Brownlow had hoped to marry.[59] This extreme distancing of the curtailed courtship plot as a possible factor in Brownlow's affection for Oliver is indicative of the extent to which Dickens marginalizes opposite-sex romance in his delineations of family formation. The affectionate recollection of both lost friend and fiancé stimulated by Oliver's physique and manner, suggests the complexity and diversity of emotional motivations for adoption.

As both Dellamora and Larry Wollf have noted, Brownlow's ardency to possess Oliver has unmistakable affinities with those less benevolent 'guardians', who are also specifically attracted by the boy's prepossessing physical appearance:

While it is suggestively interesting that Fagin regards Oliver's 'looks' as the boy's chief asset in the criminal world, it is perhaps equally remarkable that his

---

[59] The queer possibilities of sibling parity are the subject of Chapter 3.

looks should be every bit as much of an asset in the respectable world of Mr Brownlow.[60]

Dickens reinforces the structural parallels between these figures who capitalize, either financially or emotionally, on Oliver's appearance, through repeated, ostensibly ironic, references to Fagin and Brownlow in the same terms; Brownlow is introduced as an 'old gentleman', 'a very respectable-looking personage' (p. 74), a description which recalls the novel's first mention of Fagin just two chapters earlier, in the words of Jack Dawkins, as a 'spectable old genelman' (p. 62) and the title of Cruikshank's memorable plate of Oliver's entry to Fagin's household, 'Oliver introduced to the respectable Old Gentleman' (p. 65). Oliver's bodily appeal, especially in the context of Fagin's boy gang, Wolff goes on to argue, has a historical resonance with the numerous cases of boys being used in the sex trade at this time. In 1837, while Dickens was writing *Oliver Twist*, the London Society for the Protection of Young Females and Prevention of Juvenile Prostitution, established 1835, was closing down brothels prostituting girls and boys and prosecuting proprietors.[61] Two gritty filmic responses to the novel make similar connections between the realities of the contemporary sex-trade and the suspicions of 'guardianship' raised by Dickens's novel. Seth Michael Donsky's *Twisted* (1996) is set in a New York brimming with male hustlers and child prostitutes, and Jacob Tierney's *Twist* (2004) transports Oliver and the Dodger to a

---

[60] Larry Wolff, '"The Boys are Pickpockets and the Girl is a Prostitute": Gender and Juvenile Criminality in Early Victorian England from *Oliver Twist to London Labour*', *New Literary History*, 27.2 (1996), 27–49, p. 239. Richard Dellamora examines Cruikshank's illustrative support for Dickens's critique of abusive 'male mentorship', observing that the phallic depiction of Oliver is paralleled in scenes with Fagin and Bumble: 'He draws an oversized spoon directed at a forty-five degree angle from Oliver's crotch to the open mouth and popping eyes of Bumble.' 'Cruikshank's plate "Oliver introduced to the Respectable Old Gentleman" is a diptych to "Oliver asking for More" [...] As in the earlier illustration, Oliver carries an [appropriately phallic] object at an angle, not a spoon this time but a walking stick'. 'Pure Oliver, or Representation without Agency', in *Dickens Refigured: Bodies, Desires and Other Histories*, ed. John Schad (Manchester and New York: Manchester University Press, 1996), pp. 55–79, p. 58, p. 68. See also chapter 1 of *Friendship's Bonds*.

[61] Wollf and Dellamora develop an established tradition of reading Fagin as a pederast. See Steven Marcus 'Who is Fagin', in *Oliver Twist* (1965, repr. New York: Norton, 1993), pp. 478–95 and Gary Wills, 'The Loves of *Oliver Twist*' in *Oliver Twist* (1989, repr. New York: Norton, 1993), pp. 593–608.

Toronto life of teenage pimping and familial sexual abuse.[62] Though these are fringe films, explicitly marketed for a gay audience, they are in dialogue with a tradition of mainstream *Twist* movies, in which the visual commodification of boys' bodies has long been a staple. Since Lean's film followed Bumble's exclamation 'Show me the boy!' with a lingering introductory shot of Oliver's raised buttocks, *Twist* audiences have repeatedly been drawn into an uneasy relationship with all those figures who desire to appropriate and possess Oliver.

Neither Donsky nor Tierney's brutally bleak visions can accommodate a benevolent Brownlow. The homeless Canman who cares for the Oliver figure in at the start of Donsky's film is murdered,[63] and Tierney's partly Brownlowian Senator, who initially holds out the possibility of long-term help for Oliver, has a particularly ambivalent interest in him. The Senator hires the prostitute Oliver only to sit gazing at him, transposing the intense physical scrutiny of Dickens's Brownlow. It remains unclear whether this interest is a more unusual client fetish or whether the Senator is endeavouring to recover a lost relation. The Senator's interest in Oliver's family history and his fascination with the locket that Oliver wears raises the possibility of a lost heir plot, which is finally shut down when Oliver poses as the Senator's grandson to visit his family home, and is told 'You can't come to this house [. . .] I never intended to invite you to dinner.'[64] In the director's overview, Tierney explains that this moment is a deliberate break with Dickens, so that 'Oliver does not get adopted by the shadowy grandfather figure.' Tierney's memory of this adoption shows the

---

[62] *Twisted*, dir. Seth Michael Donsky, Miravista, (1996); *Twist*, dir. Jacob Tierney, Strand Releasing (2004).

[63] Scott Freer has worked on the Dickensian influence in the classic film of a child cared for by a loving tramp, Charlie Chaplin's *The Kid* (1921). Freer notes that Chaplin's favourite Dickens novel was *Oliver Twist* and that Jackie Coogan, star of *The Kid*, went on to play the part of Oliver Twist in Frank Lloyd's film of the following year, and Freer draws out the thematic and affective affinities between these projects. 'The Abandoned Child: The Dickensian Influences in Chaplin's *The Kid*' (forthcoming). Given that *The Kid* and *Twisted* share a Dickensian concern with juxtaposing the emotionally rich care provided by a tramp with the inadequate provision of child-care authorities, Donsky's film can be positioned in a thickly intertextual filmic tradition of imaginative responses to Dickens's *Oliver Twist* as the exemplary culture-text of dispossessed childhood and surrogate parenting.

[64] In 'Dickens's Queer Children' (forthcoming), Susan Zieger reads this scene, in which the door is initially opened by the Senator's actual grandchild, as a rebuke of Oliver's 'queer trespass onto family ground'.

impact of those multiple re-tellings that cast Brownlow as grandfather. In fact, Dickens's text is queerer than Tierney thinks in its refusal of biology as the basis for nurture. Throughout much of the film, however, Tierney holds open the Senator's motives, allowing the full ambivalence of Nancy's interpretation – 'Maybe he wants to take care of you' – to register. This ambiguity offers another response to the underdetermined interest of Dickens's Brownlow. This film finally makes clear the anxieties and false logic behind the various adaptations that make Brownlow into a blood relative. The explicit plot of familial sexual abuse which surrounds Dodge, shows the fantasy at work in ideas of family as safe haven from the threats of life with Fagin. By drawing out the parities between the economically and sexually exploitative forms of guardianship offered by Fagin and Brownlow, *Twist* suggests that the energy which has been dedicated to reading Fagin as a pederast in both literary criticism and earlier filmic reworkings could be as usefully directed to Brownlow's interest in Oliver.

James Kincaid has made a provocative exploration of the overdetermination of paedophilia in modern culture, pointing to the incoherency of our efforts to hold separate different forms of child loving: 'Some are sanctified; others are censured. How they are to be distinguished is never, in practice, very clear, though there is pressure to pretend that nothing could be clearer.'[65] Though Kincaid reads the end of *Oliver Twist* as a ghastly pretence that Brownlow's domestic world is 'not linked' to the institutional world or criminal sexual world, the evident, explicit overlaps between Oliver's experiences in these only partially separated milieus is what makes the novel's depiction of child loving particularly interesting.[66] Responding to Kincaid's work on the Victorian anticipation of paedophilia, Catherine Robson has suggested that we also need 'to consider what *else* that adult interest might be signifying in the period before the pronouncements of medicalized discourse effectively closed down all explanations other than the diagnosis of individual pathology'.[67] Whilst we might wish to read for the possible pederastic desires that connect Oliver's guardians, we should also recognize

[65] James Kincaid, *Child-Loving: The Erotic Child and Victorian Culture* (New York: Routledge, 1992), p. 187.
[66] Kincaid, *Child-Loving*, pp. 389–91.
[67] Catherine Robson, *Men in Wonderland: The Lost Girlhood of the Victorian Gentleman* (Princeton: Princeton University Press, 2001), p. 10.

that to do so might be regulatory – both an imposition of a later division of the affects that could and could not permissibility attach to children, and a form of the repetition of what Kincaid identifies as 'stranger danger' that strategically deflects attention away from incestuous paedophilia.[68] It is all too easy to 'other' sexual desire for children as that which resides outside the biological family, as the suspect motive for alternative family arrangements, such as those organized around an unmarried adoptive parent. Such 'reasoning' was employed in the US Children's Bureau 1938 draft of policy, which opposed spinster and bachelor adoptions on the grounds that 'the relationship developed is nearly always highly abnormal. While the relationship may not be homosexual, yet the mere presence of a child in such a home often indicates an adult in need of compensation to assist in overcoming poor adjustment to life.'[69]

PATERNAL PASSIONS: QUEER BOATS AND HANDS-ON FOSTER FATHERING IN MID-VICTORIAN FICTION

The form of child-loving that Brownlow offers to Oliver can be alternatively figured within a context of wider Victorian narratives of adoption. In many of these plots the adoptive father's desire *for* a child is so intense, an articulation of an almost physical need, that existing thinking makes it difficult to pose interpretations other than the sexual. Without rejecting this as a possible component in a range of complex motivations, I want to explore the rich emotional vocabularies employed in mid-Victorian representations of the male yearning for a child. These descriptions further disrupt received patterns of family, calling into question its gendered composition, and extending the conventional remit of exemplary masculinity. They also resist compulsory heterosexuality by decoupling this from the idealized form of domesticity.

Even those who had a different experience of family, such as foundling John Brownlow, often endorsed what now read as conventional attitudes about the superiority of the biological family and the importance of maternal care. Except in his radical refusal to stigmatize illegitimacy as

[68] Kincaid, *Child-Loving*, p. 204.   [69] Quoted by Julie Berebitsky, p. 118.

disability (another area in which his agenda coincides with Dickens's), John Brownlow's attitudes to the family are firmly conservative. His *Observations* are concerned with 'the best means of providing a substitute' for 'the assistance of both father and mother', which he describes as 'the natural agents which the beneficent wisdom of the Deity has designated as guides' (p. 3). Brownlow's interest in reinstating a system of school mistresses is, he says, in 'compliance with the rule which the general consent of society has sanctioned, that a female is the only fit monitress and instructress of a child. She best knows its feelings, and her attention and watchfulness can best direct those feelings to the right channel' (p. 11). The numbers, though, of highly positive depictions of adoptive fathering in Victorian fiction, resist this idea. Dickens's Brownlow sets a pattern for a range of domestically and emotionally adept foster fathers throughout his novels, including Jarndyce who supports the illegitimate Esther and several other orphans in *Bleak House*, Crisparkle who becomes foster father to the previously abused twins Helena and Neville Landless in *Edwin Drood* (1870), Dan Peggotty whose 'bacheldore' adoption of his orphan nephew and niece confounds the young David Copperfield (p. 40), Sol Gills who cares for his orphaned nephew Walter Gay in *Dombey and Son* (1846–8), as well as *Dombey's* memorable maritally averse Captain Cuttle (whose name, occupation and style of masculinity perhaps reference Captain Coram) who offers Florence a gentle surrogate fatherhood after she is rejected by her biological father.

Both Dan Peggotty and Sol Gills provide, to use Sedgwick's terminology, avunculate care in physically eccentric domestic spaces.[70] Young David Copperfield is perplexed by the design of both Peggotty's home and his adoptive family.[71] On his arrival at Yarmouth David initially fails to recognize that the boat can qualify as a house or habitation:

I looked in all directions, as far as I could stare over the wilderness, and away at the sea, and away at the river, but no house could *I* make out. There was a black barge, or some other kind of superannuated boat, not far off, high and dry on

---

[70] James Arnett applied Sedgwick's avunculate terminology to Gills and Cuttle in a paper entitled 'Striking Abjection, Evacuating Horror' at the 2008 conference of the British Association for Victorian Studies, 'Victorian Feeling: Touch, Bodies, Emotions', University of Leicester, 3 September 2008.

[71] I am grateful to members of my 'Before Homosexuality' special subject class, especially Nicola Cadman, for suggesting the interpretation of Peggotty's boat as queer space.

the ground, with an iron funnel sticking out of it for a chimney and smoking very cosily; but nothing else in the way of a habitation that was visible to *me*. 'That's not it?' said I. 'That ship looking thing?' (p. 36).

David's partial vision exposes the way in which only certain domestic configurations are easily legible. A similar limited perception is clear is David's struggle to understand the relational logic within the boathouse: 'Mr Peggotty [..] did you give your son the name of Ham because you lived in a sort of ark?' David discovers the error of his assumptions, finding he has misread the nature of the bonds between the boat's inhabitants: 'I was very much surprised that Mr Peggotty was not Ham's father, and began to wonder whether I was mistaken about his relationship to anybody else there' (p. 40). David, who has yet to learn the hard way that good parenting in Dickens is usually done by surrogate, is finally brought to comprehend that Dan Peggotty is a bachelor who has adopted the orphaned and destitute around him. Peggotty provides a home for Ham and Emily, 'an orphan nephew and niece' and for Mrs Gummidge, 'the widow of his partner in a boat, who had died very poor' (p. 40). Through David's growing understanding of Mr Peggotty's form of parenting, Dickens models a way in which children may come to appreciate non-heterosexual and non-reproductive forms of bonding. Peggotty and Dickens's other avunculate carers open up the queer possibilities that, as Sedgwick has argued, children often first encounter through uncles and aunts as 'adults whose intimate access to children needn't depend on their own pairing or procreation'.[72] Dickens's regular readers, alert to Dan Peggotty's position in a long line of benevolent bachelor dads in Dickens's fiction, would be quicker to appreciate avunculate possibilities than David.

The queer potential of houseboat life is similarly explored in the novel that precedes Copperfield, *Dombey and Son*. Here Sol Gills, ably assisted by his retired seafaring friend Captain Cuttle, brings up his orphaned nephew Walter in his home and ship's instrument shop, which with its careful space-saving, battening down of all loose articles and navigational tools, is 'a snug, sea-going, ship-shape concern, wanting only good sea room, in the event of an unexpected launch, to work its way securely, to any desert island in the world' (p. 47). The fishlike

---

[72] Sedgwick, *Tendencies*, p. 63.

names of Gills and Cuttle further complement the building's blurring of
the boundaries between sea and land-dwelling. The Wooden-midshipman, so called for the little wooden figure that advertises its trade, does
no business. Gills is, for the majority of the novel, outside of both
productive and reproductive economies, and as such presents a conundrum to the arch-capitalist patriarch, Mr Dombey. Dombey, whose
insistence on the value of patrilineal lines of inheritance contributes to
his fatal parenting of his own son, initially misunderstands Sol's relationship to Walter. Like David on first meeting the members of Peggotty's boathouse, Dombey mistakes Walter as 'the son of Mr Gills'
(p. 51). These misunderstandings reflect an inflexible definition of
parenting, to which Dickens's work is opposed. The unusual architectures of Peggotty's and Gills's homes give form to Dickens's various
breaks with conventional expectations of what constitutes family. In
their alternative configuration, these houseboats promise a different
experience of physical space, without the accretion of the cultural
meanings of the family house. Building on Gaston Bachelard's investigation of the lived experience of architecture and Henri Lefebvre's work
on the social production of space, queer geographers (such as David Bell
and Gill Valentine) have examined the ways that spaces are sexualized.[73]
In *Queer Phenomenology* Ahmed speaks of her experience of the way
that: 'Some spaces extend certain bodies and simply do not leave room
for others [...] "the family home" seems so full of traces of heterosexual
intimacy that it is hard to take up my place without feeling those traces
as points of pressure.'[74] Similarly Nancy Duncan's survey of gay attitudes to private space reflects a widespread disenfranchisement with
the family home as 'an extremely heterosexist and alienating site'.[75]
At their best, Dickens's shipshape domestic arrangements would
allow their inhabitants to exist without the same social pressures of a
particular life-script that directs all towards heterosexual conjugality and

---

[73] See Gaston Bachelard, *The Poetics of Space* (1958), trans. Maria Jolas (Boston: Beacon, 1992), Henri Lefebvre, *The Production of Space* (1974), trans. Donald Nicholson-Smith (Oxford: Blackwell, 1991), and, for example, David Bell and Gill Valentine (eds.), *Mapping Desire: Geographies of Sexualities* (London: Routledge, 1995).
[74] Ahmed, *Queer Phenomenology*, p. 11.
[75] Nancy Duncan, 'Renegotiating Gender and Sexuality in Public and Private Spaces', in *Body Space: Destabilising Geographies of Gender and Sexuality*, ed. Nancy Duncan (London: Routledge, 1996), pp. 127–45, p. 130.

reproduction. Foucault has discussed the particular existential possibilities presented by the boat, 'a floating piece of space, a place without a place, that exists by itself, that is closed in on itself and at the same time is given over to the infinity of the sea [. . .] In civilisations without boats, dreams dry up.'[76] Peggotty's and Gills's unusual houseboats are comfortably out of place; imbricated in the spaces of both land and sea yet fully of neither element, they powerfully suggest a renegotiation of available spaces and possible domesticities.

Dickens's queer boathouses register an architectural and emotional difference from the many unhappy, more conventionally housed biological families of his fiction. As others, such as Arthur Adrian, have observed, Dickens's oeuvre displays an 'abiding interest in the surrogate parent'.[77] Though there are cruel fosterers, including Fagin, Squeers, Creakle, the Murdstones, and Mrs Joe, the loving foster plot is one much more regularly represented in Dickens's work, presenting, as Sally Ledger has noted, a contrast to the many dysfunctional and unhappy biological families of this fiction.[78] Dickens's surrogate parent plots cross lines of class and gender, taking in a demographic cross-section from the moneyed, leisured Mr Jarndyce to the impoverished working-woman, Betty Higden, in *Our Mutual Friend*. Betty combines a financial need for the money she receives for taking in 'Minders' – 'I love children, and Four-pence a week is Four-pence' (p. 199) – and for the labour that the adopted 'love-child' Sloppy provides turning the mangle, with a fond regard for them as well as for her orphaned young grandson whom she has also taken in. As Adrian puts it, 'because they are dedicated to helping those least able to help themselves, the young victims of social injustice, Dickens's ideal surrogate parents are among his noblest characters'.[79] Betty Higden, Mrs Boffin, and Betsy Trotwood are some of the stars of this electively caring constellation.

[76] Michel Foucault, *Of Other Spaces: Heterotopias* (1967), trans. Jay Miskowiec, http://www.foucault.info/documents/heteroTopia/foucault.heteroTopia.en.html.

[77] Arthur Adrian, *Dickens and the Parent-Child Relationship* (Ohio: Ohio University Press, 1984), p. 91.

[78] Ledger examines a 'series of alternative domestic units' (including Fagin's gang, Sleary's circus, Wemmick's castle, David Copperfield's surrogate parenting by the Micawbers and later by Aunt Betsy and Mr Dick) that offset and offer refuge from 'the broken and dysfunctional families which litter the pages of Dickens's fiction.' 'Domesticity', *Oxford Reader's Companion to Dickens*, ed. Paul Schlicke (Oxford: Oxford University Press, 1999), p. 191.

[79] Adrian, p. 94.

What is striking though, in terms of the disruption of gendered expectations about nurture and the 'natural' impulse to both have and care
for a child, is the high proportion of Dickensian adoption plots that
focus on the single male.

Such plots are certainly not restricted to Dickens's fiction, although
they abound there.[80] George Eliot's two central narratives of foster
fathering, *Silas Marner* (1861) and *Felix Holt* (1866), are similarly
concerned with the exploration of masculine tenderness and men's
innate ability for childcare. In *Felix Holt* the clergyman Rufus Lyon
has an immediate skill for soothing baby Esther, who becomes his
adopted daughter. As Esther's mother, Annette, puts it, not long before
Rufus marries her, 'You do nurse baby well [. . .]. Yet you never nursed
before I came?'[81] Felix – another man who is 'never easy but when he's
got [a] child on his lap' – criticizes the argument 'that a man should
marry because he's fond of children', arguing instead that 'that's a
reason for not marrying. A bachelor's children are always young; they're
immortal children – always lisping, waddling, helpless, and with a
chance for turning out good' (p. 226). However, a major factor in
Rufus's short-lived marriage to Annette is his affinity to her baby, and
this is figured in Annette's unconventional proposal which places the
infant as a central bond in their marriage: '"We will go out and be
married – shall we not? See! and *la petite*" (the baby had never been
named anything else) "shall call you Papa – and then we shall never
part"' (p. 88). Here, although a heterosexual bond is in place in Rufus's
irresistible passion for Annette, this clearly is not the only impulse for
marriage. Here, as very often in Dickens's fiction, it becomes clear that
marriage is not exclusively motivated by cross-sex desire, but also by
male nurturing needs and desires.

Eliot's representation of the significance of the relationship between
Rufus and baby Esther in this marriage partly recalls the dynamics
of Joe Gargery's proposal to Georgiana Pirrip in *Great Expectations*
(1860–1), which emphasizes his interest in caring for her young,

---

[80] Novy observes the prevalence of foster fathering narratives in Victorian fiction,
suggesting that this gendering might have its basis in classical and Shakespearian
precedents or in an effort to give 'sympathy more cultural prestige by attributing it to
men, in whom it is taken to have a less biological basis' (*Reading Adoption*, p. 152).
[81] George Eliot, *Felix Holt: The Radical* (London: Penguin, 1995), p. 87.

orphaned brother, Pip: 'When I offered to your sister to keep company, and to be asked in church at such times as she was willing and ready to come to the forge, I said to her "And bring the poor little child. God bless the poor little child," I said to your sister, "there's room for *him* at the forge!"'.[82] Pip's reaction to this disclosure – 'I broke out crying and begged pardon, and hugged Joe round the neck', expresses his belated understanding that Joe's marital motive was that of caring for his young self. Joe's emphasis on Pip's central role in this 'courtship' – 'When I got acquainted with your sister, it were the talk how she was bringing you up by hand' (p. 48) – corrects Pip's earlier impression, so alert to the incompatibility of this couple, that his sister 'must have made Joe Gargery marry her by hand' (p. 8). Tess O'Toole, reflecting on the proliferation of adoption plots in Victorian fiction, points out that 'though the marriage plot is the novel's most familiar vehicle for reshaping the family, the adoption plot is a prominent alternative (and sometimes intersecting) paradigm'.[83] This alternative presents a potentially queer form of family formation, in which marriage and reproduction are displaced as the exclusive means of creating kinship and constructing family stories. In the Gargery family, as elsewhere in Dickens's novels, marriage clearly does not operate as a heterosexual institution, in that the most significant affective bond impelling the partnership is not that between the couple. Instead of offering a straightening mechanism (the function which is conventionally ascribed to it in responses to Victorian material), marriage itself can operate to develop non-heterosexual ties, permitting, as in Joe Gargery's case, the establishment of a foster-parent relationship, or (as will be discussed in Chapter 3) furthering homoerotic bonds.

In Eliot's *Silas Marner*, as in Dickens's Brownlow plot, the connections between parenting, marriage, and the sexual mechanics of reproduction are fully severed as the bachelor Silas becomes a father to a girl he has no biological or affinal relation to. Unlike Rufus Lyon who had no siblings, a more familiar context for male childcare, Silas is reminded of caring for his little sister as a child when Eppie totters into his home. Experiencing 'old quiverings of tenderness', Silas instinctively picks up

---

[82] Charles Dickens, *Great Expectations* (London: Penguin, 2003), p. 48.
[83] Tess O'Toole, 'Adoption and the 'Improvement of the Estate' in Trollope and in Craik', in *Imagining Adoption: Essays on Literature and Culture*, ed. Marianne Novy (Michigan: University of Michigan Press, 2001), pp. 11–34, p. 17.

the child and 'almost unconsciously uttered sounds of hushing tenderness; while he bethought himself that some of his porridge [...] would
do well to feed the child with if it were only warmed up a little'.[84] Eliot
depicts this as a divergence from expected gendered behaviour in her
record of the villagers' responses to his eagerly embraced, elective fatherhood: 'Why, there isn't many lone men 'ud ha' been wishing to take up
with a little 'un like that but I reckon the weaving makes you handier as
men as do out-door work – you're partly as handy as a woman, for
weaving comes next to spinning' (p. 128). As Marianne Novy has
proposed, Eliot's adoption narratives provide 'arguments against seeing
nurturing as an instinctive capacity determined by women's biology
alone'.[85] These examples further suggest that the hands-on nursing
father, which as John Tosh has demonstrated, was a particularly visible
and applauded figure at the end of the eighteenth century, persists as a
figure to be celebrated well into the Victorian period.[86]

Narratives of the domestically skilled and emotionally astute non-
biological father intervene in debates about the parameters of masculinity.
Just as authors, and Dickens in particular, contributed to discussions
of what constituted the gentleman by exploring the tactile aspects of
male gentleness (a subject that will receive full treatment in Chapter 5),
writers could deploy narratives of foster fathering to recommend a
nurturing masculine ideal. As Gillian Beer argues, 'for the novelist
who, like George Eliot, sets so much store by sympathy, the chosen
and unnatured bond of "fostering" is crucial'.[87] The voluntarism of tender
fatherhood here, and in instances across Dickens's fiction from *Oliver
Twist* to his 1860's Christmas books, presents a particularly compelling
endorsement of this practice. These are not characters actively forced to
single-parent by the death of a spouse or the orphanhood of a close
relative, although, as Terri Sabatos has shown, sensitive visual depictions of widowers with children at this time participated similarly in
contests over domestic masculinity. Sabatos suggests that works like
Luke Fieldes's *The Widower* (exhibited 1876) entered 'contemporary

    84 George Eliot, *Silas Marner* (Oxford: Oxford University Press, 1998), pp. 109–10.
    85 Marianne Novy, 'Adoption in *Silas Marner* and *Daniel Deronda*', in *Imagining Adop-
tion*, pp. 35–56, p. 50.
    86 John Tosh, *A Man's Place: Masculinity and the Middle-Class Home in Victorian England*
(New Haven and London: Yale University Press, 1999), p. 87.
    87 Gillian Beer, *George Eliot* (Sussex: Harvester, 1996), p. 109.

debates on the father's role in the domestic sphere, particularly as it relates to his role as caregiver, and began to diffuse anxieties about male feminization, as widowers evidently have no choice but to adopt the role of nurse to their children'.[88] Tosh has suggested that such anxieties about the relationship between nurture and femininity were relatively new, documenting a shift away from easily affectionate fatherhood through the nineteenth century: 'As the gendered nature of man and woman, of father and mother, became more polarized, there was less tolerance for paternal behaviour which appeared to encroach on the maternal role.'[89] While Tosh's nuanced account of domestic manliness does find space for the 'intimate father' as well as models of absent, tyrannical, and distant paternity, these literary celebrations of the caring male, whose provision of nurture is completely voluntary and often represented as being in response to a deep emotional need, suggest that existing accounts have under-emphasized the significance of such alternative modelling of manliness. Margaret Markwick makes a similar point in her reading of Anthony Trollope's depiction of fathering, focusing on *Dr Thorne* (1858), a novel concerned with the eponymous doctor's bachelor adoption of his niece. Markwick posits that 'it is his men bringing up children alone who reveal Trollope as the herald of the new man', but goes on to argue that this form of masculinity may not be so 'new' as it seems.[90] She suggests that we read Trollope's work as 'an historically plausible account of men's aptitude for child care, and consider whether hands-on fatherhood was not, in fact, more of a Victorian ideal than we usually acknowledge'.[91]

As well as challenging the gendering of nurturing as feminine, these narratives disrupt a biological basis for familial commitment through moving depictions of the mutual dedication of fathers and adoptive children. Trollope's bachelor Dr Thorne, who swears on the Bible to be 'father' 'and mother' to his niece Mary, has, like Eliot's foster father heroes, 'an aptitude for the society of children'.[92] He describes the times

---

[88] Terri Sebatos, 'Father as Mother: The Image of the Widower with Children in Victorian Art', in *Gender and Fatherhood in the Nineteenth Century*, ed. Trev Lynn Broughton and Helen Rogers (Basingstoke: Palgrave, 2007), pp. 71–84.

[89] Tosh, p. 87. See also pp. 91–9.

[90] Margaret Markwick, 'Hands-on Fatherhood in Trollope's Novels', in *Gender and Fatherhood in the Nineteenth Century*, pp. 85–95, p. 86, p. 89.

[91] Markwick, p. 94.

[92] Anthony Trollope, *Doctor Thorne* (London: Penguin, 1991), p. 27, 39.

passed with Mary in his refitted bachelor pad as 'perhaps the pleasantest of his life' (p. 89) and looks on her as 'his own niece, his adopted bairn, his darling, the pride of his heart, the cynosure of his eye, his child also, his own Mary' (p. 133), the multiple descriptors pointing to the difficulty of verbalizing the emotional complexity of this relationship. Eliot is similarly thorough in documenting the 'deep affections' that mean that 'Silas would rather part with his life than with Eppie' (p. 152). In *Felix Holt* and *Silas Marner* the adoptee is offered a choice between the father who has raised them and the biological father. Both Esther and Eppie choose their adoptive fathers, the latter movingly articulating the long-term intimacy and reliance that outweighs any tie of blood: 'He's took care of me and loved me from the first, and I'll cleave to him as long as he lives, and nobody shall ever come between him and me [. . .] I can't feel as I've got any father but one' (p. 167). Similarly, Trollope's Mary Thorne celebrates the fact that her marriage will not separate her from the doctor: 'What had he not done for her, that uncle of hers, who had been more loving to her than any father!' (p. 546). These emphatic conclusions queer the family in a similar way to Dickens's work, by making explicit the possibility that elective forms of family, in which heterosexual reproduction is at most a peripheral concern and exemplary parenting is performed by alternative configurations (in terms of gender, number and age of parents) to the opposite-sex couple, may be preferable to biological formations of kinship.

CHILD-LOVING IN THE CHRISTMAS NUMBERS

Dickens's most detailed delineation of a man's intense emotional attachment to his adoptive daughter appears in his now little-known *All the Year Round* Christmas number of 1865, *Dr Marigold's Prescriptions*. The tale begins with a child abuse plot reminiscent of *Great Expectations*. Dr Marigold, who is characterized by his statement: 'I love children with all my heart',[93] feels powerless to prevent his wife from

[93] Charles Dickens, *Doctor Marigold's Prescriptions* in *The Christmas Stories*, pp. 566–605, p. 576.

beating their daughter, just as Joe Gargery feels unable to protect Pip from the heavy hand of Mrs Joe. When Dr Marigold is consecutively bereaved by the death of his daughter from a fever, the suicide of his stricken wife, and finally the death of his faithful dog, he is steeped in isolation: 'Being naturally of a tender turn, I had dreadful lonely feelings on me arter this [. . .] they got me down in private and rolled upon me' (p. 580). Instead of seeking the more conventional expedient of re-marriage, Marigold comes across a neglected deaf and dumb orphan girl at a circus and is possessed by an immediate urge to adopt her. In line with what Nelson identifies as the primary emotional motivation for adoption in mid-nineteenth-century America, the circus girl is figured as a replacement for a dead child.[94] Marigold calls her 'Sophy' after his dead daughter and reflects that 'if she was more cared for and more kindly used she would be like my own child. She was just the same age that my own daughter would have been' (p. 581).

Marigold's impulsive response to the circus girl offers a fairly close reworking of the central elements of Wilkie Collins's *Hide and Seek*, an 1854 novel that Collins dedicated to his close friend, Dickens, in 'admiration and affection', and wrote, in part, while the two men were staying together in Boulogne.[95] Dickens was, unsurprisingly given his particular interest in its central theme, fulsome in his praise for *Hide and Seek*: 'I think it far away the cleverest novel I have ever seen written by a new hand [. . .] I call it a very remarkable book and have been much surprised by its great merit.'[96] In Collins's novel a sensation plot, complete with concealed identities and family secrets, is catalysed by an elective father's deep anxiety that his adopted daughter, Mary, or Madonna as he renames her, may be removed from him. On seeing Mary – who, like Dickens's 'Sophy', is deaf and dumb – performing at a circus and discovering that she is beaten by the circus owner, Valentine Blyth is immediately seized with a compulsive desire to make her his own child: 'I must take the child home with me, oh [. . .] don't say no! I'll make her happy as the day is long. I've no child of my own: I'll watch

---

[94] Nelson, *Little Strangers*, p. 16.
[95] Wilkie Collins, *Hide and Seek* (Oxford: Oxford University Press, 1999) ed. Catherine Peters, p. xxv.
[96] Charles Dickens to Georgina Hogarth, 22 July 1854, *Pilgrim*, VII, p. 366. Dickens wrote to Collins on 23 May 1854 to express his delight at the dedication (*Pilgrim*, VII, p. 335).

over her and love her and teach her all my life. I've got a poor, suffering, bed-ridden wife at home, who would think such a companion as little Mary the greatest blessing God could send her' (p. 101). Collins's articulation of Blyth's longing for a child and his gentleness – both to Mary and to other street children he encounters – places this with other fostering fictions that question the gendered affects associated with parenting. Collins, while challenging the very distinctions he draws, details Blyth's 'affections' as 'so manly in their firmness, so womanly in their tenderness, so childlike in their frank, fearless confidence' (p. 40). Though Mary does go on to have an idyllic childhood encompassed by the love of the Blyths, Valentine's ardency about adopting her complete with the frenzy of kisses with which he repeatedly embraces her, requires reassurances within the plot. Blyth, like Dickens's Brownlow, manifests an apparently undermotivated desire to parent. A respectable old friend feels it necessary to vouch for the overly passionate Valentine's 'integrity of motive' (p. 103). Such a reference is necessary given the text's fairly explicit acknowledgement of the sexual danger that young Mary is exposed to at the circus. Valentine insists that she be removed from the vicious circus master to ensure 'the sacred preservation of her purity of heart and mind' (p. 105). Valentine's passion, as Collins describes it, is, by contrast, a product of his extreme but chaste desire to have a daughter.

Hide and Seek has long been criticized as a poor imitation of Dickens's work. In its pioneering level of attention to a male emotional impulse to father a foster child, however (it predates Eliot's fiction on this theme and Dickens's most emotionally explicit treatments of this), Collins's novel clearly anticipates a central plotline in a number of Dickens's 1860s Christmas stories, as well as providing the direct inspiration for elements of *Dr Marigold's Prescriptions*. Male adoption is the central concern of Dickens's contribution to the multi-authored 1862 Christmas number, *Somebody's Luggage*, while foster parenting and the creation of a family of choice structures Dickens's parts of the Christmas numbers for the next two years, *Mrs Lirriper's Lodgings* (1863) and *Mrs Lirriper's Legacy* (1864), and is at the heart of the number he co-authored with Collins, *No Thoroughfare* (1867). Dickens's chapter of the 1862 project, 'His Boots', picks up an apparent juxtaposition that he had explored in the tender muscles of *Bleak House*'s Trooper George. In this short story a cantankerous Englishman, who has rejected his adult daughter when she had a baby outside marriage, learns how to father from the example of a gentle soldier.

Staying in an unspecified fortified French town, the English man disapprovingly observes the French soldiery 'lighting the people's fires, boiling the people's pots, minding the people's babies, rocking the people's cradles, washing the people's greens, and making themselves generally useful, in every sort of unmilitary way' (p. 470). He is particularly fascinated and irritated by a particular case of such domestic care, in which Corporal Théophile, a man of 'careful hands' (p. 476), looks after a disowned, illegitimate 'child of [. . .] no one', Bebelle. Though the barber's wife receives a small stipend to care for the girl, she has been neglected until the Corporal's arrival, when he takes her care upon himself: 'washing and dressing and brushing Bebelle [. . .] Always Corporal and always Bebelle. Never Corporal without Bebelle. Never Bebelle without Corporal' (p. 473). Observing this tender inseparability the unlikeable Englishman exclaims 'Why, confound the fellow, he is not her father!' (p. 472), 'He is not one of her relations. Not at all!' (p. 474). The Englishman's landlady, however, contests this biological (il)logic: 'The less relation, the more genteel' (p. 474). In terms that resonate with Collins's exploration of the emotional investment in foster fathering, the landlady intuits the mutual affective benefits of this partnership: 'finding the poor unowned child in need of being loved, and finding himself in need of loving' (p. 475). That blood is not the only means of forming family is a lesson that, in the redemptive mode of the Christmas narratives, the Englishman must learn in order to reclaim his humanity. He must come to understand the benefit to both child and man in such a relationship, so that when the 'gentle Corporal' (p. 480) unexpectedly dies he is ready to take on the care of Bebelle, making her toilette in 'the way in which he had often seen the poor Corporal make it' (p. 481), having learnt how to father from this tender military man. He leaves with Bebelle for England to find his 'forgiven' daughter (p. 481) and to experience family in a new way.

John Bowen has offered a compelling biographical reading of this 'fantasy of adoption' noting the tale's affinity with *Dr Marigold's Prescriptions* and the *Lirriper* stories, all of which 'explore the possible fates of illegitimate children who are not cared for by their real parents, and [. . .] engineer happy fates for them'.[97] Following Claire Tomalin's

[97] John Bowen, 'Bebelle and "His Boots": Dickens, Ellen Ternan and the *Christmas Stories*', *The Dickensian* 96.3 (2000), 197–208, pp. 203, 206.

Somebody's Luggage.

1. Charles Green, Woodcut of Corporal Théophile and Bebelle, 'Somebody's Luggage', Library edition of Dickens's Works, 1911

speculation that Dickens and Ellen Ternan had a baby sometime in 1862, that Ellen lived with the infant in France and that it died young, Bowen proposes that these stories could offer a response to and a working-through of Dickens's feelings about his own illegitimate child. This seems especially likely given that writing in these stories is frequently presented as a form of relief for the loss (in the tales, temporary or partial) of a child. The miscellaneous tales that make up the bulk of *Dr Marigold's Prescriptions* are introduced as stories written by Marigold in readiness for Sophy's return from the deaf and dumb school. The writing has a therapeutic element, easing Marigold's loneliness at the separation: '[It] kept my time and attention a good deal employed and helped me over the two years stile' (p. 585). Similarly, in the *Lirriper* stories, another tender military man who cares for an orphaned child, is said to write the composite tales of lodgers that make up the numbers to console himself while his godson is away at school.[98]

Though the biographical interpretation is persuasive, these foster father narratives clearly develop Dickens's existing attentiveness towards alternative family configurations and tender masculinities – interests that span his entire career and are much in evidence before 1862. The gentle Major Jemmy Jackman, of *Mrs Lirriper's Lodgings*, for example, has affinities with a whole range of tender martial men long celebrated in Dickens's work, and the lodging house family that he establishes with his landlady and an infant orphan resonates with numbers of Dickensian families attached by neither blood nor heterosexuality. Major Jemmy Jackman and Mrs Lirriper become godfather and grandmother to an illegitimate infant who is born and immediately orphaned in Mrs Lirriper's boarding house. Bonds of long affection, rather than romance, unite these surrogate parents, in a partnership that is reminiscent of that between Betsy Trotwood (married but separated from her abusive husband) and the single Mr Dick, who provide another form of cheerful, eccentric guardianship to David Copperfield. At the start of *Mrs Lirriper's Lodgings* the Major has boarded with Mrs Lirriper for thirteen years and in Dickens's opening of the Christmas number for the following year, *Mrs Lirriper's Legacy*, he is affectionately reinstalled as an integral feature of the lodgings: 'The Major is still a fixture in the Parlours quite as much so as the roof of the house.'[99] The lodging house

---

[98] Charles Dickens, *Mrs Lirriper's Lodgings*, in *The Christmas Stories*, pp. 502–35, p. 530.

[99] Charles Dickens, *Mrs Lirriper's Legacy*, in *The Christmas Stories*, pp. 535–66, p. 538.

becomes home to an emphatically non-sexual and non-reproductive family of choice, with landlady and lodger giving the child a suitably composite name: 'We called him Jemmy, being after the Major his own godfather, with Lirriper for a surname being after myself, and never was a dear child such a brightening thing in a Lodgings or such a playmate to his grandmother as Jemmy to this house and me' (p. 521). This idyllic community recalls the contentment of the Brownlow and Maylie adoptive households of Dickens's early novel: 'in summer we were happy as the days were long and in winter we were happy as the days were short' (p. 527). Mrs Lirriper is emphatic about this household's departure from a biological model of family, pointing explicitly to the age differential: 'This is sent to a childless old woman. This is for me to take care of' (p. 520).[100] As in *No Thoroughfare*, young Jemmy's experience of this elective family forms the basis for his vision of a larger family of choice, in which he and his favourite school friend, 'the cleverest and bravest and best looking and most generous of all the friends that ever were' (p. 534) marry two sisters and take all the lodgings of 'this Gran and this godfather, [...] that they would all live together, and all be happy! And so they were, and so it never ended!' (p. 535).

    This brief reference to an intermarriage plot that functions to preserve and enhance a male bond as well as maintaining an extended household, points to the ways in which foster family plots are consonant with Dickens's wider attention to the limits of marriage as an erotic opposite-sex bond and the broader, queer motives for family formation. As Karen Chase and Michael Levenson, observing Dickens's narrative horror of the isolated marital couple, have noted: 'more than a marriage, it is a *household* that Dickens's novels come to seek, and the conditions of the flourishing household require at least three, at least that additional one, to break the close-circuit of romantic love'.[101]

<hr/>

[100] Mrs Lirriper reiterates this, with the same emphasis on her age in *Mrs Lirriper's Legacy*: ' "My dear this baby is sent to a childless old woman." He has been my pride and joy ever since. I loved him as dearly as if he had drunk from my breast' (p. 557).

[101] Karen Chase and Michael Levenson, *The Spectacle of Intimacy: A Public Life for the Victorian Family* (Princeton: Princeton University Press, 2000), p. 94.

As this and the following two chapters attest, the reproductive hetero-sexual couple is emphatically not at the centre of Dickensian family formation. Instead his writings celebrate a broad range of elective affinities, placing such figures as the tender bachelor dad at the heart of the ideal home.

2

Serial Bachelorhood and Counter-Marital Plotting

Dickens supplements his attention to bachelor parenting with a commitment to counter-marital plotting, articulating male resistance to marriage through diverse modes, ranging from the comic to the Gothic. While Dickens has seemed the exemplar of the bourgeois Victorian novelist using the wedlock tradition as a device for social reward and closure, the security of such plots is undermined by, to use Joseph Boone's terms, a wealth of counter-traditional narratives, in which marital closure is strenuously avoided.[1] Important work has examined resistance to marital plotting from within in Dickens's fiction, noting the near ubiquity of marital disharmony.[2] This project turns from discontent to indisposition to register Dickens's explicit articulations and plotting of marital aversion. Taking the presentation of the

[1] Joseph, Boone, *Tradition Counter Tradition: Love and the Form of Fiction* (Chicago and London: University of Chicago Press, 1987).

[2] See especially Kelly Hager, 'Estranging David Copperfield: Reading the Novel of Divorce', *ELH* 63.4 (1996), 989–1019, and Hager 'Plotting Marriage: Dickens, Divorce and the Failed-Marriage Plot' (doctoral thesis, University of California, 1992). Even critics determined to maintain that 'Dickens, like many Victorian writers, felt that marriage was "the most important event and the happiest state of life"' (Margaret Dalziel, *Popular Fiction 100 Years Ago* (Philadelphia: Dufour, 1958) quoted and affirmed by Rita Lubitz, *Marital Power in Dickens's Fiction* (New York: Peter Lang, 1996), p. 115), struggle to support this. Lubitz's book offers four meaty chapters on marital dominance, avarice and other discontents, whilst only finding material enough for a noticeably slimmer single chapter on happier unions. For a similar collision between a belief in 'Dickens's vision of marriage as the desired end of human activity' and the contrary evidence of the novels see Barbara Weiss, 'The Dilemma of Happily Ever After: Marriage and the Victorian Novel', in *Portraits of Marriage in Literature*, ed. Anne Hargrave and Maurine Magliocco (Illinois: Western Illinois University Press, 1984), pp. 67–86.

congenital and celebrated bachelor Mr Lorry in the weekly instalments and monthly parts of *A Tale of Two Cities* (1859) as an opening case study, I propose that Dickens's first readers read differently for the plot. Here I tease out the queer possibilities of the serial form in which linear, teleological reading is structurally discouraged and closure is only ever a temporary cessation. By examining Dickens's fiction through the approaches recommended by book history, attentive to the conditions of publication and the varied experiences of readers, it becomes apparent that marriage and reproduction, even when present in Dickensian denouement, were not usually experienced as the author's final word.

'YOU WERE A BACHELOR IN YOUR CRADLE': MR LORRY'S CONGENITAL BACHELORHOOD

As an elderly bachelor Mr Lorry has evaded the conventional narrative trajectory most often applied to bachelor characters in literature of the time. George Cruikshank's sketch series of 1844, *The Bachelor's Own Book, or, The Progress of Mr Lambkin (gent.), in the Pursuit of Pleasure and Amusement: and also in Search of Health and Happiness* distils into twenty-four plates a familiar 'progress' trajectory, in which 'happiness' is eventually translated as marriage. Cruikshank stereotypically depicts a lonely illness attended by a hired nurse as the result of Lambkin's indulgence in the homosocial 'pleasure and amusement' of betting and heavy social drinking. Recovering his health Mr Lambkin determines upon a more staid single lifestyle 'but feels buried alive in the Grand Mausoleum Club; and contemplating an old bachelor member who sits poring over the newspapers all day, he feels horror-struck at the possibility of such a fate becoming his own and determines to seek a reconciliation with the Lady of his affections'.[3] The perceived negative social consequences of the bachelor's departure from marital domesticity are emphasized by Cruikshank's inclusion of newspapers bearing the captions 'Refuge for the Destitute', 'Home for the Housewife' and '[. . .] on Solitude' in his depiction of the un(re)productive Mausoleum Club.

---

[3] George Cruikshank, *The Bachelor's Own Book* (1844, repr. Glasgow: David Bryce, 1888), plate 22.

Cruikshank's headlines reflect contemporary concerns that bachelor-hood contributed to increased numbers of so-called 'redundant' women, and could result in more applications for charitable relief from those without families to financially support them. Demographic shifts throughout the nineteenth century resulted in a dramatic increase in the population of unmarried women (famously addressed in W. R. Greg's 1862 article 'Why are Women Redundant?') and a corresponding escalation of anxieties surrounding the volitional bachelor. Through an abrupt recapitulation to familial domesticity, Cruikshank spares Mr Lambkin from the growing stigma surrounding wilful bachelorhood. The final plate of the series, portraying Lambkin's wedding breakfast, is accompanied by an inscription that concludes with Lambkin's marriage speech: 'May the single be married and [. . .] married happily.'[4]

Such common narratives of bachelor development were faithful to the etymological origins of the term. In its earliest uses a bachelor was a noviciate, a junior in training either for fully fledged knighthood, craftsmanship or a university degree. The now most common sense of bachelor as 'an unmarried man (of marriageable age)' has, from its origins, carried an implication of incompleteness.[5] Integral to this common use (and explicit in the rarer application of 'bachelor' to 'an inexperienced person, a novice') is a sense of transgression against the imperative to marriage. In the immensely popular *Reveries of a Bachelor: Or a Book of the Heart* by American author Donald Grant Mitchell (alias I. K. Marvel) the young single protagonist, despite his ambivalence to marriage, marks elderly unreformed bachelorhood as aberrant: 'I will never [. . .] live a bachelor till sixty; never so surely as there is hope in man, or charity in woman, or faith in both.'[6] Picking up on popular rhetoric on both sides of the Atlantic, such as T. S. Arthur's 1845 description of bachelorhood as 'strange, unnatural, criminal', Howard Chudacoff has argued that 'in modern Western society, any choice of lifestyle that diverts or prevents a presumably marriageable person from the social obligation to settle

[4] Cruikshank, *Bachelor's*, plate 24.
[5] OED records 1386 as the first use of the term in this sense.
[6] I. K. Marvel, *Reveries of a Bachelor: Or a Book of the Heart* (New York: 1850), first published in England two years later (London: David Bogue, 1852), p. 65. Katherine Snyder, *Bachelors, Manhood and the Novel 1850–1925* (Cambridge: Cambridge University Press, 1999), documents the popular success of this text, which went through over 50 unauthorized editions, p. 48.

down and start a family has been considered inappropriate'.[7] In her wide-ranging exploration of bachelorhood in the British novel Katherine Snyder reaches a similar conclusion:

The polymorphic variety of negative bachelor stereotypes reveals no single trajectory of aberrance, but any number of ways in which bachelors, especially those 'old bachelors' who seemed to have run permanently off the rails of the marriage track, were seen as veering away from an acceptable performance of manhood.[8]

While both Chudacoff and Snyder register the complexity and incoherence of treatments of the bachelor, their emphasis on deviance precludes an investigation of the extent to which even respectable fiction could use the confirmed bachelor to promote and celebrate the alternative narrative trajectory of marital refusal.

Dickens's fiction, as we have seen in the previous chapter's exploration of his triumphant plotting of blissful bachelor parenting, firmly resists any simple equivalence of the bachelor with the anti-domestic. Instead his plots uncouple the assumed interconnection between marriage and domesticity, to create a space for other patterns of care and new understandings of family. Indeed, Dickens's innovative attention to the possible homeliness of bachelor life is recorded in the OED citation of two new combinations, 'bachelor cottage', Dickens's description of Mortimer and Eugene's lodgings near Hampton in *Our Mutual Friend*, and 'sweet bachelor apartment', from *Little Dorrit*. In both instances Dickens redefines bachelor life as a positive lifestyle choice, rather than a state of incompleteness.

Dickens's close friend and sometime literary collaborator Wilkie Collins presents a parallel reworking of the bachelor's literary trajectory.[9] In a mischievous 1859 article for Dickens's weekly journal *All the Year Round*, Collins rejects the repetitive, predictable plot of bachelorhood-resolved:

---

[7] T. S. Arthur, quoted in Boone, p. 279; Howard Chudacoff, *The Age of the Bachelor: Creating an American Subculture* (Princeton: Princeton University Press, 1999), p. 8.

[8] Katherine Snyder, *Bachelors, Manhood and the Novel 1850–1925* (Cambridge: Cambridge University Press, 1999), p. 28. For continuing concerns about volitional bachelorhood later in the century see John Tosh, *A Man's Place: Masculinity and the Middle Class Home in Victorian England* (New Haven and London: Yale University Press, 1999); and Tosh, 'Domesticity and Manliness in the Victorian Middle Class: The Family of Edward Benson White', in *Manful Assertions: Masculinities in Britain since 1800*, ed. Michael Roper and John Tosh (London: Routledge, 1991), pp. 44–73.

[9] For a more thorough treatment of the literary and personal relationship between Dickens and Collins see the previous chapter.

The bachelor has been profusely served up on all sorts of literary tables; but the presentation of him has hitherto been remarkable for a singularly monotonous flavour of matrimonial sauce. We have heard of his loneliness, and its remedy; of his solitary position in illness, and its remedy; of the miserable neglect of his linen, and its remedy.[10]

Collins refuses to bemoan bachelor life; instead he celebrates the diversity of a 'succession of remarkable bachelors' whose true characters – closely concealed in everyday society – unfold at night to a select exclusively male group 'in the loose atmosphere of the Bachelor Bedroom'.[11] This piece operates as the culmination of Collins's articles on bachelorhood for both of Dickens's journals. Previously in *Household Words* Collins had written a variety of short pieces critiquing marriage from the provocative perspective of the confirmed bachelor. In 'Bold Words by a Bachelor' (1856) Collins argued 'that the general idea of the scope and purpose of the institution of Marriage is a miserably narrow one'.[12] He critiques the stifling exclusivity of marriages that depend on the relinquishment of earlier ties, making an impassioned defence of the maintenance of intimate homosocial bonds – 'the truest longest-tried friends of a man's bachelor days' – after marriage. The piece explores what Jonathan Katz has suggested was a recurrent experience of loss for male romantic friends, articulating the 'shock of losing a dear friend, in order that a bride may gain a devoted husband'.[13] As Collins's bachelor persona insists: 'There are other affections, in this world, which are

---

[10] Wilkie Collins, 'The Bachelor Bedroom', *All the Year Round*, 6 August 1859, I, pp. 355–60, p. 355.

[11] Collins, 'Bachelor Bedroom', p. 355, 358.

[12] Wilkie Collins, 'Bold Words by a Bachelor', *Household Words*, 13 December 1856, XIV, pp. 505–7, p. 507.

[13] Collins, 'Bold Words', p. 506; Jonathan Ned Katz, *Love Stories: Sex Between Men Before Homosexuality* (Chicago and London: University of Chicago Press, 2001). Katz examines Abraham Lincoln's response to the engagement of his closest friend, Joshua Fry Speed, noting the articulation of 'deep love for Speed and his anger at losing his most intimate male friend to a wife – a common experience of the era's romantic men friends, as other stories show' (p. 25). Katz also quotes the hero, Ned, of Frederick Wadsworth's Loring's 1871 novel, *Two College Friends*: 'When this war is over, I suppose Tom will marry and forget me. I never will go near his wife – I shall hate her' (pp. 144–5). Xavier Mayne's early-twentieth-century study of homosexuality devotes a section to examples of 'the anguish of a Uranian when partnerless by marriage.' Mayne provides a range of poignant literary and actual accounts of male and female suicides on the marriage of their intimate friend (*The Intersexes*, pp. 544–52).

noble and honourable, besides those of conjugal and parental origin.'[14] Collins's queer decentralizing of marital and reproductive ties as the basis of relationships and affection is delivered by 'an incurably-settled old bachelor'.[15] 'An Awful Warning to Bachelors' (1858) is voiced by a similarly inveterate bachelor persona who declares: 'I have the strongest possible antipathy to being settled in life; and that, if I thought either of my eyes were capable of fixing itself on a young woman, I would shut that eye up, by an effort of will, henceforth and forever.'[16] Collins, albeit in a comic mode, expends a great deal of journalistic energy in defence of the wilfully single male. Both these pieces hold the prestigious opening article position in *Household Words*, suggesting Dickens's editorial support for their content.

Collins's enthusiastic portrayal of the variety of bachelor experience in 'The Bachelor Bedroom' is both spatially and conceptually positioned amongst Dickens's comparable novelistic ruminations on the same theme. At this time the lead fictional serial in Dickens's periodical *All the Year Round* was his *A Tale of Two Cities*, which appeared in thirty-one weekly instalments from the journal's inaugural issue on 30 April 1859 to 26 November of that year. The 6 August issue of *All the Year Round* begins with the fifteenth and exactly central instalment of Dickens's novel and closes with Collins's article, chased by an advertisement for the third monthly part of *A Tale*, which Dickens also issued separately in this format over eight months.[17] Through the figure of Jarvis Lorry in this novel Dickens offers the precise collation of bachelorhood minus the 'matrimonial sauce' that Collins's piece promotes, an overlap in purpose strongly suggested by the immediate proximity between Collins's article and the closing advert for *A Tale*. Readers of the novel in its weekly instalments would have been, then, particularly aware of the debates about the limitations of marriage and the possibilities of single life circulating in the periodical press at the time, and in which Dickens's novel and the non-fiction sections of his journal

[14] Collins, 'Bold Words', p. 505.   [15] Collins, 'Bold Words', p. 351.
[16] Wilkie Collins, 'An Awful Warning to Bachelors', *Household Words*, 27 March 1858, XVII, pp. 337–40, p. 337.
[17] This use of available space as 'free' advertising for the publisher's other current ventures was standard practice in the periodical press. See Laurel Brake *Print in Transition, 1850–1910: Studies in Media and Book History* (Basingstoke: Palgrave, 2001), p. 32.

participate. As Linda Hughes and Michael Lund put it in their important study of Victorian experiences of reading serialized fiction:

> We might even view each volume of a specific periodical [. . .] as a single text by a corporate author; for subscribers certainly read much in each issue of their favourite journal, linking together in their minds not just specific continuing stories but overlapping ongoing presentations linked together by editorial principles.[18]

Given Dickens's notorious level of intervention into contributions to his periodicals, continuities throughout and between issues were particularly pronounced.[19] As 'conductor' of the *All the Year Round* – a role of which he reminds readers in the running heads to every page, in sharp distinction to the principle of anonymity of contributions – Dickens orchestrates particular constellations of content.

The inaugural issue of *All the Year Round* includes both the opening of *A Tale of Two Cities* and a cultural tour of London, one of the two urban sites, of course, referenced in the fictional serial's title. This artistic history of the metropolis briefly takes in the 'brave old Captain Coram, who reared the Foundling, and died poor, but happy'.[20] At its inception then, *A Tale of Two Cities* is both spatially and conceptually proximate to one of Dickens's favourite model bachelors (Coram, as discussed in the previous chapter, was regularly eulogized in Dickens's fiction and journalism), and to a celebrated model of the elective reformation of family bonds by the bachelor 'who reared the Foundling',

[18] Linda Hughes and Michael Lund, *The Victorian Serial* (Charlottesville and London: University Press of Virginia, 1991), p. 9. Brake has done significant work on the interpretative possibilities opened up by a recreation of the Victorian experience of reading a serialized novel in the context of the journal in which it appeared, an experience which brought the serial into an intertextual dialogue with cover or wrapper material, advertising matter, and other contributions. She reads these various periodical components holistically and interactively, arguing that these 'hybrid texts' offer a 'model of textual heteroglossia' (*Print in Transition*, pp. 45, 27). See also Louis James, 'The Trouble with Betsy: Periodicals and the Common Reader in Mid-Nineteenth Century England' in *The Victorian Periodical Press: Samplings and Soundings*, ed. Joanne Shattock and Michael Wolff (Toronto: Leicester University Press and University of Toronto Press, 1982), pp. 349–66.

[19] For a reading of Dickens's sometimes aggressive interventions into contributors' work see Elsie Michie, *Outside the Pale: Cultural Exclusion, Gender Difference and the Victorian Woman Writer* (Ithaca: Cornell University Press, 1993), pp. 79–141.

[20] 'Haunted London', *All The Year Round*, 30 April 1859, I, pp. 20–4, p. 24.

as this playful description of Coram's pioneering philanthropic work puts it. A more explicit suggestion of potential conceptual connections between material is made through the positioning of Collins's six page disquisition on the situation of the single male in domestic space. The continuity between Collins's article and Dickens's novel is particularly apparent in the collected edition of the journal, in which the sixteenth instalment of *A Tale*, which begins the following weekly number of 13 August, is positioned on the opposite page to Collins's 'Bachelor Bedroom'. Through strategic editorial positioning, Dickens employs Collins's critique to recommend the treatment of bachelorhood in his own serial, and to prime readers for a more favourable reception of the provocative figure of the volitionally single male.[21] Collins's comic piece envisages a series of bachelor visits to a country house, positioning the unmarried man as an uncomfortable inhabitant of domestic space able only to reveal his true self, as 'another being – a being unknown to the ladies and, unsuspected by the respectable guests', in the 'select society of the [Bachelor] Bedroom'. While Collins seeks to present a new aspect of the bachelor 'in his relation to married society, under those peculiar circumstances of his life, when he is away from his solitary chambers, and is thrown straight into the sacred centre of that home circle from which his ordinary habits are so universally supposed to exclude him', Dickens's serial is at pains to reject the widespread (if clearly not quite universal) supposition that bachelorhood and the home circle are mutually exclusive.[22]

The sixteenth instalment of *A Tale of Two Cities* returns to the extended Manette family, which accommodates elderly bachelor banker Mr Lorry (who is seventy-eight during the novel's central period of action), and former nursemaid turned general carer and cook Miss Pross, as well as the father-daughter-suitor triad of Dr Manette, Lucy

---

[21] Mark Turner has made a similar case for Anthony Trollope's use of the wealth of positive bachelor discourse in periodicals of the 1860s and 70s to support his, albeit muted, novelistic affirmation of bachelorhood: 'A sense of propriety would have prevented Trollope from being any more explicit about the pleasures a man gives up by marrying, but such open proclamations were unnecessary as the discourse of the bachelor circulated in magazines and pamphlets around the time of the serialisation of *The Belton Estate*.' *Trollope and the Magazines: Gendered Issues in Mid-Victorian Britain* (Basingstoke: Macmillan, 2000), p. 117.
[22] Collins, 'Bachelor Bedroom', pp. 356, 355.

and Darnay. Mr Lorry experiences the Manette household as 'the sunny part of his life', and is described 'thanking his bachelor stars for having lighted him in his declining years to a Home'.[23] Mr Lorry's pleasure in this household is strictly one of 'his declining years', which have released him from the imperative to marriage allowing him to enter domestic life without becoming a spouse. The sixteenth weekly instalment, in which Dickens briefly celebrates Lucy Manette's marriage to Charles Darnay, is largely taken up by a lengthy elaboration of the perfect appropriateness of Mr Lorry's bachelor status:

'Dear me! This is an occasion that makes a man speculate on all he has lost. Dear, dear, dear! To think that there might have been a Mrs Lorry, any time these fifty years almost!'
'Not at all!' From Miss Pross.
'You think there might never have been a Mrs Lorry?' asked the gentleman of that name.
'Pooh!' rejoined Miss Pross; 'you were a bachelor in your cradle.'
'Well!' observed Mr Lorry, beamingly adjusting his little wig, 'that seems probable, too.'
'And you were cut out for a bachelor', pursued Miss Pross, 'before you were put in your cradle.'
'Then, I think,' said Mr Lorry, 'that I was very unhandsomely dealt with, and that I ought to have had a voice in the selection of my pattern' (p. 200).

This discussion offers an emphatic statement of Dickens's divergence from the contemporary cultural expectation of bachelor 'rehabilitation' through marriage. Although Mr Lorry pays lip service to perceptions of bachelorhood as an 'unhandsome' vocation, the end of this conversation is clearly at variance with Mr Lorry's cheerful and immediate acceptance of Miss Pross's suggestions. His 'beaming' agreement with her conception of him as a bachelor from inception suggests a pleasure in her understanding, as well as a desire to justify what was increasingly, though clearly not uncontestedly, perceived as a deviant or perverse lifestyle.

In Mr Lorry, Dickens provides a more subtle, emotionally astute delineation of the single male to that offered in his earlier comic narratives of incorrigible bachelors such as Mr Pickwick. Though fated by 'bachelor stars' Lorry anxiously describes his position as 'a

[23] Charles Dickens, *A Tale of Two Cities* (London: Penguin, 2003), p. 96, p. 103.

solitary old bachelor [. . .] there is nobody to weep for me' (p. 322). The swift correction of this statement reinforces Dickens's refusal to ally unmarried status with anti-domesticity. Sydney Carton, who has a comparable elective bond to the Manette/Darnay family, allays Lorry's fears by insisting that familial inclusion need not be routed through conjugality or blood:

'How can you say that? Wouldn't She [Lucy] weep for you? Wouldn't her child?'
'Yes, yes, thank God. I didn't quite mean what I said' (p. 322).

A celebratory image of the esteem and affection that Lorry receives from his self-elected family is incorporated within Carton's final vision of the Manettes: 'I see the good old man, so long their friend, in ten years' time enriching them with all he has, and passing tranquilly to his reward' (pp. 389–90). Readers of *A Tale* in its incarnation as monthly parts would have had Lorry's central position in the narrative and in this family confirmed and reinforced by Hablot Knight Browne's (Phiz's) illustrations. The important opening illustration of the first monthly

The Mail

2. Hablot Knight Browne, or Phiz, 'The Mail' (first illustration to the monthly parts of *A Tale of Two Cities*, June 1859)

76 *Queer Dickens*

part, 'The Mail', places Lorry in the middle foreground of the composition, spot lit by a lantern which illuminates him in an otherwise dark scene, reading a letter which plots out the mysterious meeting with Lucy that propels this instalment, the novel's central narrative, and the future of Lorry's emotional and domestic life.[24]

In Phiz's 'Under the Plane Tree', which was prominently placed as frontispiece to the first bound edition, Mr Lorry, in contrast to the peripheral Sydney Carton, appears in the centre of the family grouping. The foreground and background positioning of Lorry and Carton allows them both to be spatially allied with the trunk of the noble-looking tree whose curving branches embrace and shelter this vulnerable community of four (or five).

Carton's interest in Lorry's elective participation in this family is, of course, bound up with his own more troubled bachelor inclusion in this group, an affinity that can only be paradoxically recognized through the act of sacrifice that severs him from them. Carton's closing vision inscribes both himself and Lorry within the heart of the family. As in Phiz's 'Under the Plane Tree' Lorry is spatially at the centre of this vision of the family, while Carton's emotional involvement, signalled in the image by his gaze at Lucy (or Darnay), is only possible from a physical remove. As James Eli Adams suggests, 'although Carton celebrates domesticity, he does so in confirming his own exclusion from it, save in the pleasures of imagination. [. . .] Carton's meditation offers a vicarious experience of domesticity [. . .] in which he is a divinity freed from further responsibility in human affairs'.[25] Carton's famous last words envisage Lucy and her child, Dr Manette and Mr Lorry; he goes on to consider his continuing posthumous involvement in Lucy's and Darnay's marriage and in the lives of their blood-line:

I see that I hold a sanctuary in their hearts, and in the hearts of their descendants generations hence. I see her, an old woman, weeping for me on the anniversary of this day. I see her and her husband, their course done, lying side by side in their last earthly bed, and I know that each was not more honoured and held sacred in the other's soul than I was in the souls of both. I see that child who lay upon her bosom and who bore my name, a man, winning his way up in that path

[24] For a differently focused reading of Lorry as hero through the examination of these monthly parts see Hughes and Lund, pp. 61–74.
[25] James Eli Adams, *Dandies and Desert Saints: Styles of Victorian Manhood* (Ithaca and London: Cornell University Press, 1995), p. 59.

3. Hablot Knight Browne, 'Under the Plane Tree' (frontispiece to the first bound edition of *A Tale of Two Cities*, issued with the final double monthly number, November 1859)

of life which once was mine. I see the blots I threw upon it, faded away. I see him, foremost of just judges and honoured men, bringing a boy of my name, with a forehead that I know and golden hair, to this place – then fair to look upon, with not a trace of this day's disfigurement – and I hear him tell the child my story, with a tender and a faltering voice.

It is a far, far better thing that I do, than I have ever done; it is a far, far better rest that I go to, than I have ever known (p. 390).

This wonderful final speech, positioned in the space of closure conventionally reserved for marriage in Victorian novels, is a deeply queer statement of Dickens's total revision of the types of bonding on which family depends. Carton's death will inscribe him in a spiritual triangle with the husband and wife while quasi-paternally writing him into a line of sons who will continue to bear his name coupled with Darnay's.[26] His is the ultimate confirmation of Collins's earlier statement that 'there are other affections, in this world, which are noble and honourable, besides those of conjugal and parental origin'.

If this tragic conclusion points to the difficulties of accommodating the single male in familial space by only managing to do so posthumously, Mr Lorry's confirmed place in the Manette family points to more positive possibilities. Dickens's recourse to models of born and fated bachelorhood, predestined by 'bachelor stars', to convey the centrality of unmarried status to Mr Lorry's entire being, responds directly to contemporary debates that, in the words of Eli Adams, 'posed, and attempted to answer, a host of questions about the nature and meaning of bachelorhood: Was the bachelor born or did he acquire his bachelor traits? Was bachelorhood chosen as an act of conviction or imposed by an incident of fate? Was the bachelor's behaviour volitional or non-volitional, an issue of will or defect, badness or weakness?'[27] In his insistence on Mr Lorry's experience of bachelorhood as natural and unavoidable, Dickens resists contemporary perceptions of unmarried men as either failed or wilfully aberrant.

Sedgwick has read the nineteenth-century fictional bachelor as a visible emblem of the 'refus[al] of sexual choice, in a society where sexual choice for men is both compulsory and always self contradictory', recognizing the bachelor's potential to 'startlingly desexualise [...] the question of male sexual choice'.[28] Lorry as congenital and generally

---

[26] Though this triangulation may remind us of Sedgwick's work on the homosocial/homicidal bonds of rivalry experienced between men bonded by a mutual female love object (a structure more fully critiqued in the next chapter), Carton's sacrificial suicide offers an important, if not less tragic, alternative to murderous rivalry.

[27] Eli Adams, pp. 28–9.

[28] Eve Kosofsky Sedgwick, 'The Beast in the Closet: James and the Writing of Homosexual Panic', in *Sex, Politics and Science in the Nineteenth Century Novel*, ed.

content celibate presents an important alternative to sexuality as conceived as either same- or opposite-sex directed. An identity based on the rejection of sexual identity, is surely, in its repeated refusals, still a sexual identity. It is important to hold open this space of identity based on the resistance to models of sexuality as defined by object choice, which were soon to be articulated and culturally enshrined in the multiple but limiting categories of sexology. However, it is significant that Dickens's strategic presentation of Mr Lorry as born bachelor anticipates (albeit in a novelistic rather than a clinical register) the strategy employed by Havelock Ellis and other sexologists at the end of the century to de-stigmatize homosexuality by arguing for its non-volitional, congenital basis. As Laura Doan and Chris Waters have documented, early sexological interventions attempted to counter claims of depravity 'by deeming homosexual behaviour to be less the result of misguided choice than the outcome of an innate, congenital condition over which the individual had little control'.[29] Chris White has questioned the veracity of sexologists' congenital thesis, suggesting the tactical value of such a position: 'It is impossible to know to what extent these theorists genuinely believed in the theory of innate homo-sexuality, or to what extent it was a vital strategic device in arguing for toleration and acceptance.'[30] For those who treated heterosexual refusal with suspicion, bachelorhood was progressively associated with same-sex desire. As Snyder argues:

By the turn of the century, all forms of non-procreative sexual activity [. . .], even the *absence* of sexual activity within or beyond marriage, were coming increasingly to be seen as possible signs of homosexuality [. . .] 'Bachelor' came to be used often as an slurring insinuation against gay men or as an insider's codeword by them.[31]

Whilst this linkage became explicit during the fin de siècle after sex-ologists had officially constituted 'homosexuality', Snyder carefully

Ruth Bernard Yeazell (Baltimore and London: Johns Hopkins University Press, 1986), pp. 148–86, pp. 160, 154. For another version of this article see Sedgwick, *Epistemology*.

[29] Laura Doan and Chris Waters, 'Homosexualities', in *Sexology Uncensored: The Documents of Sexual Science*, ed. Lucy Bland and Laura Doan (Cambridge: Polity Press, 1998), p. 42.

[30] Chris White (ed.), *Nineteenth-Century Writings on Homosexuality: A Sourcebook* (London: Routledge, 1999), p. 3.

[31] Snyder, p. 33.

emphasizes the pre-existent homoerotic nuances concurrent with 'the epistemological indeterminacy of bachelorhood [that] both preceded and postdated' such medico/legal definitions.[32] Dickens's naturalization and valorization of Lorry's single status clearly demonstrates his resistance to the idea that identity *is* sexual identity and his appreciation of the insufficiency of marriage as the exclusive mechanism for domestic fulfilment.

SERIAL PUBLICATION, THE WILFULLY SINGLE MALE, AND RESISTANCE TO THE MARRIAGE PLOT

Lorry is one of a long line of Dickens's natural bachelors. Though he affably holds open the possibility that 'there might have been a Mrs Lorry, any time these fifty years almost', Miss Pross's emphatic rejection of this would come as little surprise to Dickens's regular readers who were already well acquainted with the connection between bachelorhood and marital aversion in the work of this author. In his first novel, *The Pickwick Papers* (1836–7), Dickens explicitly considers marital resistance as an expression of heteroerotic repugnance, developing this theme variously throughout his career. Beloved figures including Mr Pickwick, Captain Cuttle of *Dombey and Son* and even Eugene Wrayburn of *Our Mutual Friend*, strive hard to preserve their cherished bachelorhood, offering repeated explicit statements of hetero-repulsion throughout the long serializations of their respective novels. In these novels, particularly *The Pickwick Papers* and *Our Mutual Friend*, Dickens develops the portrayal of marital resistance as an expression of heteroerotic aversion, building up a series of connections between the refusal of marriage, heterosexual disinclination and homo-erotic desire. Through these interconnections Dickens also challenges the linear narrative shape most regularly attributed to the Victorian novel, uncoupling the association of marriage with narrative finality.

In another important conversation with Miss Pross, Mr Lorry (as befits a serial character) questions the originating moment of narrative, disputing Miss Pross's sense of plot chronology. Having demurred at Miss Pross's analysis that he was responsible for instigating the novel's

---

[32] Snyder, p. 33.

action – 'I began it, Miss Pross?' – Lorry airily notes the problem of identifying the opening incident from which events proceed: 'Oh! If *that* was beginning it –' (p. 99). Early readers of *A Tale of Two Cities* experienced a similarly blurred sense of beginnings and endings, whether they read the weekly instalments, in which the novel was spatially and conceptually embedded in the journal's other matter, the monthly parts, which physically detracted from the physical weighing of distance travelled through the novel's whole, or even a bound edition, subject to numerous collections in sets of complete works. By this point in Dickens's career his work seemed inexhaustible, an impression that Dickens was keen to confirm, as, for example, in his *All the Year Round* advertisements for the monthly parts of *A Tale of Two Cities*, which emphasized the continuities between this and his earlier productions:

Now ready, price 1s.,
Uniform with PICKWICK, DAVID COPPERFIELD, BLEAK
HOUSE, &c.

Dickens's insistence on the uniform presentation of the monthly parts across his different novels clearly contributed to a readerly sense of his work as shooting forth in a process of continuous growth. A reviewer of the first monthly part of *Our Mutual Friend* for the *Sun* put it like this: 'The "two green leaves" dear to us all by reason of so many delightful recollections are putting forth anew, this once, appropriately enough, in the spring time.'[33] This reviewer quotes Dickens's own organic rhetoric, placed in prefaces to the novels, which, in themselves, endeavoured to create a sense of a reciprocal relationship between himself and his readers.[34]

Continuities between Dickens's fictions were enhanced by the autonomous existence with which many readers imbued his creations. From the beginning of Dickens's career characters took on an identity beyond

---

[33] *Sun*, 2 May 1864, quoted by Jennifer Hayward, *Consuming Pleasures: Active Audiences and Serial Fictions from Dickens to Soap Opera* (Kentucky: University Press of Kentucky, 1997), p. 55.

[34] See for example Dickens's closing comments about *David Copperfield*, first printed with the final monthly part and inserted in the single volume edition as a preface: 'Instead of looking back, therefore, I will look forward. I cannot close this Volume more agreeably to myself, than with a hopeful glance towards the time when I shall again put forth my two green leaves once a month, and with a faithful remembrance of the genial sun and showers that have fallen on these leaves of *David Copperfield* and made me happy' (repr. Penguin edn, p. 9).

the page, as an 1837 review for the *National Magazine* explained: 'The characters and scenes of this writer have become, to an extent undreamed of in all previous cases, part of our actual life. Their individualities whether mental or external, are as familiar to us as those of our most intimate associates, or our most frequent resorts.'[35] As Amy Cruse argued in an early account of experiences of reading Dickens, 'some of the younger Victorians grew up in such close familiarity with the Dickens people that these became their intimate life companions, meeting them at every turn of the road'.[36] Dickens actively encouraged readers' experiences of a personal intimacy with characters, regularly referring to his own sense of familial relationships or friendships with his creations (such as David Copperfield, whom he famously described as a 'favourite child' in the preface to the novel in the 1867 'Charles Dickens' edition of his works, the third and final collected edition that Dickens authorized during his lifetime). Dickens also used other characters to present explicit models for reading as a method for forming elective communities. Master Humphrey, the titular bachelor of Dickens's weekly serial *Master Humphrey's Clock*, for example, envisages himself as part of a fictional family who crowd around his solitary chair: 'I have sons and daughters and grandchildren and we are assembled on some occasion of rejoicing common to us all.'[37] Similar constellations of characters drawn from across the range of Dickens's writing are common, as Jennifer Hayward has argued, in visual depictions such as W. H. Beard's 'Dickens Receiving his Characters' (1874).[38]

This (authorially encouraged) blurring of the boundaries between Dickens's fictional projects extends the general indeterminacy of the serial form, in which aspirations to closure are repeatedly exposed as

---

[35] Quoted by Hayward, p. 37.

[36] Amy Cruse, *The Victorians and Their Books* (London: George Allen and Unwin, 1935), p. 171. Cruse gathers a wealth of instances in which Victorian diarists and autobiographers used Dickens's characters to conceptualize their own experiences. She quotes, for example, Francis Barnard's perception of his nursery governess as 'a Cornelia Blimber' and his description of his severe childhood illness as a time when he 'acted Paul Dombey to the life.' Such intimate engagement with Dickens's characters has a long and continuing history, as recent novels such as Lloyd Jones's *Mister Pip* (London: John Murray, 2007) demonstrate.

[37] Dickens, *Master Humphrey's Clock*, III (London: Chapman and Hall, 1840), Issue 88, p. 422.

[38] Hayward, p. 66.

mythic. D. A. Miller has produced a thorough theoretical critique of the belief in closure as a totalizing power of textual organization. He argues that novels published in parts, which demonstrate their 'length serially, in the regularly broken line between letters, chapters, instalments, and even whole works', offer a particularly clear exposé of the way in which 'the narratable is stronger than the closure to which is it opposed.'[39] Or as Brake has suggested through scholarship of history of the book: 'the termination of completed magazine serials and the "loss" of characters, world, and plot which ends with the serial are mitigated in magazine serialization by the continuation of the periodical in which the serial appeared, and by the periodical's supply of a new fictional world for immediate consumption by the bereaved reader'.[40] Serials offer a particularly attenuated experience of closure. They materially demonstrate the incompleteness of ending in the novels carried by them, disrupting the marital denouement so associated with the genre. Serialization, then, can productively destabilize what queer narratologists have described as 'narrative heteroideology'. Judith Roof, for example, has critiqued 'narrative's heterosexually friendly shape', identifying a dominant 'reproductive narrative trajectory' that insists on a plot impetus towards 'joinder or synthesis' and 'the ensuing (re)production – of people, of goods, of narrative'. Roof argues that 'as an organising structure, narrative plays a large part in the stubborn return of a particularly heterosexual normativity'.[41] The Victorian novel has widely been interpreted as a particularly stubborn heterosexual form, finally concerned with marriage, birth (and death), while Dickens has been perceived as the exemplary writer in that genre, determined to impose a closing celebrant vision of marital hearth and home in defiance of earlier counter-plotting that might militate against this. Whatever queer energies Dickens's plots might mobilize, existing criticism has

[39] D. A. Miller, *Narrative and Its Discontents* (Princeton: Princeton University Press, 1981), pp. 277, 266.
[40] Brake, p. 51.
[41] Judith Roof, *Come as You Are: Sexuality and Narrative* (New York: Columbia University Press, 1996), pp. 106, 112, xxix. For an earlier critique of the way in which heterosexuality operates as a default mode in narrative construction and interpretation – 'no one speaks of 'heterotextuality' because there is no need to' – see Jacob Stockinger, 'Homotextuality: A Proposal', in *The Gay Academic*, ed. Louie Crew (Palm Springs: ETC, 1978), pp. 135–51, p. 138.

argued, they are firmly contained and closed down by the end of his novels.[42] My reading of Dickens's serial bachelors explores instead the spaces held open for this counter-marital, counter-reproductive narrative, a plot insistently re-opened and cumulatively explored across Dickens's career.

The conventionality of Dickens's closures should not, in any case, be overstated. As in the previous chapter's consideration of the celebration of the formation of an adoptive, single-parent family as the crowning achievement of *Oliver Twist*, or in the example of *A Tale of Two Cities* where Carton's last words articulate a queer vision of non-heterosexual and non-marital family formation, Dickens's closures, even where marriage is a central component, often express the author's ambivalence towards this version of finality. *Bleak House* and *Great Expectations*, to take just two of the most famous examples of the fissured Dickens ending, both present a case for the insufficiency of closure. In Esther's unfinished final utterance, 'they can very well do without much beauty in me – even supposing –' (p. 989), *Bleak House* leaves open both syntax and meaning. This narrative indeterminacy is specifically also an indeterminacy of heterosexual resolution. Although the ostensible completing device of Esther and Allan Woodcourt's marriage is nominally in place, the ceremony fails to convince.[43] Here, even

---

[42] The most extended example of this type of interpretation is offered in Mary Armstrong's doctoral thesis (supervised by Sedgwick), 'What Can You Two Be Together?', in which she argues that 'these narratives are characterized by the work of maintaining perversities (usually female homoerotic desires) and then orchestrating their dissolutions'; 'female-female desire, once it appears to block or undo heterosexual romance, is defused through abrupt marriage and deaths' (pp. 14, 15). In what is, in many ways, a pioneering thesis, Armstrong also argues for the instability of heterosexual structures and their emotional hollowness, making a clear distinction between 'heterosexual (romance/marriage) plots' and the 'heterosexual desire' which is so rarely a corollary of such structures in Dickens's work (pp. 12–13). This, however, is at variance with Armstrong's reliance on traditional marriage and romance to recoup and diffuse homoerotics. For a differently focused rendering of the belief that Dickens's novels retreat to a conservative reliance on the (narrowly conceived) family as a solution to social ills see Marianna Torgovnick, *Closure in the Novel* (Princeton: Princeton University Press, 1981). See also the critical readings of *Pickwick* as finally offering a recapitulation to marital plotting cited later in this chapter.

[43] Mark Turner has read this indeterminate 'ending' as Dickens's specifically urban appreciation of 'the never-ending uncertainties thrown up by a disorientating city in which there is "fog everywhere"'. *Backward Glances: Cruising the Queer Streets of New York and London* (London: Reaktion, 2003), p. 26.

an apparently celebratory union presents a studied hollowness that undermines, even while avowing, more positive sentiments. Sally Ledger has identified the domestic set pieces which close the novel as 'very staged and self-conscious': 'the new Bleak House at the novel's close is presented to us almost as a stage set, it is painstakingly crafted (by Mr Jarndyce, as a proxy for Dickens), and thereby draws attention to itself as a constructed object rather than a naturally occurring phenomenon'.[44]

The plausibility of marriage as a natural completing structure is similarly challenged by the two endings of *Great Expectations*. On the advice of Bulwer Lytton, Dickens altered his original ending in which Pip and a remarried Estella meet accidentally and fleetingly, provoking Pip's concluding reflection on their mutual suffering. The revised ending as published apparently coheres more closely with traditional romance (and indeed novel) structures by, albeit ambiguously, suggesting a continued union between the pair in Pip's famous last words: 'I saw the shadow of no parting from her' (p. 484). Paradoxically, though, this capitulation to readerly demands for closure through heterosexual union (Bulwer Lytton anticipated that readers would be disappointed by the original ending) poignantly dramatizes not only the insufficiency of that union, but invalidates perceptions of marriage as the only closure, as an opposite alternative is both possible and plausible. As D. A. Miller argues, this is confirmation that the ending does not regulate the narrative leading up to it, a demonstration of the relative unimportance of closure in Dickens's scheme for the novel: 'That the text can issue in either of two opposite resolutions points up the indeterminacy with which [. . . it] has been invested. The appropriateness of each ending is thus bound to bespeak a certain inappropriateness as well.'[45]

These specific examples are complimented by the displacement of marital satisfaction in the endings of those novels largely concerned with the celebration of bachelorhood. In *The Pickwick Papers* and *Our Mutual Friend* maritally averse plots are not fully reined in by Dickens's partial capitulations to nuptial closure. The undercutting of heterotextual logic

---

[44] Sally Ledger, 'From Queen Caroline to Lady Dedlock: Dickens and the Popular Radical Imagination', *Victorian Literature and Culture* 32.2 (2004), 575–600, p. 594.
[45] D. A. Miller, p. 274.

within these novels is further developed by the counter-plotting favoured by seriality. The serialized form held open the possibility for multiple plot directions and conclusions. Early plagiarists (as Dickens perceived them), or adaptors (to use a term that recognizes the creative contribution required in such acts of refashioning), were adept at inventing endings for Dickens's still running works. Much to Dickens's frustration his novels were subject to a plethora of stage and prose piracies; indeed, an effort to foil this lively industry was one factor in his shift from monthly to weekly part publication.[46] Mid-work adaptations, as with the two opposite but possible resolutions to *Great Expectations*, suggest that the possibilities of plot exceed any authoritative moment of closure. Such plagiarisms rely on a different method of reading for the plot that is not determined by an ending against which all previous possibilities are revised,[47] but is open to the multiple directions in which narrative might issue.

   Publication in instalments not only allows a dialogue between the various contents of a periodical, it also contributes to a sense of continuation, as characters, never wholly tied to the text in which they (first) appear, have an ongoing imaginative currency for regular readers, especially those readers eager to foster relationships of long gestation through many instalments by incorporating fictional characters into their own social circle. As Hughes and Lund have argued, the prolonged period of serial reading made an affective difference to the experience of ending: 'Although the happy ending certainly had a resonance over time for Victorian readers after the novel concluded, modern evaluations of the text have given too much weight to this small part

---

[46] See Robert Patten, 'Publishing in Parts' in *Palgrave Advances in Charles Dickens Studies* ed. John Bowen and Robert Patten (Basingstoke: Palgrave, 2006), pp. 11–47, p. 33; Louis James, *Fiction for the Working Man 1830–50: A Study of the Literature Produced for the Working Classes in Early Victorian Urban England* (Oxford: Oxford University Press, 1963). Peter Ackroyd's biography recounts Dickens's distress at seeing one of the six 1838 London stage productions of *Oliver Twist* (the novel as serialized by Dickens was not completed until the next year). Dickens, unable to bear the liberties taken, 'lay down in his box from the middle of the first act until the end of the play'. *Dickens* (London: Sinclair Stevenson, 1990), p. 276.

[47] This, in a broad sense, is the trajectory of narrative interpretation charted by Peter Brooks. He acknowledges that, particularly dramatically in serialized novels, the 'drive toward the end is matched by an ever more deviant, transgressive, tension-filled resistance to the end', and recognizes the artifice of endings but asserts that 'still we read in a spirit of confidence and also a state of dependence, that what remains to be read will restructure the provisional meanings of the already read'. *Reading for the Plot: Design and Intention in Narrative* (Harvard: Harvard University Press, 1984, repr. 2002), pp. 147, 23.

of the total event.' As they observe, these readers would have been alert to the potential for continuation and development, 'with possible (probable) renewed engagement later (in other novels)'.[48] Though Hayward finds evidence of a desire for tidy denouement in reviews of *Our Mutual Friend* as it appeared in parts, Dickens's authorial practices, as well as the material form of the serial, worked to undermine the ideal of a definitive ending.[49]

The clearest example of this is offered in Dickens's resurrection of the popular Mr Pickwick, Sam, and Tony Weller as sales quickly tailed off for his weekly sole-authored fiction miscellany, *Master Humphrey's Clock*, which ran from 4 April 1840 to 4 December 1841. Dickens would again resurrect these and other popular characters in his extensive public reading tours. The selection of Mr Pickwick to enter as 'Master Humphrey's Visitor' in the journal's fifth week was, however, conceptually coherent as well as commercially astute. Dickens is clearly on the defensive against commercial interpretations in his preface to the complete three volume edition of *Master Humphrey's Clock*: 'When [the author] sought to interest his readers in those who talked, and read, and listened, he revived Mr Pickwick and his humble friends; not with any intention of reopening an exhausted and abandoned mine, but to connect them in the thoughts of those whose favourites they had been, with the tranquil enjoyments of Master Humphrey.'[50] In a canny piece of intertextuality Dickens signals this possible engagement to his readers by having the circle of single men, who take the roles of narrators and listeners in the weekly's loose framing device, recognize Mr Pickwick, complete with the gaiter's to which they are 'quite attached' (I, p. 72), as an 'old friend' (I, p. 51). Mr Pickwick's popularity, in terms of sales figures and public affection, granted legitimacy to what had begun as a decidedly strange framework for the telling of miscellaneous tales, focused around the disabled, elderly, and socially isolated bachelor character of Master Humphrey.

Master Humphrey is detached from his local community, having long 'led a lonely, solitary life'. On his arrival in the area, the neighbours form prejudicial suspicions, which seem to be fuelled both by Master Humphrey's physically hunched form and his solitariness: 'I was a spy, an infidel,

---

[48] Hughes and Lund, pp. 44, 289.

[49] Hayward, pp. 55–8.

[50] Dickens, 'Preface', *Master Humphrey's Clock*, I. Brake reads the insertion of Pickwick and the Wellers as a shrewd sales ploy, p. 46.

4. George Cattermole, Illustration of the first meeting between Master Humphrey and Mr Pickwick (*Master Humphrey's Clock*, issue 5, May 1840)

a conjuror, a kidnapper of children, a refugee, a priest, a monster. Mothers caught up their infants and ran into their houses as I passed; men eyed me spitefully, and muttered threats and curses' (I, p. 2). Though local relations have improved through Master Humphrey's irrepressible acts of social benevolence, his narrative is open to similarly pejorative judgements from the weekly's readers; the first 'correspondent' in the journal's short-lived letters column (clearly an authorial strategy for introducing alternative fictional voices) makes this assessment of Master Humphrey's briefly narrated life story: 'You must have been a queer fellow when you were a child, confounded queer' (I, p. 23). This queer fellow is only drawn into the companionship that forms the basis for the storytelling circle when he encounters another solitary elderly gentleman seated alone in a public house on Christmas day. This encounter with the deaf gentleman, as he is described throughout the serial, changes the current of Master Humphrey's life, inaugurating the narrative events of which the *Clock* is composed:

5. Hablot Knight Browne, Hearthside illustration of Master Humphrey and the Deaf Gentleman (*Master Humphrey's Clock*, issue 3, April 1840)

'There should be a freemasonry between us' said I, pointing from himself to me to explain my meaning – 'if not in our grey hairs, at least in our misfortunes. You see that I am a poor cripple.'
I have never felt so happy under my affliction since the trying moment of my first becoming conscious of it, as when he took my hand in his with a smile that has lighted my path in life from that day (I, p. 28).

Inspired by this friendship, Master Humphrey and the deaf gentleman invite two other elderly single men to join their narrative club, Jack Redburn, a bachelor who is 'remarkably fond of children' and 'the best and kindest nurse in sickness' (characteristics particularly approved by Dickens), and Owen Miles, a widower. Two chairs are left spare in case we 'should find two men to our mind', a device that allows Dickens to

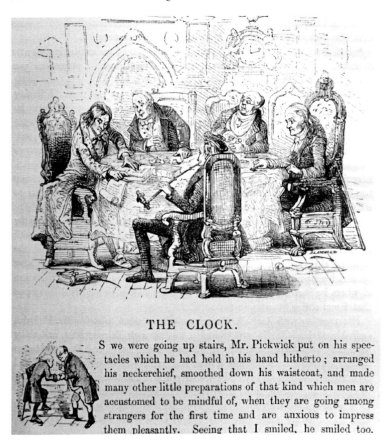

THE CLOCK.

S we were going up stairs, Mr. Pickwick put on his spectacles which he had held in his hand hitherto ; arranged his neckerchief, smoothed down his waistcoat, and made many other little preparations of that kind which men are accustomed to be mindful of, when they are going among strangers for the first time and are anxious to impress them pleasantly. Seeing that I smiled, he smiled too.

6. George Cattermole, Illustration of the story-telling circle including Mr Pickwick (*Master Humphrey's Clock*, issue 7, May 1840)

generate further narrative by bringing in suitable occupants as the weekly format demands. By filling one of these vacant seats, the figure of Pickwick lends a legitimacy to the bachelor narratives, on which the running of the *Clock* depends.

Indeed, the fictional serial that Dickens developed as another response to the poor commercial fortunes of the *Clock, The Old Curiosity Shop* (1840–1), also includes male figures characterized by their single status, and the action pauses over emotionally charged scenes of bachelor intimacy. The novel's mysterious 'single gentleman', who is searching for Nell is revealed to be Master Humphrey and, in an additional (less clunking) affinity between novel and framing device, Dickens briefly introduces a figure called 'the bachelor'. This character cares for the widowed clergyman of the diocese where Little Nell's journey finally ends. 'The bachelor', 'a little old gentleman', cohabits with the clergyman, in a direct anticipation of the domestic arrangements of two of the *Clock* circle, Jack Redburn and the widowed Owen Miles, who live together in Master Humphrey's house, after his death. *The Old Curiosity Shop* pauses over a scene of the domestic idyll experienced by the bachelor and the clergyman: 'He had been his college friend and always his close companion; in the first shock of his grief had come to console and comfort him; and from that time they had never parted company. The little old gentleman was the active spirit of the place; the adjuster of all differences, the promoter of all merry-makings'.[51]

This scene of the domestic harmony and emotional intimacy of single men resonates with the direct framing narrative of *Master Humphrey's Clock*, as well as with the promotion of bachelorhood offered by *The Pickwick Papers* and embodied in immediate proximity to *The Old Curiosity Shop* through Mr Pickwick's position in the group of listeners. The importation of Pickwick and the male Wellers into *Master Humphrey's Clock* allows, then, for an overt acknowledgement of the continuities between Dickens's work and an encouragement of readerly practices that invest characters with independent life. It also allows a continuation and (as we shall see) modification of central themes of *The Pickwick Papers*, including the concept of natural bachelorhood, antipathy to maritally inclined women, and bonds of absolute fidelity between men.

This example provides a clear instance of the queer possibilities of serialization. While the serial in its paralleling of capitalism and its participation in the creation of mass markets may seem to lack queer credentials, in its intervention into narrative structure, its mediation of the relationship between readers and author, and its generic dexterity, it has evident queer potential.[52] As an unflattering 1851 notice in the

---

[51] Charles Dickens, *The Old Curiosity Shop* (London: Penguin, 2000), p. 395.
[52] See Norman Feltes for a convincing reading of the affinities between serialization and capitalism as similarly requiring an investment of time and money underwritten by a

Prospective Review for *David Copperfield* and Thackery's *Pendennis* put
it: the serial form affords 'the greatest excuse for unlimited departures
from dignity, propriety, consistency, completeness and proportion
[. . .] Nine tenths of readers will never look at it or think of it as a
whole'.[53] Through the explicit intertextuality of *Pickwick*, the *Clock*,
and *The Old Curiosity Shop*, marriage as a device for closure is entirely
displaced, as a superfluity of bachelor plots become the occasion for the
generation and continuation of narrative.

BACHELORHOOD BESIEGED: PICKWICK'S PERIL

The central incident of *The Pickwick Papers*, both spatially and conceptually, is the trial famously brought against Mr Pickwick for 'Breach
of Promise'. In another interconnection between contemporary treatments of marriage inside and outside fiction, this episode drew directly
upon a sensational public dramatization of marital discontent in the
'criminal conversation' or adultery trial of Norton vs. Melbourne, on
which Dickens had reported for the *Morning Chronicle*.[54] Through
its eponymous hero, the circle of initially single men who make up
the Pickwick club, and a wealth of interpolated tales concerned with
marriage and its discontents, this rambling novel offers a sustained
exploration of the parameters of the cultural association of ideal masculinity with marriage, experimenting with the possibility of a socially
endorsed election of bachelorhood. Pickwick is horrified to discover
that his landlady, Mrs Bardell, has misconstrued his uncharacteristic
agitation about appointing a man-servant as a proposal of marriage. In
his eagerness to secure the powerfully charismatic Sam Weller (the locus

confidence in long-term reward, *Modes of Production of Victorian Novels* (Chicago:
University of Chicago Press, 1986), and Peter Brooks, *Reading for the Plot*, on the
commercial and consumerist drive behind part publication, pp. 146–7.

[53] '*David Copperfield* and *Pendennis*', *Prospective Review*, July 1851, repr. in *Dickens:
The Critical Heritage*, ed. Phillip Collins (London: Routledge and Keegan Paul, 1971),
pp. 264–6, p. 264.

[54] Richard Altick provides an account of journalistic and novelistic responses to the
Norton trial in *The Presence of the Present: Topics of the Day in the Victorian Novel*
(Columbus: Ohio State University Press, 1991), pp. 148–52. For a more detailed
exploration of Dickens's response to this see Sally Ledger, *Dickens and the Popular
Radical Imagination* (Cambridge: Cambridge University Press, 2007), Ch. 2.

of sexual magnetism in this novel, attracting the attentions of men and women of all classes through an appealing 'ease and freedom for which he was remarkable') to his personal service, Pickwick's behaviour becomes 'most mysterious and unaccountable':

> He paced the room to and fro with hurried steps, popped his head out of the window at intervals of about three minutes each, constantly referred to his watch, and exhibited many other manifestations of impatience, very unusual with him. It was evident that something of great importance was in contemplation, but what that something was not even Mrs Bardell herself had been enabled to discover.[55]

Mr Pickwick's election of the domestic offices of this male servant in preference to the homely provision of a wife is registered throughout the novel as a departure from an ideal of marital masculinity.[56] Sergeant Buzfuz's court case for the plaintiff employs a model of appropriate manliness as compulsory heterosexuality, critiquing Pickwick's ability to resist his landlady and his 'intention of gradually breaking off from' her as 'unmanly' (p. 454). Indeed, as Buzfuz again emphasizes, Pickwick's very appearance to defend himself at this trial signals his deviation from approved masculine behaviours: 'It would have been more decent in him, more becoming, in better judgement and in better taste, if he had stopped away' (p. 452). Ginger Frost has observed the illumination of gender roles in both actual and fictional breach of promise trials during this period. Participants in these public dramatizations of the failure of marital ideology regularly emphasized perceived infringements of "proper' manliness and womanliness'.[57] Indeed, gendered behavioural codes made it very difficult for accused male jilters to respond to the allegation, because 'the very act of defending the action was (at base) accusing the plaintiff of lying'.[58]

Pickwick's strenuous efforts to resist Mrs Bardell's marital advances are repeatedly marked as inexplicable, as, for example, in the perplexed responses of Mrs Bardell's friends as voiced to Sam:

[55] Charles Dickens, *The Pickwick Papers* (London: Penguin, 2003), pp. 521, 159.
[56] For alternative explorations of Mr Pickwick's choice of Sam in preference to Mrs Bardell see Brian McCuskey ' "Your Love-Sick Pickwick": The Erotics of Service', *Dickens Studies Annual* 25 (1996), 245–66, and John Glavin, 'Pickwick on the Wrong Side of the Door', *Dickens Studies Annual* 22 (1993), 1–20.
[57] Ginger Frost, *Promises Broken: Courtship, Class and Gender in Victorian England* (Charlottesville and London: University Press of Virginia, 1995), p. 40.
[58] Frost, *Promises*, p. 44.

'And your master, young man, a gentleman with money, as could never feel the expense of a wife, no more than nothing [...] why, there ain't the faintest shade of an excuse for his behaviour. Why don't he marry her?'
'Ah,' said Sam, 'to be sure; that's the question' (p. 349).

This hanging question is only intensified by Mrs Bardell's perfect fulfilment of the homely standards that elsewhere in Dickens's fiction apparently constitute the domestic ideal. That Mrs Bardell is well qualified for the status of 'angel in the house' is clear from her description as 'a comely woman of bustling manners and agreeable appearance, with a natural genius for cooking, improved by study and long practice into an exquisite talent. [...] Cleanliness and quiet reigned throughout the house; and in it Mr Pickwick's will was law' (p. 159). The home that Mrs Bardell offers conforms exactly to Margaret Lane's description of Dickens's ideal household model:

An essentially modest home, not rich or ostentatious [...] but warm, bright, clean, a pattern of good management and homely virtues. Cleanliness is repeatedly insisted upon, as it was in Dickens's own domestic arrangements at all periods of his life. [...] Domestic skill, in short, is one of the essential virtues of a Dickens heroine.[59]

By Michael Slater's reasoning also, Mrs Bardell should present ideal marriage material: 'Dickens's presentation of admirable wives does not rise much above the level of efficient housewifery with much emphasis on the creation of neatness and order, comfort, and the provision of plenty of food.'[60] Indeed, such skills are presented as the most effective provocation to matrimony within *The Pickwick Papers*. The interpolated 'Bagman's Tale' that follows the catalogue of Mrs Bardell's domestic attributes, features a similarly widowed landlady whose offer of choice viands to the traveller Tom Smart exacerbates his marital intentions towards her: 'His admiration of the widow increased as she spoke. Thoughtful creature! Comfortable provider!' (p. 194) Mr Pickwick's emphatic rejection through Mrs Bardell of even the most ideal marital scenario provides compelling evidence of Dickens's awareness of the insufficiency of a celebrated model of marriage from the very beginning of his novelistic career.

[59] Lane, 'Dickens on the Hearth' p. 155.
[60] Slater, *Dickens and Women* (London: Dent, 1983), p. 312.

The narrator's careful disclaimer, 'we [. . .] beg it to be distinctly understood that we indulge in no hidden sarcasm upon a married life' (p. 369), is constantly exposed as disingenuous as, comically and poignantly, farcically and melodramatically, the dysfunction of marriage provides the impetus for almost every plot line. Dickens exploits the inclusive structure of this miscellaneous novel, which accommodates interpolated tales, multiple genres and a fecundity of diverse characters, to provide a comprehensive survey of marital aversion and discontent. 'Central' incidents include the negotiation of a separation by the flirtatious Mrs Pott and provide numerous opportunities for what Hager has described as 'Wellerisms' from both Sam and his unhappily remarried father 'on the subject of that dreaded state of matrimony which abound throughout the novel'.[61] When the death of Susan releases Mr Weller Senior from his second bout of marital disharmony, he recoils in horror from the attentions of local single women: 'It's a horrid sitiwation. I'm actiwally drove out o'house and home by it' (p. 694). This scenario exactly parallels Pickwick's panicked retreat from Mr Ben Allen's aunt: 'The truth is that the old lady's evidently increasing admiration was Mr Pickwick's principal inducement for going. He thought of Mrs Bardell; and every glance of the old lady's eyes threw him into a cold perspiration' (p. 642). Pickwick is similarly brought out into a cold sweat by the bedroom farce at The Great White Horse Inn. Here he mistakenly goes to bed in the wrong room, discovering too late that he has confused Miss Witherfield's sleeping quarters for his own: 'Mr Pickwick almost fainted with horror and dismay. Standing before the dressing glass, was a middle-aged lady in yellow curl-papers, busily engaged in brushing what ladies call their "back hair" [. . .] "I never met with anything so awful as this" thought poor Mr Pickwick, the cold perspiration starting to drop upon his nightcap. "Never, this is fearful"' (p. 301). In their doubled abhorrence towards maritally inclined women, the portly pair of Mr Pickwick and Mr Tony Weller demonstrate the broad scope for heterosexual aversion across class boundaries.[62]

The reappearance of Mr Pickwick, Sam, and Tony Weller in *Master Humphrey's Clock* allows for a continuation and revision of this theme of

[61] Hager, 'Plotting Marriage', pp. 18–19.
[62] James Kincaid describes this duo as 'a kind of unit [...] the first two points in the trinity of flesh that defines the erotic reading of this novel; Tony Weller, Mr Pickwick and the Fat Boy'. 'Fattening Up on Pickwick', *Novel* 25 (1992), 235–44, p. 243.

nuptial repugnance. In his new incarnation Tony Weller offers an energetic account of his efforts to escape the 'most awful' advances of a 'livin wider' on a railway journey, and, in a mode of somatic horror familiar from *Pickwick*, has 'perspiration breaking out upon his forehead' at the thought that Master Humphrey's housekeeper might also be a widow (I, pp. 72, 71). However, here the misogynistic dimension to such humour is tempered as Tony Weller finds himself attracted by the attributes of this housekeeper, who, unmoved by Weller's opinion, favourable or otherwise, has her own agenda and forms a happy match with the local barber. The anti-marital rhetoric subtly shifts from the problematically sexist humour generated by an antipathy to women seeking marriage, to an assertion of the naturalness of volitional bachelorhood. In *Master Humphrey's Clock* Tony Weller finally announces 'his determination to "take arter the old un in all respects" from which I infer that it is his intention to regulate his conduct by the model of Mr Pickwick, who will certainly set him the example of a single life' (III, p. 425). This reassertion of Pickwick's incontrovertible single status anticipates the portrayal of Mr Lorry's congenital bachelorhood.

Within *The Pickwick Papers* Mr Pickwick's rejection of marriage is similarly illuminated and contextualized by complementary textual strands, including the range of normative to aberrant marital attitudes conveyed through the often gothic and fantastical mode of the interpolated tales. While the first two interpolations present case-studies of spousal cruelty and wifely suffering, other interpolations such as the paired 'A Tale Told by a Bagman' and 'The Story of the Bagman's Uncle', offer an alternative exploration of marital inducement and resistance. In 'A Tale Told by a Bagman', the bagman has a dream which reveals the bigamous intentions of his rival, effecting his successful courtship of an eminently marriageable Bardell-esque landlady. Later in the novel his uncle has a dream which has the opposite effect, revising this marital outcome. The uncle fantasizes that he has heroically rescued a damsel in distress, who promptly exacts his promise never to marry anyone but her: 'He remained staunch to the great oath he had sworn to the beautiful young lady refusing several eligible landladies on her account, and died a bachelor at last' (p. 659).

This final dream comprises a mysteriously underdetermined prohibition against marriage, which prevents the uncle from connubially converting his apparently 'great admiration for bright eyes, and sweet faces, and pretty legs and feet' (p. 653).[63] The uncle's employment of his phantasmal commitment as a shadowy explanation for his perceived failure to marry demonstrates the cultural demand that bachelors justify their single status. The Bagman's anxious response to his uncle's bachelorhood similarly points to the ambivalent social position of the volitionally single male. The bagman emphasizes his uncle's complicity with heterosexual models of desire, reiterating the uncle's penchant for kissing barmaids (p. 657) and repeatedly insisting that the uncle's bachelor status has no hereditary impact on his own heterosexual virility: 'In short he was fond of the whole sex. It runs in our family, gentleman – so am I' (p. 653).

The opposite marital effects of these two dreams condense Mr Pickwick's own trajectory away from marital expectation towards a justification and celebration of the hetero-resistant pattern of living offered by bachelorhood. As Brian McCuskey puts it, 'weddings do provide occasion for much merrymaking among the Pickwickians, but the novel leaves little doubt that bachelorhood is to be greatly preferred to married life.'[64] The comedy arising from Pickwick's heterosexual aversion is carefully buttressed by a more serious framework of statements that position Mr Pickwick's refusal of compulsory heterosexuality as central to his sense of self. Mr Winkle, even in his flurried state, is able to commit firmly to the official record of the trial that Pickwick had never 'contemplated matrimony' – 'Oh no; certainly not' (p. 461). Pickwick himself provides an equally emphatic message in his response to the question of whether he has ever proposed: '"Never", said Mr Pickwick with great energy, "never"' (p. 314). At the close of the novel the social and generic expectation of Pickwick's personal marital conclusion is 'strenuously' quashed for a final time: 'Some (among whom was Mr Tupman) were

---

[63] *Master Humphrey's Clock* includes similarly bizarre and macabre tales in which there are comparable underdetermined bars to otherwise promising marriages. Sam Weller, for example, in his role in the downstairs storytelling group 'Mr Weller's Watch' that mirrors the upstairs club, tells a Pygmalion style tale of a hairdresser who refuses to marry until he meets the living counterpart of a blonde dummy in his shop. Having found his ideal woman the courtship is proceeding well until he introduces his fiancé to the dummies, and she immediately transfers her attention to a handsome male mannequin – 'my affections is set on that manly brow' (I, pp. 99–102).
[64] McCuskey, p. 251.

disposed to think that Mr Pickwick contemplated a matrimonial alliance, but this idea the ladies strenuously repudiated' (p. 748).

Although Pickwick himself succeeds in maintaining bachelor status, existing readings have none-the-less perceived the close of the novel, in which the fortunes of the novel's pairs marital and otherwise are detailed, as a belated recapitulation to conventional marital closure:

> The end of *Pickwick*, with its comic reconciliation and celebration of multiple marriages, suggests that *Pickwick* has been a domestic novel with a traditional marriage plot all along [. . .] Pickwick's release from the Fleet is a pact with such a plot, a pact that transforms the bachelor Pickwick, who stands as a figure of transgression in a society that seems to insist on the nuclear patriarchal family, into Cupid, a transcendental facilitator of marriages.[65]

Gina Marlene Dorre reiterates the popular belief that Pickwick's 'orchestration of the proper couplings of two of his companions, which sees them into happy marriages, verifies his work as a patriarch and resolves the menace of his potentially transgressive sexuality'.[66] The final coupling that the novel discusses, though, is that of Pickwick and Sam, their mutual fidelity offering a reworking of the terms of the marriage ceremony: 'On this, as on all other occasions, he is invariably attended by the faithful Sam, between whom and his master, there exists a steady and reciprocal attachment, which nothing but death will sever' (p. 754). The reprise of this relationship in *Master Humphrey's Clock* allows a continuation beyond this happy ending in a restatement of Sam's dedication to Pickwick: ' "Oh! Sam" replied Mr Pickwick "is the same as ever. The same true, faithful fellow that he ever was. What should I tell you about Sam, my dear Sir, except that he is more indispensable to my happiness and comfort every day of my life" ' (I, p. 52). Male relationships of mutual devotion that surpass marriage are similarly a concern of the central characters of this weekly. As Master Humphrey says of his intimacy with the deaf gentleman, 'such attachment and devotion as he has shown to me'; 'We have gone on strengthening in our friendship and regard and forming an attachment which,

[65] Mara Fein, 'The Politics of Family in *The Pickwick Papers*', *ELH* 61 (1994), 363–79, p. 374.
[66] Gina Marlene Dorre, 'Handling the "Iron Horse": Dickens, Travel and Derailed Masculinity in *The Pickwick Papers*', *Nineteenth Century Studies* 16 (2002), 1–19, p. 10.

I trust and believe, will only be interrupted by death, to be renewed in another existence' (I, p. 28). Unbreakable bachelor bonds, then, are seen in the textual superfluities of the serialized *Pickwick* and *Clock* to supersede marriage as the ultimate achievement of narrative.

Pickwick's, like Mr Lorry's, bachelorhood can be read as a sexual choice in its resistance to the non-choice of compulsory heterosexuality. However, the intensity of Pickwick's admiration for his charming servant also has a homoerotic dimension, carefully forged by Dickens through the structural association of Pickwick and Sam with the male couple who provoke a vehement homophobic response in this novel. McCuskey suggests that the triumphant finale of *The Pickwick Papers* is only possible because the intimacy between master and man is firmly differentiated from the provocative relationship between Alfred Jingle (conman and chameleon who variously tricks and outmanoeuvres the Pickwickians) and his friend and sidekick Job Trotter. As McCuskey argues, the difficulty of categorizing this relationship 'causes a great deal of confusion and anxiety in the novel. No one can be sure if the two men are master and servant or not; Sam refers to Jingle as 'friend or master, or whatever he is' and Lowten, the legal assistant, similarly terms Job 'that servant, or friend, or whatever he is'.[67] As an ambiguous, difficult-to-label relationship, the bond between Jingle and Job becomes the locus for explicit articulations of anxiety about the boundaries of male friendship. Such concerns are particularly fuelled by the self-sacrificing nature of Job's acts. When Jingle is committed to the Fleet debtor's prison, Job voluntary follows him: 'Following close at his [Jingle's] heels, came Mr Job Trotter, in the catalogue of whose vices, want of faith and attachment to his companion could at all events, find no place' (p. 605). This neatly parallels the moving fidelity of Sam Weller to Mr Pickwick, who has entered the Fleet several chapters earlier. Sam has himself arrested in order to join his master, an act which Pickwick fully values: 'Mr Pickwick felt a great deal too much touched by the warmth of Sam's attachment, to be able to exhibit any manifestation of anger or displeasure' (p. 583).

The careful doubling of these two incarcerated pairs is made explicit in the image of the two-by-two procession through the jail of Pickwick and Jingle, followed by Sam and Job (p. 606).

---

[67] McCuskey, p. 263.

Job's dedication to Jingle reaches new heights of expression when Pickwick benevolently pays the debt for which Jingle has been imprisoned and finds work for him on an estate in Demerara. Job insists that 'he must go along with the other one', sacrificing a less arduous and better paid job opportunity in London to do so (p. 701). Job's self-denying insistence that he accompany his friend to begin this new and arduous life in the West Indies provokes Lowten's articulation of the novel's most open representation of homophobic anxiety:

'He says that he's the only friend he's ever had, and he's attached to him, and all that. Friendship's a very good thing in its way; we are all very friendly and comfortable at the Stump, for instance, over our grog, where every man pays for himself, but damn hurting yourself for anybody else, you know! No man should have more than two attachments – the first to number one, and the second to the ladies; that's what I say – ha ha!' (p. 701)

Lowten disparagingly describes Job as 'a soft chap' and as 'downright sneaking'. This phobic reaction, however, is counteracted by an opposing response from the novel's highest moral authority. Pickwick's 'glistening eyes' at Job's fidelity to 'the only friend he ever had', marks and sanctions an alternative response to this attachment (p. 701). Pickwick, as a selfless character who is appalled by, rather than attached to, 'the ladies', clearly fails in the same way as Job and Jingle to conform to Lowten's restrictive prescription for permissible relations. McCuskey is unconvincing in his attempt to demonstrate that the novel ensures that this type of suspicion is 'deflected away from Pickwick's and Sam's attachment to each other.'[68] To distinguish responses to this partnership from the anxious attempts to establish the boundaries of the friendship between Job and Jingle, McCuskey cites Mr Magnus's uncertainty about whether their relationship is one of friendship, quoting Pickwick's equivocal response: '"Not exactly a friend", replied Mr Pickwick in a low tone. "The fact is, he is my servant, but I allow him to take a good many liberties"' (p. 293). This exchange, however, better serves to illustrate the similarly permeable boundaries, and parallel difficulties of recognizing and defining the parameters, of both pairings.

Pickwick provides controversial support for the continuing relationship of Job and Jingle, ignoring his solicitor's disapproval of what he views as a

---

[68] McCuskey, p. 263.

misplaced generosity – 'You have already lost upwards of fifty pounds' (p. 703) – to fund their joint emigration to the West Indies. Pickwick's final acts of benevolent family formation are not then, as previous approaches have tended to suggest, exclusively focused on effecting conventional marriage. Pickwick also negotiates the future cohabitation of Job and Jingle, and arranges his own bachelor domesticity alongside Sam and his family, appointing Sam's wife Mary as housekeeper and accommodating their children.[69] The family of choice that Dickens establishes around Pickwick in the much celebrated society of the Dulwich villa where 'everything was so beautiful' (p. 751), is typical of his complex portrayals of non-marital and non-reproductive desires, expressed and lived within a broadly heterosexist society through diverse adaptations and appropriations of conventional marital and family structures.

THE UNTENABILITY OF BACHELOR DOMESTICITY?: QUEER SPACES AND EUGENE WRAYBURN'S DEATHBED CONVERSION

In *Our Mutual Friend* Dickens offers a more tragic rendering of the difficulty of establishing a domestic space in which attachments between men can be fully lived out. Eugene's final reparative capitulation to marriage with Lizzie, who he has 'pursued' in a desultory way despite her being the locus of sexual attraction in the novel, is upstaged by the expression of the intensity of male intimacy. As in *The Pickwick Papers*, it is bonds between men that are most emphatically celebrated, in contrast to the muted treatment of marriage, in this novel's final pages. Eugene's non-proposal (Jenny Wren has to intuit that the word he cannot bring himself to say is 'wife', p. 722) is explicitly positioned as a dying man's final effort to make amends by placing 'Lizzie and [. . .] reparation before all' (p. 720) – 'If my dear brave girl will take me, I feel persuaded that I shall live long enough to be married, dear fellow' (p. 723). The successful completion of the ceremony immediately incites Eugene to a death wish, totally incongruous, as Lizzie is aware,

---

[69] Glavin has seen the arrival of Sam's wife and their offspring as militating against 'any simplistically homoerotic reading of this structure', p. 13.

with the 'happy' occasion: 'Would you believe [. . .] that on his wedding day he told me that he almost thought the best thing he could do
was to die?' (p. 790) This subdued capitulation to marriage is at variance
with the vibrant declarations of love between Eugene and his partner in
law and intimate friend Mortimer Lightwood, with whom he has
cohabited throughout the novel. Mortimer's statement of feeling on
what he sees as his execution of Eugene's final command dramatizes the
difficulty of both speaking and fulfilling such a love: '[H]e may die with
his request ungratified, with his last wish – intrusted to me – we have
long been much more than brothers – unfulfilled. I shall break down, if
I try to say more' (p. 717). The broken clauses in this parenthetical
admission of the extent of their relationship demonstrate the difficulty
of saying so much. Mortimer does though find a voice with which to
speak his feeling for Eugene, describing himself as 'the friend who has
always loved you, admired you, imitated you, founded himself upon
you, been nothing without you, and who, God knows, would be there
in your place if he could' (p. 719). Eugene reciprocates with an avowal
of his need for physical contact with his beloved friend: 'Touch my face
with yours, in case I should not hold out until you come back. I love you
Mortimer' (p. 723).

Eugene's longing for perhaps a final moment of contact with Mortimer
is in distinct contrast to his expressed abhorrence for the female 'touch'. In
one of his many earlier fireside scenes with Mortimer, Eugene has made it
clear that he has a physical antipathy to the marital schemes proposed by
the paternal authority he sarcastically refers to as M. R. F. (my respected
father): 'M. R. F. pre-arranged for myself that I was to be the barrister I am
(with the slight addition of an enormous practice, which has not accrued),
and also the married man I am not [. . .] Considering myself sufficiently
incongruous on my legal eminence, I have until now suppressed my
domestic destiny' (p. 149). Mortimer's suggestion that Eugene meet the
unspecified woman proposed by M. R. F. implies that physical attraction
may overcome Eugene's marital objections. Eugene emphatically rejects
this scheme and the potential for opposite-sex attraction it represents:
'Anything to carry out M. R. F.'s arrangements, I am sure, with the
greatest pleasure – except matrimony [. . .] No, there is no help for it;
one of the prophetic deliveries of M. R. F. must forever remain unfulfilled.
With every disposition to oblige him, he must submit to a failure' (p. 150).
The typically languid Eugene's uncharacteristic decisive vehemence on

this single issue is explained through a direct reference to heterosexual disinclination:

'Touching the lady, Eugene.'
'There M. R. F. ceases to be amusing, because my intentions are opposed to touching the lady' (p. 149).

Eugene sees the marriage that M. R. F. advocates as his only route to 'domestic destiny', and duly self-prescribes a heavy dose of what he perceives as the trappings of the marital home by liberally applying its paraphernalia to the chambers that he shares with Mortimer:

[M]iniature flour-barrel, rolling-pin, spice-box, shelf of brown jars, chopping-board, coffee-mill, dresser elegantly furnished with crockery, saucepans and pans, roasting jack, a charming kettle, an armoury of dish-covers. The moral influence of these objects, in forming the domestic virtues, may have an immense influence upon me; not upon you, for you are a hopeless case, but upon me. In fact, I have an idea that I feel the domestic virtues already forming (p. 282).

The elaborate costuming of this 'very complete little kitchen [. . .] in which nothing will ever be cooked' (p. 281), operates in a similar way to the crafted staginess of the set-piece marital home in *Bleak House*. Both moments draw attention to the artifice involved in an inflexible model of marital domesticity as a natural, inevitable destiny. Though Mortimer is 'a hopeless case', Eugene is optimistic of a cure for his preference for bachelor life: 'I am doing all I can towards self-improvement [. . .] Sensible of my deficiencies, I have surrounded myself with moral influences expressly meant to promote the formation of the domestic virtues' (p. 293).

The idyllic home life of Eugene and Mortimer, whether in chambers or in their 'joint establishment' of a 'bachelor cottage near Hampton' (a celebratory coinage that the OED attributes to Dickens) exposes the illogic of Eugene's persistent equation of domesticity with marriage. Eugene and Mortimer's comfortable inhabitation of domestic space allows them to pass as normative representatives of Dickensian home life, as in Margaret Lane's inclusion of 'the enveloping warmth of that confidential fireside' shared by the bachelor barristers in her account of Dickens's domestic ideal of 'cleanliness, domestic order and efficiency, [complete with] the little woman, a troop of happy and untroublesome children', and also to be spotted as 'Dickens's closest approach to a gay couple.'[70] Despite his pleasure in Mortimer's company, Eugene perceives their home arrangements to be ultimately untenable, fantasizing instead an alternative space for prolonged domestic intimacy. M.R.F's proposal of a wife for Eugene brings his contentment at life with Mortimer into crisis, and Eugene's expression of his antipathy to 'touching the lady' is immediately preceded by his vision of an eccentric alternative domestic scenario in which he and Mortimer, removed from all other society, keep a lighthouse together: 'It would be a defined and limited monotony. It would not extend beyond two people. Now, it's a question with me, Mortimer, whether a monotony defined with that precision and limited to that extent, might not be more endurable than the unlimited monotony of one's fellow-creatures' (p. 148). Dickens carefully establishes a disparity between Eugene's employment of ennui as a device to avoid wedlock – 'Could I possibly support it? I, so soon bored, so constantly, so fatally?' – and his contradictory lighthouse fantasy of 'a monotony of two'. Eugene meets Mortimer's charge of inconsistency with a request that his friend remember the imagined context: 'In a lighthouse. Do me the justice to remember the condition. In a lighthouse' (p. 150). This vision of exclusive, uninterrupted male/male cohabitation is necessarily isolated from a society, whose marital structure resists the longevity of such pairings:

'If we were on an isolated rock in a stormy sea,' said Eugene, smoking with his eyes on the fire, 'Lady Tippins couldn't put off to visit us, or better still, might put off and get swamped. People couldn't ask one to wedding breakfasts. There would be no Precedents to hammer at, except the plain-sailing Precedent of keeping the light up. It would be exciting to look out for wrecks' (p. 148).

Notorious contemporary sexual dissident Algernon Swinburne recorded a similar yearning as Charles Sprawson has documented: 'Swinburne had always wanted to live in a lighthouse – so long as it was miles out to sea and difficult to get at.'[71] This scenario had a strong imaginative appeal for Dickens. He first thought to begin *Martin Chuzzlewit* (1843–4), a novel that makes use of the alternative space of Mississippi swampland to explore

[70] Lane, 'Dickens on the Hearth', p. 163; Graham Robb, *Strangers: Homosexual Love in the Nineteenth Century* (London: Picador, 2003), p. 210.
[71] Charles Sprawson, *Haunts of the Black Masseur: The Swimmer as Hero* (London: Vintage, 2002), p. 97.

male intimacy, in a lighthouse off the Cornish coast, and he placed a pair of lighthouse keepers at the centre of visions of convivial Christmases present in *A Christmas Carol*: 'But even here, two men who watched the light had made a fire, that through the loophole of in the thick stone wall shed out a ray of brightness on the awful sea. Joining their horny hands over the rough table at which they sat, they wished each other Merry Christmas in their can of grog.'[72] Lighthouses continue to be an important site in contemporary queer thought. In Jeanette Winterson's novel *Lighthousekeeping* (2004), for example, which is concerned with many varieties of queer space, a bachelor lighthouse keeper takes in an orphaned girl.[73] As an imperfect but more practical alternative to lighthouse keeping, Eugene and Mortimer settle for a 'boating summer'.

Lighthouses, like the bachelor boats discussed in the previous chapter, are sites with a particularly attenuated relationship to wider society, interstitial spaces of imaginative possibility. In Dickens's work these unusual physical spaces often accommodate non-marital and non-reproductive domestic units. This is true of bachelors Sol Gills and Captain Cuttle, whose partnership endures beyond their avunculate parenting of the now adult Walter Gay at the end of *Dombey and Son*. Cuttle – another figure who experiences 'profuse perspiration' at the horror of a nuptial encounter, feeling a 'shadowy terror that he might be married by violence' (p. 923) – narrowly avoids wedlock, a fate reserved for his more hapless friend Bunsby, who is legally joined to Cuttle's formidable widowed landlady Mrs Mac Stinger against his will, having been unable to 'sheer off', as the Captain suggests, from the altar (p. 925). Though Dombey does conclude with a number of marriages,

---

[72] For more on Dickens's early lighthouse plans for *Martin Chuzzlewit* see his letter to Forster, early August 1842, *The Letters of Charles Dickens*, vol. III: 1842–1843, Pilgrim Edition, ed. Madeline House, Graham Storey and Kathleen Tillotson (Oxford: Clarendon Press, 1974), p. 303, and to Southwood Smith, 22 October 1842, in which he arranges to visit 'the very dreariest and most desolate portion of the seacoast of Cornwall' (*Letters*, III, p. 356). Charles Dickens, *A Christmas Carol* collected in *A Christmas Carol and Other Writings* (London: Penguin, 2003), p. 86.

[73] Jeanette Winterson, *Lighthousekeeping* (London: HarperCollins, 2005). Winterson's determinedly intertextual novel perhaps references a central Dickensian celebration of bachelorhood in the typical lunch enjoyed by the lighthouse family of keeper and adopted daughter, 'Chops and tomato sauce' (p. 37). This same menu is an important piece of evidence in *Pickwick's* Breach of Promise trial, the legal proceeding against Pickwick's effort to maintain his bachelor status.

including Walter's (who, disappointingly, fails to capitalize on the queer possibilities of his upbringing), it also formalizes the bond between bachelors as they become business partners; above the Wooden-Midshipman, the figurehead for their queer boat-house, 'these names shine refulgent, GILLS AND CUTTLE' (p. 943).

Dickens's fiction, though committed to a denaturalization of marriage as destiny and the exploration of non-marital experiences of domesticity, cannot comfortably accommodate the bachelor of perceived marriageable age. Prolonged enjoyment of a family of choice is possible in some particular, architecturally eccentric spaces; otherwise it is reserved for those elderly single males whose age has released them from the imperative to marry. Though the tragic bachelor plots of Sydney Carton and Eugene Wrayburn temper the celebration of the incurable bachelorhood of figures such as Mr Pickwick, Master Humphrey, Captain Cuttle, and Mr Lorry, the spaces that Dickens's fiction continually creates for the bachelor hero points to the more radical trajectory of his work. Through seriality, connections with non-fictional recommendations of bachelor life, explicit reanimations of earlier characters, and the implicit connections drawn between a long line of bachelors, marriage as a device for closure is rejected and the heterosexual shape that has been attributed to the Victorian novel is broken up in favour of plots that eschew marriage and reproduction. Dickens's plots, however, do not only challenge the sufficiency of connubial bonds, they also (as the next chapter will elaborate) question the extent to which marriage itself is a heterosexual mechanism.

3

Families of Choice: Homoerotic Intermarriage and Sibling Triangulation

Throughout his career Dickens was fascinated by the limitations of the family as defined and formed by marriage and reproduction. He consistently explores alternative domestic spaces and bonds. In this chapter I examine the queer possibilities inherent even within the putatively heterosexual family, exploring Dickens's exposure of the multiple motivations, including the homoerotic, that can coalesce as factors determining marital choice. I focus upon one particularly rich strategy through which Dickens destabilizes the operation of marriage as a straightening mechanism: in-lawing. Throughout Dickens's work prohibited desire for a member of the same sex is often quite transparently redirected or extended to an opposite-sex sibling. Here I explore three early triads: Bob Sawyer, Ben and Arabella Allen in *The Pickwick Papers*, Smike, Nicholas and Kate Nickleby, and John Westlock and Tom and Ruth Pinch in *Martin Chuzzlewit.* I consider these (homo)erotically suggestive triangles of male suitor, brother, and sister in the expansive context of Victorian concepts of family. By stressing the numerous economic and erotic investments that structure inter-marital plotting, Dickens's fiction unravels the pervasive current logic that posits heterosexuality as the primary determinant of, or central motive for, family formation. Instead, his novels explore the multiple motives behind the formation of families of choice. In his emphasis on the homoerotic potential of the familiar situation of in-law intimacy Dickens is queer, not in his rendering of a scenario which transgresses an always imagined family norm, but in his fascination with the possible congruity of opposite-sex and same-sex desire *within* marriage and family. In delineating the easy slippage of desire from a male to a female sibling,

Dickens also complicates gendered boundaries, showing the proximity, rather than the opposition, of masculinity and femininity.

This chapter explores a different form of queer triangulation to that famously discussed by Sedgwick in *Between Men*. Sedgwick explores instances in which the homoerotic relationship is one of rivalry, triangulated around a woman. I argue that once we recognize an alternative, familial triad, then it becomes clear that in the Victorian period there was not always or necessarily a 'radically discontinuous relation of male homosocial and homosexual bonds'.[1] In suitor/brother/sister triangles ties of rivalry give way to relations of affinity – more benevolent and life enhancing, but no less eroticized than those triads documented by Sedgwick. Dickens's works dramatize the sexual content of in-law bonds not covertly through violent contact, but overtly in the explicitly presented parallels of attraction offered by opposite-sex siblings.

In his repeated delineation of a male character's compulsive shift of attention from a close male friend to his (most often) physically similar sister, Dickens leans on – and then proceeds to expose the homoerotic possibilities within – two central Victorian beliefs about siblinghood. Siblings, even of the opposite sex, were thought to possess both physical and temperamental parity. As Valerie Sanders puts it, 'in the nineteenth century, family ideology saw siblings of both sexes as being more like than unlike one another, even in looks. A sibling was a part of the home life, assumed to have the same fundamental values . . . and the same memories of shared experiences.'[2] Sanders amasses a wealth of evidence to demonstrate that even opposite-sex 'Victorian siblings in literature were regarded as being more alike than different', since it was the case that most novelists of that period writing 'about sibling pairs . . . stressed the similarities between the brother and sister' (pp. 132, 136). The extent to which Dickens and his contemporaries were alert to the potential physical interchangeability of sibling bodies is apparent in widespread public anxiety about the transfer of desire from one (female) sibling to another. Debates around the 1835 legislation prohibiting marriage to a deceased

---

[1] Sedgwick, *Between Men*, p. 5.
[2] Valerie Sanders, *The Brother-Sister Culture in Nineteenth-Century Literature* (Basingstoke: Palgrave, 2002), p. 81. For a historically focused account of sibling parity see Leonore Davidoff, *Worlds Between: Historical Perspectives on Gender and Class* (Oxford: Blackwell, 1995), pp. 208–9.

wife's sister highlighted the potential substitutability of sisters, and thus rehearsed contemporary attitudes about sibling similarity.[3] Meanwhile, a variety of fictional and personal documents (novels, poems, letters, diaries, and biographies) were beginning to explore the gender-dismantling parity of opposite-sex siblings. This cultural prioritizing of familial sameness over expected gender difference creates a space for homo-affirmative plotting in Dickens's work.

While physical resemblance as a consequence of shared blood was often over-determined in the Victorian imagination, the expected parallels of character were, in part, a consequence of a powerful strand of sororal ideology, which recommended that a good sister should learn to mould her wishes to those of her brother, sharing and imitating his desires. Through readings of conduct literature and fiction of this period Leila Silvana May observes the many ways in which adolescent sisters were instructed in the subordination of their wishes within the family: 'She is taught that she must defer to and minister to her brother, and understands that eventually she might have to reject a beloved suitor if her brother disapproves of him.'[4] The ultimate, maritally coercive, implication is clear: 'She must learn to identify the desire of the (br)other, and then come to identify it as her own' (p. 19). In Dickens's fiction, as well as in actual instances of the time, these aspects of sibling ideology provide an enabling frame-work for the experience and continuation of homoerotic desires within the ostensibly heterosexual family. Domestic ideologies of siblinghood allowed both fictional men and their historical counterparts to create a homoerotically motivated family of choice through betrothal to the suggestively similar sister of their closest male friend. Ideas of the parity of sibling bodies and minds enabled various challenges to the emotional and erotic precedence of marital relations. Through the repetition of sibling transference across his career, Dickens pioneered an influential

---

[3] Jane Waller's thorough examination of fictional responses to the deceased wife's sister controversy concludes that, given the cultural investment in the paradigm of sororal similarity, 'the idea that the man would be attracted to both sisters seems almost taken for granted' (*Two Sisters Loving One Man: the Victorians and the Sisterly Ideal*, MA dissertation, Birkbeck College, University of London, 2003, p. 4).

[4] Leila Silvana May, *Disorderly Sisters: Sibling Relations and Sororal Resistance in Nineteenth Century British Culture* (Lewisburg: Bucknell University Press, 2001), p. 18.

model for corporeal, homoerotic articulation which was thereafter eagerly employed by his contemporaries, including Thomas Hughes and Mary Elizabeth Braddon, and later in overt representations of same-sex desire by pioneering early twentieth-century writers who endeavoured to treat homosexuality with candour.

'HE LOVED A DAUGHTER OF OUR HOUSE': CONTEMPORARY MODELS OF INTER-FAMILIAL DESIRE

Dickens's fiction both draws upon and anticipates wider literary explorations, and actual experiences of homoerotic in-lawing. His first, Pickwickian treatment of in-lawing clearly expands upon an earlier example of such plotting from Edward Bulwer Lytton's 1828 novel *Pelham*. The novelist was one of Dickens's most admired contemporaries, and the two authors became firm friends, co-founding the 'Guild of Literature and Art'.[5] In *Pelham*, the eponymous hero imperfectly transfers his excessive enthusiasm for Reginald Glanville – 'I thought as I looked at him, that I had never seen so perfect a specimen of masculine beauty, at once so physical and intellectual' – onto Reginald's sister, Ellen.[6] After he has been introduced to her, Pelham describes himself (giving the familiar, telling precedence to his response to the male sibling) as 'full of hope, energy, ambition – of interest for Reginald Glanville – of adoration for his sister' (p. 193). Bulwer Lytton's construction of Pelham's offer of marriage makes clear that this is a proposal for prolonged male cohabitation. An implausible plot in which Reginald is suspected of murder allows Pelham to recommend a furtive life overseas with his prospective brother-in-law, interrupted only by brief visits to Ellen, who will be left in England:

---

[5] Adam Roberts, 'Bulwer Lytton', *Companion*, pp. 63–4. For Dickens's enthusiasm for Bulwer Lytton's work see Collins, 'Dickens's Reading'; *Catalogue of the Library of Charles Dickens*, ed. J. H. Stonehouse.

[6] Edward Bulwer Lytton, *Pelham, or Adventures of a Gentleman* (London: Routledge, 1848), p. 119.

I told him all that had just occurred between Ellen and myself. 'And now', said I, as I clasped his hand, 'I have a proposal to make, to which you must accede: let me accompany you abroad: I will go with you to whatever corner of the world you may select. We will plan together every possible method of concealing our retreat . . . I will tend upon you, watch over you, bear with you, with more than the love and tenderness of a brother . . . you shall have me by your side till – till –' (p. 257).

This scheme neatly exposes this marriage and emigration as devices to allow the brothers-in-law an increased intimacy. Ironically, given Bulwer Lytton's anxiety that Dickens should make his fiction fulfil conventional romantic expectations, this novel may have provided a template for Dickens's development of a wide range of familial scenarios that operate through the homoerotic device of in-lawing. Bulwer Lytton's prose also contains devices that Dickens was to use in portraying the intensity of male relations throughout his career. The marital language of 'a proposal' anticipates those to-the-death male partnerships considered in the previous chapter that rework the terms of the marriage ceremony to emphasize the way in which male bonds supplant, or at least supplement, those of husband and wife. Similarly the familial language of a relationship comparable to, or beyond, the fidelity of brotherhood is typical of climactic moments in Dickens's work in which the emotional intensity of male bonds is finally articulated.[7] In-lawing plots give legal legitimacy to a rhetoric of intimate brotherhood, as close male friends are rendered, in law, one blood. This shift from fantasized fraternity to ratified brotherhood exerted a powerful appeal for Dickens and many of his contemporaries.

Indeed, the brother-in-law tie cemented one of the most powerful historical models of male friendship in the period, that between the biblical David and Jonathan. As documented in the first and second books of Samuel, Jonathan loved David, who was married to his sister Michal, 'as his own soul' (I Samuel, 18:1) and 'delighted much' in him (I Samuel, 19:2). In the second book of Samuel, David laments

---

[7] See, for example, Mortimer's avowal of his feeling for Eugene in a scene discussed in detail in the previous chapter: 'we have long been much more than brothers' (p. 717). Master Humphrey and the deaf gentleman are similarly described as having 'grown to be like brothers' (I, p. 5).

Jonathan's death, in a language also applicable to many of Dickens's male friendships which supersede (even marital) relationships with women:

> I am distressed for thee, my brother Jonathan;
> Very pleasant hast thou been unto me:
> Thy love to me was wonderful,
> Passing the love of women
>
> (II Samuel: 1:26)

By the end of the nineteenth century, as Richard Dellamora has noted, homoerotic interpretations of this relationship were common, with artists such as the American John Singer Sargent drawing out the erotic implications of their familial bond. Sargent's illustration, 'The Parting of Jonathan and David' (c.1895) to accompany I Samuel: 20: 42, 'the Lord be between me and thee, and between thy seed and my seed for ever', fuses the textual vision of the continuation of these intermingled bloodlines with an image of the two men strained together in a moment of breast to breast rapture. Though Sargent prepared the picture for a new illustrated edition of the Bible, it was not used. Dellamora, following the Sargent scholar Trevor Fairbrother, attributes this to a new anxiety about male friendship following Oscar Wilde's trail for gross indecency in 1895, at which Wilde referred to the biblical example of David and Jonathan to contextualize his relationships with young men.[8] Wilde's invocation of this model signified ambivalently, as references to David and Jonathan earlier in the Victorian period had, both to advocate the nobility of male friendship, and to signal its homoerotic intensity. Dinah Craik's 1856 novel *John Halifax, Gentleman*, for example, framed her depiction of an emotionally and physically intense male friendship with biblical references to the 'David and Jonathan' friendship, 'surpassing the love of women'.[9] Yet reviewers responded uncomfortably to Craik's portrayal, comparing the relationship to a male/female romantic courtship.[10] Reviews of *In Memoriam: A. H. H.*

---

[8] Dellamora, *Friendship's Bonds*, frontispiece.

[9] Dinah Craik, *John Halifax, Gentleman* (Gloucestershire: Nonsuch, 2005), pp. 16, 152.

[10] See, for example, 'Novels by the Author of John Halifax', *North British Review* 29 (1858), 466–81: 'during the early part of the tale, it is difficult to suppress a fear that Phineas Fletcher will fall hopelessly in love with John Halifax, so hard is it to remember that Phineas is of the male sex'.

(1850), Alfred Tennyson's idyll for his dead friend (and brother-in-law to be) Arthur Hallam, referenced David and Jonathan in a similarly ambiguous way. In a riposte to *The Times* reviewer's infamous critique of the poem's tone of 'amatory tenderness', and 'feminine application' – 'Is it Petrarch whispering to Laura?' – F. W. Robertson asserted, quoting II Samuel: I1: 26: 'It may be well also to recollect that there is a precedent for this woman-like-tenderness, against whose authority one who condemns so severely the most distant approach to irreverence will scarcely venture to appeal.'[11] Similarly Charles Kingsley's review of the elegy celebrated this Biblical instance alongside classical and Shake-spearian accounts as examples of the 'depth and vehemence of affection' possible in male friendships.[12] These reviews, albeit defensively, brought the parallel brother-in-law relationship of David and Jonathan into debates about the appropriateness of and limits to romantic bonds between men. Though Dickens does not use this language for his male intimates, he does create a David and James (Steerforth) with a wish to be united through a sister.

Dickens's literary and cultural precedents for the intensity of brother-in-law bonding were supplemented by high profile biographical examples, which point towards the significance of in-lawing in determining spousal selection during this period. The intended marital triangle of Tennyson (Dickens's most beloved poet) and his closest friend, Hallam, who was affianced to Tennyson's favourite sister, Emily, is perhaps the best known actual example of such a triadic relationship. In April 1830, a year after meeting Hallam at Cambridge University, Tennyson invited his best friend to the family home. Hallam's report of an early visit is tellingly constructed: 'I am now at Somersby, not only as the friend of Alfred Tennyson, but as the lover of his sister.'[13] The motives for Hallam's engagement have received much scrutiny, with many biographers sharing Peter Levi's conclusion that this 'was how his affection for Alfred resolved itself'. Robert Bernard Martin argues that Hallam's

[11] Anonymous review of *In Memoriam*, *The Times*, 28 November 1851, reprinted in *In Memoriam: A Casebook*, ed. John Hunt (Basingstoke: Macmillan, 1970), p. 104; F. W. Robertson, 'Two Lectures on the Influences of Poetry on the Working Classes', reprinted in *In Memoriam: A Casebook*, p. 118.
[12] Charles Kingsley, review of *In Memoriam*, *Fraser's Magazine*, September 1850, reprinted in *Tennyson: The Critical Heritage*, ed. John Jump (London: Routledge, 1967).
[13] Quoted by Christopher Ricks, *Tennyson* (Basingstoke: Macmillan, 1989), p. 34.

'deep affection for Alfred had predisposed him to choose one of the daughters of the Rectory . . . thus knitting still more tightly the bond of their friendship'.[14] Christopher Ricks's biography of Tennyson portrays Hallam's instantaneous response to Emily, arguing that 'Hallam's sonnets to Emily in April and May 1830 show that he immediately loved her' (p. 34).[15]

This sudden infatuation is closely paralleled in accounts of another famous triangular engagement of the period. In his memoirs, William Michael Rossetti recounts efforts made by members of the Pre-Raphaelite Brotherhood to reinforce their artistic fraternity though intermarriage. He records James Collinson's 'immediate' love for the sister of his favourite 'brother', Dante Gabriel Rossetti: 'James Collinson, about the time of the

[14] Peter Levi, *Tennyson* (Basingstoke: Macmillan, 1993), p. 58; Robert Bernard Martin, *Tennyson: The Unquiet Heart* (Oxford: Faber, 1980), p. 103. Similarly Garrett Jones suggests that 'Arthur actually needed this double bonding in order to anchor his emotions more firmly in their own [male] relationship.' *Alfred and Arthur, an Historic Friendship* (Hertford: Authors Online, 2001), p. 44.

[15] The extent to which this relationship, and Tennyson's account of it in *In Memoriam*, can be interpreted as homoerotic continues to generate critical controversy. Jack Kolb recently expressed reservations about the queer bias in selective presentations of Tennyson's and Hallam's biography by such pioneers of sexuality studies as Alan Sinfield and Richard Dellamora. In the vein of his 1981 edition of Hallam's letters, in which he hoped that epistles to Emily would 'put such [homoerotic] suspicions finally to rest – if indeed such things are still suspect', Kolb continues to cite Hallam's engagement to Emily Tennyson as a piece of 'pertinent data that these critics seldom – if ever – mention' Kolb, ed., *The Letters of Arthur Henry Hallam* (Columbus: Ohio State University Press, 1981), p. 17; 'Hallam, Tennyson, Homosexuality and the Critics,' *Philological Quarterly*, 79.3 (2000), 365–96, p. 387. However, Hallam's and Tennyson's representations of their triangulated relationship, particularly when read in a wider contemporary context of homoerotic in-lawing, make ambiguous the heterosexuality that Hallam's engagement is held to represent.

Emily Tennyson's relationship with Arthur Hallam's sister, Ellen, after his death, provides an important and poignant example of the similar emotional benefits of sibling substitution for women. Until Ellen's untimely death in 1837, Emily found great consolation in imagining slippage between brother and sister, describing this in an 1835 letter:

In listening to thee imagination has often left me to suppose 'twas the voice of my beloved Arthur, thy sentiments and manner are so like his, that I loved when sitting by thy side to close my eyes, and lose myself in this delicious dream – Dear, dear Ellen, how could I part from thee? – how could I find strength of mind sufficient to tear myself from thy embrace, and look my last on those eyes of tender light! (Quoted by Jones, p. 106)

Given the corresponding intensity of this relationship, Jones suggests that it offers a 'mirror to the friendship between their two brothers, although in this case, Ellen became for Emily a surrogate Arthur' (p. 106).

formation of the PRB (in early 1848), was introduced to Christina, then aged seventeen, in our family circle, and he immediately fell in love with her . . . He explained his feeling to Dante Gabriel, who, with perhaps too headlong a wish to serve the interests of a 'Pre-Raphaelite Brother', represented the matter to Christina and advocated Collinson's cause.'[16]

Like Collinson, Hallam was eager to cement brotherly bonds and was sensitive to the supplementary appeal of the wider 'family circle'. Martin proposes that Hallam experienced the endearing informality, warmth and impetuosity of the 'Tennysons *en masse*' as a welcome contrast to the sterner atmosphere of his own home: 'Hallam seems to have fallen in love at once, but with the whole family rather than a particular member' (p. 100). His regard was affectionately returned. Tennyson's young sister Matilda, who was thirteen when Hallam first visited, said of the whole family later: 'we were all in love with him from the first'.[17] Dickens's own relationship with the Hogarth family fulfilled a similar search for support and affection that were not provided by his existing relatives. Fred Kaplan's biography posits that Dickens 'wanted a family he could identify with, who would provide the intimacy and stability that his own lacked'. As Kaplan suggests, Dickens's offer of marriage to Catherine Hogarth was largely determined by his longing to be part of that family 'who welcomed him warmly and whose warmth he returned'.[18]

The public suspicion excited by a wider, potentially erotic, attachment to extended family received voice in the Deceased Wife's Sister controversy. After the so-called Lyndhust Act of 1835, marital law legislated against the possibility of a transfer of a bereaved husband's affection from wife to sister-in-law, deeming such relationships as falling within the prohibited degrees of affinity. Diane Chambers argues convincingly for the wider cultural significance of ensuing debates about the legality or incestuous nature of such marriages, which were 'fought on the political scene almost annually for most of the Victorian period'.

---

[16] William Michael Rossetti, *Some Reminiscences*, 2 vols. (London: 1906), I, p. 71. Collinson and Christina Rossetti had a difficult, on-off engagement, during which Collinson attempted to abandon the Catholic faith. After Collinson found himself unable to permanently alter his religion Rossetti finally terminated the engagement. This conclusion suited Rossetti's own apparent preference for sororal over opposite-sex intimacies.

[17] Quoted by Jones, p. 42.   [18] Kaplan, *Dickens*, pp. 67, 66.

As Chambers suggests, the whole of this controversy 'was about the potential for triangular desire'.[19] In their exploration of these debates Karen Chase and Michael Levenson identify Dickens's enthusiasm for narratives of desire transference from one sister to another.[20] Such plotting is most explicit in his 1846 Christmas Book, *The Battle of Life*, in which a younger sister, Marion, sacrifices her suitor to the older sister, Grace, who also loves him. Before running away and faking her own sexual fall Marion leaves a letter of instruction to Grace: 'praying and beseeching me, as I loved her, and as I loved you, not to reject the affection she believed (she knew, she said) you would transfer to me when the new wound was healed, but to encourage and return it'.[21] Suitor Alfred understandably follows Marion's plot of transference as Dickens's novella systematically erases any physical or behavioural difference between the sisters: '[Grace's] face was so like Marion's as it had been in her later days at home, that it was wonderful to see' (p. 222). Chase and Levenson detect similarly explicit instances of heterosexual sororal exchange in Jonas Chuzzlewit's sudden cruel switch of attention from Charity to Mercy Pecksniff in *Martin Chuzzlewit* and in the blessing that the dying Dora Copperfield bestows on the romantic future of her husband and her quasi-sister Agnes in *David Copperfield*. As I argue below, both novels are simultaneously concerned with the possibility that desire can be transferred or extended to siblings of the opposite sex. Dickens redirects the imaginative potency adhering to controversial sister-switch plots at this time of the Deceased Wife's Sister debates, onto homoerotic transfers, as he widens the question of which desires can be accommodated within the family.

The widely noticed Deceased Wife's Sister controversy had direct implications for Dickens in his later career. A belief that desire could readily be mapped from one sister to another probably contributed to the accusations of sister-in-law incest that were circulated around him

---

[19] Diane Chambers 'Triangular Desire and the Sororal Bond: The Deceased Wife's Sister Bill,' *Mosaic* 29.1 (1996), 19–36, pp. 19–20. For more on how these debates contributed to wider contests about definitions of incest, including discussions of the legality of marriages between cousins, see Elisabeth Rose Gruner, 'Born and Made: Sisters, Brothers and the Deceased Wife's Sister Bill,' *Signs* 24.2, (1999), 423–47.

[20] Chase and Levenson, *The Spectacle of Intimacy*.

[21] Charles Dickens, *The Battle of Life* (London: Penguin, 1985), pp. 220–1.

after his separation from Catherine.[22] Dickens forcefully repudiated
these physical allegations. From his intense relationships with Catherine's sisters, however, Dickens would have been acutely aware that
emotional attachments to siblings-in-law could be more heartfelt than
marital bonds. Michael Slater speculates about the particular appeal of
the Hogarth siblings in Dickens's attraction to this family unit: 'The
actual sister-sister relationship always seems to have charmed him
(if Catherine Hogarth had been sisterless would that have diminished
her attractiveness in his eyes, one wonders?)'[23] The much-contested
erotic nuances of Dickens's relationships with Mary and Georgina
Hogarth are less important here than the personal appreciation of
inter-marital attachments that Dickens acquired through his wider
relations with his wife's family. Dickens's own experience of marriage
into a family of choice provided him with a personal understanding of
the importance of other family members in the selection of a marital
partner. He would also have been aware of these wider structures of
affinity from his parents' marriage; Dickens's mother was sister to his
father's best friend and colleague. As John Forster put it in the first
biography of Dickens, 'his father, John Dickens, a clerk in the Navy-pay
office [. . .] had made acquaintance with the lady, Elizabeth Barrow,
who became afterwards his wife, through her elder brother, Thomas
Barrow, also engaged on the establishment at Somerset House.'[24]

While Dickens's first-hand experience of the emotional bonds between in-laws is ever present in his fiction, the complex bonds between
Hallam and the Tennyson family inspired the century's single most
extended literary exploration of such interrelationships: Alfred
Tennyson's long elegy for Hallam, *In Memoriam, A. H. H.* This work
provides particular insight into the complex motivations that made
brother-in-law-hood so desirable for Dickens's contemporaries. Without wanting to read this rich and polyvalent work as only, or even
centrally, a statement of desire, it is important to recognize the significance of the brother-in-law bond in the queer cultural legacy of this text.
As Matthew Sweet has demonstrated, the homoerotic dynamic of this
elegy was emphasized in many later nineteenth-century writings on

---

[22] For an account of these allegations, see Kaplan, pp. 389–94.
[23] Michael Slater, *Dickens and Women*, p. 367.
[24] Forster, I, p. 1.

homosexuality.[25] While it is impossible to ascertain how far Dickens interpreted *In Memoriam* as homoerotic confession, his attentive re-reading of the poem certainly provided him with an explicit confirmation of the advantages of intermarriage for men in love with another male.[26] In the epilogue to his actual brother-in-law, Edward Lushington, Tennyson expresses his absolute delight at the prospect of forming such a bond with Hallam:

> Nor have I felt so much of bliss
> Since first he told me that he loved
> A daughter of our house
>   (Epilogue, lines 6–8).[27]

Poem eighty-four of *In Memoriam* offers a fantasy vision of the benefits of this relationship, had Hallam lived to marry Emily. Tennyson envisages a permanent domestic attachment and the continued intellectual stimulus of a life that would be officially 'link'd with thine in love and fate' (line 38, p. 50):

> I see myself an honor'd guest,
>   Thy partner in the flowery walk
>   Of letters, genial table-talk,
> Or deep dispute, and graceful jest
>   (lines 21–4, p. 50).

Tennyson pictures many such emotional benefits, including the privilege of becoming uncle to Hallam's sons, traditionally a particularly significant and intimate alliance. In an explicit acknowledgement of the physicality enabled by the creation of family ties Tennyson describes Hallam as 'A central warmth diffusing bliss/ In glance and smile, and

---

[25] The hero of an 1878 erotic novel *The Monomaniac of Love*, for example, 'keeps his hair in "the style" displayed in the photographs of Mr Tennyson', and is described as being 'a regular Mary-Ann' for his preference for Tennysonian coiffure (quoted in Sweet, *Inventing*, p. 201).

[26] 'Tennyson's 1842 *Poems* became "very favourite reading with him"; in 1844 Dickens was still reading them again and again, and exclaiming "What a great creature he is" [and later] "Lord what a blessed thing it is to find a man who can write"' (Collins, 'Dickens's Reading', p. 140). Robin Gilmour reinforces this, noting that Tennyson 'was the one poet after Shakespeare [...that Dickens] read and re-read most carefully in adult life' ('Dickens, Tennyson and the Past', *Dickensian* 75 (1979), 131–42, p. 131).

[27] Alfred Tennyson, *In Memoriam A. H. H.* (New York: Norton, 1973), p. 86.

clasp and kiss,/ On all the branches of thy blood' (lines 6–8, p. 49). Such familial embraces can now include Tennyson, as he insists that through intermarriage their blood lines are commingled: 'Thy blood, my friend, and partly mine' (line 9, p. 49). This imaginative vision was supported by contemporary legislation that, in treating bonds of affinity and consanguinity as identical, rendered brothers-in-law of one blood.[28]

Dickens's fictions resonate with, and variously anticipate and build upon, these wider literary treatments of elective families. He even, through his practice of recognizing his literary admirations in his sons' names, accommodates such material within his own family in the childish figures of Alfred Tennyson Dickens and Edward Bulwer Lytton Dickens. Dickens was, though, to go beyond his literary heroes in his career-long commitment to exploring and queering in-law bonds.

'YOU HAVEN'T GOT A SISTER HAVE YOU?': IN-LAWING DESIRE IN DICKENS'S FICTION

Dickens's novels insistently explore what was a familiar marital pattern in this period, unpacking the diverse motivations behind such unions. Early in *The Pickwick Papers*, trainee surgeon Ben Allen becomes infatuated with the idea of becoming a brother (in-law) to his boyhood friend and now fellow medical apprentice, Bob Sawyer. These 'very particular friends' strive to inject permanence into their professional and personal relationship through intermarriage (p. 391). Dickens's first in-law plot unfolds as one of the many, characteristically abortive, marital plots of the episodic *Pickwick*. Ben and Bob's romance, which has blossomed around the enabling figure of Ben's sister, Arabella, also has clear connections to Bulwer Lytton's earlier rendering of a plot of intermarriage and male emigration.

Ben Allen strenuously urges his sister to comply with his desires by marrying the man of his choice. Ben's expectations, though resisted as excessive by the text, are consonant with the strand of nineteenth-century sororal ideology, under which sisterly wishes were subordinated in order for a sister to fully enter into her brother's desires. Such

---

[28] For a detailed exploration of the many overlaps in legal treatment of marital and blood relations see chapters 1 and 2 of Sybil Wolfram, *Inlaws and Outlaws: Kinship and Marriage in England* (London and Sydney: Croom Helm, 1987), especially pp. 16–20.

thinking is clearly behind Ben Allen's comically overstated belief that his sister's destiny, and the destination of her dowry, is entirely determined by his own economically and erotically conflated desires. In what looks very much like a classic case of gift-giving, Ben highlights for Bob the men's shared financial interest in the match: 'You must make yourself, with as little delay as possible, master of Arabella's one thousand pounds... She has it when she comes of age, or marries. She wants a year of coming of age, and if you plucked up a spirit she needn't want a month of being married' (p. 633). Claude Levi-Strauss famously documents such kinship transactions when he specifically thinks of the positions occupied by sisters (as well as daughters) in exogamy:

> The total relation of exchange which constitutes marriage is not established between a man and a woman, where each owes and receives something, but between two groups of men, and the woman figures only as one of the objects of the exchange.[29]

Gayle Rubin has provided a feminist account of such transactions, memorably describing them as 'traffic in women': 'If it is women who are being transacted, then it is the men who give and take them who are linked, the woman being a conduit of the relationship rather than a partner to it.'[30]

As Rubin's account implies, emotional as well as economic investments may participate in such transactions.[31] Here, and throughout his oeuvre, Dickens plays with the complex, potentially homoerotic,

---

[29] Claude Levi-Strauss, *The Elementary Structures of Kinship*, trans. James Hare Bell, John von Sturmer and Rodney Needham (Boston: Beacon, 1969), p. 115.

[30] Gayle Rubin, 'Notes on the 'Political Economy' of Sex', in *Toward an Anthropology of Women*, ed. Rayna Reiter (New York: Monthly Review Press, 1975), pp. 157–210, p. 174. Similar efforts of brother and suitor to gain a dowry appear in the *The Old Curiosity Shop*, where Fred Trent designs to access his sister's inheritance by 'persuad[ing], or if the word sounds more feasible, forc[ing] Nell to a secret marriage' with his best friend Dick Swiveller (p. 64), and in *Great Expectations* in Arthur Havisham's and Compeyson's conspiracy to defraud Arthur's half-sister, Miss Havisham. In both cases mysterious other motives are alluded to but not specified, and the plans are unfulfilled. Dickens's most thorough denouncement of such an employment of sisters as objects of exchange is presented through the sensitive depiction of Miss Havisham's trauma at the total disregard of her emotions in this male collusion for profit. Although figured as such by male schemers, the women involved never actually become 'a conduit of the[ir] relationship.'

[31] Marcus's more recent reading of Levi-Strauss finds the traces in his account of a homosexual impetus behind brother-in-law formation. Although Levi-Strauss associates homosexuality with immaturity, implying that it will be displaced by marriage, he acknowledges that in some groups the potential 'brother-in-law is the one with whom,

motivations of forging in-law ties, devaluing the sufficiency of the monetary motive as a complete explanation. In their social history of the Victorian period, Leonore Davidoff and Catherine Hall temper their focus on economic aspects of intermarriage by acknowledging the importance of prior intimacy with the other family members of a future spouse:

Intermarriage also sealed relationships of friendship. Rebecca Solly, a Unitarian from Essex, deeply desired that her best friend would become her 'sister', which she eventually did by marrying one of Rebecca's elder brothers. Men too, prized friendship which they confirmed by marriage. George Gardner married the sister of his childhood playmate and adult friend, James Soanes, despite her malformed spine (p. 221).

While not all experiences of in-lawing were as unproblematic as Davidoff and Hall's brief example suggests, marrying into an intimate friend's family often provided a desirable means of maintaining control over this central relationship and protecting its continuity.[32] Such motives certainly informed Ellen Nussey's instigation of her brother's proposal to her particular friend Charlotte Brontë. Although Brontë rejected Henry Nussey's suit on the grounds of incompatibility of temperament, her letter to Ellen demonstrates her reluctance to relinquish the benefits of in-lawing: 'Now my dear Ellen there were in this proposal some things that might have proved a strong temptation – I thought if I were to marry so, Ellen could live with me and how happy I should be.'[33] As the humorous mode of *Pickwick* makes clear, Ben and Bob's anticipation of their future happiness through the inter-marital recognition of the life-long friendship, combined with a certain financial greed and professional nepotism, are the *only* motivating factors in Bob's courtship of Ben's sister:

as an adolescent, one indulges in homosexual activities' (quoted by Marcus, *Between Women*, p. 196).

[32] Emily Dickinson, for example, experienced extreme difficulty in reconciling her desire to formalize her relationship to Sue Gilbert by becoming sisters (in-law), with her trauma at the inevitable sharing of this intimate friend that marriage would demand. For further exploration see Lillian Faderman, 'Emily Dickinson's Letters to Sue Gilbert,' *Massachusetts Review* 18.2 (1977), 197–225; and John Cody *After Great Pain: The Inner Life of Emily Dickinson* (Massachusetts: Belknap Press, 1971).

[33] *The Letters of Charlotte Brontë*, ed. Margaret Smith, 3 vols. (Oxford: Clarendon Press, 1995–2004), I, p. 187. For further details of this proposal and Ellen Nussey's encouragement of it, see Rebecca Fraser *Charlotte Brontë* (London: Methuen, 1988), p. 119.

'I designed 'em for each other; they were made for each other, sent into the world for each other, born for each other . . . There's a special destiny in the matter, my dear Sir; there's only five years' difference between 'em, and both their birthdays are in August' . . . Mr. Ben Allen, after a tear or two, went on to say, that, notwithstanding all his esteem and respect and veneration for his friend, Arabella had unaccountably and undutifully evinced the most determined antipathy to his person (p. 511).

Arabella has long expressed her aversion to her brother's intended. Nonetheless, the two men's shared memories of her earlier disdain for Bob's boyish advances demonstrate the extent to which the peripheral presence of a sister enables increased male intimacy:

'You have loved her from a child, my friend – you loved her when we were boys at school together, and even then she was wayward, and slighted your young feelings. Do you recollect, with all the eagerness of a child's love, one day pressing upon her acceptance two small carraway-seed biscuits and one sweet apple, neatly folded into a circular parcel with the leaf of a copy book?'
'I do,' replied Bob Sawyer.
'She slighted that, I think?' said Ben Allen.
'She did,' rejoined Bob. 'She said I had kept the parcel so long in the pockets of my corduroys, that the apple was unpleasantly warm.'
'I remember,' said Mr. Allen, gloomily. 'Upon which we ate it ourselves, in alternate bites' (p. 634).

Bob Sawyer's abortive wooing of Arabella Allen permits his actual courtship of her brother, as Arabella's rejection of the offering enables a male sharing of what have been explicitly identified as love gifts.

In the context of both the strictly gendered Victorian economy of consumption – in which women were warned against displays of appetite, especially for fattening sweet stuffs and symbolically sinful fruit snacks – and the novel's own firm designation of apples as boyish fare, suspicion is cast on Bob's intended recipient.[34] Bob selects gifts which are less suitable for the courting of Arabella than for the wooing

[34] On the Victorian gendering of alimentary appetites see Gail Turley Houston, *Consuming Fictions: Gender, Class and Hunger in Dickens's Novels* (Carbondale and Edwardsville: Southern Illinois University Press, 1994) and Helena Michie, *Flesh Made Word: Female Figures and Women's Bodies* (Oxford and New York: Oxford University Press, 1987) For *Pickwick's* reinforcement of the strict gendering of food consumption see, for example, the case related at Bob Sawyer's bachelor party of

of her more corpulent brother, whose 'stout, thick-set' body is a marker of his apparently insatiable appetite (p. 392). Arabella's inevitable rejection of these edible presents results in a male sharing of food, a reliable index of emotional bonding in Dickens's fiction. While Ben and Bob go on to enjoy a long career of shared oral indulgence in a novel which persistently conflates sexual and alimentary appetites,[35] their pleasure in mutually recounting this scene is especially suggestive. The erotic connotations of mutual eating are intensified in their reminiscence of eating the rejected love gifts together in 'alternate bites', with the corresponding close mouths and shared saliva that would necessarily result from such a method of consumption. Arabella is repulsed by the proffered goods as a bodily extension of Bob; in his trouser pockets they have spent too long in close proximity to his body (more specifically to his genitals), until the 'apple was unpleasantly warm.' Importantly, Ben has none of these scruples, readily eating the literal fruit of Bob's loins. The symbolism of male genitalia is strengthened by the specific details of foodstuffs offered. While the intimately warmed apple represents phallic forbidden fruit, the 'two small carraway-seed biscuits' substitute for the testicular seed-producers of Bob's body. Lest this seem an overly juicy interpretation, the pattern by which an intermediary sister facilitates the oral pleasures of her brother and his male favorite is reinforced through its reiteration in the famous brother-sister-suitor triangle of Tom Pinch/ Ruth Pinch/ John Westlock in Dickens's *Martin Chuzzlewit*, to which I will return.

Dickens's delineation, then, of Arabella's longstanding antipathy to her brother's election of her future husband, allows for an expression of the erotic (as well as commercial and pecuniary) male investments in a relationship enabled through the socially acceptable framework of courtship with a view to intermarriage. At the same time, however, Dickens exposes and critiques the gender inequities of the ideology of

---

a boy who, only two minutes after his leg had been removed from its socket, ate 'five apples and a gingerbread cake' (p. 422).

[35] Indeed, a key part of the evidence for Pickwick's amorous intentions towards Mrs Bardell as presented by Sergeant Buzfuz is a letter in which Pickwick requests 'Chops and Tomata sauce' (p. 454), and the rounded figure of Mr Wardle's servant, the Fat Boy, provides a constant embodiment of the varieties of insatiability. James Kincaid observes that 'the most pointed of the novel's erotic impulses' circulate around this corpulent character ('Fattening Up on Pickwick,' *Novel* 25 (1992), 235–44, p. 243).

sororal subordination that structures Ben's familial bullying: 'She *shall* have you or I'll know the reason why – I'll exert my authority' (p. 634). Arabella's just objections to her brother's uncharacteristically forceful behaviour on this issue – 'so unkind, so unreasonable' (p. 526), 'so violent, so prejudiced . . . so, so anxious in behalf of his friend, Mr. Sawyer' (p. 629) – are upheld by the novel's rotund moral centre, Mr Pickwick, who prefers to advance the cause of the lady's own preferred suitor, his young protégé, Mr Winkle. As documented in the novel's wrap-up, Arabella and Mr Winkle are ultimately married, while Ben and Bob emigrate to Bengal: 'both gentleman having received surgical appointments from the East India Company' (p. 753).

Denied the permanence, social sanction and recognition that brother-in-law status would grant their relationship within British domesticity, Ben and Bob seek an alternative setting within which their attachment can be experienced without mediation. Like Job and Jingle, another alliterative couple, whose relationship is considered to exceed the parameters of domestic respectability, Ben and Bob's plot ends with emigration.[36] Their relocation points to the limits of the comfortable accommodation of homoeros within Victorian society. While imaginative and actual room existed in Victorian families for same-sex relationships structured along very specific lines, for a wide variety of practical and personal reasons such spaces often proved insufficient in Dickens's fiction and beyond.

The Pickwickian triangle of Bob Sawyer, Ben, and Arabella Allen presents a good early example of Dickens's attention to the homoerotic possibilities of in-lawing, to which he was to return throughout his career. In his first novel Dickens draws upon and critiques the wider social expectation that a sister match her desires to those of her brother, even and especially in the election of a husband. *Pickwick* only lightly touches upon a related aspect of contemporary domestic ideology, which held that the opposite sex sibling bond was 'one in which gender difference [was . . .] rendered secondary to the tie of blood likeness, familiarity and friendship'.[37] Dickens uses the (unmet) cultural expectation of sibling

---

[36] See Chapter 2 for a discussion of the various responses that the novel offers to the relationship between Job and Jingle. Chapter 4 returns to the significance of emigration as destiny for these figures and explores the broader erotic significance of overseas relocation.

[37] Joseph Boone and Deborah Nord, 'Brother and Sister: The Seductions of Siblinghood in Dickens, Eliot and Brontë', *Western Humanities Review* 46.2 (1992), 164–88, p. 165.

parity to humorous effect in *Pickwick*, as Ben Allen comically proffers his body to Arabella's preferred suitor as a reminder of her desired form:

'Perhaps my features may recall her countenance to your recollection?' Mr. Winkle required nothing to recall the charming Arabella to his mind; and it was rather fortunate that he did not, for the features of her brother Benjamin would unquestionably have proved but an indifferent refresher to his memory (p. 511).

Here the narrator invokes, without imaginatively capitalizing on, the gender-bending possibilities of a widespread belief in sibling body-doubles.

Previous critical attention has attached to only one of Dickens's many ruminations on the suggestive (homo)erotic triangle of suitor, brother and sister – that of Steerforth, David, and David's quasi sister Emily in *David Copperfield*. In this novel Steerforth's seduction of Emily is foreshadowed in a memorable bedroom scene while the boys are at school together. Steerforth fantasizes an imaginary sister of David, 'a pupil younger than himself who had taken his fancy' (p. 279):

'You haven't got a sister, have you?' said Steerforth yawning.
'No,' I answered.
'That's a pity,' said Steerforth. 'If you had one, I should think she would have been a pretty, timid, little, bright eyed sort of girl. I should have liked to know her' (p. 90).

Here, the actual existence of a sister is not necessary for homoerotic articulation. As Oliver S. Buckton has convincingly argued, this scene 'suggests that the expression of desire is actually for David himself, no less timid and bright eyed than his imaginary sister, whom Steerforth, using a word inevitably carrying biblical connotations, would like to "know"'.[38] David's reciprocal desire for Steerforth is here expressed through his identification with the schoolmaster's daughter's permissible love, which allows David to catalogue those aspects of Steerforth that appeal to him most:

---

[38] Oliver S. Buckton, '"The Reader Whom I Love": Homoerotic Secrets in *David Copperfield*', *ELH* 64.1 (1997), 189–222, p. 202. For briefer analysis of this transfer see E. Pearlman's use of the implicit body doubling of David and Emily to answer the question 'What exactly does Steerforth find attractive in Em'ly? Steerforth is more interested in David than he admits, and of all the daisies in the field he chooses a girl most like David – his "sister".' 'David Copperfield Dreams of Drowning', *American Imago* 28.4 (1971), 391–403, p. 402.

I heard that Miss Creakle was regarded by the school in general as being in love with Steerforth; and I am sure as I sat in the dark, thinking of his nice voice, his fine face, and his easy manner, and his curling hair, I thought it very likely (p. 89).

David's observation of the pair walking together focuses on details of Steerforth's appearance and reiterates his sense of a parity of 'romantic feelings' (p. 291) for the older boy that he shares with Miss Creakle: 'When Steerforth, in white trousers, carried her parasol for her, I felt proud to know him; and believed that she could not choose but adore him with all her heart' (p. 93).[39] Steerforth's rhetorical use of David's non-existent sister enables a similar acknowledgement of his appreciation of his friend's body. Dickens's careful sequencing of this conversation places Steerforth's avowal of his desire 'to know' the body double of David *after* his discovery of David's sororal lack. In her absence, Dickens reveals the extent to which the sister is employed as a device through which inter-male desire may be voiced. Under these strategically sequenced conditions Steerforth offers a brief vision of a male physical union that, in this enabling imaginative realm, is not finally displaced by the intervention of a sanctioning female.

Such a union is here restricted to the bounds of male fantasy. As Buckton observes, it receives only a symbolic enactment in the seduction of Little Emily, whom Steerforth selects 'as his desired object precisely because she, as David's figurative sister, *resembles* the primary object of desire that is prohibited as an erotic choice' (p. 209). The efficacy of substituting Emily for David is demonstrated when David, through his quasi-familial relationship to the Peggottys, is asked to read out Emily's letter of departure. In this performance David ventriloquizes seduction by Steerforth, narrating the shame and hope of this outlawed liaison through a first person voice that suggests Steerforth's magnetic attraction for both Emily and David (p. 419).

The particular erotic re-direction that takes place in Steerforth's fantasy of David's sister is a queer manoeuvre that fascinated Dickens throughout his career. Whilst this chapter explores the in-lawing interconnections of Dickens's earlier work, Dickens's attention to the queer possibilities of suitor/sibling triads persists to the end: such configurations are developed

[39] Throughout the novel David makes numerous hyperbolic expressions of his appreciation of Steerforth's 'handsome face and figure' and 'so graceful, so natural, so agreeable' manner (pp. 105, 291), emphasizing the 'power of attraction' or 'kind of enchantment' of the friend he describes as 'so irresistible' and 'engaging' (pp. 105, 279, 121).

in the Gradgrinds' connections with Harthouse in *Hard Times* (1854); the parallel romance of Charley Hexam and Bradley Headstone, in which they seek to enmesh Charley's sister, Lizzie, in *Our Mutual Friend*; and perhaps most explicitly in the telepathically shared mutual attachments of the 'identical' Landless twins in *The Mystery of Edwin Drood*. In this final novel's bald statements of the parity of Neville and Helena Landless's romantic feeling for the highly appealing Rosa Bud, Dickens's exploration of the homoerotic possibilities of opposite-sex sibling love plots reaches its culmination. Dickens's regular readers, particularly attuned (as explored in the previous chapter) through the prolonged, often explicitly intertextual experience of serial reading to continuities across his work, were well placed to recognize the recurrence of this plot. As Peter Brooks has argued, repetition has major narrative significance, allowing 'us to see how the text and reader put energy into forms where it can be mastered, both by the logics set in motion by plot, and by interpretative effort'.[40] Through cross-textual transcoding Dickens draws attention to in-lawing, allowing the more and less detailed depictions of such triangular relationships to resonate with other instances. Across his career Dickens amasses a particularly detailed account of the complexity of in-lawing desires.

'SISTER! [. . .] IS SHE VERY LIKE YOU?': FAMILIES OF CHOICE IN *NICHOLAS NICKLEBY*

The heady combination of Steerforth as suggestive schoolboy and seducing sailor has rendered *David Copperfield* an acceptable site for queer interpretation. More controversial, however, is the recognition of the parallels between Steerforth's homoerotic bedroom rhetoric and a much more fully fleshed example of such plotting in the earlier *Nicholas Nickleby*. Smike's imaginative use of the information that his beloved friend Nicholas has a sister operates as a direct precursor to Steerforth's more sophisticated homoerotic oratory:

'Sister! . . . Is she very like you?' inquired Smike.
'Why so they say,' replied Nicholas, laughing, 'only a great deal handsomer.'

[40] Brooks, *Reading*, p. 123.

'She must be very beautiful,' said Smike, after thinking a little while with his
hands folded together, and his eyes upon his friend.
'Anyone who didn't know you as well as I do, my dear fellow, would say you
were an accomplished courtier,' said Nicholas.
'I don't even know what that is,' replied Smike, shaking his head. 'Shall I ever
see your sister?' (p. 359)

The imaginative critical investment in Smike as a reform- provoking
icon of child abuse tends to obscure the novel's later emphasis on his
effortful adult expressions of sexual agency.

Traditionally, critics have tended to interpret Smike as 'worship[ing
. . .] his deliverer' and exhibiting a 'dog-like devotion' to Nicholas.[41] The
canine comparison, which frequently recurs in critical descriptions of
Smike, obscures the actual complexity of his multi-faceted and very
human response to Nicholas. Combined with his gratitude, loyalty, and
deep affection is a specifically physical admiration of Nicholas's body.
Smike is repeatedly depicted silently gazing upon Nicholas (pp. 147, 251),
and even watching his friend sleep (p. 162). Physical admiration is half
expressed in Smike's admission of his almost magnetic attraction to
Nicholas: 'I tried to go away today, but the thought of your kind face
drew me back' (p. 251); 'I only want to be near you' (p. 162). Smike's
valiant and repeated efforts to speak his love for Nicholas reach their
culmination when the possibility of a physically similar sister is presented.
Without meeting Nicholas's sister, Smike can be certain that 'she must be
very beautiful', an assumption based entirely on the pattern of his friend's
body which he has so closely observed. Similarly, Steerforth's conviction
that David's sister would be 'a pretty, timid, little, bright eyed sort of girl,'
is based on the same fantasy of finding all the physical delights of the male
friend repeated in a body which can be permissibly desired. In his depictions of Smike's and Steerforth's anticipated desire, Dickens reflects the
languages of compulsion and immediacy characteristic of contemporary
real-life accounts, such as those of Hallam and Collinson, in which love for

[41] A. J. Coppock, 'Smike', *Dickensian* 35 (1939), 162–3, p. 163; Nicholas Bentley,
Michael Slater, Nina Burgis, (eds.), 'Smike', in *The Dickens Index* (Oxford: Oxford
University Press, 1988), p. 240. Roy Ball, one of the few to argue for a greater complexity
to Smike's character as 'an early and at least partially successful attempt by Dickens to
produce a personality developing through self-realization', suggests that Smike's 'dog-
like affection for Nicholas and his family matures into a real friendship for Nicholas and
a love for Kate' ('The Development of Smike', *Dickensian* 62 (1966), 125–8, p. 126).

a friend's sister is so sudden as to seem pre-determined. At the moment that he meets the 'pretty sister,' about whom he has 'so often asked' (p. 423), Smike is predictably smitten, to an extent that he cannot bear to witness Kate's courtship by her future husband.

Smike's anticipation of Kate's beauty is entirely appropriate given the novel's considerable investment in a wider cultural expectation of sibling parity, as well as its interest in the broader social and economic motivations for intermarriage. Alongside the inclusion of two sets of identical same-sex twins – the Kenwigs girls and the Cheeryble brothers, who have barely 'a perceptible difference between them' (p. 432) – the narrative devotes considerable energy to outlining the parallel attractions of both Nicholas and Kate Nickleby:

> As the brother and sister stood side by side with a gallant bearing which became them well, a close likeness between them was apparent, which many, had they only seen them apart, might have failed to remark. The air, carriage, and very look and expression of the brother were all reflected in the sister, but softened and refined to the nicest limit of feminine attraction (p. 672).

Dickens's narrator observes this doubling of physique and manner throughout. Ralph Nickleby, relying on the expected feminine pliancy of the sister, is surprised by the similarity in temperament between opposite sex siblings: ' "There is some of that boy's blood in you, I see," said Ralph, speaking in his harshest tones, as something of the flashing eye reminded him of Nicholas at their last meeting' (p. 355). Added to the same blood is a shared history of 'all the happy days . . . all the comfort and happiness of home' (p. 249), which makes the pair virtually indistinguishable within the domestic setting. Indeed Mrs Nickleby considers her children to be so interchangeable that she can request that one of her offspring substitute for both in order to please visitors: 'Kate, my dear, you must be both Nicholas and yourself' (p. 605).

Such parity creates a suggestive confusion of emotion in Nicholas's future wife, Madeline Bray, who first desires (to become) a Nickleby when she is tenderly nursed by Kate. In a remarkably explicit rendering of the familial expandability of female desire, Dickens has Madeline shift her 'warmer feeling' from sister to brother:

> What wonder . . . if with the image of Nicholas so constantly recurring in the features of his sister that she could scarcely separate the two, she had sometimes found it equally difficult to assign to each the feelings they had first inspired,

and had imperceptibly mingled with her gratitude to Nicholas some of that warmer feeling which she had assigned to Kate (pp. 680–1).

Madeline struggles both to distinguish the sibling bodies and to separate her inter-mingled emotional responses to each.[42]

Interwoven with this suggestive attention to sibling resemblance as romantic motive is a related concern with the wider familial and economic attractions of intermarriage. We learn, for example, that the benevolent Cheeryble brothers have planned a double wedding of a type Davidoff identifies as common, where 'two brothers from one family would marry two sisters from another.'[43] Dickens demonstrates that the interconnections forged here are the primary aim; when one of the sisters inconveniently dies the whole strategy is abandoned and the second sister marries another man of her choice, while the brothers choose permanent cohabiting bachelordom (p. 565). Nicholas himself fantasizes openly about socially advancing intermarriage as the culmination of a successful career path:

'Suppose some young nobleman who is being educated at the Hall, were to take a fancy to me, and get his father to appoint me his travelling tutor when he left, and when he got back from the continent, procured me some handsome appointment... And who knows, but when he came to see me when I was settled (as he would of course), he might fall in love with Kate, who would be keeping my house – and – marry her, eh!' (p. 41)

In a cruelly ironic reworking of this rosy vision, the young man of the Hall who 'take[s] a fancy' to Nicholas, and who subsequently recognizes this commitment by falling in love with Kate, is of course the abused and destitute Smike. The conversation, in which the absent body of the sister is so transparently the means that communicates Smike's previously muted physical admiration of Nicholas, takes place after the friends have fled together from the abuses of Wackford Squeers's establishment for those boys whose natal parents choose not to accommodate them.

The readily expandable Nickleby family holds out the promise of an emotionally centered, alternative domesticity. As a counter to what

---

[42] This situation bears out Marcus's findings that in literature and life-writing of the period intense, often eroticized, relations between women could catalyse marital unions, after which they could be sustained and even strengthened (*Between Women*, see especially ch. 2).

[43] Davidoff, *Worlds Between*, p. 214.

Families of Choice   131

Mr Squeers perversely calls his 'parental and affectionate treatment'
('Mrs. Squeers and myself are a mother and father to every one of
them' p. 67), Nicholas movingly offers Smike a home: 'When I talk
of homes . . . I talk of mine – which is yours of course . . . When I speak of
home, I speak of the place where – in default of a better – those I love are
gathered together' (p. 423).[44] While this family can accommodate
socially marginal figures such as the hard-up single landlady Miss La
Creevy and the eccentric and impoverished Newman Noggs, the place it
affords Smike is less secure. Michie has justly expressed frustrations with
a plot, which having held out the promise of an elastic ideal of domestic
kinship, suddenly tightens to exclude its most vulnerable new member.
Michie rightly rejects an entirely affirmative reading of this novel's
'capacious sense of family' by dwelling on the questions 'Why can't
Smike marry Kate?' and 'Why must Smike die?':

> Smike's presence is a consistent reminder of the porousness of family. While
> this porousness is a virtue for most of the novel, it cannot and must not survive
> the marriage plot, where all relations, including Nicholas's to the Cheeryble
> brothers must be rerouted through the law and through marriage.[45]

Though in-lawing can provide a way of linking marital and homoerotic
plotting, exposing the queer spaces within the institution of marriage that
only masquerades as sealed and straight, Dickens never acknowledges
Smike as an acceptable suitor for Nicholas's 'pretty sister'. In consequence,
Smike cannot realize his fantasy of legally enshrined brotherhood with
Nicholas, and so dies of a broken heart. Though Dickens allows Smike a
brief, exclusively male Arcadia, being nursed and cared for by Nicholas in
an idyllic and remote rural setting, there is no recovery from his desire,
which here proves to be terminal.

Similarly tragic is the fate of Steerforth, who meets a retributive death
after his exploitative seduction of David's stand-in, Little Emily. These
conclusions seem to cohere with a long literary tradition of queer
tragedy, in which a heterosexist society leads to the eventual annihila-
tion of gay desires and selves. Dickens's multiple re-drawings of the
brother/sister/suitor triangle, however, allow him to imagine a variety of

---

[44] My Postscript includes a reading of the affirmative reading of families of choice
presented by Doug McGrath's 2002 film *Nicholas Nickleby*.
[45] Michie, 'From Blood to Law', pp. 135, 139.

denouements, including more affirmative conclusions in which the family of choice remains triumphant. In *Martin Chuzzlewit*, for instance, a novel which appeared between *Nickleby* and *Copperfield*, John Westlock is united to live happily ever after with his life-long intimate friend Tom Pinch, through marriage to Tom's similar sister, Ruth Pinch.

BLISS AND BEEFSTEAK IN THE TRIANGULAR PARLOUR: *MARTIN CHUZZLEWIT* AND THE REJECTION OF QUEER TRAGEDY

The formation of *Chuzzlewit's* happy triangle characteristically takes place as part of Dickens's wider scrutiny of domestic configuration. In what is perhaps the novel's most radical domestic experiment, the eponymous hero and his loyal manservant, Mark Tapley, try their hands at business- and home-building in fetid Mississippi swampland. As I will argue more thoroughly in Chapter 5, the alternative domesticity of this American 'Eden' provides the setting for the consolidation of physical and highly tender male bonds through mutual nursing, and offers a variation on the kind of to-death fidelity apparent in the relationship enjoyed by Pickwick and Sam. On home ground, another of the novel's hopeful young men, John Westlock, stars in an alternative plot of queer domesticity. John pays his first addresses to Ruth in the Pinches' aptly configured home, with 'the triangular parlour and the two small bed-rooms' (p. 564), one of Dickens's many unusual domestic architectures that reflect the arrangement of relationships within. John is yet another suitor who follows the compulsive pattern played out in so many fictional and biographical accounts of the period. It only takes 'a glimpse' of his closest friend's sister for John to wish to be immediately in Tom's place, being kissed by her (p. 553). Following the cumulative logic of Dickens's fiction, this sororal consummation is the inevitable longing of such a close male friend. Tom and John, like *Pickwick's* Ben and Bob, are friends of long duration, and are repeatedly reunited through feast scenes of much anticipated shared oral indulgence. John's introductory meeting with Tom's sister is structured around a demonstration of her culinary abilities in the preparation of a beefsteak pudding. Ruth, as pudding impresario, finally satisfies their shared appetites, proving herself to be a domestic goddess equally able to cater to the needs of both men.

Prior to this meeting – in parallel with both Smike's and Steerforth's anticipations of sisterly bodily beauty – John's romantic imagination has been inspired by the mere concept of his friend's sister. The pictorial graffiti of 'Tom's Corner' of the room the two young men have shared at Pecksniff's suggests John's earlier fantasy of a sister figure as a particularly suitable relative to mediate their otherwise too intense relationship:

Every pupil had added something, even unto fancy portraits of his [Tom's] father with one eye, and of his mother with a disproportionate nose, and especially of his sister: who always being presented as extremely beautiful, made full amends to Tom for any other joke (p. 474).

On meeting Ruth Pinch, John ruminates on the physical superiority of the real over the fantasized sister, describing the portraits as 'gross-libels, and not half pretty enough: though . . . the artists always made those sketches beautiful, and he had drawn at least a score of them with his own hands' (p. 573). This subtle admission reveals John's emotional investment in the bare concept of 'Tom's sister', the relational designation that is applied to Ruth more often than her own name. Ruth's body fulfils the longings of this principal fantasist, providing him with a female incarnation of his beloved friend. Although the similarity between Tom and Ruth is not expressed through an exact physical transposition, Ruth echoes the kind, cheerful, and gentle manner which most characterizes her brother, delivering herself with 'Tom's own simplicity and Tom's own smile' (p. 140): 'There was something of her brother, much of him indeed, in a certain gentleness of manner, and in her look of timid trustfulness' (p. 138). Given her similarity to Tom and her inseparableness from him, Ruth both embodies the most admired attributes of her brother and guarantees the permanence of a male in-law connection forged through her marriage.

Ruth, who is able to cater to the immodest alimentary requirements of these two men is figured, through a sequence of significant feasting scenes, as simultaneously facilitator and substitute. *Chuzzlewit*, like *Pickwick*, institutes an erotic economy of eating, and John and Tom, echoing Ben and Bob, are united through emotionally charged scenes of mutual gustatory gratification. After enduring a harrowing separation

(Tom likens the coach that bears John away from Pecksniff's to 'some great monster [. . .] more exulting and rampant than usual' in the seizure of such a 'prize', p. 35), they are reunited in a cosy scene of feasting, in which previously only fantasized pleasures of the palate are realized:

'I have ordered everything for dinner, that we used to say we'd have, Tom,' observed John Westlock.

'No!' said Tom Pinch, 'Have you?' (p. 196)

They dine at great expense on an elaborate bill of fare of soup, fish, side dishes, top and bottom, birds, and sweets. Such rich variety of foodstuffs was recommended in sample entertaining menus of the time, such as that provided by Catherine Dickens under the pseudonym of Lady Maria Clutterbuck. In *What Shall We Have for Dinner?* Catherine Dickens proposes similarly digestively-challenging menus to the spread laid on by John Westlock. Clutterbuck's recommended fare for a large dinner party included 'Mushroom Patties, Lobster Cutlet, Lamb's Cutlet with cucumber sauce, Rabbit curry smothered with white sauce, Roast Haunch of Mutton, Boiled Fowl and Tongue, Spinach, New Potatoes, Salad, Duckling, Guinea Fowl, Asparagus.'[46] Importantly, these menus are addressed to wives as an alimental strategy for keeping their husbands at home. In the preface the Clutterbuck persona outlines the damaging impact of poor catering on marital relations, blaming unappetizing dinners for 'making the Club more attractive than the Home, and rendering "business in the city" of more frequent occurrence than it used to be in the earlier days of [. . .] connubial experience'.[47] Lady Clutterbuck prides herself on the success of her administration to her husband's stomach: 'I am consoled in believing that my attention to the requirements of his appetite secured me in the possession of his esteem until the last.'[48] Given Dickens's well documented love of fine dining this comical frame has its basis in an actual concern of his household. Whether composed by Dickens as a conduct book for his wife, or by Catherine as a darkly humorous recognition of

---

[46] Lady Maria Clutterbuck (alias Catherine Dickens), *What Shall We Have for Dinner?* (London: Bradbury and Evans, 1852), p. 42.

[47] Clutterbuck, p. vi. Slater believes that this preface was authored by Dickens on his wife's behalf (*Dickens and Women*, p. 132). For a detailed discussion of the Clutterbuck project and Dickens's own appetites see Susan M. Rossi-Wilcox, *Dinner for Dickens: The Culinary History of Mrs Charles Dickens's Menu Books* (Totnes: Prospect, 2005).

[48] Clutterbuck, p. v.

her husband's needs, the preface establishes a slippage between the culinary and the connubial.

This contemporary cultural endorsement of the maxim linking male hearts and stomachs gives a romantic dimension to John Westlock's repeated provision of such ideal menus for Tom Pinch's gratification. The realization of the fantasized feast 'at the very first hotel in the town' (p. 193) is followed by another food fuelled reunion at John's lodgings. John's articulations of delight at seeing Tom are interpolated with his persistent encouragement of the appetite of his unexpected guest:

> While he was delivering himself of these words in a state of great commotion, John was constantly running backwards and forwards to and from the closet, bringing out all sorts of things in pots, scooping extraordinary quantities of tea out of the caddy, dropping French rolls into his boots, pouring hot water over the butter (p. 533).

When Tom tucks into these 'irreconcilable and contradictory viands', John contemplates 'his visitor's proceedings, with infinite satisfaction' (p. 534). In John's persistent anxiety about his friend's alimental gratification he conforms closely to the Clutterbuck model of a wife whose appeal is measured by her ability to cater, a scale of worth familiar from the discussion of the marital merits of various 'comfortable providers' in *Pickwick*. Indeed, only after observing Ruth Pinch's competence at simultaneously catering for both himself and Tom does John relinquish his 'attention to the requirements of his [friend's] appetite'.

John first enters the Pinch's aptly proportioned home on the occasion of Ruth's beefsteak pudding experiment. His flattery of Ruth's culinary capacity as 'such an agreeable domestic occupation, so very agreeably and skilfully pursued' (p. 568) coheres with the strategically over-egged joke that he and Tom entertain 'tremendous expectations' of this pudding (p. 570). Though comically over-inflated, John's courtship of Ruth is structured around a constant repetition of pudding puns that focus on the oral satisfaction of the two men.[49] In a mirroring of Bob

---

[49] Chapters 39 and 45 are liberally seasoned with pudding humour, including John's significant slip, where the distracting pudding displaces his actual meaning (p. 571). These jokes culminate in the men's hyperbolic enjoyment of Ruth's successful substitution of flour and eggs for suet, which forces Tom to 'stop [...] in Temple Bar to laugh; and it was no more to Tom, that he was anathematized and knocked about by the surly passengers, than it would have been to a post; for he continued to exclaim with unabated good humour "flour and eggs! a beefsteak pudding made with flour and eggs!" ' (p. 647).

Sawyer's alimental gifts to his best friend's sister, John's first offering to Ruth is the 'merry present of a cookery-book [...] with the beefsteak-pudding leaf turned down, and blotted out' (p. 582). Given the reiter-ated culinary currency of descriptions of the emotional bonds between John and Tom, Ruth's status as successful caterer further marks her intermediary function in the male relationship. The pudding scene seduces through its dramatization of Ruth's ability to play the domestic goddess for both men, allowing John to relinquish his elaborate and unusually gendered housekeeping by joining this family of choice.

Images of the triadic configuration of his relation to the Pinches domi-nate John's proposal to Ruth: 'Tom had not come in. They entered the triangular parlour together, and alone' (p. 764). This persuasive (il)logic of lone togetherness in the absence of Tom is clarified by the newly engaged couples' fervent inclusion of Tom in their future arrangements. Immediately after the proposal 'they began to talk of Tom again' (p. 764):

'Leave Tom! That would be a strange beginning. Leave Tom, dear! If Tom and we be not inseparable, and Tom (God bless him) have not all honour and all love in our home, my little wife, may that home never be!' (p. 765)

Ruth's corresponding eagerness to maintain her sibling relationship, 'I could never leave Tom' (p. 765), has often been read as suggestive of incestuous longing. Robert Lougy, for example, convincingly argues that 'Hablot K. Browne's brilliant final illustration is visual testimony to the novel's refusal to separate brother and sister, as they are bound together in a *ménage à trois* legitimized by Ruth's marriage to John Westlock, itself a screen for deeper motives that we find articulated in Ruth's insistence to her future husband that she will not tolerate separation from her brother.'[50] Lougy's account of the 'deeper' erotics that structure this triangle, however, obscures John's investment in Tom's presence. John's desire to include Tom is expressed with ardency equal to his declaration of love to Ruth; indeed,

[50] Robert Lougy, 'Repressive and Expressive Forms: The Bodies of Comedy and Desire in *Martin Chuzzlewit*,' *Dickens Studies Annual* 21 (1992), 37–61, p. 57. Similarly, Alexander Welsh has argued that 'if anyone, it is really Tom who has discovered the sexual attraction of his sister'. *The City of Dickens* (Oxford: Clarendon, 1971), p. 150. Slater reinforces this perception: '[Dickens's] account of the Pinches settling into their new home reads as though he were writing about a couple of self-conscious newly-weds. It is just as well, one might feel, that Tom's friend, John Westlock, enters when he does to provide another target for Ruth's demure looks' (p. 364).

his proposal is nullified unless Tom is equally involved – without him 'may that home never be'. While incest may be another motive for brother/sister/ suitor patterns, in Dickens's representations of such triangles it is an incomplete explanation which should not be allowed to elide the homo-erotic. An appreciation of the incestuous desire between the Pinches is not, however, incompatible with a reading of desire between John and Tom. These interlocking erotic attachments may explain why this scenario is ultimately successful. Not coincidentally, this triangle is also unusual in that its female member has her own (incestuous) erotic motive, and is at no point figured as exploitable portable property between brother and husband.

The imaginative space of *Martin Chuzzlewit*'s triangular parlour allows a happy realization of contemporary yearnings for the proximity and emotional intimacy of brother-in-law-hood. Still more affirmative is Dickens's continued commitment to articulating the homoerotic possibilities of in-law bonds throughout his career: a queer strategy that had a demonstrable influence upon his contemporaries and succes-sors. Avid first readers of Dickens's works, such as Thomas Hughes and Mary Elizabeth Braddon, adopted the device of sibling substitution in their own representations of same-sex desire. Dickens's account of schoolboy sexuality in *David Copperfield* directly influenced Hughes's employment of a female body double to enable barely mediated same-sex expression of physical admiration in *Tom Brown's Schooldays* (1857). Hughes's biographers point to his debt to *David Copperfield* as a source for the 'new literary genre' of the school story, identifying Dickens's novel as presenting a rare example of a school setting in a form traditionally less concerned with the experiences of childhood.[51] In Hughes's novel – which overlaps closely with *David Copperfield* in its representation of a schoolboy relationship between an older, protective male and his younger more delicate and explicitly effeminate charge, Arthur – the protagonist finds himself compulsively attracted to his younger friend's mother. To bring it into tolerable limits, Tom Brown's

---

[51] E. Hack and W. Armytage, *Thomas Hughes: The Life of the Author of Tom Brown's Schooldays* (London: Ernest Benn, 1952), p. 91. Hughes, who met Dickens in 1844, was an attentive reader of his work, building his characters into his imaginative world as is clear from his fusion of fiction and news in his musing over whether 'Mr Pickwick was *man* enough for what I fancy the staple of the Adirondack Club' (p. 174).

desire must be expressed through two removes: 'He couldn't help wondering if Arthur's sisters were like her.'[52]

Similarly, Dickens's work, especially *Nicholas Nickleby*, contributed to the century's most critically discussed example of brother/sister/suitor triangulation in Braddon's *Lady Audley's Secret*. In Braddon's novel, Robert Audley famously resolves his intense attachment to fellow Etonian and 'most intimate friend' George Talboys, through marriage to George's sister, Clara – who in looks and demeanor he finds 'so like the friend whom he had loved and lost'.[53] While this Victorian instance receives a high level of critical visibility it had a direct precedent in Dickens's work, by which Braddon was hugely influenced. Braddon received advice from her printer in her early career deliberately to imitate the 'human interest' created by Dickens's fiction. She also had a strong personal response to *Nicholas Nickleby*, describing it as 'so bright and vivid' and recounting that after she had read her copy 'there was not a dry page'.[54] By the end of the nineteenth century, the device of sibling mapping had become character-istic of those pioneering British novels that first attempted an overt presentation of homosexuality, including E. M. Forster's *Maurice* (1971) and Evelyn Waugh's *Brideshead Revisited* (1945). Edward Clarke's *Jaspar Tristram* (1899) offers an additional, now less well known, example, with a clear debt to Dickens's now most famous instance of the homo-erotic sibling motif. In the distinctly Copperfieldian atmosphere of his schoolboy bedroom, Clarke's protagonist tells stories into the night to attract the attention of his beloved Els. As soon as Jaspar meets Els's sister he is able to articulate the physical aspect of his fascination with the boy: 'It was always of her brother that she reminded him [. . .] For though not nearly so good-looking, she had yet the same broken eyebrows which in him he had been so fond of and the same laughing eyes; even the few tiny

[52] Thomas Hughes, *Tom Brown's Schooldays* (Oxford: Oxford University Press, 1999), p. 321.

[53] Mary Elizabeth Braddon, *Lady Audley's Secret* (London: Penguin, 1998) pp. 95, 203. The pioneering work of Ann Cvetkovich and Richard Nemesvari has engendered a range of readings which take up and reinforce the thesis that Robert's desire for Clara is a technique through which his attraction to George is avowed. Cvetkovich, *Mixed Feelings: Feminism, Mass Culture and Victorian Sensationalism* (New Brunswick: Rutgers University Press, 1992); Nemesvari, 'Robert Audley's Secret: Male Homosocial Desire in *Lady Audley's Secret*', *Studies in the Novel* 27.4 (1995), 515–28.

[54] Jennifer Carnell, *The Literary Lives of Mary Elizabeth Braddon* (Hastings: The Sensation Press, 2000), pp. 202, 88.

freckles which Els had had and which had exercised upon him *such a curious charm*, were now reproduced in her and with the same effect [... Her] face [...] was so troublingly like that of the boy to whom, a boy, he had been devoted.'[55] Forster's novel – written in 1913–14 but carefully suppressed until the year after his death – similarly uses the physical resemblance of brother and sister to explore the multiplicity of desire. Durham, who has had an explicitly homoerotic (although deliberately not homosexual) relationship with the eponymous Maurice, wishes for marriage and conformity. Unable to cope with a social climate of shame and secrecy, Durham decides that 'he and his friend would arrange something that should include women'.[56] Whilst such a triangulation is anathema to the homosexually committed Maurice, Durham sees a possibility for 'transition' in Maurice's sister, Ada, who has 'Maurice's voice, his nose, [...] the mouth too, and his good spirits and good health'. In Ada, Durham 'saw features that he knew, with a light behind that glorified them. He turned away from the dark hair and eyes to the unshadowed mouth or to the curves of the body, and found in her the exact need of his transition. He had seen more seductive women, but none that promised such peace.'[57] Similarly, Waugh's novel examines a wide range of erotics from the explicitly homosexual to the more suggestive relationships between Charles, his adored friend Sebastian Flyte, and Sebastian's sister, Julia. Charles is specifically attracted by 'the physical likeness between brother and sister', repeatedly explaining to Julia that Sebastian 'was the forerunner' to his interest in her.[58] Dickens fiction, then, occupies an

---

[55] Edward Clarke, *Jaspar Tristram*, (London: Heinemann, 1899), pp. 216–17.
[56] E. M. Forster, *Maurice* (London: Edward Arnold, 1971), p. 111.
[57] Forster, *Maurice*, p. 113–14.
[58] Evelyn Waugh, *Brideshead Revisited* (London: Penguin, 1970), p. 245 (for example). Iris Murdoch's modification of a model of 'identical' twins in her 1958 novel *The Bell* suggests a gradual rejection of sibling transference as homosexual solution in an era beginning to permit fuller experiences and expressions of same-sex desire. In this novel Murdoch relates the disgust of a lover of a male twin when he meets the female counterpart. The protagonist, Michael, is 'confronted by the head of Nick set on the body of Catherine'. *The Bell* (London: Chatto and Windus, 1961), p. 109. In this encounter Murdoch emphatically critiques an earlier model of homosexual body substitution: 'It might be thought that since Nature by addition had defeated him of Nick, at least by subtraction it was now offering him Catherine: but this did not occur to Michael except abstractly and as something someone else might have felt' (pp. 110–11). Indeed Michael is repulsed by the possibility of transference: 'Michael felt that he was the victim of some appalling conjuring trick. He found her, as he found all women, unattractive and a trifle obscene, and the more so for cunningly reminding him of Nick' (p. 111).

important position in a two-directional queer literary genealogy, as Dickens appropriated fictional and actual examples of in-lawing to consolidate an influential motif for the expression of homoeros within the family. The wider employment of this plot, particularly by those authors whose particular debt to Dickens's work can be identified, is evidence that through cross-textual reiteration Dickens did produce readers competent in apprehending and recognizing the homoerotic hermeneutic of in-law triangles. Those readers who became writers attest to the continued potency of Dickens's pioneering model for expressing same-sex desire.

The widespread cultural commitment to in-lawing demonstrates that Dickens and his contemporaries did not necessarily conceive of heterosexual bonds as the primary determinant of marital choice. They were energetic in their efforts to construct actual and fictional families which consolidated and sustained homoeroticism. To recognize this is to give up long-cherished beliefs about the inherently socially transgressive nature of same-sex desire, and to thus reconstrue the Victorian family as a site of queer possibility. Dickens, as the central representative of nineteenth-century canonicity, bespeaks the enthusiasm with which his culture could incorporate and celebrate sexual diversity.

4
Homotropics: Queer Travels and New Homelands

British domestic space did expand, in perhaps surprising ways, to accommodate those whose desires did not fit a model of family centred on marriage and reproduction. As previous chapters have shown, Dickens uses practices of adoption and the celebration of celibacy to deprivilege reproduction at the same time as his depictions of intermarriage emphasize the significance of wider, often more eroticized ties, to the relatives of a spouse. Dickens emphasizes the possibility of queer space through the development of a range of eccentric domestic architectures, including boathouses, lighthouses, and the triangular home inhabited by the Pinch/Westlock trio. Such strategies and accommodations, however, are clearly partial and unevenly available. In his homotropical plots of emigration, itinerancy, and extended overseas travel, Dickens acknowledges the limits to the (doubly) domestic accommodation of same-sex desire, recognizing the potential dissidence of homoerotics and negotiating alternative constructions of domesticity overseas. Though, as we have seen, the domestic and familial are not antithetical to the queer in Dickens's imagination, emigration in these novels, as in wider Victorian culture, also permits the exploration of anti-domestic lifestyles. Rudi Bleys has suggested that historically travel and emigration constitute 'a privileged territory of homosexuals, and of a particular group among them, defending its integrity against a western strategy directed toward the domestication of sexuality – domestication, as a way of both excluding all forms of social and sexual life that don't fit the imperatives of a procreative family, and promoting the house as its privileged, exclusive and private domain against an ambulatory, nomadic and dionysiac sexuality'.[1] Here I explore those desires that cannot be fully expressed and experienced at home, attending to the erotically connotative locations at which specific characters cluster. In examining the significance of these sites, I work towards a historically and geographically nuanced understanding of the premise advanced by Karl Miller that for many individuals in the nineteenth century 'national ambivalence and sexual ambivalence were one and the same: the change of country [...] was caused or conditioned by a search for the exotic partner, for a love that was domestically unspeakable'.[2] This chapter, then, gives space to Dickens's representation of asocial and ambulatory forms of eroticism.

Whilst departing and returning emigrants and travellers feature in almost all of Dickens's novels, these 'foreign' elements have received little attention.[3] Grace Moore's recent work on *Dickens and Empire* functions as an important corrective to this, making a concerted effort to recognize and understand Dickens's undeniable, if complicated, racial prejudice.[4]

The traditional lack of critical emphasis on the significance of other countries in Dickens's fiction is at odds with a widespread appreciation of the importance of travel and new locales to his imaginative world. Nicola Bradbury has pointed to the dual connotations of a geographical move away from the domestic in Dickens's writing: 'The word "abroad"

---

[1] Rudi Bleys, 'Homosexual Exile: The Textuality of the Imaginary Paradise, 1800–1980' in *Gay Studies from the French Cultures*, ed. Rommel Mendès-Leite and Pierre-Olivier de Busscher (New York: Haworth Press, 1993), pp. 165–82, p. 166.

[2] Karl Miller, *Doubles: Studies in Literary History* (Oxford: Oxford University Press, 1985), p. 221.

[3] Andrew Sanders has, for example, asserted that 'the world beyond western Europe and North America figures only minimally in his work'. 'The Dickens World' in *Creditable Warriors 1850–1876*, ed. Michael Cotsell (London: Ashfield, 1990), pp. 131–42, p. 133. The marginalization of such elements reflects a modus operandi in which, as Edward Said has observed, 'writers' ideas about colonial expansion, inferior races, or "niggers" [are relegated] to a very different department to that of culture, culture being the elevated area of activity in which they "truly" belong and in which they did their "really" important work.' *Culture and Imperialism*, 4th edn (London: Vintage, 1994), p. xiv.

[4] See Grace Moore, *Dickens and Empire: Discourses of Class Race and Colonialism in the Works of Charles Dickens* (Aldershot: Ashgate, 2004), and 'Reappraising Dickens's "Noble Savage"', *Dickensian* 98.3 (2002), 236–44. Moore demonstrates that the critical dismissal of this piece 'as a mere testimony of Dickens's growing racism in this period' leads to widespread understatement of Dickens's more positive contributions to debates on race, including his continued commitment to the abolitionist cause ('Reappraising', p. 236).

has two potential inflections: overseas, foreign, alien; or at large, free. Dickens explores both of these areas of meaning, and also how they might intersect.[5] Bradbury, in line with existing approaches to Dickens's travel writing, focuses on the imaginative potential of journeys which permit 'psychological and even philosophical exploration'.[6] As John Drew has put it 'the effects of motion on the mental processes, and the fundamental similarity between physical displacement or trajectory and wanderings of flights of the imagination seem to be concepts underlying many of Dickens's sketches and essays about travelling and travellers.'[7] Various commentators have observed Dickens's metaphoric use of foreign locales to offer comment on domestic reform.[8] However, this emphasis tends to obscure Dickens's literary investment in specific overseas sites as providing a space for alterity from the values of home. A distilled form of this strategy is available in Dickens's most readily recognized travel fiction, *Martin Chuzzlewit*. The sojourn of the younger Martin and his faithful servant Mark Tapley in America (which becomes the setting for emotional and physical male intimacy, discussed in Chapter 5) is prefaced by an explicit reference to emigration as a nomadic alternative to conventional domesticity in the history of Mr Todgers, 'who, it seemed, had cut his matrimonial career rather short, by unlawfully running away from his happiness, and establishing himself in foreign countries as a bachelor' (p. 134).[9] This figuring of Todgers's pleasure-tripping as both transgressive and (sexually) liberating suggests a sexually dissident dimension to what Andrew Sanders has

---

[5] Nicola Bradbury, 'Dickens and James: "Watching with my Eyes Closed": The Dream Abroad', *Dickens Quarterly* 17.2 (2000), 77–87, p. 77.

[6] Bradbury, p. 81.

[7] John Drew, 'Voyages Extraordinaires: Dickens's "Travelling Essays" and *The Uncommercial Traveller*' (part one of two), *Dickens Quarterly* 13.2 (1996), 76–96, p. 87.

[8] See especially John Drew, and Anthony Chennells, 'Savages and Settlers in Dickens: Reading Multiple Centres' in *Dickens and the Children of Empire*, ed. Wendy Jacobson (Basingstoke: Palgrave, 2000), pp. 153–72.

[9] Todgers's overseas excesses set a pattern for Dickens's errant husbands. After Miss Betsy Trotwood pays off her abusive husband, 'and effect[s] a separation by mutual consent', he emigrates: 'He went to India with his capital, and there, according to a wild legend in our family he was once seen riding an elephant, in company with a Baboon; but I think it must have been a Baboo – or a Begum' (*David Copperfield*, p. 13). Maritally separated Mr Sparsit in *Hard Times* also opts for emigration, relocating to France where he dies of excessive alcohol consumption.

recognized as a yearning for 'something beyond' in Dickens's preoccupation with travel narratives as both writer and reader.[10]

Dickens was obsessed with travel literature from boyhood, repeatedly recording the appeal of such writings through a range of partially biographical personae. David Copperfield's reflection on his 'greedy relish for a few volumes of Voyages and Travels' (p. 60) is echoed in journalistic pieces: 'Such books have had a strong fascination for my mind from my earliest childhood; and I wonder it should have come to pass that I have never been round the world, never have been shipwrecked, ice environed, tomahawked or eaten.'[11] Dickens's 'ardent interest in voyagers and travellers' informed his ambitious trans-Atlantic crossings and extended European tours, as well as his work as novelist, travel writer, editor and journalist. As well as incorporating fictional treatments of foreign scenes in almost all of his novels, Dickens authored two dedicated travelogues *American Notes* (1842) and *Pictures from Italy* (1846), commissioned and printed numerous travel pieces as the editor of two weeklies, and confirmed his statement in a piece for *Household Words*, 'we have outgrown no story of voyage and travel', by adopting the persona of the 'Uncommercial Traveller' in *All The Year Round* for a series of sketches that ran throughout the 1860s.[12] John Forster's recollection of Dickens spending the summer of 1848 reading 'a surprising number of books of African and other travel for which he had an insatiable relish' is borne out by catalogues of Dickens's library.[13] Drew offers a detailed record of the numerous volumes of travel literature in the Sotheran's sale catalogue, concluding that such material accounts 'for the largest section of books of one particular description purposefully acquired by Dickens during his

[10] Sanders, p. 133. Todgers's libidinal excesses are implied in his phallic name. It is not unlikely that Dickens was drawing upon crude Yorkshire dialect slang (revived, as the *Bloomsbury Dictionary of Contemporary Slang* would have it, 'by students, alternative comedians, etc., in the 1980s') given his penchant for penis punning in this novel, which is often observed in relation to Tom Pinch's delighted manipulation of his 'simple little organ' (p. 461). Chase and Levenson suggest that in innuendos on Tom's instrument 'Dickens plays (shamelessly) on the sexual pun' (p. 93). For further examination of Tom's organ see Michael Steig, 'The Intentional Phallus: Determining Verbal Meaning in Literature', *Journal of Aesthetics and Art Criticism* 36 (1977), pp. 51–61.

[11] Charles Dickens, 'The Long Voyage', *Household Words*, 31 December 1853, repr. in *Dickens' Journalism*, vol. III: *'Gone Astray' and Other Papers from Household Words, 1851–59*, ed. Michael Slater (London: Dent, 1998) p. 181.

[12] Charles Dickens, 'Where We Stopped Growing', *Household Words*, 1 January 1853, quoted by Drew, p. 76.

[13] Quoted in *Dickens's Journalism*, III, p. 180.

lifetime'.[14] When George Henry Lewes visited Dickens in 1838, he was somewhat under-whelmed by the young author's library of 'nothing but three-volume novels and books of travel'.[15] Whilst Lewes found the collection shockingly unstudious, his observation that 'a man's library expresses much of his hidden life' gestures suggestively towards the covert release valve that Dickens was to find in both reading and writing of 'something beyond' domestic shores.[16]

Both literary critics and social historians have most readily detected the (homo)sexual element of this 'something beyond' at the close of the nineteenth century. Robert Aldrich, for instance, examines the lives of (most often late) Victorian colonial explorers who 'channelled energies into expeditions and homoerotic friendships rather than "normal" married life [. . .] prefer[ring] the camaraderie of male assistants to the pleasures of a wife.'[17] As John Tosh puts it, the empire in the period 1870–1900, was a major site of the male 'flight from domesticity': 'The empire was run by bachelors; in the public mind it represented devotion to duty or profit (and sometimes pleasure), undistracted by feminine ties.' Thus 'empire was actively embraced by young men as a *means* of evading or postponing the claims of domesticity'.[18]

Historical and literary perspectives come together in periodizing the fin de siècle as the moment when 'the wilderness' became a site of freedom from compulsory heterosexuality for both real and fictive colonists. Elaine Showalter, for example, positions the 'revival of [male quest] "romance" in the 1880s', investigating the questers' desire 'to evade heterosexuality altogether' in novels by Rider Haggard, Rudyard Kipling, and Joseph Conrad.[19] Aldrich does cite many earlier nineteenth-century examples of the cultural

---

[14] Drew, p. 77.

[15] George Henry Lewes, 'Dickens in Relation to Criticism' (1872), quoted by Leon Litvack, 'What Books Did Dickens Buy and Read? Evidence from the Book Accounts with his Publishers', *Dickensian* 94.2 (1998), 85–130, p. 85.

[16] Litvack, 'Books', p. 85.

[17] Robert Aldrich, *Colonialism and Homosexuality* (London and New York: Routledge, 2003), p. 2.

[18] John Tosh, *A Man's Place*, p. 175, p. 177.

[19] Showalter, *Sexual Anarchy*, p. 82. Joseph Boone's survey of protagonists 'existing outside the boundaries of matrimonial definition or familial expectation' in American quest romance similarly clusters around the end of the nineteenth century, although he also includes Herman Melville's *Moby Dick* (1851), demonstrating the fruitfulness of this approach when applied to earlier texts (*Tradition Counter Tradition*, p. 226).

association of particular locations with same-sex practice. He suggests, however, that such a linkage became most visible at the turn of the century:

By the late nineteenth century, a widespread belief circulated in Europe that homosexuality (and other sexual deviance) was endemic in the non-European world. The perception, and (to a limited extent) the reality, of the empire as a homosexual playground must not be underestimated. Homosexual men fleeing legal persecution in Britain, Germany and the Netherlands (and cultural disapprobation if not persecution in France) often found a warm welcome in the colonies.[20]

Miller also acknowledges that the association of expatriation with a queer turn away from conventional family life 'is evident at earlier points in the history of this literature', but he argues that 'in the Nineties the tendency came to a head'.[21] The heightened visibility of sexually motivated migration at the fin de siècle is intimately related to the travels of particularly colourful individuals, including André Gide (1869–1951), and Jean Genet (1910–86).[22]

Even more significant than these memorable figures, however, is the conceptual connection between the apparent increase in sexually motivated travel and the discursive formation of the homosexual. As Boone argues: 'it is no coincidence that the decade that saw the creation of the pathological category of the homosexual intensified the search for non-European outlets, such as Algeria, for sexual energies increasingly persecuted within Western culture'.[23] The notoriety of these later queer pilgrimages is intensified by the uneven critical attention bestowed on those instances of homosexuality that appear at the time when it was so constituted. The academic emphasis on both literary male romance questers and famous homosexual travellers from the turn of the century

[20] Aldrich, *Colonialism*, p. 5.   [21] Miller, p. 225.
[22] Miller, p. 331. Jonathan Dollimore takes a similar focus in his survey of *Sexual Dissidence*, arguing that 'Gide's experience in Africa is one of the most significant modern narratives of homosexual liberation.' *Sexual Dissidence: Augustine to Wilde, Freud to Foucault* (Oxford: Clarendon, 1991), p. 12. Miller provides an alternative late-nineteenth and early twentieth century list: 'Stevenson, Sharp, Henry James, Wharton, Conrad, Wilde, Yeats, Frost and then Eliot' (p. 221). Similarly, Boone allows his prehistory of the homoeroticizing of North Africa to be eclipsed by what he reverently describes as the 'legend' of Gide, Oscar Wilde, Alfred Douglas and E. M. Forster. 'Vacation Cruises: or the Homoerotics of Orientalism', *PMLA* 110.1 (1995), 89–107.
[23] Boone, 'Vacation Cruises', p. 105.

tends to obscure longer traditions of queer diaspora, encompassing what is often surprisingly explicit earlier material such as 'textual evidence of a fascination with the Near East's rumoured homoeroticism scattered through commentaries that reach back to the time of the crusades'.[24] Ian Littlewood, while recognizing the conceptual dominance of these late nineteenth-century figures, does explore the earlier homotropics integral to the diverse erotic opportunities of the Grand Tour (a declining tradition by the nineteenth century), and the legacy of previous sexual explorers such as Byron.[25]

Dickens, although dismissive in his correspondence of Byron's 'gloomy greatness', clearly internalized many of the productions of the foremost poet of his youth, repeatedly quoting him.[26] In his library at Gad's Hill he kept two editions of Byron's complete works (1829 and 1837) as well as a later edition of *Childe Harolde*. Importantly, Dickens's travellers paraphrase and refer to Byron at key moments of departure and return. As Kathryn Chittick has recorded:

Martin Chuzzlewit while in America, receives a letter from a young poet, enquiring about boat-fare to England and 'any critical observations that have ever presented themselves to your reflective faculties' on *Cain*. [. . .] Micawber, embarking for Australia, translates Byron into the familial plural with 'our Boat is on the shore, and our Bark is on the sea.'[27]

Here Micawber adapts a poem that Byron included in a letter that he sent while on his liberating overseas travels to his intimate friend, Thomas Moore. Byron's poem, in full, combines an expression of an urgent need for escape despite the dangers of ocean and desert(stanza three) with a love for this friend and implied sorrow at their parting: 'Were't the last drop in the well, / As I gasp'd upon the brink, /Ere my fainting spirit fell, / 'Tis to thee that I would drink.'[28] Dickens's familiarity with this poem and its position in his conception of parting and emigration suggests his awareness of Byron's travels as a response

---

[24] Boone, 'Vacation Cruises', p. 92.

[25] Ian Littlewood, *Sultry Climates: Travel and Sex* (London: Murray, 2001), p. 131, p. 107.

[26] Katthryn Chitick, 'Lord Byron', *Companion*, p. 65.

[27] Chittick, 'Byron', p. 65.

[28] Byron, *To Thomas Moore*, 10 July 1817, collected in *Byron: A Self Portrait: Letters and Diaries*, ed. Peter Quennell, 2 vols. (London: Murray, 1950), II, p. 413.

to social liminality. His appreciation of Byron as traveller is further suggested by his plan in 1844 to rent Byron's former villa near Genoa.[29] Louis Crompton has documented Byron's own close association of travel with sexual, particularly homosexual, freedom. He cites Byron's letter to Matthews just before he left for Greece, which 'shows [...] that both anticipated that his visit there would lead to homoerotic adventures'.[30] Indeed, before this extended tour Byron 'had made no direct or open allusions to homosexuality in his correspondence; now he recurs repeatedly to the subject'.[31] Byron famously described the Turkish baths he visited as 'marble palace[s] of sherbet and sodomy',[32] continually reinforcing the already firmly established association of the Orient with same-sex sexuality: 'In England the vices in fashion are whoring and drinking, in Turkey, Sodomy and smoking. We prefer a girl and a bottle, they a pipe and a pathic. – They are sensible people.'[33] Dickens would almost certainly have been aware of the sexual nature of Byron's experiences abroad. Andrew Elfenbein argues that during the earlier part of the Victorian period, knowledge of Byron's bisexuality circulated as an 'open secret', well known to particular circles including members of Dickens's social set such as close friend William Macready.[34]

In his fiction Dickens openly refers to ambiguities of gender and sexuality surrounding Byron. A controversial wax figure of Lord Byron appears in *The Old Curiosity Shop*, under the inventiveness of the exhibitor of waxworks, Mrs Jarley, whose slight adjustments of costumes and props allow her mannequins to undergo complete character transformations:

[29] Chittick, 'Byron', p. 65. Instead Dickens secured another villa for twelve months in Genoa, where he was powerfully reminded of Byron. See *Pictures from Italy* collected in *American Notes and Pictures from Italy* (London: Oxford University Press, 1957), p. 259, pp. 324–5.

[30] Louis Crompton, *Byron and Greek Love: Homophobia in Nineteenth Century England* (Berkeley: University of California Press, 1985), p. 109.

[31] Crompton, p. 126. Crompton acknowledges his anachronistic use of 'homosexuality', but deploys the term to refer to sexual relations between men.

[32] 12 August 1819, *Byron's Letters and Journals*, ed. Leslie Marchand, 12 vols. (Cambridge: Harvard University Press, 1973–1982), VI (1976), p. 207. Quoted by Crompton, p. 142.

[33] 3 May 1810, *Byron's Letters*, I, p. 238. Quoted by Crompton, p. 143.

[34] Andrew Elfenbein, *Byron and the Victorians* (Cambridge: Cambridge University Press, 1995), p. 212. Elfenbein discusses Macready's knowing embarrassment when asked to comment on the cause of Byron's marital separation.

Mr Pitt in a nightcap and bedgown, and without his boots, represented the poet Cowper with perfect exactness; and Mary Queen of Scots in a dark wig, white shirt-collar, and male attire, was such a complete image of Lord Byron that the young ladies quite screamed at it. Miss Monflathers, however rebuked this enthusiasm, and took occasion to reprove Mrs Jarley for not keeping her collection more select, observing that His Lordship had held certain free opinions quite incompatible with wax-work honours, and adding something about a Dean and Chapter, which Mrs Jarley did not understand (pp. 221–3).

Elfenbein describes this scene as a 'fictional representation of Byron's androgyny', one of many contemporary depictions that 'drew attention to his femininity' and Norman Page reads the schoolmarm's disapproval as an only slightly masked reference to Byron's scandalous reputation, which meant that the authorities of Westminster Abbey would not allow him to be buried there, or, later, for a statue of the poet to be placed there.[35] The waxwork's easy transition from Queen to Lord, effected through nothing more than 'a dark wig, white shirt-collar, and male attire', offers a vivid, Butlerian exposure of gender as performative, 'in the sense that the essence or identity that [it] otherwise purport[s] to express are *fabrications* manufactured and sustained through corporeal signs and other discursive means'.[36] Dickens was, as discussed in the previous chapter, more broadly interested in dismantling a culturally imposed opposition of masculinity and femininity by exposing the parity of male and female bodies and behaviours, a technique that he sustains through explorations of the resemblance of male and female siblings. His choice here of Byron is apt, as Byron famously refused to be constrained by conventional categories or styles of gender or sexuality. Dickens typically portrayed Byron as exerting a strong charismatic force over both men and women, as, for example, in the early sketch 'Horatio Sparkins', when the mysterious Byronic hero enters the ballroom:

'How like Lord Byron!' murmured Miss Teresa.
'Or Montgomery!' whispered Miss Marianne.
'Or the portraits of Captain Cook! ' suggested Tom.[37]

---

[35] Elfenbein, *Byron*, p. 65; Norman Page, notes to the Penguin edn, p. 565.
[36] Butler, *Gender Trouble*, p. 173.
[37] Charles Dickens, 'Horatio Sparkins' in *Monthly Magazine*, February 1834, repr. *Dickens's Journalism*, vol. I: *Sketches by Boz and Other Early Papers, 1833–39*, ed. Michael Slater (London: Dent, 2000), p. 348.

This enthusiastic comparison of the same figure to Byron and Captain Cook, the age's most eminent explorer, again emphasizes the importance of travel to Dickens's eroticized conception of Byron. Throughout the century knowledge of Byron's sexual relations with men, and women, increased, and by the 1890s Oscar Wilde speculated on a homoerotic tension between Byron and Shelley and compared himself to Byron in *De Profundis* as another figure 'hounded from British society because of sexual misconduct'.[38] Despite the much more heavily documented sexing-up of foreign travel at the close of the nineteenth century, this example demonstrates that an association of travel with a revolt from domestic, especially sexual, constraints was firmly established by the period of Dickens's career.

EARLY EROTICIZED TERRAIN: THE EAST AND WEST INDIES

From Dickens's first novel, a suggestive link is forged between same-sex desire and emigration. As discussed briefly in Chapter 2, *The Pickwick Papers* features two intimate male couples who are relocated at the novel's close to colonial outposts: Alfred Jingle and Job Trotter who move to Demerara, and Ben Allen and Bob Sawyer who emigrate to Bengal. These emigration plots draw on a complex range of contemporary connotations of economic and sexual dissidence that were already circulating at the end of the 1830s. Emigration is widely read as a device for closure – a move outside the domestic centre of the novel, which is often seen, as Leon Litvack suggests, as operating in a similar way to marriage or death, as a way of 'tying up loose ends.'[39] Such 'loose ends', in Victorian culture, are often the bodies of those who cannot be smoothly woven into the social fabric. These othered bodies include the criminal – those escaping the law and those convicts transported under it (such as Jack Dawkins, the artful dodger, who is transported for life in *Oliver Twist*, book 3, chapter 6); the financially insolvent (best represented by the debt-ridden Micawber family who are relocated to

[38] Elfenbein, p. 237.
[39] Leon Litvack, 'Emigration and Colonization', *Companion*, pp. 221–3, p. 223.

Australia at the end of *David Copperfield*); and, of course, most pertinently for Dickens given his involvement with Urania Cottage, fallen women, prostitutes, and other sexual dissidents. This latter category is most memorably represented by *David Copperfield*'s Martha and Em'ly who embark for New South Wales on the same vessel as the Micawbers. In Dickens's fiction, emigration can also complete the narratives of those who for the most part live alternative lives in Britain, such as the Crummles acting family who exchange the stage for the New World of America at the end of *Nicholas Nickleby* (p. 594).

Dickens had a particular investment in the promotion of emigration as a response to unsanctioned female sexuality. In *Oliver Twist* Dickens opens the possibility of prostitutes beginning again abroad, although at this early stage of his career Nancy is also offered a domestic alternative: 'a quiet asylum, either in England, or, if you fear to remain here, in some foreign country'.[40] By 1847 when Dickens opened Urania Cottage, his 'Home for Homeless Women', his attitude had hardened and the refuge was offered for the indivisible 'reclamation and emigration of women'. Believing that for such women 'there could be little or no hope in this country' Dickens admitted 'only those who distinctly accepted this condition: That they came there to be ultimately sent abroad'.[41] Through novelistic figures such as Martha and Little Em'ly who begin new lives in Australia, Dickens promoted this course of action for 'fallen women' in his fiction. Anny Sadrin argues that connotations of fall inevitably attach to exiled characters, even when they are otherwise exonerated of sexual misconduct, as with faux-adulteress Edith Dombey: 'This confidential revelation of her innocence is unlikely to disperse the whiff of scandal that surrounds her and makes her presence in London undesirable [...] Her retreat to Italy is unquestionably a golden exile compared to Martha's or Little Em'ly's (not to mention Alice Marwood's), but it nonetheless contaminates her through associations and gives her the status of a fallen woman'.[42]

---

[40] Charles Dickens, *Oliver Twist* (London, Penguin, 2003), p. 340.
[41] Charles Dickens, 'Home for Homeless Women', *Household Words*, 25 April 1853, repr. in *Dickens's Journalism*, III, p. 128.
[42] Anny Sadrin, 'Why D.I.J.O.N? Crossing Forbidden Boundaries in *Dombey and Son*', in *Dickens, Europe and the New Worlds*, pp. 14–21, p. 18.

The association of foreign relocation with what was perceived as anti-social sexuality is strengthened in this period through the widespread familial strategy of sending those whose desires did not fit (often lucrative) marital plans on extended overseas tours. Davidoff and Hall offer a variety of instances of what was a typical deployment of foreign travel as an antidote to sexual disgrace at home, such as the case of 'John Howard Galton, the youngest of a Birmingham banking family and the darling of his mother [who] became involved in an affair at the age of twenty-three and was packed off to the continent as rumours circulated of an illegitimate baby born in Ireland. He returned to make a good marriage with the daughter of a leading manufacturer.'[43] In *Pickwick* Dickens makes a somewhat ironic use of this trope of familial sexual coercion to encourage marital choice. Attempting to force his sister's selection of partner into line, literally, with his own, Ben Allen threatens to 'take her abroad for a while and see what that'll do' (p. 512). Arabella manages to resist her brother's choice and without this intermarriage to sanction his relationship with Bob Sawyer the two men opt to relocate. In this they follow a parallel tradition of homosexual emigration and travel, such as that which had already achieved a certain notoriety as practised by figures such as William Beckford and Lord Byron.[44]

This range of subjects and activities variously deemed to be outside the social, resonates with a definition of queer favoured in one branch of current queer theory, as those 'bodies and knowledges that exist outside the boundaries of sanctioned time and space, legal status, citizen-subjecthood, and liberal humanism'.[45] Although, as previous chapters have argued, Dickens emphatically does not yoke queer to the asocial or

[43] Leonore Davidoff and Catherine Hall, *Family Fortunes: Men and Women of the English Middle Class 1790–1850* (London: Hutchinson, 1987), p. 523.

[44] See Crompton, pp. 118–120 on Beckford's expedient flight to the continent in the late eighteenth century after being accused of sexual relations with another man. Crompton also records how Beckford's home in exile formed a central part of what can be seen as Byron's queer foreign pilgrimage: 'It was ironic that Byron, on his first arrival in Europe, should have been immediately reminded of another wealthy and literate bisexual who had been forced to flee abroad' (p. 130). Aldrich argues that Beckford's 'expatriation was not unusual for men of his sexual and cultural inclinations and wealth'. *The Seduction of the Mediterranean* (London and New York: Routledge, 1993), p. 70.

[45] Eng *et al.*, 'Queer', p. 13.

antisocial, in this accretion of instances of repudiated activities, including the criminal, economically eccentric, and the sexual, and grouped together through the practice of emigration, Dickens's fiction also explores a form of queer based on antithesis to, and removal from, domestic society. Dickens's diverse emigration plots, including those featuring same-sex intimates, draws homoerotic desire into a wider constellation of behaviours that cannot be accommodated at home. In her reading of *David Copperfield*, Patricia Plummer argues that 'eventually Dickens resorts to a convenient trick by shipping the disorderly elements of fallen women and the non-conformist Micawber family off to Australia'.[46] Plummer's phrase 'disorderly elements' points to the combination of economic and sexual concerns that very often come together in nineteenth-century attitudes towards emigration as a suitable solution to a range of perceived social problems. Within his many emigration narratives Dickens includes numbers of same-sex pairs, whose disorderliness is explicitly linked to the intensity of their mutual attachment. I will suggest that Dickens strategically uses the contemporary associations adhering to emigration and travel to explore a range of dissident behaviours, including the homoerotic – making such plots much more than a 'convenient [narrative] trick' or tidy 'tying up of loose ends'.

As we have seen, the first of Pickwick's alliterative pairs, Jingle and Job, have an ambiguous relationship that defies conventional terms of description. The bond between them becomes the locus for explicit articulations of anxiety about the boundaries of male friendship, a concern particularly fuelled by the self-sacrificing nature of Job's acts. Having voluntarily followed Jingle into the Fleet debtors' prison, Job determines to follow his friend and one-time master across the world. When Pickwick pays the debt for which Jingle has been imprisoned and finds an opening for the insolvent man to begin again on an estate, probably sugar cane farming, in Demerara (an act presented as a

---

[46] Patricia Plummer, 'From Agnes Fleming to Helena Landless: Dickens, Women and (Post-) Colonialism' in *Dickens, Europe and the New Worlds*, ed. Anny Sadrin (Basingstoke: Macmillan, 1999), pp. 267–82, p. 275. As Moore notes, Dickens was not averse to employing this technique to purge his own family of its 'disorderly elements': 'He frequently exiled troublesome members of his large family to make a new start in the colonies. As Forster wrote of the Dickens family in 1860, "Charley is in the Far East, Sydney is at sea, Walter in India, Alfred in Australia, whither he is planning to send another boy to join him"' (*Dickens and Empire*, p. 1).

benevolent solution to the social problems presented by Jingle's penury and uncanny chameleon ability for self refashioning) Job insists that 'he must go along with the other one'. As the legal clerk Lowten observes, Job gives up a remunerative clerkship ('eighteen bob a-week and a rise if he behaves himself') in London for 'something on the same estate; not near so good, Perker says, as a convict would get in New South Wales, if he appeared at his trial in a new suit of clothes' (p. 701). With debtors' incarceration as a prelude to their emigration and this reference to the involuntary deportation of convicted felons, the impoverished pair become associated with the two conceptually and numerically dominant emigrant groups: the economically insufficient and transportable criminals.

During the period of Dickens's career, emigration was increasingly discussed as a possible solution to the perceived problem of working-class overpopulation. It was advanced as a resolution to problems posed by poverty itself, as a means of expelling unemployed and dissident workers from the domestic economy, reducing home political tensions under the soothing ideology of 'civilizing' colonized peoples through an increased British presence abroad.[47] Dickens sympathized with Caroline Chisholm's promotion of emigration as a relief to domestic poverty, advocating this cause in the first issue of *Household Words*. In their preface to the co-authored article, 'A Bundle of Emigrant's Letters', Dickens and Chisholm position the alleviation of severe hardship as the primary design of Chisholm's Family Colonization Loan Society: 'It is melancholy to reflect that thousands of British subjects should wander about, more like spectres than beings of flesh and blood; and that hundreds should die from starvation, while our vast colonies could provide abundantly for them.'[48] Ken Lewandosi makes a convincing argument for the slippage in the mid-nineteenth century 'between the object of transportation and the object of emigration – the convict and the poor – a slippage that helped sustain the earlier ideology of projecting the

---

[47] See entries on 'Emigration and Colonisation' and 'Travel and Exploration' in *Companion*, and Nan Dreher, 'Redundancy and Emigration: The "Woman Question" in Mid-Victorian Britain', *Victorian Periodicals Review* 26.1 (1993), 4–8.
[48] 'A Bundle of Emigrants' Letters', *Household Words*, 30 March 1850, I, p. 19.

socially dangerous as far out of the light as possible'.[49] He argues that articles in *Household Words* 'reveal a remarkable consistency in promoting free emigration as a solution to the widespread social ills thought to result from both criminality and poverty'.[50]

The emigration of Job and Jingle is not, however, exclusively, or even primarily, associated with criminality or poverty, but with their status as a pair. Whilst they are associated with the eminent emigrant categories of pauper and criminal, discussions about their mutual relocation focus on their relationship as 'a worthy couple' (p. 704). Job's self-sacrificing insistence on remaining with Jingle provokes the most explicit homophobic anxiety of the novel; Lowten's description of Job's selfless attachment as 'downright sneaking'. As discussed more fully in Chapter 2, Lowten goes on to detail his perception of the deviancy of this pairing: 'no man should have more than two attachments – the first to number one and the second to the ladies' (p. 701). This phobic reaction, however, is counteracted by Pickwick's support of the pair, and his emotional response to what the novel also suggests is a noble attachment in various declarations of fidelity between Job, Jingle, and their benefactor: ' "He means to say," said Job, advancing a few paces, "that if he is not carried off by the fever, he will pay the money back again. If he lives, he will, Mr Pickwick. I will see it done. I know he will, Sir," said Job, with great energy, "I could undertake to swear it" ' (p. 703). Pickwick's emotion at such avowals signals an understandably homophilic reaction, given the emotional and erotic overlaps between Job and Jingle's relationship and the to-death fidelity of this eponymous bachelor hero and Sam Weller.

The cross-referential intimacies of male pairs in this novel are further developed in the parallel emigration of similarly alliterative 'intimate friends' Ben and Bob, who depart under parallel circumstances of bankruptcy, four chapters after Job and Jingle. Before leaving the country Ben and Bob have sought to mediate their relationship domestically thorough in-lawing. When this fails, emigration is offered as an

---

[49] Ken Lewandosi, 'A New Transportation for the Penitentiary Era: Some *Household Words* on Free Emigration', *Victorian Periodicals Review* 26.1 (1993), 8–18, p. 10.

[50] Lewandosi, p. 8. *The Pickwick Papers* further iterates this conservative association in the inference made through Job's brother, Dismal Jemmy, that voluntary relocation is also related to criminality: 'He emigrated to America, Sir, in consequence of being too much sought after here, to be comfortable; and has never been heard of since' (p. 703).

alternative means of negotiating the relatively narrow spaces available for homoerotic experience within British domesticity: 'Mr Bob Sawyer, having previously passed through the Gazette, passed over to Bengal, accompanied by Mr Benjamin Allen, both gentlemen having received appointments to the East India Company. They each had the yellow fever fourteen times, and then resolved to try a little abstinence, since which period they have been doing well' (p. 753). The shared experience of fever and languages of mutuality – 'both', 'each', 'they' – that characterize this short report clearly intensify the association of this male pair with that other inseparable 'worthy couple', Job and Jingle. In sending those abroad whose attachment is regarded by other characters as suspiciously 'soft', and those who have sought (but failed) to domesticate their intense relationship through intermarriage, Dickens's first novel clearly establishes a homoerotic resonance to mutual relocations of male pairs.[51]

Pickwick ends with a summing up of the various characters' destinies – in this catalogue, as discussed in Chapter 2, the conventional closure devices of emigration and marriage appear in proximity to Dickens's establishment of alternative elective communities. The pairing of Bob Sawyer and Ben Allen in Bengal appears alongside that of 'Mr and Mrs Winkle' and 'Mr and Mrs Snodgrass' (pp. 752–3). Dickens's concluding list of the novel's pairs suggests an erotic parity between nuptials and emigration. This mutual male pairing (like their counterparts Job and Jingle) are implicated in a same-sex marriage which can be lived outside the boundaries of Britain. In this first novel, the homoerotic resonances adhering to both Job and Jingle and Ben and Bob productively reverberate, offering additional suggestiveness to the details of both emigrant pairs. Beyond this novel, Dickens's regular readers could recognize the strategic repetition of such a plot-line – using a method of cross-referential reading that serial readers, used to suspending their reading and holding complex plots in mind over time, would be particularly adept at. Such readers could bring a set of pre-established homoerotic connotations to their encounter with the many Dickensian emigrations of same-sex pairs.

---

[51] See Chapter 3 for a thorough exploration of Dickens's rendering of the homoerotic relationship between Ben and Bob, and their foiled efforts to become brothers-in-law.

In his second novel Dickens again deploys the West Indies as a site of perceived freedom from social, including sexual, constraints. Diana Archibald has demonstrated that the Caribbean had its own distinct significance in a contemporary literature that capitalized 'on the image of Latin America as a wild and dangerous land' and Paul Sharrad has observed the recurrence of references to the Caribbean in *Oliver Twist*.[52] Mrs Bedwin tells Oliver about her son 'who was clerk to a merchant in the West Indies, and was also such a good young man, and wrote such dutiful letters home four times a year' (p. 106). This is also the location to which Brownlow pursues Edward Leeford, alias Monks (p. 260), who deploys his estate in the West Indies as a retreat whenever it is necessary 'to escape the consequences of vicious courses here' (p. 413). Sharrad has speculated on the imaginative significance of this locale: 'It may be that Dickens deliberately connected Monks with the West Indies to indicate moral degeneracy by association with the slave trade, but it is far more likely that he simply saw the tropics as a natural metonym for physical, mental and moral degeneration as Charlotte Brontë was to do later in the decade with *Jane Eyre*.'[53] After Brownlow's settlement we learn that 'Monks, still bearing that assumed name, retired with his portion to a distant part of the New World; where having quickly squandered it, he once more fell into his old courses, and, after undergoing a long confinement for some fresh act of fraud and knavery, at length sunk under an attack of his old disorder, and died in prison. As far from home died the chief remaining members of Fagin's gang' (p. 451). Criminality again links these experiences of voluntary and forced movements overseas.[54] As the very different, mercantile example

---

[52] Diana Archibald, *Domesticity, Imperialism and Emigration in The Victorian Novel* (Missouri: University of Missouri Press, 2002), p. 16. Archibald cites the tempestuous contemporary example of Harriet Martineau's *Demerara* (1839), in which the hurricane operates as a physical embodiment of the rage of black slaves. A later instance is cited from Wilkie Collins's *Armadale* (1866), which opens with a Caribbean murder. Paul Sharrad, 'Speaking the Unspeakable: London, Cambridge and the Caribbean', in *Describing Empire: Post Colonialism and Textuality*, ed. Chris Tiffin and Alan Lawson (London and New York: Routledge, 1994), pp. 201–17.

[53] Sharrad, p. 209.

[54] This reference to the transportation of convicts from Fagin's gang resonates with the deportation of the Dodger and the description of the returned felon Kags, who 'arrived sooner than was expected from foreign parts, and is too modest to want to be presented to the Judges on his return' (p. 367).

of Mrs Bedwin's merchant son demonstrates, this location has various, and competing significances. It is conceived as both a commercially significant trade-region and a perceived dystopia or arcadia (depending on one's point of view) of moral laxity.

THE FOREIGN VICE: EUROPE AND DICKENS'S HOMOTROPICAL IMAGINATION

As Rudi Bleys has argued, queer travel and migration 'does not occur in a political vacuum [. . .] the destinations and professional occupations of most travellers reflect the colonial constellation'.[55] Dickens's novels bear out this geographical pattern, with exiled figures largely relocating to the colonies, to areas that Dickens knew from first-hand experience, America, France, and Italy, and in his later work to Egypt, a country that became increasingly fascinating to the British throughout the nineteenth century, by virtue of its antiquities and its geographical position as a trade route to colonial India. While the similarities between the *Pickwickian* pair of relocations establish a homoerotic referent to such moves, there is clearly a qualitative difference between Ben and Bob's continuance of their semi-professional hack work as surgeons in Bengal, a British protectorate under the rule of the East India Company, Jingle and Job's estate work, in what was perceived as the wilder terrain of the Caribbean, in the newly abolitionist colony of British Guyana, and Monks's incognito escapes to the more vaguely specified West Indies. While Sharrad's focus upon the Monks plot results in an understandably critical reading of Dickens's use of this area, it is clear from the parallel movement of Job and Jingle that Dickens also perceived the potential for more homophilic freedoms under what appeared to Victorian authors as an alternative, almost unregulated Caribbean morality. The perceived wildness of sites such as the Caribbean combined suggestively with a belief in the relaxation of social mores outside of Britain to form spaces for queer exploration.

As Crompton argues, by the Georgian period there was an established and repeatedly articulated dogma about 'the absolute foreignness of

---

[55] Bleys, 'Homosexual Exile', p. 167.

same-sex attractions'.[56] This othering of homoerotics did not extend equally to all foreign countries, but clustered associatively around particular locales. An early eighteenth-century tract, 'Plain Reasons for the Growth of Sodomy in England', firmly places the blame with Italy, the alleged 'mother and nurse of sodomy' and with France, a country that is apparently disproportionately successful in producing nuns who are 'criminally *amorous* of each other in a Method too gross for Expression'.[57] Similarly Daniel Defoe's popular poem 'The True Born Englishman' (1701), which Dickens owned and which was reprinted in Walter Scott's 1840 collected edition of Defoe's work, assigns sexual aberrance to Italy: 'Lust chose the torrid zone of Italy / Where Blood ferments in Rapes and Sodomy.'[58] So acceptable was this jingoistic citation of Italian vice, that Defoe's other works capitalized on its popular success, advertising under this title. Dickens's own copy of Defoe's *Jure Divino*, itemized in the Stonehouse catalogue, bears the heading 'by the author of The True Born Englishman'. These sentiments are reiterated in a 1749 work, which asks: 'Have we not Sins enough of our own, but we must eke 'em out with those of Foreign nations, to fill up the cup of our abominations? ' In this vein, the author asserts that in Italy 'the Master is oftener intriguing with his Page than a fair Lady', offers various accounts of lesbianism in French nunneries, and concludes that such behaviour is spreading, and has ' "got footing" among English women of quality, and is practised in Twickenham as well as in Turkey.'[59]

Dickens repeatedly uses the two European countries that he knew well from personal visits, and which had the most firmly established erotic associations, Italy and France, as connotative sites for the relocation of sexually dissident characters. Littlewood describes how the

[56] Crompton, p. 52.
[57] 'Plain Reasons for the Growth of Sodomy in England' (c.1728), quoted by Littlewood, p. 28. The author participates in the often anti-Catholically motivated popular construction of the French lesbian nun, an anti-papist strategy exemplified by Diderot's eighteenth-century novel *La Religieuse*.
[58] Daniel Defoe, 'The True Born Englishman', *The Novels and Miscellaneous Works of Daniel De Foe*, ed. Walter Scott, 6 vols. (London: Bohn, 1854–1856), V (1855), pp. 434–63, p. 435.
[59] 'Satan's Harvest Home: or the Present State of Whorecraft, Adultery, Fornication, Procuring, Pimping, Sodomy . . . and Other Satanic Works, Daily Propagated in this Good Protestant Kingdom', quoted by Hyde, pp. 82–3.

increasing speed of travel and the growing association of sex and tourism encouraged by notorious figures, especially Byron, resulted in an increasing number of Victorians who 'began to use the Continent as a refuge where pleasure could be snatched in the discreet intervals of a virtuous working life. The most immediate focus for such trips was Paris, a city whose reputation was well established by the end of the eighteenth century.'[60] It is likely that in the 1860s Dickens used Paris, or perhaps a French port town, in exactly this way as a discrete site for his affair with Ellen Ternan.[61] He certainly enjoyed liberating, perhaps sexually experimental, trips to Paris with Wilkie Collins in the mid 1850s, mischievously proposing a trip together to Paris in 1854 as an opportunity for 'a career of amiable and unbounded license in the metropolis. If you will come and breakfast with me about midnight – anywhere – any day – and go to bed no more until we fly to these pastoral retreats – I shall be delighted to have so vicious an associate.'[62] Dickens's playful tone reflects widespread British fascination with (and disapprobation of) the perceived immorality of French culture, most fully expressed in long-running debates about French novels. As an 1845 review for *Blackwood's Magazine* put it: 'vice and licentiousness are exhibited with vast power' by 'the modern romance writers of France – Victor Hugo, Janin, Madame Dudevant [George Sand], and Sue'.[63] An 1854 piece in *Household Words*, 'Paris with a Mask On', describes a 'general love of extravagance' and profligacy – by three in the afternoon 'every Parisian has had his breakfast' – detailing instances of cross-dressing in the masked carnival: 'surely there is nothing very funny or very commendable, or even harmless in that'.[64] Despite this moralistic tone, Dickens clearly enjoyed the pleasure-tripping opportunities that the city offered. Early in 1855 Dickens wrote to the proprietor of the Comedie-Française to arrange similar excitements for his return visit with Collins. He requests help in finding a more flexible hotel than his usual choice, the Hotel Brighton: '[T]here they expect one to dine at

[60] Littlewood, p. 120.
[61] See Claire Tomalin, *The Invisible Woman: The Story of Nelly Ternan and Charles Dickens*, 2nd edn (London: Penguin, 1991), pp. 135–8.
[62] Charles Dickens to Wilkie Collins, 12 July 1854, *Letters*, VII (1993), p. 366.
[63] 'The Historical Romance', *Blackwood's Magazine*, September 1845, p. 356.
[64] Douglas Blanchard Jerrold, 'Paris With a Mask On', *Household Words*, 29 April 1854, IX, pp. 245–8.

home [...] whereas we are coming to Paris expressly to be always looking about us, we want to dine wherever we like, every day [...] I want it to be pleasant and gay, and to throw myself en garcon on the festive diableries de Paris.'[65] Such 'festive diableries', as Dickens and his contemporaries were well aware, included sex tourism including spots for 'lesbian diversions' widely advertised in Bachelor Guides to the city, part of the famously seamy side of Parisian life that Thomas Cook advised his patrons to shun.[66] The popular association of Paris with sex between women was further fuelled in this period through rumours widely circulated about Marie Antoinette.[67]

In Dickens's fiction Italy and France figure prominently as libidinous sites. Steerforth's heterosexual seduction tour ends, for example, in the purportedly sodomitic locale of Naples, where he becomes especially restless and abandons Emily, his mistress, in favour of the homosocial pleasures of a Mediterranean sailing tour.[68] Edward Leeford, Oliver Twist's, and Monks's adulterous father, dies in Rome (p. 411), and Leeford's legal wife (Monks's mother), who is strongly indicted for her ability to conceal and forget her marriage and live 'wholly given up to continental frivolities', resides in Paris (p. 410). Similarly, the site for Edith Dombey's apparently adulterous tryst with Carker is Dijon.[69] Dickens's most legible 'lesbian' figure, Miss Wade, is associated with both these eroticized countries and with a rootless lifestyle of constant relocation; itinerant and socially ostracized, 'Miss Wade mostly lives abroad' (p. 517). She travels in Italy, (p. 630, p. 633), a locale also chosen

---

[65] Charles Dickens to Philocles Regnier, 3 February 1855, *The Letters of Charles Dickens*, vol. VII: 1853–1855, Pilgrim Edition, ed. Madeline House, Graham Storey, Kathleen Tillotson and Angus Easson (Oxford: Clarendon Press, 1993), pp. 522–3.

[66] Littlewood, p. 122.

[67] Terry Castle provides a detailed account of the circulation of these rumours, observing their currency and longevity into the nineteenth century: 'Lesbian diarist Anne Lister, visiting Paris in 1825, reported hearing from one of her female lovers there that "Marie Antoinette was accused of being too fond of women".' *The Apparitional Lesbian: Female Homosexuality and Modern Culture* (New York: Columbia University Press, 1993), p. 131.

[68] For an account of the homotropical history of Naples see Frank Bowning, *A Queer Geography: Journeys Toward a Sexual Self* (New York: Crown, 1996), ch. 2.

[69] Sadrin makes a case for the inevitability of a French setting for scenes of sexual impropriety in this period, and Plummer argues that the relocation of characters in *Oliver Twist* is complemented by the naming of Oliver's unmarried mother, Agnes Fleming. Fleming, meaning a native of Flanders, associates her, as a fallen woman, with continental vice (p. 270).

in *Little Dorrit* by both the villainous Blandois and Miss Wade's former seducer Gowan, and first meets Harriet (called Tattycoram by the Meagles family) in the feverish region of Marseilles. Miss Wade and Harriet later return to France, and the port town of Calais is the setting for the most open revelations of their relationship. Here Miss Wade gives Arthur Clennam her 'History', which details her intense attachments to women and her illicit sexuality with Gowan as a context for her defiant declarations of independent cohabitation: 'We have been living together ever since, sharing my small means' (p. 643); 'Sir, whether you find me temporarily and cheaply lodging in an empty London house or in a Calais apartment, you find Harriet with me' (p. 632).

For an intermediate time Miss Wade and Harriet have furtively occupied an unmarked, dark, and apparently empty London flat, where their out-of-place possessions and travel accoutrements mark their itinerancy even at this moment of temporary stasis:

The lady whom they had come to see, if she were the present occupant of the house, appeared to have taken up her quarters there, as she might have established herself in an Eastern caravanserai. A small square of carpet in the middle of the room, a few articles of furniture that evidently did not belong to the room, and a disorder of trunks and travelling articles, formed the whole of her surroundings (p. 318).

On his return to the London house, Clennam finds that the couple have vanished, discovering only 'that Miss Wade was gone, that the waifs and strays of furniture were gone' (p. 323). With no more affiliation to home, either in a national or domestic sense, than such inanimate 'waifs and strays', Miss Wade takes the similarly domestically alienated Harriet to a site specifically reserved for such national 'outlaws'. Clennam eventually traces and pursues them to Calais, arriving at what is described as a magnet for 'all the French vagabonds and English outlaws in the town (half the population)' (p. 626). As Michael Hollington observes, the manuscript originally put this proportion at 'three fourths', suggesting even more explicitly the outlaw status of Miss Wade and Tattycoram.[70] The 'countrymen' that Arthur Clennam encounters in Calais are described through one of the century's most prominent metaphors for sexual excess, as having 'a straggling air of having at

[70] Michael Hollington, 'France', *Companion*, p. 249.

one time over-blown themselves, like certain uncomfortable kinds of flowers, and of being, now, mere weeds' (p. 627). The port town is variously marked as a site on the edge; with a ghostly 'meagre lighthouse', it is an 'oozy' place, struggling to remain distinct from 'the undermining and besieging sea' (p. 626). Here Dickens employs a geographically connotative strategy similar to that used in Henry James's *The Bostonians* (1886). In this novel, as Castle has observed, Olive takes Verena to Paris 'in the hope that living on a "continent of strangers" will make them "cleave more closely to each other"'. In his use of such 'suggestive surroundings' Castle argues that James draws on a Zolarian tradition in which France itself becomes one of the 'various objects and "props" associated [...] with deviance and homosexual love'.[71] In Dickens's setting of Miss Wade's most triumphant declaration of her same-sex relationship in this explicitly marginal site of 'outlaws', he draws upon an existing association of France with lesbianism that allows Calais to operate as a prop, contributing further to the visibility of homoerotics in this expatriated partnership. Miss Wade's geographical relocation extends her resistance to conventional forms of sociality – she repulses the friendly advances of Mr Meagles just as she has rejected the proffered fellowship of other pupils at school. The outsider position cherished by Miss Wade reflects a correlation observed by Bleys in narratives of homosexual exile, in which a 'particular intimacy exist[s] between "homosexual" sensibility and the restlessness provoking the geographical move towards other countries'.[72] This important example demonstrates that homoerotics in Dickens's work can become visible as the anti-social and exterior. Miss Wade and Dickens's other homotropical emigrants provide important counter-examples to the instances of queer domestic experience and expression explored elsewhere in this book.

Whilst many individuals benefited from a relaxation of censures against same-sex desire when they travelled overseas or emigrated, recent critics have cautioned against any simplistically celebratory reading of the potential freedoms of homotropics.[73] Jarrod Hayes raises the con-

---

[71] Castle, *Apparitional*, p. 168, p. 167.
[72] Bleys, 'Homosexual Exile', p. 165.
[73] Sedgwick's extremely muted interpretation of positive homoerotic possibilities of foreign locales injects a useful degree of caution. She describes such locations as 'a male

cern that representations of foreign homosexuality as playing away may not present any challenge to the compulsory and privileged nature of heterosexuality at home, merely operating as 'the escape hatch for activities Western heterosexuality abjects'.[74] Diana Archibald makes a similar point about the literary deployment of emigration in the nineteenth century: 'Certain British authors often brought their texts to the margins as a way to shore up their own ideological centres.'[75] Shannon Russell argues that this conservative separatist ideology informs exile in Dickens: 'Dickens's use of emigration as a narrative solution in *David Copperfield* exposes his adherence to perceptions of the colonies as the place for those who cannot be morally or materially accommodated in the Old World. He sanctions the view that some people should be kept separate.'[76] It is important to be wary of the conservative agenda very often behind the expulsion of particular groups. However, uses and experiences of emigration during this period were diverse and contradictory. In her study of the recruitment of middle-class single women for transportation to areas of the 'New World', Archibald modifies her initial separatist thesis, arguing that while conservative promoters may well have hoped to eradicate un(re)productive spinsters, the women themselves often welcomed the liberating imaginative and practical possibilities presented by emigration.[77] In one of many conceptual contradictions, emigration was simultaneously associated with prostitutes and spinsters; figured as a way of accommodating both excess and surplus sexuality. Nan Dreher's research supports and extends Archibald's argument for competing deployments and appropriations of overseas relocation. She finds that despite its basis in conservative ideology, 'emigration offered an opportunity for some redundant

place in which it is relatively safe for men to explore the crucial terrain of homosociality. There are limits, but in these imagined subject territories, as to some degree in real ones, the schism of homophobia is not the most visible feature of geography' (*Between Men*, p. 198).

[74] Jarrod Hayes, *Queer Nations: Marginal Sexualities in the Maghreb* (Chicago and London: University of Chicago Press, 2000), p. 31.

[75] Archibald, p. 4.

[76] Shannon Russell, 'Recycling the Poor and the Fallen: Emigration Politics and the Narrative Resolutions of *Mary Barton* and *David Copperfield*', in *Imperial Objects: Essays on Victorian Women's Emigration and the Unauthorised Imperial Experience*, ed. Rita Krandis (New York: Twayne, 1998), pp. 43–63, p. 45.

[77] Archibald, pp. 10–11.

women to escape the situation, and the colonies served as a testing ground for more flexible social prescriptions that subsequently returned to Britain. Ironically, conservative efforts to strengthen British ideology and extend it to the colonies fatally strained it.[78] Dickens's own representations of emigration stage a similar ideological contest. Though in his journalism on prostitution Dickens unambivalently recommends emigration as social panacea, his fiction complicates this apparently conservative position through the repeated suggestion that overseas relocation also offers erotic freedom and provides opportunities for alternative lifestyles.

'GOING UP THE NILE AND SEEING WONDERS': EGYPT AND THE HOMOEROTIC FANTASIES OF NINETEENTH-CENTURY BRITAIN

Sedgwick's analysis of '*Edwin Drood* and the Homophobia of Empire' focuses on Dickens's final unfinished novel and uses a framework of later nineteenth and early twentieth-century theories and experiences of overseas homosexuality, articulated by the infamous figures of Richard Burton and T. E. Lawrence. She demonstrates that there is much mileage in positioning *Edwin Drood* against the narratives of these later imperial adventurers who, as Suvendrini Pevera has documented, 'produce male homosexuality as an oriental, and particularly Middle Eastern practice'.[79] Without noting the anachronism, Sedgwick uses Burton's theory of a 'Sotadic Zone' of allegedly endemic non-Western homosexuality propounded in the famous 'Terminal Essay' of his *Thousand Nights and a Night* (1885–8), to explicate the penetrative homosexual imagery of Dickens's 1870 work: 'Rosa may munch serenely on her sticky Turkish Lumps-of-Delight candy; but for the English male, there is more at stake in Turkish pleasures. At stake, for instance, in the opium dream of the novel's first paragraph, is a Sultanly habit of impaling men on spikes. Burton describes some related Oriental habits.'[80] To observe the textual

[78] Dreher, p. 6.
[79] Suvendrini Pevera, *Reaches of Empire: The English Novel from Edgeworth to Dickens* (New York: Columbia University Press, 1991), p. 112.
[80] Sedgwick, p. 189.

anachronism of this reading is not to invalidate its appreciation of Dickens's use of specific locales to express sex between men.

Following Sedgwick, critics have read Dickens's final novel as a site where the 'concentric model' of empire, a 'structure of hierarchical asymmetry, with the metropolis at the centre, and colonies or other supplementary economies at the periphery of the knowable universe', is most rigorously challenged.[81] Through the dark figure of opium-soaked Jasper orientalized homosexuality is brought home. As Pevera argues:

Embracing the 'unclean spirit of imitation' lodged in opium, Jasper succumbs indiscriminately to the degraded ways of the Chinese, Turks and Lascars. These ways, of which opium is the signifier, encompass a whole spectrum of 'oriental' 'vices', among them effeminacy, homosexuality, and 'thugee'.[82]

The foreignness that renders Jasper's intense feeling for his nephew visible as homoeros, has continuities in the relationship that the repatriated Helena Landless enjoys with the English Rosa. Given the broader homotropical economy of this specific work and Dickens's oeuvre more widely, Helena's upbringing in Ceylon and her indeterminate race is central to the signification of her homoerotic desire.[83] The gender confusion engendered by Helena's twinship with Neville is intensified by a 'foreign' childhood during which she repeatedly 'dressed as a boy, and showed the daring of a man' (p. 64). Such behaviour accords with British travellers' accounts such as that of Charles Dilke, who discovered Ceylon to be a site at which pre-existing gender assumptions were challenged. In the record of his 1866 trip to Ceylon

---

[81] David Faulkner, 'The Confidence Man: Empire and the Deconstruction of Muscular Christianity in *The Mystery of Edwin Drood*' in *Muscular Christianity: Embodying the Victorian Age*, ed. Donald Hall (Cambridge: Cambridge University Press, 1994), pp. 175–93. Plummer makes a similar point, arguing that in *Edwin Drood* what she sees as a typical resolution technique of 'shipping the chaotic characters happily off to the colonies', is reversed: 'The novel begins with a description of the influx of chaotic elements from the colonies' (p. 275).
[82] Pevera, p. 112. This echoes Sedgwick's observation of the three things that become articulated, but remain entangled, in Jasper's reveries under the 'Un-English' substance, 'his love for his nephew, his need to do violence, and the rhythm of sexual desire' (p. 189, p. 188).
[83] In a working note Dickens pondered 'Mixture of Oriental blood – or imperceptibly acquired mixture in them?' Quoted by Tim Dolin, 'Race and the Social Plot in *The Mystery of Edwin Drood*' in *The Victorians and Race*, ed. Shearer West (Aldershot: Scolar, 1996), pp. 84–101, p. 85.

(published 1869) Dilke observed that wives were 'far more rough and "manly" than their husbands' and resolved to 'set down everybody that was womanly as a man, and everyone that was manly as a woman'.[84]

In this most oriental novel Dickens also returns to Egypt, a site loaded with competing contemporary connotations. Relocations to Egypt in *Edwin Drood, Hard Times,* and *Great Expectations* reflect a growing British fascination with this country, fuelled by the opening of the 'Egyptian Hall' in 1809, Giovanni Belzoni's discoveries of temples and tombs, on which Dickens wrote a *Household Words* piece in 1851, the search for the source of the Nile (about which Dickens owned several books), and British trade interests in the region which provided a direct route to colonial India. Economic interests in the area were developed through the construction of railway routes in the 1850s and the opening of the Suez canal in 1869, the main factor behind the British occupation of the country from 1882.[85] Edwin Drood – whose failure properly to value the Bud or Pussy reserved for him is central to the plot – contemplates the resolution of his heterosexual ambivalence through a speedy marriage to Rosa Bud, after which he will 'go engineering in the East'.[86] This will resolve his lack of enthusiasm for his fiancé, whose otherwise widely appealing body functions as the locus for avowed desire in the novel. Indeed, Edwin perceives the perversity in his lack of ardour, insisting that given free selection he 'would choose Pussy from all the pretty girls in the world' (p. 18). The later suggestion that Edwin may prefer Helena Landless, another orientalized dark figure, whose twinship with her brother Neville creates an explicit physical and psychical parity of male and female bodies, does little to bolster his insufficient performance of heterosexual lust. Dickens presents the movement east to Egypt as a way to resolve Edwin's deficient desire. In his wish to 'wake up Egypt a little' (p. 72), Edwin expresses the magnetic draw that this country exerts on a number of Dickens's romantically dissident later male characters. While Edwin is a poor fit in a society that endorses marriage and reproduction, his earlier

---

[84] Charles Dilke, *Greater Britain: Charles Dilke Visits Her New Lands 1866 and 1867*, ed. G. Blainey (Sydney: Methuen Haynes, 1985), p. 168.

[85] For more on the cultural significance of tomb discovery and the Suez Canal see Hyangji Park ' "Going to Wake Up Egypt": Exhibiting Empire in *Edwin Drood*', *Victorian Literature and Culture* 30.2 (2002), 529–50.

[86] Charles Dickens, *The Mystery of Edwin Drood* (London: Penguin, 2002), p. 21.

counterpart, Harthouse, exhibits inappropriate urges of the opposite type. After Harthouse's failed seduction of the married Louisa in *Hard Times*, he is compelled 'to go up the Nile [...] going in for camels' (p. 229). This movement suggests the wider association of the Orient, especially through popular images of the seraglio, with hetero- as well as homosexual 'excess'.[87] In *Great Expectations* Dickens continues to use relocation to Egypt both to resolve and articulate those male desires incompatible with marriage and reproduction.

Egypt, and the orient more generally, had a powerful association with same-sex desire in the Victorian period. By relying on infamous turn-of-the-century writers to buttress her interpretation of the homophobia of empire, Sedgwick withholds from her reading of *Edwin Drood* the contemporary cultural homoeroticizing of specific locales that occurred before and during Dickens's career. As evidence amassed by Aldrich, Bleys, Boone, Collette Colligan, Jeffrey Schneider, and others demonstrates, Burton's theories did not emerge from nowhere. Instead, Burton's 'Sotadic Zone' tapped into existing national fantasies and beliefs to crystallize a variety of earlier discourses that attempted to map same sex praxis.[88] Indeed, Burton had himself formulated many of his 'Sotadic' theories some thirty years before they finally reached publication in his version of the *Nights*. He had hoped to share his 'curiosity for marriage customs and sexual practices of different nations', including such material in the notes to his *Personal Narrative of a Pilgrimage to al Madinah and Meccah*. However, the publisher of this 1855 travel book 'suppressed it all as "garbage"'.[89]

[87] See Colette Colligan's discussion of the 'Victorian harem fantasy' which proliferated in an obscene print culture that repeatedly produced tales along the lines of *The Lustful Turk* (1828). ' "A Race of Born Pederasts": Sir Richard Burton, Homosexuality, and the Arabs', *Nineteenth Century Contexts* 25 (2003), 1–20, pp. 6, 16. Dickens provides an explicit version of this fantasy in his portion of the 1859 collaborative Christmas story 'The Haunted House'. Haunted by the phantom of childhood memory, the adult protagonist fantasizes of when he was a schoolboy and proposed to a friend that they 'should have a seraglio', through which they would become 'blessed in the smiles of eight of the fairest of the daughters of men': 'The other creature assented warmly. He had no notion of respectability, neither had I. It was the custom of the East, it was the way of the good Caliph Hauron Alraschild [...] the usage was highly laudable and most worthy of imitation.' *The Christmas Stories*, pp. 221–52, pp. 246–7.
[88] See, for example, Aldrich, *Colonialism*, p. 51, Colligan, p. 5.
[89] Fatma Moussa-Mahmoud, 'English Travellers and the *Arabian Nights*', in *The Arabian Nights in English Literature*, ed. Peter Caracciolo (Basingstoke: Macmillan, 1988), pp. 95–110, p. 106.

Said reads the (perceived) availability of 'a different type of sexuality' as central to the appeal of the Orient to nineteenth-century Europeans:

Just as the various colonial possessions – quite apart from their economic benefit to metropolitan Europe – were useful as places to send wayward sons, superfluous populations of delinquents, poor people, and other undesirables, so the Orient was a place where one could look for sexual experience unobtainable in Europe. Virtually no European writer who wrote on or travelled to the Orient in the period after 1800 exempted himself or herself from this quest.[90]

Despite Said's inclusion of Flaubert, who famously wrote home of his Egyptian 'experiments' in sodomy, and '"Dirty Dick" Burton' in his list of prominent questers, he refuses to name the powerful cultural conjunction of sex between men and the Orient. Jeffrey Schneider argues that 'although Said seems unable and/or unwilling to move beyond euphemisms in his discussion of "Oriental sex", the British had no problem whatever in identifying the form of sexuality they most often, and traditionally associated with the Orient – sodomy (more specifically, sodomitical relations between men)'.[91] This link is re-forged repeatedly throughout the period, most explicitly in candid private letters such as those Flaubert sent from Egypt in 1850: 'One admits one's sodomy and talks about it at the dinner table. Sometimes one denies it a bit, then everyone yells at you and it ends up getting admitted [. . .] The opportunity hasn't presented itself yet: nonetheless we are looking for it.'[92] In a later letter Flaubert has availed himself of an opportunity for sodomy and hopes to repeat the experience, avowedly for reasons of further exploration rather than pleasure. Earlier, Byron had penned a more enthusiastic sodomitic correspondence during his travels in the Mediterranean and Albania. These private accounts reflect with exuberant explicitness a more muted nineteenth-century public discourse of Oriental homosexuality. Public accounts typically combined climatic, moral, and racial assumptions with a strong vein of religious prejudice, repeatedly echoing 'the claim first made during the Middle Ages that a close affinity existed between

---

[90] Said, p. 190.
[91] Jeffrey Schneider, 'Secret Sins of the Orient: Creating a (Homo)Textual Context for Reading Byron's *The Giaour*', *College English* 65.1 (2002), 81–95, p. 82.
[92] Quoted and trans. Hayes, p. 30. For further discussion see Aldrich, *Colonialism*, pp. 329–330.

sodomitical practices and Islam'.[93] Jeremy Bentham, for example, stated
in the late eighteenth century (published 1838) that 'even now, wherever
the Mahometan religion prevails, such practices ["crimes against nature"]
seem to be attended with but little disrepute'.[94] This link was reinforced in
travel writing and informed anxieties about the sexual 'corruption' of
Europeans stationed in Islamic countries for military and trading purposes.[95] Particular concern focused on the 'pernicious effects of service in
North Africa, and fraternisation with Arabs on French morals' given the
'widespread visibility of *moeurs arabes* among French regiments during the
occupation of Algiers in 1830'.[96]

Whilst this potent combination of xenophobia and homophobia
could be deployed punitively (Crompton argues that the accusation of
un-Englishness was used to justify the severity of 'punishment for the
individual who strayed so far from the national norm' in practising
sodomy[97]), personal accounts show that this ideology could be enabling
and liberating. The textual othering of homosexuality as a foreign vice
permitted, as Schneider has suggested, 'representation [which] was not
seen as a threat at all'.[98] Thus, a writer like Byron could consciously
draw on a shared cultural imagination of Oriental homosexuality,
selecting very specific settings 'as a means of alerting his reader to the
"queer" possibilities at work in the text'. As Schneider argues, 'it is
precisely because the Orient is so clearly constructed as a (homo)textual
universe that such a hermeneutic is possible'.[99]

A parallel argument can be made for Dickens's repeated selection of
Egypt as queer locale. Dickens was imaginatively engaged with
homoerotic Orientalism, especially as routed through the figure of
Byron and explicit translations of the *Arabian Nights*, which had such
a rich effect on his imagination. Contemporary interests in Egyptian
antiquities, geography, and trade, did not displace the longer association
of the Orient with sex between men, a link suggestively reinforced for

[93] Rudi Bleys, *The Geography of Perversion* (New York and London: Cassell, 1996),
p. 163.
[94] The *Works of Jeremy Bentham*, ed. John Bowring, 11 vols. (1838–43, repr. New
York: Russell and Russell, 1962), I, p. 175.
[95] For bibliography of nineteenth-century travel reports of Arab same-sex praxis
see Bleys, p. 112.
[96] Aldrich *Colonialism*, p. 329, Bleys, p. 112.
[97] Crompton, p. 55.   [98] Schneider, p. 85.   [99] Schneider, p. 93.

Dickens in some of his most cherished literature. Though the homo-erotic content of *The Arabian Nights* was yet to be explicitly revealed in Burton's infamous translation (published fifteen years after Dickens's death), like Byron's about-to-become-public-knowledge bisexuality, awareness of this material can be seen to circulate as an open secret during the period of Dickens's career. The importance of the medieval Persian classic to Dickens's imagination is apparent from the wealth of quotation and allusion from this work throughout his fiction. As Sanders puts it, 'these tales kept his fancy, like David Copperfield's, alive and spurred "the hope of something beyond" the limits of place and unhappy times. The "beyondness" of these stories seems always to have been associated with the exotic and the wonderful, with magic and luxury.'[100] Michael Slater continues this dissociation of the erotic from the Arabian exotic, despite the powerful conceptual link between the two in Victorian culture: 'The strong erotic element in the *Nights* tends to disappear [. . .] in Dickens's fond reminiscences about them.'[101] As Muhsin Jassim Ali documents, however, anxiety about the sexual mate-rial of these tales was repeatedly expressed during Dickens's lifetime in reactions to Galland's translation as 'coarse' and 'indecent'.[102] Signifi-cantly, Dickens gives fulsome praise to this edition in the opening of his satire 'The Thousand and One Humbugs', apparently rejecting prudish calls for further bowdlerization.[103] Competing calls 'for a faithful but decorous version' drew national attention to the perceived sexual ex-cesses of the *Nights*. Robert Fergerson, for example, paradoxically called for a complete *Nights* in 1825, but quickly restricted the demand to only the 'translatable' tales, 'for some of the *escapades* of the Asiatic writers are too free for our Northern ears'.[104] Thus knowledge of the sexual content of the *Nights* circulated along with a wider cultural linkage of the Orient and same-sex praxis, making this text, as Boone suggests, a powerful player in queer imaginaries:

---

[100] Sanders, p. 133.
[101] Michael Slater 'Dickens in Wonderland', in *The Arabian Nights in English Literature*, ed. Peter Caracciolo (Basingstoke: Macmillan, 1988), pp. 130–42, p. 133.
[102] Muhsin Jassim Ali, *Scheherazade in England* (Washington DC: Three Continents Press, 1981), p. 120.
[103] 'The Thousand and One Humbugs', *Household Words*, 21 April 1855, repr. *Dickens's Journalism*, III, p. 292.
[104] Ali, p. 120.

This work has served, since its transmission to the West in 1704, as one of the subliminal conduits through which the myth of a homoerotic Near East has entered Western consciousness [...] The presence of same sex relations – however obscured by reticent translators before Sir Richard Burton – has inspired the imaginative *and* actual journeys of a countless number of adept gay or bisexual readers-between-the-lines such as William Beckford, Lord Byron and Pierre Loti, for whom these tales, like the Arabic Orient itself, has always promised an outlet for sexual energies suppressed within homophobic European culture.[105]

In *Great Expectations* Dickens demonstrates his own participation in this wider queer interpretation of *Arabian Nights*, structuring the emotional and physical intensity of Pip's relationship with Herbert around an imaginative and actual journey to Egypt: '[Herbert] could sketch airy pictures of himself conducting Clara Barley to the land of the Arabian Nights, and of me going out to join them (with a caravan of camels I believe) and of our all going up the Nile and seeing wonders' (p. 416). Just as the anticipated death of the stricken Eugene facilitates the most explicit declarations of love between men in Dickens's next novel, *Our Mutual Friend*, Herbert's impending departure to run his company's eastern office in Cairo incites a male crisis of separation, enabling Pip's admission that with the loss of Herbert he 'felt as if [his] last anchor were loosening its hold' (p. 416). Herbert's leave taking of the man he pet-names 'Handel' permits an even greater revelation of mutual feeling:

'My dear Handel I shall soon have to leave you [...] We shall lose a fine opportunity if I put off going to Cairo, and I am very much afraid I must go, Handel, when you most need me.'
'Herbert, I shall always need you, because I shall always love you; but my need is no greater now, than at any other time.'
'You will be so lonely' (p. 449).

Herbert rightly interprets Pip's emotional reliance on him. Herbert's previous business trip to Marseille permits a similar revelation of Pip's otherwise unspoken feeling: 'I was alone, and had a dull sense of being alone [...] I sadly missed the cheerful face and ready response of my

---

[105] Joseph Boone, 'Rubbing Aladdin's Lamp' in *Negotiating Lesbian and Gay Subjects*, ed. Monika Dorenkamp and Richard Henke (New York and London: Routledge, 1995), pp. 149–77, pp. 151–2.

friend' (p. 313). Herbert leaves for Cairo only after urging Pip to 'come to [him]', with reassurances that this is also the ardent desire of his fiancé:

'Clara and I have talked about it again and again,' Herbert pursued, 'and the dear little thing begged me only this evening, with tears in her eyes, to say that if you will live with us when we come together, she will do her best to make you happy, and to convince her husband's friend that he is her friend too. We should get on so well, Handel!' (p. 450)

William Cohen has emphasized the erotic freight of Herbert's 'impulse, almost immediately upon becoming reacquainted with Pip, to christen him "Handel"' in significant relation to 'his own surname, Pocket, the usual receptacle for hands in the novel'.[106] The men's parting permits further emphasis on this suggestive spatial affinity, as Dickens makes it clear that Handel's home is where his Pocket is. After Herbert's departure, Pip returns to their previously shared lodgings: '[I] went to my lonely home – if it deserved the name, for it was now no home to me, and I had no home anywhere' (p. 451). Indeed Herbert's choice of 'Handel for a familiar name' (p. 179) that simultaneously encodes their friendship and Pip's better self – 'We are so harmonious and you have been a blacksmith' (p. 178) – also brings this partnership into line with an established Dickens heritage of alliterative male couples who experience homotropics together (Ben and Bob, Jingle and Job, Martin and Mark). Herbert and Handel have previously fantasized the resolution of their respective financial or emotional embarrassments through emigration. Herbert's dream of evading his debts by 'buying a rifle and going to America, with a general idea of compelling buffaloes to make his fortune' (p. 273) has a darker echo in Pip's longing to flee from Magwitch 'and enlist for India as a private soldier' (p. 338). Here the emotional interdependence of the two men becomes explicit, as neither wish to begin anew in a 'New World' without the support of the other. Pip explicitly acknowledges this mutual emotional reliance, remaining in Britain only because of 'the knowledge that Herbert must soon come back' (p. 338).

Pip, Herbert, and Clara finally settle in a triangular cohabitation in Cairo, forming a trio in which Pip's participation is unsanctioned by familial bonds. This home is reminiscent of the domestic threesome

---

[106] Cohen, *Sex Scandal*, p. 58.

enthusiastically effected through intermarriage by Tom and Ruth Pinch
with John Westlock in *Martin Chuzzlewit*, who agree that without such
a *ménage* 'may that home never be' (p. 765). While a business relation
between Herbert and Pip operates as ostensible rationale, the text firmly
signals the queerness of this household. Pip's earlier intuition that
Herbert 'and his affianced [. . .] had naturally not been very anxious
to introduce [him as] a third person into their interviews' (p. 371),
clearly flags the unusualness of the final triadic arrangement under
which Pip 'lived happily with Herbert and his wife' (p. 480). Indeed,
Peter Brooks has read Pip's final affection for Magwitch 'and his
acceptance of a continuing existence without plot, as celibate clerk for
Clarrikers' in Cairo as the 'real ending' of *Great Expectations*.[107] Pip's
life with Herbert and Clara offers an emigrant experience of a family of
choice, in a reworking of domesticity that promises similar possibilities
to that Gayatri Gopinath attributes to queer diaspora: 'alternative forms
of collectivity and communal belonging that redefine home outside of a
logic of blood, purity, authenticity, and patrilineal descent'.[108]

In Dickens's original ending Pip re-visits England after eight years to
find Estella married, and we assume beyond the realms of the reported
action to return to his domestic contentment in Egypt. The revised,
published ending extends Pip's Egyptian life to eleven years, giving it
greater significance. This deliberately prolonged, settled bachelordom
perhaps adds greater ambiguity to the famously uncertain reunion with
Estella. In both versions Pip firmly states his intention not to marry. On
Biddy's unspecified insistence that 'you must marry', Pip reports Herbert
and Clara's similarly vague lip-service to this conventional ideology: 'So
Herbert and Clara say, but I don't think I shall, Biddy. I have so settled
down in their home, that it's not at all likely. I am already quite an old
bachelor' (p. 481). The reference to marriage as institution rather than any
potential wife exposes the emptiness of this social proscription, combining
suggestively with Pip's self-designation as an 'old bachelor' to emphasize
his departure from a model of family constituted by marriage. This empty
marital model reiterates the social compulsion that propels Pip to seek

[107] Brooks, *Reading*, p. 137.
[108] Gayatri Gopinath, *Impossible Desires: Queer Diasporas and South Asian Public
Cultures* (Durham and London: Duke University Press, 2005), p. 187.

marriage with Biddy, a figure for whom he has previously tried to discipline himself into an appropriate marital enthusiasm:

'If I could only get myself to fall in love with you [...] If I could only get myself to do it, *that* would be the thing for me.'
'But you never will, you see,' said Biddy (p. 131).[109]

It also echoes the sense of unavoidability apparent in Herbert's apologia to Pip for his engagement, a topic he cautiously introduces under the justification that 'the children of not exactly suitable marriages are always most particularly anxious to be married.' His fiancée remains an entirely depersonalized figure who is, by implication, no more significant to Herbert than the partners compulsively selected by his child siblings in precocious alliances of convenience: 'Little Altick in a frock has already made arrangements for his union with a suitable young person at Kew. And indeed, I think we are all engaged, except the baby' (p. 251). The humour here does not detract from the unhappy sense of fatality that pervades this bizarre announcement of what has been assumed to be the crowning achievement of the domestic novel. Indeed, in language suggestive of erotic deflation, Pip observes that his friend had 'become curiously crestfallen and meek, since we had entered on the interesting theme' (p. 252). Throughout the rest of the novel Clara's appeal to Herbert as someone 'so much needing protection' is undermined through similarly negative narration. Pip, for example, uses litotes, a double negative rhetoric, to describe the engagement as one he 'would not have undone [...] for all the money in the pocket book' (p. 376).

The textually celebrated union of Herbert and Pip in Egypt is in sharp contrast to their unenthusiastic attempts to enter matrimony. This continued cohabitation of intimate male friends, despite one's marriage (and that not to his friend's sister!) is unique in Dickens's fiction, and only possible outside the more rigid parameters of British domesticity. Egypt as a queer signifier, like the other eroticized terrains discussed here, renders the homoerotic dynamic of this relationship visible at the moment of expulsion from Britain. Emigration plots allow for an exploration of queer desires that do not cohere with

---

[109] See also J. M. Léger on Pip's unconvincing 'fiction' of desire for Biddy ('The Scrooge in the Closet', p. 210).

domestic life scripts, providing a space for the narratives of wilful itinerants such as Miss Wade. Homotropics are a significant component in Dickens's delineation of same-sex desire, and present an important balance to Dickens's affirmative explorations of homoerotic strategies which allow same-sex relationships to be lived within Britain.

5

'It is impossible to be gentler':
The Homoerotics of Nursing
in Victorian Culture

This chapter explores Dickens's strategic queer use of nursing, an intensely eroticized practice in his culture. Nursing reformers, from the 1840s onwards, anxiously debated the sexual dangers and temptations of this new profession at the same time as respectable novelists deployed nursing as a staple courtship narrative and pornographers cashed in on the imaginative possibilities of medical drama. Throughout Dickens's novels same-sex nursing operates as a central, reiterated behaviour through which both male and female characters legitimate their physical contact and express their excitement at such intimate touching. While Dickens's scenes of male nursing draw on a cultural eroticization of nursing for their sexual suggestiveness, such treatment also queers twenty-first-century understandings of Victorian gender divisions, asking us to reassess categories of masculinity, femininity and emotional and tactile literacy. Literary and historical instances of male nursing, as well as wider forms of restorative male tactility with which the next chapter is concerned, have tended to get under a critical radar more attuned to acts of masculine aggression. In these two chapters I will suggest that Dickens's career long preoccupation with the gentle, often nursing, male reflects a much broader, historically elided, Victorian concern with tender masculinities. I endeavour to rethink the interrelated categories of masculinity and male homoeroticism through scrutiny of the previously under-examined figure of the tactile man. I will suggest that the extremely tender expressions of desire offered in Dickens's scenes of same-sex nursing provide an alternative frame of interpretation to that passed forward by the influential homoerotic violence thesis, outlined in the introduction to this project. Through an exploration of the Victorian sexualization of nursing I will argue that Dickens deploys this eroticizing of nurse/patient roles throughout his fiction to develop more affirmative, tender strategies for articulating same-sex desire.

Widely circulating concerns about the gendered erotics of nursing constitute the sickbed as another culturally eroticized realm. It comes as little surprise that many of the Victorian narratives that explore the homotropical possibilities of spatially and socially alternative domesticities are also interested in the sick-room setting, which was similarly experienced as a space of relaxed mores, and provided opportunities for societal and familial refashioning. Catherine Judd, Alison Bashford, and Miriam Bailin have detailed the heterosexual possibilities of the nineteenth-century actual and literary sickroom, a space in which, as Bailin observes, 'confidences are exchanged, clothes removed or readjusted, soothing caresses administered to aching limbs, and basic wants given utterance – all of this within the bedroom turned sickroom, a site suggestive of the intimacies which those activities both disguise and express'.[1] Bailin also provides compelling accounts of the alternative communities and family groupings that sufferers such as Florence Nightingale and Harriet Martineau were able to gather around them in their sickrooms, in preference to their relatives by blood or marriage. While the sickroom could operate as permissive, tangential site of familial refashioning and sexual license, the very familiarity of fictional and biographical sickroom narratives shows this, at the same time, to be a central, staple experience of Victorian culture. While homotropical narratives found queer spaces by going outside of British domestic experience, the sickroom, as a permissive space *within* the Victorian household, provided home-ground for practical and imaginative reworkings of sexuality, gender, and social relationships.

Dickens as both eminent sufferer and his family's principal domestic nurse (as documented in his daughters' enthusiastic testimonies) had a personal appreciation of the transformative power of such physical

---

[1] Miriam Bailin, *The Sickroom in Victorian Fiction* (Cambridge: Cambridge University Press, 1994), p. 23. See also Catherine Judd, *Bedside Seductions: Nursing and the Victorian Imagination, 1830–1880* (Basingstoke: Macmillan, 1998), pp. 33–4; Alison Bashford *Purity and Pollution: Gender Embodiment and Victorian Medicine* (Basingstoke: Macmillan, 1998).

care in intimate relationships. He was never entirely robust in health; he recounted that he was a 'delicate' child 'soon hurt, bodily or mentally', and suffered throughout his life from 'violent spasmodic attacks'.[2] Ackroyd suggests a very plausible psychological dimension to these attacks, which have been variously put down to kidney stones, renal colic or epilepsy: 'In Dickens's case, these youthful spasms or fits of agony seem frequently to have occurred at times of crisis or anxiety.'[3] In the autobiographical fragment printed in Forster's biography, Dickens recounts enduring a particularly acute instance of his 'old attacks of spasm' when working at Warren's Blacking factory as a child:

Bob Fagin was very good to me on the occasion of a bad attack of my old disorder. I suffered such excruciating pain that time, that they made a temporary bed of straw in my old recess in the counting-house, and I rolled about on the floor, and Bob filled empty blacking-bottles with hot water and applied relays of them to my side half the day. I got better, and quite cosy towards evening, but Bob (who was much bigger and older than I) did not like the idea of my going home alone, and took me under his protection.[4]

Dickens's reaction to what he viewed as a forced companionship with Bob and the other boys labouring at the blacking warehouse has always been read as one of great shame, worked out through the attribution of Bob's surname to one of his most unpalatable figures.[5] Buckton reads Dickens's accounts of the blacking factory as a discourse of shame deriving from the '"low" company in which he had been observed', 'the companionship he has [had] to endure' and 'the unsettling intimacy of male bodies with which it [...was] associated'.[6] However, the physical intimacy that Dickens experienced under the protective Bob's gentle attentions to his suffering body is given a more positive reincarnation in the many depictions of tender male nursing in Dickens's fiction.

---

[2] Ackroyd, p. 68, p. 49.　　[3] Ackroyd, p. 50.

[4] Forster, *The Life of Charles Dickens*, I, p. 40.

[5] See, for example, Ackroyd: 'Although it seems that even by Dickens's own account Bob Fagin was gentle and considerate to him, his very presence evoked a horror greater than any gratitude Dickens might have felt – the horror of being part of the poor' (p. 78).

[6] Buckton, 'The Reader Whom I Love', p. 196.

MARTIN CHUZZLEWIT AND THE HIDDEN
HISTORY OF MALE NURSING

Reflecting both the health hazards of overseas travel and different national attitudes towards the gendering of nursing, Dickens's novels continue a long-association of same-sex nursing with foreign travel or relocation. In *Pickwick* both emigrant pairs, discussed in detail in the previous chapter, are associated with the illness that was a typical concomitant to travel to 'the frontier'.[7] Job anticipates the health risks of life in the Caribbean, fearing that Jingle could be 'carried off by the fever' (p. 703), while in Demerara medical students Ben and Bob 'each had the yellow fever fourteen times' (p. 753). In *Martin Chuzzlewit* Dickens was to develop these brief references into a thorough exploration of the camaraderie and support between men that was central to survival in perilous overseas locations.

Dickens would have been particularly aware of the benefits of good health when writing *Martin Chuzzlewit* after his miserable affliction on voyages across the Atlantic. In *American Notes* Dickens offers a hyperbolic account of his suffering, describing himself as 'excessively sea-sick': 'Not sea-sick, be it understood, in the ordinary acceptation of the term: I wish I had been: but in a form which I have never seen or heard described.'[8] Dickens's particular concern with health after this experience is apparent in his inclusion, in the travelogue, of an impassioned call for legislation to ensure a medical attendant on cross-Atlantic ships. He hoped that this would alleviate the 'sickness of adults, and deaths of children on the passage', which he had observed as 'matters of the very commonest occurrence' (p. 224).

Having survived a bilious sea voyage, Mark Tapley and the younger Martin Chuzzlewit set up home in another exemplary site of sickness. Through mutual nursing these men are able to save one another from the fatal pestilence of Eden. The tenderness of this (yet another!)

---

[7] Aldrich qualifies his celebration of the erotic possibilities of the colonies, acknowledging that the prevalence of tropical hazards and potentially fatal diseases meant that such locations were 'not homosexual paradise' (*Colonialism*, p. 408).

[8] Charles Dickens, *American Notes and Pictures from Italy* (London: Oxford University Press, 1957), p. 13.

alliterative pair in the 'New World' (anti-)paradise has a suggestive resonance with more explicitly homoeroticized locations. Andrew Sanders notes that 'Eden was almost certainly based on Cairo, Illinois. "Dismal Cairo" appears in *American Notes* as a "hotbed of disease, an ugly sepulchre"'.[9] Indeed this seems very likely, given Dickens's repeated horrified references to this location, which he also describes as 'the detestable morass called Cairo' and 'ill-fated Cairo' in the travelogue (pp. 187, 246). On their return, Mark reinforces this oblique link between locations, describing 'the Atlantic ocean and the Red Sea [as] being, in that respect, all one' (p. 619). This reference to Egypt allows the homotropical connotations of this site to attach to Martin and Mark's transatlantic experience. Their Eden sojourn brings together two forms of queer space, as Dickens unites the possibilities of homotropics with those of the sickroom.[10]

Dickens was particularly appalled by the fetid and often fatal conditions that settlers around the Mississippi had to endure. He visited a woman in 'this blighted place' who had watched 'her children, one by one, die here of fever, in the full prime and beauty of their life' (*American Notes*, p. 186). The centrality of Dickens's concern with public health is demonstrated in the final remarks of *American Notes*, which focus on the need for 'common precautions' to avoid unnecessary illness in a country of 'so many great rivers, and such opposite varieties of climate' (p. 251). Linda Sabin has explored the range of male nursing practised in this Mississippi region during the nineteenth century. She documents the work of the Howard Association, founded in the early 1830s to give relief during the numerous epidemics of this period. Members would 'organise relief, hire nurses, and in many cases give temporary nursing care themselves'.[11] Sabin records the mutual nursing undertaken by male volunteers who cared for one another as they also sickened in the 1843 yellow fever epidemic at Rodney, Mississippi. It is likely that Dickens would have been familiar with such

---

[9] Sanders, 'The Dickens World', p. 141.
[10] See the previous chapter for a full discussion of the exoticizing and (homo) eroticizing of specific overseas locations, including Egypt. In *Great Expectations*, which will be discussed fully later, Pip and Herbert Pocket experience the parallel liberations of both London sickroom and Egyptian domesticity.
[11] Linda Sabin, 'Unheralded Nurses: Male Care Givers in the Nineteenth Century South', *Nursing History Review* 5 (1997), 131–48, p. 134.

organizations, making Eden/Cairo the perfect, feverish site for the reciprocal care of Mark and Martin.

On Dickens's travels in both America and on the Continent he encountered instances of unofficial and more organized male nursing. In the prison at Philadelphia he witnessed male inmates nursing one another: 'Some two or three had prisoner nurses with them, for they were very sick; and one, a fat old negro whose leg had been taken off within the jail had for his attendant a classical scholar and an accomplished surgeon, himself a prisoner likewise.'[12] This use of the prison population to nurse one another was similar to the practice employed in sex-segregated institutions in Britain at this time.[13] From his visits to establishments such as prisons and workhouses Dickens was aware of institutional practices of male nursing.

During the nineteenth century men were increasingly pushed to the margins of nursing in Britain. Although, as Carolyn Mackintosh argues, 'men have had a place in nursing for as long as records are available', 'their contribution has been perceived as negligible, largely because of the dominant influence that the nineteenth-century female nursing movement has had on the occupation's historical ideology'.[14] In what he identifies as 'the first book written about and for men in nursing' Chad O' Lynn discusses the historical lack of recognition of male nurses, and the difficulties this causes for the men who comprise 5.4 per cent (about 10 per cent in the UK) of the US nursing profession today.[15] Histories of

---

[12] *American Notes*, pp. 103–4. *Pictures from Italy* includes accounts of various nursing fraternities. Dickens describes the Cappucini Monks as 'the best friends of the people. They seem to mingle with them more immediately, as their counsellors and comforters, and to go among them more when they are sick' (p. 296). Similarly, he records that one of the 'commonest offices' of secular, egalitarian 'brotherhood', Campagnia della Misericordia, was 'to attend and console the sick'. Members of this fraternity also administered to victims of accidents: 'their office is to raise the sufferer and bear him tenderly to hospital' (p. 431).

[13] See Carolyn Mackintosh, 'A Historical Study of Men in Nursing', *Journal of Advanced Nursing* 26.2 (1997), 232–6.

[14] Mackintosh, p. 232. For a history of male nursing in ecclesiastical movements (such as those observed by Dickens in Italy) and in the hospitals of the Byzantine Empire see Vern Bullough, 'Men in Nursing', *Journal of Professional Nursing* 10.5 (1995), p. 267.

[15] Chad O'Lynn and Russell E. Tranbarger, (eds), *Men in Nursing: History Challenges and Opportunities* (New York: Springer, 2007), opening dedication. Figures from 2000 taken from Chad O'Lynn, 'Men Working as Rural Nurses: Land of Opportunity' in *Rural Nursing: Concepts, Theory and Practice*, ed. Helen Lee and Charlene Winters (New

nursing have understandably been dominated by approaches that value the profession as a historically rare space in which could be celebrated for developing skills and careers. As Vern Bullough (and others) have suggested, nursing discourses that constitute women as ' "natural" care-givers and healers' 'helped women break through the male monopolies of power and establish what came to be regarded as a woman's profession'.[16] Foremost icon of 'New' or reformed nursing, Florence Nightingale, was invested in simultaneously professionalizing and feminizing nursing, making it a more respectable field of work for women to enter. Although in her *Notes on Nursing: What It is and What it is Not* (1859) she challenged the idea of a natural, untrained aptitude for nursing, providing guidance on 'the proper use of fresh air, light, warmth, cleanliness, quiet' etc., she firmly gendered such provision: 'Every woman is a nurse.'[17] Indeed, in her critique of military hospitals, Nightingale strongly implied that male was precisely what nursing 'is not' or should not be:

I solemnly declare that I have seen or known of fatal accidents, such as suicides in *delirum tremens*, bleedings to death, dying patients dragged out of bed by drunken Medical Staff corps men, and many other things less patent and striking, which would not have happened in London civil hospitals nursed by women. [. . .] Were a trustworthy *man* in charge of each ward [. . .] the thing would not, in all probability have happened. But were a trustworthy *woman* in charge of the ward, or set of wards, the thing would not, in all certainty have happened.[18]

Nightingale developed this attitude in her correspondence, celebrating reforms that 'take all power over the nursing out of the hands of men, and put it into the hands of one female trained head'.[19] This was certainly not an unchallenged view; it was contested by a variety of contemporary accounts (discussed later in this chapter) that repre-sented the sympathy and efficiency of male nurses, especially in battle-field contexts. Attention to the way that nursing reforms enabled

York: Springer, 2006), pp. 232–47, p. 233 and Christine McCarthy, 'Nursing a Female Bias', BBC News, 12 May 2000, http://news.bbc.co.uk/1/hi/uk/746218.stm.
    [16] Vern Bullough, 'Men, Women, and Nursing History', *Journal of Professional Nursing*, 10.3 (1994), p. 127.
    [17] Florence Nightingale, *Notes on Nursing: What it is and What it is Not* (London: Duckworth, 1970), p. 6, preface.
    [18] Nightingale, *Notes*, p. 23.
    [19] Quoted in B. M. Dossey, *Florence Nightingale: Mystic, Visionary, Healer* (Spring-house PA: Springhouse, 1996), p. 291.

a professionalization of a (largely) female work force has meant that there is almost no research into the histories and often complex representations of male nurses, many of whom provided such physical ministration under different names. Throughout the nineteenth century male orderlies, corps men, and attendants performed nursing duties before and alongside the 'New' nurse in both general and military hospitals as well as dominating the profession in asylums.[20]

Bashford has further suggested that the symbolism deployed by the interrelated movements for sanitary and nursing reform excluded men to mobilize potent gendered images of the new nurse as a 'middle-class figure of efficiency, neatness and whiteness': 'The story of old and new nurses resonated far more deeply around issues of purity and pollution if constructed in terms of a shift between types of women, types of female bodies' (pp. 21, 33). The story of Victorian nursing reform is regularly cast as a classed replacement of Sairey Gamp, the caricatured 'Old' working-class nurse of Dickens's *Martin Chuzzlewit*, by the (upper-) middle-class lady with the lamp, Florence Nightingale.[21] In *Chuzzlewit*,

---

[20] Judd briefly acknowledges this enormous omission (p. 160), and Fiedler, (p. 102) and Bashford (pp. 93–4) recognize the gradual replacement of male nurses, and orderlies while maintaining a focus on the 'new' women of nursing. On the proliferation of men in asylum nursing see Mackintosh, p. 238 and David Wright, 'The Dregs of Society? Occupational Patterns of Male Asylum Attendants in Victorian England', *International History of Nursing Journal* 1.4 (1996), 5–20. Wright's work on the Earlswood Asylum for Idiots, near Redhill in Surrey, challenges the belief that men, particularly ex-soldiers, were hired to fulfil a need for strong-armed men to physically control patients. At Earlswood, where the majority of new inmates were children below age twelve, Wright identifies a variety of other pragmatic benefits provided by a labour supply of ex-soldiers as 'a reserve of unmarried men, already of similar pay and expectations, who had been disciplined to long hours and monotonous work' (p. 10). Using treatment and dismissal records, he also disputes the preconception that such attendants were more likely to treat patients with roughness or brutality. For an account of the very gradual feminizing of military nursing see Anne Summers, *Angels and Citizens: British Women as Military Nurses, 1854–1914* (London: Routledge, 1988): 'Twenty-five years after the Crimean War, the British army employed barely a dozen female nurses. In 1898, a year before the Anglo-Boer War, there were still only seventy-two' (p. 2). As Summers notes, for most of the nineteenth century 'the regular Army Nursing Service was almost hidden from public view' (p. 2).

[21] See Bashford, (p. 21), Judd (p. 34) and Tooley. Tooley argues that 'what *Uncle Tom's Cabin* was to the abolition movement, *Martin Chuzzlewit* was to nursing reform' (p. 46) and Toshikatsu Murayama justly describes Gamp as 'the most famous or notorious nurse in English literature.' Toshikatsu Murayama, 'A Professional Contest Over the Body: Quackery and Respectable Medicine in *Martin Chuzzlewit*', *Victorian Literature and Culture* 30.2 (2002), 403–20, p. 403. Whilst Gamp was most often held

Dickens uses the infamous figures of hired nurses, Gamp and her hospital nursing friend Betsy Prig, to heighten the importance of effective, loving nursing. In this novel he calls for the eradication of 'disciples of the Prig school of nursing (who are very numerous among professional ladies)' (p. 666). As Toshikatsu Murayama observes, 'no doctor or nurse can give proper treatment to the numerous sick people in this text full of physical disorders.'[22] In old Martin Chuzzlewit's choice of Mary as medical attendant, Murayama notes the preference for amateur nursing over all the text's suspect official medical practitioners. The majority of amateur, unpaid nursing in the novel is, however, performed by men. Dickens's counter to Sairey Gamp, in a novel deeply concerned with health and sanitation, is not a middle-class Nightingalesque woman, but a cross-class act of mutual male care. In examining Martin's moral rehabilitation at the hands of his servant Mark Tapley, I will begin to make a case (which is continued in the next chapter's attention to *Bleak House*'s gentle General George and the figure of Joe Gargery as healing blacksmith in *Great Expectations*) for Dickens's use of tactile care to expand the social category of the gentle man. Male nursing narratives, I will suggest, cross and complicate boundaries of class, gender, and sexuality.

Dickens's treatment of male nursing in *Martin Chuzzlewit* is fitting, given the novel's simultaneous concern with care of the body, corporeality, and with a wide range of variously eroticized male bonds. Participating in the wider fascination with embodiment in Victorian studies, various recent commentators have observed that this novel's 'fictional landscape is filled with bodies, often dismembered or fragmented.'[23] Lougy reads *Martin Chuzzlewit* as a subversive Bakhtinian assault on the integrity of an 'entirely finished, completed, strictly limited body' and

---

up as a demonic figure of all that was bad about unreformed nursing, it is important to recognize the enabling effect she had for some actual female nurses such as Louisa Alcott. Alcott frames *Hospital Sketches* with a Sairy Gamp quote and makes comic comparison between herself and Gamp throughout, alleviating the horrors of military hospital through humour: '[I go] armed with lavender water, with which I so bespinkled myself and the premises, that, like my friend, Sairy, I was soon known among my patients as the nurse with the bottle'. Louisa M. Alcott, *Hospital Sketches* (1863 repr. Massachusetts: Harvard University Press, 1960), p. 29.

[22] Murayama, p. 403.
[23] Lougy, 'Repressive and Expressive Forms', p. 39.

Bowen sees it as 'a text persistently troubled by the limits of the human, by people who may be monsters or animals or machines'.[24] The Martin/ Mark dyad is part of an interconnecting set of intimate male attachments that Dickens explores within this fleshy novel; he also devotes considerable attention to Martin's relationship with Tom Pinch, and Tom's own prolonged domestic intimacy with John Westlock.[25]

The lovable, ostensibly selfless Mark Tapley enlists himself in Martin's service when Martin is at his lowest ebb. Though the novel provides a variety of explanations for Mark's attention to Martin, they uniformly fail to convince. As Barickman *et al.* observe, 'Tapley's "humour", the idea that marriage to Mrs Lupin would be so pleasant that he could take no credit for his cheerfulness, is another contrivance to avoid the perils of traditional sexual roles and rituals in this society.'[26] Mark abandons the conventional domestic comforts offered by Mrs Lupin to follow Martin, endeavouring to justify Martin's magnetic effect on him through recourse to normative romance structures. However, Mark's chivalrous resolve to deserve Mary Graham's commendation through good service to her beloved fails to satisfy, only placing a further strain on the fiction of Mary as provoking the desires of all those men whose primary commitments are evidently to other men (p. 235).[27] Indeed the explanation that Mark offers to Martin clearly dramatizes his under-motivation: 'Here I am with a liking for what is venturesome, and a liking for you, and a wish to come out strong under circumstances as would keep other men down: and will you take me, or will you leave me' (p. 225). Mark's desire 'to come out strong' (which has him writing 'jolly' on a slate in the extremity of his illness, p. 498), is

[24] Lougy, 'Repressive and Expressive Forms', p. 39; Bowen, *Other Dickens*, p. 211.
[25] As discussed in Chapter 3, Dickens allows Tom and John to form the most effective in law bond of his canon.
[26] Barickman *et al.*, *Corrupt Relations*, p. 106. Mrs Lupin, another widowed landlady, offers the same ideal of womanly provision that (as discussed in Chapter 2) characterized the litigious Mrs Bardell of *The Pickwick Papers*. Mark's initial flight from her in favour of male company parallels Pickwick's horror at the prospect of marriage, even to one who exhibits exemplary wife material.
[27] In her relation to the interconnected male attachments of Tom Pinch, Martin, and Mark, the figure of Mary (similarly to that of Rosa Bud in *Edwin Drood*) acts as a sponge that absorbs their aberrant desires through their professions of longing for her. Ultimately she becomes oversaturated, the novel implying the insufficiencies of exclusive heterosexuality through a simple numbers game which loads three men (or four, counting the audacious Pecksniff) onto only one woman.

here shown to operate in other modes than the comic. As a figure whose actions are always avowedly under-motivated, Mark exploits his reputation for apparently arbitrary action to sanction his particular interest in the man he has a 'liking for'.

Estranged from both his wealthy grandfather and from Pecksniff the pretender, Martin is literally succoured by Mark's generous care: '[T]here was something in the fellow's merry face, and in his manner – which with all its cheerfulness was far from being obtrusive or familiar – that quite disarmed him. He had lived a solitary life too, for many weeks, and the voice was pleasant in his ear' (p. 224). 'Quite disarmed' by Mark's charms, Martin responds to his proposal with the involuntary compulsion typical in Dickens's accounts of same-sex attachments: 'His anger melted away *in spite of himself*' and 'he *could not help* thinking, either, what a brisk fellow this Mark was, and how great a change he had wrought in the atmosphere of the dismal little room already' (p. 225, p. 226, emphasis added). Though not feminized in speech or looks, Mark eagerly takes on the role of domestic goddess, meriting the description 'brisk' which is usually reserved in Victorian fiction for the 'little woman'. Catering for Martin in the London garret, he extends his role as caring provider on the outward voyage of The Screw to America. On their return journey, Mark's abilities as bodily nurturer are officially acknowledged as he obtains a place as ship's cook.[28] The caring roles of cooking and nursing are attributed to women in the Victorian imaginary, despite being frequently performed by men. Importantly, the rare accounts of male nursing that do exist support Dickens's representations of gentle, intuitive, masculine efficiency. Various historical and literary commentators emphasize the sensitivity of these practitioners, destabilizing the gender ideologies through which Victorian

---

[28] In 'The Haunted House' Dickens similarly attributes culinary skill to the male figure who excites particular male approval, making Jack Governor into 'Chief Cook':

I have always regarded Jack as the finest looking sailor that ever sailed. He is grey now, but as handsome as he was a quarter of a century ago – nay, handsomer. A portly, cheery, well-built figure of a broad-shouldered man, with a frank smile, a brilliant dark eye, and a rich dark eyebrow. I remember those under darker hair, and they look all the better for their silver setting (p. 237).

This story also offers the suggestion that the men have endeavoured to resolve such physical admiration through in-lawing: 'Jack once had that bright eye of his on my sister' (p. 241).

and current commentators conventionally ascribe this emotionally literate role to women.

In opposition to Nightingale's critique of the thoughtless brutality of medical corps men, the very differently circumstanced Creole nurse Mary Seacole wrote of the tender care between men that she encountered in the Crimea. Seacole, a skilled and experienced Jamaican nurse whose offer of Crimean service to Nightingale was famously rejected, now receives the attention she deserves for her remarkable independent venture to the Crimea. There from the base of her general store, eatery and sometime makeshift hospital, 'The British Hotel', she provided the soldiery with much needed provisions, medical care and field nursing. Seacole's Crimean experience contradicted her belief, expressed early in her 1857 memoir and travelogue that 'only women know how to soothe and bless' sickbeds.[29] In the context of the Crimea, Seacole's efforts to gender effective nursing as feminine become destabilized by her frequent acknowledgements of the tenderness of the men she saw caring for their fellow soldiers in appalling conditions, often without basic medical supplies. She speaks, for instance, of 'the Christian sympathy and brotherly love shown by the strong to the weak' at the sick wharf: 'The task was a trying one and familiarity, you might think, would have worn down their keener feelings of pity and sympathy; but it was not so' (p. 88). Coming after her accounts of 'rough bearded men [who would] stand by and cry like the softest-hearted women at the sights of suffering', Seacole's assertion about the biological superiority of a woman's touch seems more than a little strained: 'Only women could have done more than they did who attended to this melancholy duty; and they, not because their hearts could be softer, but because their hands are moulded for this work' (p. 88, p. 90).

Across the Atlantic, Louisa M. Alcott had made similar claims to those of Mary Seacole for the sympathy and tenderness of those men who attended to one another in the military hospital where she nursed during the American Civil War. This was, of course, the arena for the century's only famous male nurse, Walt Whitman, whose particular blend of practical, emotional and erotic response to his patients will be discussed in more detail in the following chapter. It has been estimated

---

[29] Mary Seacole, *The Wonderful Adventures of Mrs Seacole in Many Lands* (London: Penguin, 2005), p. 70.

that as many as seventy-five percent of all nurses in this war were male. As Colin McDuff explains, 'many were enlisted men or convalescing soldiers who were designated to look after their comrades, and as such their aptitude for work varied'.[30] Although Alcott was critical of the use of 'sleepy half-sick' convalescents as nurses, she requested that these be replaced, not with women, but with 'strong, properly trained, and cheerful men'.[31] After the feminization of military nursing had begun to accelerate, Sarah Tooley's 1906 history of British nursing continues the case for the emotional sensitivity of male orderlies of military hospitals, even while acknowledging the possible problems of such personally felt commitment. She describes these men, many of whom were convalescent or retired soldiers, as 'kind and sympathetic to their sick comrades': 'It would not have been easy to persuade an orderly who had fever himself, that he was not qualified to nurse a comrade similarly afflicted.'[32] Tooley even goes on to suggest that the empathy and skills of soldiers and military seamen uniquely equipped them as medical carers:

There was little he could not do for a sick mate on board ship, and experience thus gained made him a useful and intelligent nurse, when drafted into the wards of a hospital. A sailor, too, is so much accustomed to the exercise of skill and ingenuity at sea, that it serves him well on land [. . .] Nelson dying in the cockpit of the *Victory,* had tender and devoted nurses in his brave comrades, who knew how to minister to his needs in the last hour as they had rallied to his call for England's sake.[33]

[30] Colin Macduff, 'Meeting the Mother Man: Rediscovering Walt Whitman, Writer and Nurse', *International History of Nursing Journal* 3.2 (1997–8), 32–44, p. 35. For further details see Susan Reverby, *Ordered to Care: The Dilemma of American Nursing, 1850–1945* (New York: Cambridge University Press, 1987).
[31] Alcott, *Hospital Sketches* pp. 64, 66.
[32] Sarah Tooley, *The History of Nursing in The British Empire* (London: Bousfield, 1906), p. 174.
[33] Tooley, p. 193. Admiral Nelson's dying moments recur in accounts of physical male care. There is both historical legitimation of male tenderness as well as possible homoerotic frisson in Nelson's famous last words, 'Kiss me Hardy', and in the imagined scene of male intimacy and camaraderie surrounding him. Santanu Das has identified moments at which this historical scene of care and sacrifice was invoked by soldiers in the First World War, *Touch and Intimacy in First World War Literature* (Cambridge: Cambridge University Press, 2005), p. 122. See also Das, 'The Dying Kiss: Intimacy and Gender in the Trenches of the First World War', in *The Book of Touch* ed. Constance Classen (Oxford and New York: Berg, 2005), pp. 188–97.

Louisa Alcott records similarly positive experiences of being greatly assisted in her Civil War nursing duties by the unofficial care performed by patients. Alcott rewarded convalescents – such as Fritz, 'the big Russian' – for their timely tenderness:

The Prussian, with a nod and a smile, took the lad [a distressed twelve year old soldier] away to his own bed, and lulled him to sleep with a soothing murmur, like a mammoth humble bee. I liked that in Fritz, and if he ever wondered afterward at the dainties which sometimes found their way into his rations, or the extra comforts of his bed, he might have found a solution of the mystery in sundry persons' knowledge of the fatherly action of that night.[34]

Alcott's description of this action as 'fatherly' suggests her need to dissociate this example of bed sharing from the more homoerotic behaviours of the sickroom. From Alcott's description the ward emerges as a distinctly eroticized space, home to incidents of bodily anxiety (such as her nervousness about washing the men and their embarrassed responses) and intense male relationships, including one that she describes as 'a David and Jonathan sort of friendship': 'The Jonathan who so loved this comely David came creeping from his bed for a last look and word [. . .] They kissed each other, tenderly as women, and so parted for poor Ned [the Jonathan figure here] could not stay to see his comrade die.'[35]

Alcott, as is typical in efforts to delineate male tenderness, falls back on a shared cultural understanding of the sensitivity of women to describe a male emotional intimacy for which there was no masculine metaphor. The lack of nomenclature is similarly apparent in Mary Seacole's description of men crying 'like the softest-hearted women at the sights of suffering'. Their observations of the bodily care that male patients provided for one another, however, consistently challenge this conventional gendering of emotional and tactile literacy.

As his household's principal nurse in times of family sickness, Dickens himself was to complicate the common image of the domestic goddess or ministering angel in the house. His daughters' testimonies to his healing power, suggest that Dickens balanced his supreme

---

[34] Tooley, p. 48.
[35] Tooley, pp. 30–1, p. 49, p. 56. For detail of the erotic currency of 'David and Jonathan' relationships, see Chapter 3.

episodes of suffering (such as his immoderate experience of sea-sickness) with a particular skill for domestic nursing. According to Mamie Dickens's somewhat hyperbolic reminiscences of her father, Dickens had a deft hand for the suffering, and a restorative touch: 'His sympathy, [...] with all pain and suffering, made him quite invaluable in a sick-room. [...] I can remember now, how the touch of his hand – he had the most sympathetic touch – was almost too much sometimes – the help and hope in it making my heart full to overflowing.'[36] Lucinda Hawksley's biography of Dickens's second daughter, Katey, reveals Katey's comparable enthusiasm for being nursed by her father. In a severe childhood illness Katey would only allow her father to attend her, and Dickens pushed aside his rigorous work schedule in order to do so. As Hawksley observes, this reveals, an often less apparent 'compassionate, tender side to his character'.[37] Anne Thackeray Ritchie, who was close friends with Katey from childhood, records a visit to Katey's sickbed when they were young women. She met Dickens coming away from the sickroom: '[Katey] has told me since then that in those miserable days his very coming seemed to bring healing and peace to her as she lay and to quiet the raging fever [...] That curious life giving power of his struck me then no less than always before.'[38]

Dickens endeavoured also to exert his 'curious life giving power' through mesmerism, most famously providing what was intended to be a therapeutic course over several months for Madame de la Rue. Dickens had observed the apparent curative effects of the practice at first hand, witnessing John Elliotson's mesmeric operations at University College Hospital in 1838. From the 1840s to the end of the century mesmerism was widely recommended as a form of treatment for ailing family members. As Alison Winter points out, the domestic sickroom was viewed as a particularly appropriate space for mesmerism, which usually involved movements that skimmed over the body: 'the intimate bodily contact involved in producing the magnetic trance was less a breach of propriety when it was carried out within the sickroom,

---

[36] Mamie Dickens, *My Father as I Recall Him*, 1897, ch. 1.

[37] Lucinda Hawksley, *Katey: The Life and Loves of Dickens's Artist Daughter* (London: Random House, 2006), p. 39.

[38] Anne Thackeray Ritchie, 'Charles Dickens as I Remember Him', *Pall Mall Magazine* 49, March 1912. Collected in *From the Porch* (New York: Charles Scribner's Sons, 1914), p. 42.

because the invalid was used to extensive physical contact with nurses and other care givers'.[39] Dickens succeeded in his first effort at mesmerism on his wife, Catherine, first making the attempt on the tour of America that provided material and inspiration for *American Notes* and *Martin Chuzzlewit,* and where Dickens, presumably, felt at greater liberty to risk potential failure. His most extended mesmeric endeavours were also conducted overseas. Dickens mesmerized Madame de la Rue in December 1844 and January 1845 in Genoa, then over some weeks from a distance as he concentrated on his patient at set times on his Italian tour; he returned to Genoa for further more proximate treatment sessions from April to June. Catherine Dickens's understandable jealousy of the mutual reliance between 'humble servant and physician' and 'patient' (as Dickens termed himself and Madame de la Rue), and the later accusations that this relationship had an erotic dimension, accusations which Dickens flatly denied, showed the sexual currency that attached similarly to acts of mesmerism and of nursing.[40] As Kaplan puts it, 'in the public mind, potential sexual power and exploitation were implicit in the relationship between the operator and his subject, between the strong willed Victorian male and the potentially hysterical female'.[41] Though mesmeric relationships could be differently gendered – indeed Dickens had apparent success in aiding the recovery of his artist friend, John Leech, after an accident – the wealth of visual depictions of male practitioners and female patients at this time reflect the imaginative gendering of these positions.[42] Through the responses to his treatment of Madame de la Rue, Dickens acquired a personal insight into the erotic connotations of practitioner/patient relations.

Dickens was perceived to have, and certainly believed he possessed, a particular aptitude for healing. Perhaps drawing upon a personal experience of the diverse gratifications of the sickroom as a site for (variously) sympathy, reconciliation, power relations, and sexual frisson, Dickens bestows the power of 'sympathetic touch', as Mamie Dickens might describe it, upon numbers of male nursing heroes throughout his

[39] Alison Winter, *Mesmerized: Powers of Mind in Victorian Britain* (Chicago: University of Chicago Press, 1998).
[40] Kaplan, *Dickens and Mesmerism,* p. 77.
[41] Kaplan, *Dickens and Mesmerism,* pp. 34–5.
[42] See Kaplan on Dickens's mesmerism of Leech, p. 71.

career. In his fiction Dickens presents an idealized vision of curative contact between men, which heals ruptures beyond the physical.

'DEVOTED TO HIM HEART AND HAND': EDENIC MALE NURSING

In Eden, a terrain that precludes more conventional forms of care, Mark Tapley and Martin Chuzzlewit offer one another crucial, life-preserving nursing. Eden is another site on the remotest edge of the social. The water and 'black ooze' (p. 363) that threaten to submerge this sickly settlement anticipate the lubricity of the 'oozy' port, menaced by 'the undermining and besieging sea', that Miss Wade selects as her home with Harriet. Dickens describes America in his travel writing as a country 'which our vagabonds do so particularly favour', reworking this description in *Little Dorrit* where Calais appears as gathering place for 'French vagabonds and English outlaws'.[43] Though marked as unpleasant unregulated hinterlands, these marginal spaces are variously recouped in Dickens's fiction as sites for the experience of emotional and erotic freedoms. Martin and Mark's fortune-seeking venture as a result of straitened domestic finances qualifies them as economic outcasts, of the type best represented later by the Micawber family. However, their physical intimacy also positions them among the many sexually dissident male emigrants of Dickens's corpus. As with Herbert and Handel later, life overseas allows Martin and Mark to experience an alternative form of domesticity. They 'set up house in the Eden settlement', Barickman *et al.* argue, 'in a masculine travesty of the first marriage relationship'.[44]

Lougy has briefly observed the homoerotic effect of Eden as a wilderness environment that mirrors the common site of male bonding in texts more readily placed in the genre of male quest romance:

One of the most striking differences between the English and the American episodes of the novel is the copious absence of women in the latter. In the male-dominated community of Elijah Pogram, Scadders, Hannibal Chollop, and Major Pawkins, there is no room for Sairy Gamp, Betsy Prig or the numerous female figures that populate the English landscapes of the novel. In part,

---

[43] *American Notes*, p. 77.   [44] Barickman *et al.*, p. 105.

Dickens's images remind us of those homoerotic bonds delineated by nineteenth-century American writers such as Melville, Whitman and Mark Twain.[45]

It is significant that the absent women that Lougy actually names are those that seek to monopolize the potentially lucrative domestic sickbed through their 'one off, one on' method of perpetual attendance (p. 672). Mark and Martin's emigration to the unpromising Eden – 'so choked with slime and matted growth was the hideous swamp which bore that name' (p. 360) – removes them from all female contact, literally delivering them into one another's hands.

As the scene of exclusive male cohabitation and nursing, this site becomes an unlikely Arcadia, paralleling the remote relocation of Smike and Nicholas Nickleby which enables their select caring partnership, away from all possibility of female participation.[46] *Nicholas Nickleby* also offers an important, though much briefer, recognition of the erotics of inter-female nursing. It is, after all, at the time that she is being nursed by Kate that Madeline Bray first desires (to be) a Nickleby. In the same scene that Dickens explores Madeline's confusion of her romantic feeling for the male and female Nickleby siblings (as discussed in Chapter 3) he also details the intensity of sickroom relations: 'Who, slowly recovering from a disorder so severe and dangerous, could be insensible to the unremitting attentions of such a nurse as gentle, tender, earnest Kate? [. . .] What wonder that days became as years in knitting them together?' (p. 680) Or, as Mrs Nickleby puts it, Kate 'has been constantly at Madeline's bedside – never were two people so fond of each other as they have grown' (p. 686).

The homoerotics of this briefer plot of physical care parallel the more central plot of this novel, the action of which largely derives from

[45] Robert Lougy, 'Nationalism and Violence: America in Dickens's *Martin Chuzzlewit*', in *Dickens and the Children of Empire*, pp. 105–15, p. 111. As is typical of existing observations of homoeroticism in Dickens's work, this possibility is quickly side-lined. In the next sentence Lougy abruptly changes direction: 'But something else, I think, is going on as well.'

[46] For the significance and longevity of Arcadian ideals in 'the homosexual literary tradition' see R. S. Fone Byrne, 'This Other Eden: Arcadia and the Homosexual Imagination', pp. 13–34, and Stuart Kellog (ed.), 'The Uses of Homosexuality in Literature' in *Literary Visions of Homosexuality* (Philadelphia: Haworth Press, 1983), pp. 1–12, p. 4. Gregory Woods has discussed the related queer possibilities of desert islands in 'Fantasy Islands: Popular Topographies of Marooned Masculinity' in *Mapping Desire: Geographies of Sexualities*, ed. David Bell and Gill Valentine (New York and London: Routledge, 1995), pp. 126–48.

Nicholas's refusal to watch Smike being beaten. Nicholas intervenes to cut short Squeers's malicious caning, the first blow of which has Smike 'wincing from the lash and uttering a scream of pain' (p. 156). Nicholas's refusal to 'stand by and see it done' – 'Wretch [. . .] touch him at your peril!' – is the catalyst for his exclusive, tender care of Smike throughout the rest of the novel. The men's escape from Dotheboys Hall allows Nicholas to provide Smike with much needed emotional and physical attention. Smike attempts to reciprocate, combining his appreciation of Nicholas's body (discussed in Chapter 3) with solicitude about his physical wellbeing: ' "You grow" said the lad, laying his hand timidly on that of Nicholas, "you grow thinner every day; your cheek is pale, and your eye more sunk. Indeed I cannot bear to see you so, and think how I am burdening you" ' (p. 231). The mutual physical attentiveness of these male friends is underscored by the casting of Smike in a medical role in the Crummles's production of *Romeo and Juliet*. After his debut performance 'Smike was pronounced unanimously, alike by audience and actors, the very prince and prodigy of Apothecaries' (p. 318).

Inevitably it is Smike, rather than Nicholas, who withers away, and whom Nicholas takes into the country to die. This rural relocation creates an exclusive, idyllic site of male nursing. Notably no female carers accompany them from London or are mentioned in their country retreat. Nicholas himself appears to take sole care of his ailing friend, initially driving or walking with him to favourite spots and later wheeling or carrying him into the orchard: 'He had brought Smike out in his arms – poor fellow! A child might have carried him then – to see the sunset, and, having arranged his couch, had taken his seat beside it. He had been watching the whole of the night before, and being greatly fatigued both in mind and body, gradually fell asleep' (p. 713). These practical details of Nicholas's night watching and resulting exhaustion combine with descriptions of him taking 'his old place by the bedside' (p. 715) to create a picture of his assiduous nursing care of his friend.

Despite the unpromising location, the survival of Martin Chuzzlewit and Mark Tapley through mutual nursing triumphantly reworks the ultimately tragic conclusion to *Nickleby's* earlier pastoral idyll, providing a more celebratory image of male care. Martin's sojourn in Eden ostensibly functions as a painful education in humility and selflessness. However, inextricable from these lessons is his eroticized regard for the man who saves him. Martin falls into 'an aggravated kind of fever'

(p. 488), which the ever affectionate Mark responds to with a height-ened compassion: "I said you must be ill', returned Mark tenderly, 'and now I'm sure of it' (p. 366). Mark undertakes 'all his various duties of attendance on Martin', receiving some rudimentary training in nursing from a sickly settler: 'They had some medicine in their chest; and this man of sad experience showed Mark how and when to administer it, and how he could best alleviate the sufferings of Martin' (p. 488). The extremity of Martin's fever as he hovers 'very near his death', effects a revelation of Mark's attachment as he forgets all the irritations of living with Martin: 'He remembered nothing but the better qualities of his fellow-wanderer, and was devoted to him heart and hand' (p. 496). This heartfelt devotion is shown to be mutual when Mark falls ill of the same disease, the fever moving from one male body to the other, causing a reversal of nurse/patient roles: 'Whenever Martin gave him drink or medicine, or tended him in any way, or came into the house returning from some drudgery without, the patient Mr Tapley brightened up, and cried: "I'm jolly, sir: I'm jolly!" ' (p. 496).

Martin's character recovery takes effect through his careful observa-tion and treatment of his laid-up servant:

Now when Martin began to think of this, and to look at Mark as he lay there, never reproaching him by so much as an expression of regret; never murmuring; always striving to be manful and staunch; he began to think, how it was that this man who had had so few advantages, was so much better than he who had had so many? And attendance on a sick bed, but especially the sick bed of one whom we have been accustomed to see in full activity and vigour, being a great breeder of reflection, he began to ask himself in what they differed (p. 496).

Martin's soul searching legitimizes his close scrutiny of his patient, and admiration of Mark's efforts to be 'manful and staunch'. That character recuperation is effected through Martin's nursing of the man who had nursed him, suggests than male tenderness is both a physical practice, which can be learnt, and a transmissible affect, which can be caught.[47] Dickens's sickrooms, in which nurse/patient relations are frequently reversed, provide exemplary sites for this kind of contagion, as his

---

[47] For debates about the transmissibility of modes of feeling see Teresa Brennan, *The Transmission of Affect* (Ithaca: Cornell University Press, 2004), and Lisa Blackman, 'Is Happiness Contagious?' *New Formations* 63 (2008), 15–32.

male figures acquire new repertoires of tenderness from those men who care for them.

While already circulating connotations of the eroticism of nursing adhere to Mark and Martin's physical intimacy, their relationship also queers a still limited twenty-first-century perception of Victorian gender divisions. As Mary Poovey, Martha Vicinus, and Bashford suggest, nineteenth-century nursing reformers were able to carve this field out as a legitimate space for women's work by emphasizing the supposedly peculiarly feminine qualities of domestic nurturing, and foregrounding religious and philanthropic ideals of self-sacrifice.[48] However, the many male nursing narratives of Victorian literature – of which Dickens's novels are representative – similarly emphasize these qualities, suggesting that for many, nurture was a legitimate masculine quality as well. Mark Tapley risks the ultimate self sacrifice in catching Martin's fever himself, narrowly avoiding the fatal conclusion that Charlotte Yonge reserved for her nursing hero in *The Heir of Redclyffe*. In this 1853 novel (which was hugely popular in the nineteenth century and ran to twenty-two editions in as many years) the hero contracts his patient's fever, and is only able to save his patient at the expense of his own life. Mark Tapley, of course, survives, having benefited from a course of nursing that redeems the man he loves. His effect on Martin is that of moral regeneration, a power typically attributed to ministering middle-class women.

In their mutual nursing Martin and Mark break down the class boundary between servant and served, between 'the new master and the new man'(p. 229) and between 'Chuzzlewit and co' (p. 364) to become partners. Dickens fashions the Edenic sick-chamber as the site for a fantasy of equality and class harmony. When both men recover through the assiduous care of the other, they wait out their passage away from Eden with an intensified, bedtime intimacy: 'Often at night when Mark and Martin were alone, and lying down to sleep, they spoke of home, familiar places, houses, roads and people whom they knew' (p. 499). Nancy Aycock Metz has read homesickness as the central contributor to emigrant illnesses, positioning Eden as the site where

---

[48] As Poovey observes, Nightingale's 'personality traits [including her phenomenal organisational ability and the clout she wielded through her wealth, class position, and a politically influential family] considered 'masculine' or abrasive simply disappeared from popular representations', *Uneven Developments*, p. 172; see also chapters 2 and 3 of Martha Vicinus, *Independent Women: Work and Community for Single Women, 1850–1920* (London: Virago, 1985), especially pp. 86–7.

Martin 'comes face to face with his own nostalgic grief for England, and inextricably for the English domestic ideal'.[49] However, Martin's character-reformation at this wilderness location also provides a critique of the limitations of 'the English domestic ideal'. The explicit liberation of a better and truer self here is mirrored by the more covertly expressed experience of erotic freedom. Aycock's conclusion that Dickens 'harboured the dark suspicion that emigration itself was a malady for which the only cure was "home"'[50], is belied by the repeated assertion throughout Dickens's career that emigration offered scope for much-needed alternative ways of living.

Unusually for Dickens's fiction, Mark and Martin do return 'home', but their negotiation of conventional domesticity is continued beyond their homecoming. On their return the narrative ostensibly works to reprioritize Martin's relationships, re-pairing him with Mary. Martin, however, hardly expresses the ardour of a returning lover, having to be reminded by Mark that his first course of action is 'to see Miss Mary, of course' (p. 518).[51] Moreover, Martin continues to gain his greatest pleasure from pleasing Mark (p. 699) and is unable to suppress frequent hyperbole on the virtues of his friend, focusing on his physical restoration at Mark's hands: 'But for this faithful man [. . . who] has been, throughout, my zealous and devoted friend; but for him, I must have died abroad' (p. 627). Mark similarly provides a moving account of the continued mutuality of their relationship. He offers a staunch denial of any suggestion that Martin may doubt his fidelity: 'We have been that sort of companions in misfortune; that my opinion is, he don't believe a word of it' (p. 746). Given the life-preserving intensity of their overseas connection, Mark and Martin's relation is never fully repatriated. Their companionship tempers the marital structures into which they are

---

[49] Nancy Aycock Metz, '"Fevered with Anxiety for Home": Nostalgia and the New Emigrant in *Martin Chuzzlewit*, *Dickens Quarterly* 18.2 (2001), 49–62, p. 60.

[50] Metz, p. 60.

[51] Martin's insufficient enthusiasm parallels his entire lack of concern at leaving Mary. As Barickman *et al.* observe, on his departure 'young Martin hardly gives a thought to Mary Graham; he seems more intent on fleeing all the pressures of social life in England, including the complexities of sexual relations' (p. 104). Mark is similarly reluctant in his final incorporation into the fabric of the domestic novel through marriage to Mrs Lupin. Mark's surrender to this belated desire smacks of the self-disciplining visible in Pip's hugely postponed proposal to Biddy.

inserted, as Dickens insists on the longevity and superior vibrancy of the male bond. *Martin Chuzzlewit* stringently critiqued American manners and morals. The chapter in which Martin first disembarks in America memorably lampoons the press as 'The New York Sewer', 'The New York Stabber' etc. (p. 249) and immediately rails against political corruption, brawling, materialism and more. Many felt that the novel added insult to the still smarting injury of *American Notes*, in which Dickens's deep disappointment at the operation of fledgling democracy – 'This is not the republic of my imagination', as he famously wrote to Macready[52] – communicated itself most forcefully as personal, somatic horror. While various British travel writings on America expressed distaste for the widespread practice of tobacco chewing and spitting, Dickens's disgust at expectoration (which, characteristically, reached its height when he observed the spit pools carpeting the Senate in Washington) cohered with a whole range of bodily dis-ease that he experienced while travelling in America. In the travelogue he records his horror of being grabbed by forward, and socially 'inferior' Americans, who did not observe the same distanced class decorum that Dickens experienced as natural in England: 'Some gentlemen were only satisfied by exercising their sense of touch; and the boys (who are surprisingly precocious in America) were seldom satisfied, even by that, but would return to the charge over and over again' (p. 127). With physical barriers removed, Dickens recalls a particularly disturbing instance of a man who, fascinated by Dickens's fur coat, insistently came close to touch the fabric, 'that he might have the satisfaction of passing his hand up the back, and rubbing it the wrong way' (p. 168). Similar somatic revulsion was induced by the spectacle of bodily intermingling as steamship passengers happily availed themselves of the communal comb, toothbrush and washing facilities, which were often in alarming proximity to the eatables (pp. 147, 166).

Given this sometimes overwhelming anxiety about physical contact in *American Notes* it is startling that Dickens selects America, indeed the part of America that, with its swampy porousness and concomitant sickliness, caused him the greatest revulsion, as the site for one of the

[52] 22 March 1842, *Letters*, III, pp. 155–60, p. 156.

most extended depictions of restorative touching in his corpus.[53] Eden, albeit temporarily, is the site for the physical and moral rehabilitation of the hero, the ground upon which an entirely positive, life-preserving bond between men is forged and consolidated, and a space for the suspension and re-working of divisive social relations. This suggests a more curative role for *Martin Chuzzlewit*, as Dickens uses the Martin/ Mark plot to acknowledge the more positive, liberating aspects of a relaxation of strict social and bodily distance. Though Eden is a site to escape from, only a temporary and deeply qualified paradise, its lessons are brought home. Martin suffers no relapse into self-absorbed snobbery, insisting instead on the value of 'his friend' Mark, beyond class categories.

'A HIGHLY EROTICISED FIGURE': THE CULTURAL SEXUALIZATION OF VICTORIAN NURSING

Dickens's narratives of same-sex nursing draw attention to the complex inter-relationships between healing, touch, and eroticism. The instances of tender male/male nursing with which his fiction is particularly concerned, expose the limitations of existing assessments of Victorian masculinity. Nursing offers a context for affirmative male/male contact, but only through a reversal of a strictly (albeit imaginatively) gendered practice of medical care that carried a heavy, contemporary freight of erotic connotation and was subject to severe scrutiny throughout the period of Dickens's career. In the late 1830s and 1840s when Dickens wrote *Nicholas Nickleby* and *Martin Chuzzlewit*, nursing already had a particular erotic currency. Laurence Sterne's bawdy *Tristram Shandy* (1759–67), for example, drew upon the kinds of intimate bodily contact required in nursing for many a lusty double entendre. This novel, which Dickens enjoyed, supplements a central concern with groinal injury

---

[53] For detailed examples of the widely iterated view that Dickens used Mississippi mud metonymically to reflect his wider sense of American malaise see R. S. Edgecombe, 'Topographic Disaffection in Dickens's *American Notes and Martin Chuzzlewit*', *Journal of English and Germanic Philology* 93 (1994), 35–54; Robert Lawson Peebles 'Dickens Goes West' in *Views of American Landscapes*, ed. Mark Gridley and Robert Lawson Peebles (Cambridge: Cambridge University Press, 1989), pp. 111–25.

with a subplot in which Corporal Trim falls in love with his nurse after she has administered a passion-inducing rubbing to his leg wound.[54] During the 1850s, however, sexual anxieties surrounding nursing gained greater prominence as nursing reforms accelerated. At the same time, writers sought to recoup the horrors of the Crimean war through popular romance narratives, giving nursing a newly enhanced erotic and connubial profile.

Judd has closely examined the sexual concerns that surrounded nursing, both before and after Victorian reforms:

'Nightingale' or 'new-style' nurses were created in the mid-nineteenth century in part to counteract what was seen as the renegade sexual transgressions of the 'old-style' pauper or working-class nurses [...] Due to the focus on the working-class nurses' supposedly 'dangerous' sexuality, claims about the ostensible purity and asexuality for the new-style or 'saintly' nurse were crucial elements within the mid Victorian nursing reform movement. However [...] the saintly nurse was in and of herself a highly eroticised figure, and Victorian writers and reformers remained at least tacitly aware of the inherent eroticism contained in representations of the 'saintly' new-style nurse.[55]

Judd traces a long literary history of eroticized female nursing, bolstering examples of libertine usage with a more conventional novelistic tradition.[56] She argues that the conceptual weight of such a tradition meant that 'the "purity" of the pious, middle-class nurse [was] undermined continually by a variety of conventional erotic associations'.[57] Indeed,

---

[54] Laurence Sterne, *The Life and Opinions of Tristram Shandy, Gentleman* (London: Penguin, 2003), pp. 520–1. For details of Dickens's reading of, and influence by Sterne, see Mark Turner, 'Sterne', *Companion*, p. 551.

[55] Judd, pp. 33–4. Bashford similarly observes the eroticization of New nurses, whose uniforms quickly became associated with another, anxiety provoking public woman, the prostitute (pp. 57–60).

[56] Judd, pp. 42–3.

[57] Judd, p. 44. Judd's careful collection of data to demonstrate the sexual anxieties surrounding nursing from 1829–80, neatly historicizes a broader cultural eroticization of nursing that persists to date. A short 1983 piece exploring popular imaginings of nursing concludes that sex and intimacy persist as major metaphors for nursing:

Nursing is a metaphor for intimacy. Nurses are involved in the most private aspects of people's lives, and they cannot hide behind technology or a veil of omniscience. Nurses do for others publicly what healthy persons do for themselves privately. Nurses, as trusted peers, are there to hear secrets, especially the ones born of vulnerability [...] Nursing is a metaphor for sex. Having seen and touched the bodies of strangers, nurses

critics have confidently applied such 'conventional erotic associations' to decode the only very lightly veiled sexual nuances in literary depictions of *female* nursing of *male* patients. John Wiltshire, for example, details the paradox through which bodily care both exposes and sanctions heterosexual desire in Jane Austen's *Persuasion* (1818): 'Nursing concern for the body becomes the permissible vehicle in which awakening (or latent) desire can find a plausible and socially sanctioned, because apparently sexually neutral expression.'[58]

Nursing figures prominently in Victorian courtship narratives, frequently appearing as a prelude to connubial conclusion. Bailin lists 'Amy Dorrit and Arthur Clennam, Jane Eyre and Rochester, Lizzie and Eugene Wrayburn, Aurora and Romney Leigh as 'just a few of the couples who are permitted the intimacy of sickroom relations' (p. 23). As Chase and Levenson put it in their reading of Tennyson's *The Princess* (1847), at the moment that Ida decides to nurse the broken Prince, the marital 'resolution of the poem is assured'.[59] Dickens's contemporary Charles Reade played upon the almost inevitable progression from nurse/patient to conjugal relations in his long serial novel, which was hugely popular at the time, *The Cloister and the Hearth* (1861). Thinking that the landlady of a pub they pass would make his beloved friend and travelling companion a most suitable wife, Denys lambastes himself for his failure to incapacitate the hero and leave him

are perceived as willing and able sexual partners. Knowing and experienced, they, unlike prostitutes, are thought to be safe.
Claire Fagin and Donna Diers, 'Nursing as Metaphor', *New England Journal of Nursing* 309 (1983), p. 116–17.
    Leslie Fiedler reinforces this conceptual link between nursing and prostitution in his analysis of the erotic treatment of nursing in popular culture: 'Nurses preside at the bedsides of males – privileged, even required, unlike other members of their sex except for prostitutes, to touch, handle, manipulate the naked flesh of males [...] In the popular arts, nurses are typically portrayed as pursued by or pursuing patients, making passes at or being approached by interns or residents.' 'Images of the Nurse in Fiction and Popular Culture' in *Images of Nurses: Perspectives from History, Art and Literature*, ed. Anne Hudson Jones (Philadelphia: University of Pennsylvania Press, 1988), pp. 100–12, pp. 101–2. Reflecting persistent representations of the nurse as pursued, current US slang includes the phrase 'the Nightingale effect' to refer to the phenomenon of patients falling in love with their nurses (see discussion on VICTORIA, October 2003).
    [58] John Wiltshire, *Jane Austen and the Body* (Cambridge: Cambridge University Press, 1992), p. 173.
    [59] Chase and Levenson, *Spectacle of Intimacy*, p. 131.

invalided at the mercy of the landlady's ministering charms: 'A truer friend than I had ta'en and somewhat hamstrung thee. Then hads't thou been fain to lie smarting at the "Tete d'Or" a month or so, yon skittish lass had nursed thee tenderly, and all been well.'[60]

In the realist, lyrical and comic modes, then, intimate care is both prelude to, and an integral part of marriage. As the anonymous pamphlet (which Nightingale owned) 'Notes on Nurses' states: 'By most men it would be considered an advantage to have a *nursing* wife – a wife who understood how to tend him in sickness, how to administer effectually to the little patients of the nursery.'[61] As this pamphlet suggests, nursing was also associated with concomitant female familial relationships. Not purely a wifely virtue, the ability to heal was also held to be an essential attribute of the good mother and sister, as advice writer Sarah Stickney Ellis emphasized.[62] While not *all* instances of nursing in the period amplify the available erotic resonance, nursing was a recurrent feature in romance plots. Wilkie Collins's 1854 novel *Hide and Seek*, which he dedicated to Dickens, boldly re-gendered such curative relations in his delineation of a nursing husband. Collins's aptly named gentle man Valentine Blyth expresses himself 'just as ready to be' his debilitated wife's 'nurse as to be her husband. I am willing to take her in sickness and in health as the Prayer Book says'.[63] Valentine's reference to this standard marital text, suggests that physical care was both mandated and commonly seen as a component of marriage.

In the period during and after the Crimean War, a reassuring confusion of nursing with romance, which helped to distract from the notorious dire medical provision and poor health of British soldiers in this conflict, proliferated to the extent that Florence Nightingale felt compelled to criticize this romanticization in her *Notes on Nursing*: 'Popular novelists of recent days have invented ladies disappointed in love or fresh out of the drawing-room turning into the war hospitals to find their wounded lovers, and when found, forthwith abandoning their sick-ward for their lover, as might be expected. Yet in the estimation of the authors, these ladies were

[60] Charles Reade, *The Cloister and the Hearth* (Sherborne: Traviata, 2005), p. 330.
[61] 'Notes on Nurses', Florence Nightingale Archive, London. Quoted by Chase and Levenson, p. 132.
[62] See Sarah Stickney Ellis, *The Women of England: Their Social Duties and Domestic Habits* (London: Fisher and Son, 1839), pp. 23–4, 41.
[63] Wilkie Collins, *Hide and Seek* (Oxford: Oxford University Press, 1999), p. 36.

none the worse for that, but on the contrary were heroines of nursing'
(p. 75). Kristine Swenson has explored the genre of 'medical romance' in
this period – a still flourishing subject, to judge by the range of Mills and
Boon titles in a series with this name – suggesting that 'the story's protagonist must be a romantic heroine with typical feminine virtues; her desire to
serve her country is entangled with her desire for love'.[64] Perhaps the most
memorable example of such plotting is found in Charles Kingsley's *Two
Years Ago* (1857), in which the heroine who has fallen in love with a doctor
she has nursed back to health follows him to Scutari to offer her nursing
services and accepts his marriage proposal. Similar tales, purportedly based
on actual experiences, appeared in contemporary periodicals. In, for example, 'The Hospital Nurse: An Episode of the War, founded on Fact', which
appeared in *Fraser's Magazine* in January 1855, the bereaved heroine
prepares for 'a mission of love' in the Crimea while imagining the blessing
that her deceased fiancé would have bestowed on this venture.[65]

    The various romantic, erotic and connubial connotations that ad-
hered to nursing narratives both drew upon and contributed to discern-
ible sexual anxiety about actual nursing scenarios. The author of a
humorous 1871 magazine piece 'Bachelor Invalids and Male Nurses'
nods to this in a typically equivocal reference: 'Women are generally
placed at some disadvantage when attending a bachelor, owing to the
marked isolation of bed-rooms in family dwelling houses [. . .] They
may possess superior capacities for nursing; but often act injudiciously,
in letting their fondness for the pursuit carry them away.'[66] The
potential for such nurse/patient fraternizations, and the wider issue of
how to deal with nurses' sexualities deeply concerned Nightingale. In
her 1858 *Subsidiary Notes as to the Introduction of Female Nursing into
Military Hospitals in Peace and in War*, she wrote of the need for
architecture and practices to 'obviate the great demoralisation conse-
quent on the nurses, patients, and men-servants congregating in
numbers several times daily'. Nightingale goes on to suggest that there

---

    [64] Kristine Swenson, *Medical Women and Victorian Fiction* (University of Missouri
Press: Columbia and London, 2005), p. 39.
    [65] 'The Hospital Nurse: An Episode of the War, founded on Fact', *Fraser's Magazine*,
January 1855, vol. 51, pp. 96–105, p. 98.
    [66] 'Bachelor Invalids and Male Nurses', *Once a Week*, 7 October 1871, vol. 8,
pp. 317–21, p. 320. Snyder also quotes this piece as part of her consideration of the
constitution of the bachelor invalid, *Bachelors*, pp. 64–5.

is no one with whom 'the Nurse' can be trusted, as she gestures towards same-sex eroticism as one of many potential intimacies made possible by this environment: 'Do not let Nurses "congregate" with the orderlies *or* each other, [as] associating the nurses in large dormitories tends to corrupt the good, and make the bad worse [. . .] Give the Nurse plenty to do so that mischief will not tempt her.'[67]

In a somewhat different register, the imagined insatiable promiscuity of members of the medical profession exploiting their privileged access to the body was a going concern for contemporary pornographers. As Gowan Dawson has observed, writers of obscenity literature were alert to, and repeatedly utilized 'the sexual ambiguities particular to certain medical and scientific practices and forms of discourse', so that 'medical tropes' became 'a recurrent feature of Victorian pornography'.[68] As suggested by the inclusion of 'A Surgeon's Diary' in 1828 erotic compendium, *The Festival of the Passions, or Voluptuous Miscellany,* the entries 'The Doctor' and 'Doctor Graham's Advice to the Ladies' in lascivious Victorian serial *The Rambler's Magazine,* and the 1881 novel *The Amatory Experiences of a Surgeon,* the sick-bed was a salacious, rather than sacrosanct domain for many nineteenth-century writers and readers.[69] The way that sickbeds present an eroticized site in both obscene and more respectable literature bears out Sharon Marcus's finding that 'pornography is not the sexual underbelly of culture; rather, pornography and mainstream culture share an erotic repertoire'.[70]

Nursing is certainly a key note in the 'erotic repertoire' of Victorian culture, and its sexual resonances are in no way diminished when nurse and patient are of the same-sex. As a major metaphor for erotic contact in nineteenth-century fiction more widely, nursing in Dickens's own novels operates as an explicit index to the growing, pre-coital intimacy of pre-marital couples such as the *Old Curiosity Shop's* Dick Swiveller and the Marchioness, Little Dorrit and Arthur Clennam, and Lizzie Hexam and Eugene Wrayburn in *Our Mutual Friend.* Indeed, eroticism is so integral to sickroom episodes that in detailing Dickens's opposite-sex

[67] Quoted by Judd, p. 37.
[68] Gowan Dawson, *Darwin, Literature and Victorian Respectability* (Cambridge: Cambridge University Press, 2007), p. 128.
[69] See Peter Mendes, *Clandestine Erotic Fiction in English, 1800–1930: A Bibliographic Study* (Aldershot, Scolar, 1993).
[70] Marcus, p. 114.

nursing scenes Bailin is at pains to demonstrate his effort to forestall 'possible suggestions of dalliance' by emphasizing the 'innocence' of caring figures such as Little Dorrit.[71] Alongside these heterosexual plots, Dickens's many scenes of same-sex nursing draw in complex ways upon the erotic connotations of nursing, simultaneously exploring other and complementary forms of emotional and bodily intimacy.

This chapter certainly does not seek to strengthen any simplistic equation of male nursing with homosexuality – a reductive assumption still commonly made, as Colin Macduff and John Evans have shown: 'The persisting predominant image of the male nurse as homosexual is based on the idea that nursing is woman's work, and mistakenly assumes a correlation between non-acceptance of gender role and non-conformity in terms of sexual preference.'[72] There is clearly much work to be done on a thorough history of men in nursing, with a definite space within that history for a study of the homoerotic experience of nurse and patient roles. However, as this and the following chapter endeavour to suggest, Dickens's representations of healing tactility present a complex range of social and gender issues, within which the celebration of homoeroticism is just one interesting component.

'TOUCH ME': NURSING AND THE AFFIRMATION OF MALE/MALE DESIRE

In 1860 when the erotics of nursing had reached a particular cultural prominence, Dickens was to begin the novel that offered his most sustained and multi-faceted attention to male nursing. In *Great Expectations* Dickens delineates many of the protagonist's central bonds with other men through variously nuanced acts of healing. While Pip's

[71] Bailin, p. 103.
[72] Macduff, p. 41. John Evans offers a detailed exploration of the ongoing assumptions about gender and sexuality that mean that 'men in the nursing profession continue to be stereotyped as anomalies, effeminate or homosexual.' 'Men in Nursing: Issues of Gender Segregation and Hidden Advantage', *Journal of Advanced Nursing* 26.2 (1997), 226–31, p. 228. Evans concludes that male nurses now often choose, or are tracked into, 'more masculine specialisms', particularly areas of technical expertise that are not 'associated with feminine nursing traits – specifically the need to touch and the delivery of intimate care at the bedside'.

treatment by Joe and his physical care for Magwitch operate in modes not overtly erotic, Pip's healing by Herbert presents the most explicitly sexualized incident of male nursing of Dickens's career. This highly affirmative documentation of homoerotic touch stands as culmination of the variously restorative acts already discussed.

The homoerotic resonances of Dickens's nursing narratives act as a curative corrective to a long-held critical bias towards moments of violence in queer readings. Brutal interpretations have drawn on the assumption, widespread in queer studies, that expressions of same-sex desire present a threat to, or radical break with, respectable culture. In Sedgwick's exploration of the 'strongly homophobic mechanisms' that Gothic texts exert, moments of brutal male contact function simultaneously as the expression and punishment of impermissible desire.[73] Under this thinking of the homosexual as the antisocial, that which must be aggressively repudiated in order for homosociality to be maintained, critical attention has focused on instances where same-sex desires energetically break out as acts of destruction and violence. William Cohen, for instance, has offered such interpretations of fight scenes between men and between women in *Great Expectations*, examining the eroticism of the fisticuffs between Pip and Herbert and the lethal deathmatch of Molly and her love rival. Such readings also draw on a long literary critical tradition of reading for the repressed. Those, albeit brutal, scenes of intimate physical contact orchestrated through fighting offer moments when sublimated same-sex desires can be simultaneously expressed and repressed; at the moment that the bodies suggestively touch, that contact is recouped as a more socially acceptable form of same-sex interaction, most often heterosexual rivalry. Violence has been a popular mode in historicist and psychoanalytic approaches to all sexualities because it both looks like, and does not look like, sex; it is both a recognizable potential component of sexual practice and a familiar coding of the erotic.[74] If we recognize, however, that homoerotics are not necessarily antithetical to or discontinuous with

[73] Sedgwick, *Between Men*, p. 92.
[74] Reductive conflations of sex and violence in the reading of heterosexuality have bled into homoerotic interpretations. In his reading of *Martin Chuzzlewit*, for example,

Victorian social mores, more tender, but no less prevalent, expressions
of same-sex desire can be recognized. In the final section of this chapter I
turn to the ever ailing body of Pip in *Great Expectations*, to suggest that
healing, rather than harming, is Dickens's dominant homoerotic mode.
Queer readings of *Great Expectations* repeatedly argue that Pip's
central male relationships are played out through acts of harm.[75] The
positive concomitant of healing through which Pip's interlocking relations with Herbert, Joe, and Magwitch are explored and differentiated
has, therefore, been critically understated. Pip's restorative relationship
with Herbert Pocket is charted through a series of overtly homoerotic
nursing incidents, which act as a preface to their Egyptian relocation at
the close of the novel. These repeated restorative acts exert a curative
force over the range of homoerotics delineated by the text, allowing a
homotropic reading of the type that Cohen had feared the proliferation
of fisticuffs would circumvent: 'Pip's pugilistics with Herbert,
Drummle and Orlick (as well as Magwitch's with Compeyson) represent a form of contact too close for comfort: however ecstatically and
erotically charged one may suspect these passages of being, the form
they take – of increasingly savage violence – must sit uneasily with any
cheerfully homotropic reading.'[76]

Cohen does observe in the later friendship of Pip and Herbert that
the novel allows for a 'now far gentler touching' which 'can be more
frankly denoted'. He briefly describes the 'bodywork' that Herbert (who
has developed 'the peculiar knack [. . .] for tending to Pip's hands')
performs on his friend. Cohen sees this more frank denotation of gentle
touching as an index of the greater suppression of eros, viewing physical

---

psychoanalytic critic Lougy suggests that the novel's 'libidinised sites [are] identified by
bloody wounds, flushed faces, and tumescent organs, testifying to unspoken narratives'.
Although Lougy is astute to other such bodily sites, his typical preference for 'the erotic
dynamics of violence' leads him to read exclusively for 'libidinised sites marked by the
sudden appearance of blood'. His reading of 'the ways in which the body speaks' through
suffering prevents him from recognizing the positive, restorative physicality that takes
place in Eden ('Repressive and Expressive Forms', pp. 40, 51, 48).

[75] See Sedgwick on Orlick's 'lurking, skulking, following in the rear of other men',
especially Pip (*Between Men*, p. 132); Cohen on Magwitch's initially paedophilic 'man-
handling of Pip' (*Sex Scandal*, p. 59); Léger on the flagellatory erotics that structure Pip's
relationship with Joe ('The Scrooge in the Closet', chs. 2 and 4).

[76] Cohen, p. 54.

'tending' as part of a process through which 'youthful belligerence is rehabilitated as properly sublimated, adult male homosociality'.[77] This chapter, however, posits nursing as a *more* culturally visible form of erotic contact than combat.

In *Great Expectations* fisticuffs are immediately displaced by Herbert's particular predilection for nursing Pip. Even in their initial pugilistic encounter Herbert is more concerned with healing than harming his adversary. Pip reminisces that in this fight Herbert 'seemed to have no strength, and he never once hit me hard' (p. 92). Indeed, Herbert proves himself most efficient as a sponge boy, promptly providing 'a bottle of water and a sponge dipped in vinegar. "Available for both"' (p. 91). Later, when Pip is badly burnt, Herbert readily transposes this caring role into their adult relationship. Drawing on his aptitude for bodily treatment he becomes 'the kindest of nurses', blending efficiency with 'tenderness': '[A]t stated times [he] took off the bandages, and steeped them in the cooling liquid that was kept ready, and put them on again, with a patient tenderness that I was deeply grateful for' (p. 404). Throughout this chapter, Dickens places increasing emphasis on the gentle physicality of Herbert's nursing; a bodily contact interspersed with, and ostensibly sanctioned by, a vocal exchange about the men's respective love interests. This alleged heterosexual interest is repeatedly interrupted by tender exchanges between the two men. Herbert's comment about the need to 'take care' of his fiancé, for instance, is immediately followed by his actual bodily care of Pip: 'How can I take care of the dear child otherwise? – Lay your arm out upon the back of the sofa, my dear boy, and I'll sit down here, and get the bandage off so gradually that you shall not know when it comes. I was speaking of Provis' (p. 405). The slippage between wife and friend is further emphasized by Herbert's similar naming of them as 'the dear child' and 'my dear boy'. The greater intimacy of the possessive formulation applied to Pip again points to the erotic dynamic of their London bachelor lodgings. Herbert's relation of Provis's history, which Pip recognizes as the back-story of Estella's parentage, provides the frame for two competing interpretations of Pip's reaction to this simultaneous revelation of his own flesh and revelation of Estella's blood line. Herbert's bed-side story

---

[77] Cohen, pp. 54, 59, 58.

while he nurses is repeatedly punctuated by physical responses from Pip, who 'shrink[s]', breathe[s] quickly', and is 'rather excited' (pp. 405–407). Pip insistently attributes his bodily reactions to Herbert's narrative, disavowing the physical effect of their intimate contact: ' "Does it strike too cold on that sensitive place?" "I don't feel it" ' (p. 406). Herbert, however, provides an alternative explanation in his repeated intuition that Pip's 'sensitive place[s]' are reacting to his treatment:

'My poor Handel, I hurt you!'
'It is impossible to be gentler, Herbert' (p. 406).

Pip typically subsumes this physical acknowledgement under his desire for narrative, partially veiling this deeply intimate admission with further questions: ' "Yes? What else?" '

The heterosexual interest ostensibly behind Pip's feverish physical excitement paradoxically provides extra opportunities for male contact: 'Herbert bent forward to look at me more nearly, as if my reply had been rather more hurried or more eager than he could quite account for. "Your head is cool?" he said, touching it' (p. 405). Pip embraces the bodily dynamics of the nurse, patient relationship, asking Herbert to assess his state through scrutiny and contact:

'Look at me.'
'I do look at you, my dear boy.'
'Touch me.'
'I do touch you, my dear boy' (p. 407).

This restorative, erotically connotative touching and looking is re-enacted in a further scene of nursing between the two men, when Herbert rescues Pip from Orlick's malevolent grasp:

I saw my supporter to be –
'Herbert! Great Heaven!'
'Softly,' said Herbert. 'Gently, Handel. Don't be too eager' (p. 430).

Once again, Pip exhibits excessive eagerness at Herbert's physical support. This scene prefaces yet another spate of nursing, in which Herbert improvises bandages (p. 430) and acquires medicine for Pip (p. 432), with the assistance of Startop, who plays the role of auxiliary nurse. Nursing justifies the tender touching of Herbert and Pip, whilst providing a culturally suggestive context for Pip's expression of excitement at such contact.

In the prioritizing of healing over violence as erotic mode, *Great Expectations* reworks Dickens's much earlier exploration of inter-male nursing in *Nicholas Nickleby*, in which Nicholas's desire to spare Smike from pain and abuse becomes the catalyst for his sustained physical care of his fragile friend. *Great Expectations* also develops two of the central queer themes of *Martin Chuzzlewit*. As with Martin and Mark, Herbert and Handel's intimacy is explored in both homotropical and sickroom settings. Caring bodywork across Dickens's corpus establishes another positive motif for homoerotic articulation, demonstrating the insufficiency of brutal readings and the limitations of interpretations that position Dickens as homophobic. While queer readings can, and often have, been made of flagellation and other physical attacks, the preponderance of physically restorative narratives read in a cultural context of the Victorian sexualization of nursing, show that tenderness is at least an equally established part of Dickens's homoerotic vocabulary.

Such instances also suggest another way in which same-sex desire was compatible with nineteenth-century domesticity. As proposed through the in-lawing narratives of Chapter 3, Dickens and his contemporaries did recognize some – albeit not entirely explicit – modes in which homoerotics could be incorporated into, and even celebrated within, the Victorian home. While it would be reductive to suggest that nursing contacts operate exclusively to enable an otherwise prohibited physical proximity, in a discipline dominated by a criticism that privileges the erotics of aggression, it is crucial to recognize the proliferation of alternative, and no less culturally eroticized, ways of more tender touching.

6

The Gentle Man's Queer Touch: Reparative Masculinities

Dickens's same-sex nursing narratives draw, as the previous chapter has shown, on a wider eroticization of nursing to enhance their homoerotic suggestiveness. Such tender, restorative contact provides a crucial balance to instances in which same-sex desire is expressed as brutality, offering a highly positive mode for homoerotic expression. This chapter extends the focus further from the sexual, examining the wider affirmations and queer effects of male touch.

The popular linking of male homoerotic desire with force reflects and contributes to a wider critical orthodoxy that posits an intimate relationship between masculinity and aggression. This chapter builds upon Carol Christ's foundational essay, in which she recognizes the widespread ambivalence amongst writers such as Tennyson, Patmore, and Newman towards 'a society that valued and rewarded male aggressiveness'.[1] Despite the development of nuanced attention to the multiplicity of Victorian masculinities in the decades since Christ's article, the critical overdetermination of the relationship between militarism and masculinity persists in work on this period and in a more general cultural association of manliness with violence.[2] The overstatement of

---

[1] Carol Christ, 'Victorian Masculinity and the Angel in the House' in *A Widening Sphere: Changing Roles of Victorian Women*, ed. Martha Vicinus (1977, repr. London: Methuen, 1980), pp. 146–62, p. 160.

[2] For militaristic overdetermination see, for example, Peter Stearns: 'For men, the nineteenth century, effectively launched and ended by major wars, was a militant, indeed military century', *Be a Man: Males in Modern Society* (New York: Holmes and Meier, 1979, repr. 1990), p. 189; and Mark Girouard: '"Fighting" was one of the most honourable words in the vocabulary', *The Return to Camelot: Chivalry and the English Gentleman* (New Haven and London: Yale University Press, 1981), p. 281. Such approaches contribute to work such as that by Joseph Kestner on the phallocentric

masculine aggression is related to a wider reluctance to embrace more gentle tactility. As Constance Classen notes, 'one of the ideological barriers to writing about touch in culture is the customary Western emphasis on the brute physicality of touch'.[3] This chapter takes up several ambivalent characters and spaces from *Bleak House* and *Great Expectations* through which Dickens reverses readerly expectations about the militaristic or forceful male. In these novels a shooting gallery and a battery are reworked as spaces of masculine benevolence, and a trooper and a blacksmith are delineated as ideal gentle men. These representations, I will suggest, call into question, or queer, a whole range of interrelated attitudes about masculinity, sexuality, class, and aggression.

Carolyn Dinshaw's concept of 'queer touch' is useful in thinking through the way that tender, nurturing contact between men exposes the limitations of gender categories. Dinshaw is interested in queer, particularly in tactile encounters, for its 'disillusioning, demystifying effects', 'disorientating and rendering strange what has passed until now without comment': 'It makes people stop and look at what they have been taking as natural, and it provokes an inquiry into the ways that "natural" has been produced by particular discursive matrices of hetero-normativity.'[4] Critiqued for her apparent definition of queer, as that which is not the 'norm', Dinshaw points towards her more enabling 'notion of a residue after the imposition of categories', looking not only at that which appears deviant but at that which is currently unaccountable, 'the remainder, the leftover', after existing terms and understandings have been applied.[5] As observed briefly in the preceding chapter's attention to the lack of nomenclature for masculine tenderness, gentle

militarism of nineteenth-century art, with its worrying conclusion that 'inevitably, maleness and male bonding catalyse aggression, which may or may not be manifest in violence; team sports, war, imperialism and organizational competition are forms of such aggression. *Masculinities in Victorian Painting* (Aldershot: Scolar, 1995), p. 18.

    [3] Constance Classen (ed.) *The Book of Touch*, 'Fingerprints: Writing about Touch' (Oxford and New York: Berg, 2005), pp. 1–9.

    [4] Carolyn Dinshaw, 'Chaucer's Queer Touches/ A Queer Touches Chaucer', *Exemplaria* 7.1 (1995), 75–92, pp. 77–79. Dinshaw further elaborates on the significance of tactility in 'provok[ing] perceptual shifts' in *Getting Medieval: Sexualities and Communities, Pre and Post Modern* (Durham and London: Duke University Press, 1999), p. 151.

    [5] Carolyn Dinshaw, 'Got Medieval?' in response to a forum on her 1999 book in *Journal of the History of Sexuality* 10.2 (2001), 202–12, p. 208.

male tactility presents one such 'residue after the imposition of categories'. Instances of restorative male touching, do, however, abound.
The proliferation of examples in the novels of the 1850s and 60s suggest
that statistically this is a normative activity in the mid-Victorian novel,
even though it deviates from what has been imagined about the
gendered behaviour of the period. The tenderness of Dickens's men is
not only, then, culturally eroticized, it also enacts a queer touch, destabilizing classed pre-conceptions of the Victorian male, reaching out to
unaccounted, more gentle masculinities.

MAKE LOVE NOT WAR: TROOPER GEORGE'S SHOOTING GALLERY HOSPITAL

The provocative figure of George the Trooper in *Bleak House* brings
together militarism with particular skill in nurturing, showing that these
attributes are not necessarily antithetical. His military profession is
written legibly into the text of his body. Though now retired from the
army, he habitually holds himself 'as if the full complement of regula-
tion appendages for a field day hung about him' (p. 433), a bearing
instantly interpreted by other characters throughout the novel:

He is a swarthy browned man of fifty; well made, and good looking; with crisp
dark hair, bright eyes, and a broad chest. His sinewy and powerful hands, as
sunburnt as his face, have evidently been used to a pretty rough life. What is
curious about him is, that he sits forward on his chair as if he were, from long
habit, allowing space for some dress or accoutrements that he has altogether laid
aside. His step too is measured and heavy, and would go well with a weighty
clash and jingle of spurs. He is close-shaved now, but his mouth is set as if his
upper lip had been for years familiar with a great moustache; and his manner of
occasionally laying the open palm of his broad brown hand upon it, is to the
same effect. Altogether, one might guess Mr George to have been a trooper once
upon a time (p. 341).

George, with this literal stiff upper lip, is poised between apparently
antithetical models of masculinity. He anticipates the bluff, never-say-
die masculinist heroics of late century imperialist figures such as Baden
Powell and the fictional creations of Rider Haggard and Rudyard
Kipling. At the same time, however, he is positioned in a tradition,

most celebrated in the eighteenth century, and most associated with Samuel Richardson and his hero of sensibility, Sir Charles Grandison – the man of feeling.

Shortly after this physical description Dickens provides an insight into George's emotional life by depicting his response to the various entertainments offered by Astley's theatre. Dickens endows George with his own great enthusiasm for the circus, presenting him as his ideal audience:

Being there, [he] is much delighted with the horses and the feats of strength; looks at the weapons with a critical eye; disapproves of the combats, as giving evidences of unskilful swordsmanship; but is touched home by the sentiments. In the last scene when the Emperor of Tartary gets up into a cart and condescends to bless the united lovers, by hovering over them with the Union-Jack, his eye-lashes are moistened with emotion (p. 349).

As Malcolm Andrews observes in his book on Dickens's public readings, Dickens always loathed what he called a 'frigid', 'freezing' audience.[6] In his own performances he was delighted and energized if spectators would engage emotionally, following his injunctions to laugh and cry freely. In keeping with Dickens's entirely positive delineation of his character, George is moved to tears by the theatrical combination of romantic and patriotic ardour, and is 'touched home by the sentiments'.

After this theatre trip George returns to his unconventional home, in the premises of his business, the shooting gallery. Though ostensibly the space in which men's bodies are honed in the weapons and warfare training that instils one normative model of masculinity, the shooting gallery has complex uses that undercut its ostensibly militaristic function. In an extension of the conjunction of martial and tender qualities that come together in the body of George, his shooting gallery becomes refuge and hospital to numbers of the novel's down-and-outs. It is the final resting place for Gridley, a chancery suitor driven to despair and exhaustion by the legal system, and for Jo the homeless orphan crossing sweeper. The gallery is also the setting for the prolonged and particularly poignant relationship between George and another socially dispossessed man, Phil Squod, for whom it becomes home. Phil's damaged body records the violence, neglect, abuse and accident, for which it seems to have been a

[6] Malcolm Andrews, *Charles Dickens and His Performing Selves: Dickens and the Public Readings* (Oxford: Oxford University Press, 2006), p. 71.

magnet. Disfigured by the drunken violence of the tinker who brings him up, burnt and scorched while working in a forge and in an accident at a gasworks, Phil concludes: 'I have been throwed, all sorts of styles, all my life!' (pp. 421–2). Only George picks him up off the street, finding Phil 'in a nightcap' 'and hobbling along with a couple of sticks', after he has been literally blown up by an accident at a firework factory (p. 421). The usually taciturn Phil becomes animated in recounting what to him, and within the economy of the novel, is an extraordinary act of kindness:

'When you stops, you know,' cries Phil [. . .] 'and says to me, "What, comrade! You have been in the wars!" I didn't say much to you, commander, then, for I was took by surprise that a person so strong and healthy and bold as you was, should stop to speak to such a limping bag of bones as I was. But you says to me, says you, delivering it out of your chest as hearty as possible, so that it was like a glass of something hot, "What accident have you met with? You have been badly burnt. What's amiss old boy? Cheer up and tell us about it!" Cheer up! I was cheered already! I says as much to you [. . .]' (pp. 421–2).

The physically restorative effect that George has on Phil, so that even to hear him speak is like consuming a 'glass of something hot', is continued at the shooting gallery. Phil watches George washing and finds it 'sufficient renovation for one day, to take in the superfluous health his master throws off' (p. 418). Phil's experience of the health giving properties of George's very presence recalls the accounts, discussed in the previous chapter, of Dickens's vital emanations, resonating with Dickens's own apparent mesmeric abilities and with what Anne Thackeray Ritchie described as his 'curious life giving power', in the sickrooms of family members and friends.

Phil, who is on his knees lighting a fire, is depicted as rapturously gazing up at the dripping bare torso of his friend:

bare-headed and bare-chested, [. . .] shining with yellow soap, friction, drifting rain, and exceedingly cold water. As he rubs himself upon a large jack-towel, blowing like a military sort of diver just come up: his crisp hair curling tighter and tighter on his sunburnt temples [. . .] – as he rubs, and puffs, and polishes and blows, turning his head from side to side, the more conveniently to excoriate his throat, and standing well bent forward, to keep the wet from his martial legs (p. 417).

Phil's admiration reflects a complex blend of feelings for George, in which the erotic is commingled with gratitude, loyalty, and the experience of physical recovery. The sensual dynamic of this primarily restorative relationship, which begins when Phil is literally on his last legs having been

blown up, requires careful handling. Indeed, the physical need at the heart
of all the healing narratives considered in this and the previous chapter
always extends beyond the sexual. In the very different context of the First
World War, Santanu Das has offered a nuanced exploration of the
formation of preservative intimacies:

> In the trenches of the Western Front, where life expectancy could be a short as a
> couple of weeks, same-sex ardour, bodily contact and (in some cases) eroticism
> should not be understood solely in contrast to heterosexuality, not viewed only
> through the lenses of gender and sexuality. Such intimacy must also be understood
> *in opposition to* and *as a triumph over* death: it must be seen as a celebration of life, of
> young men huddled against long winter nights, rotting corpses and falling shells.[7]

As Das's tactile history of this conflict suggests, in contexts where
trauma, physical peril and the daily possibility of death come together
with the formation of intense male bonds, existing understandings of,
and language for, such relationships will inevitably be insufficient.

In *Bleak House*, George's rejection of marriage adds further to the
complexity of his partnership with the man whose life he has saved. The
exclusivity and committed fidelity of his relationship with Phil suggest
that this has replaced the more conventional bond. George is one of the
many idealized bachelor heroes of Dickens's fiction (a category discussed fully in Chapter 2). When Mrs Bagnet scolds George for his
failure to marry, reminding him of a suitable match he could have
made, George replies: 'It was a chance for me, certainly [. . .] but I shall
never settle down into a respectable man now. Joe Pouch's widow might
have done me good – there was something in her – and something of
her – but I couldn't make up my mind to it' (p. 440). Feeling that he
'shouldn't have been fit for' matrimony, as 'such a vagabond' (p. 444),
George elects to share a 'vagabond way' of life with Phil (p. 723) whom
it suits. This version of 'vagabonding' (the term also used in *Martin
Chuzzlewit*, with similar homoerotic resonance, for the outlaws who flee
to the male world of Eden) is oddly compatible with absolute fidelity. At
the end of the novel, when George decamps to Chesney Wold, Phil is
installed there as groom. George retains his heroism, despite departing
from the all the parameters of respectable masculinity as defined by
(re)productivity. As well as insisting on bachelorhood George is

[7] Das, *Touch and Intimacy*, p. 118.

economically unsuccessful, and at one point financially insolvent; and his most significant, and sometimes eroticized, relationship is with a totally dispossessed man, whose body he nurtures.

Trooper George is the unsung hero of a novel that stringently critiques not only the corrupt and corrupting legal process but a wider social malaise, which, as Paul Schlicke and others have argued, 'is the result of irresponsible denial of human relationships'.[8] George's response to the many socially alienated and physically suffering figures of *Bleak House* offers a model of benevolence endlessly expanding through concentric circles. When the dying Jo is brought to the shooting gallery, George places him in the hands of his auxiliary Phil: 'Here is a man, sir, who was found, when a baby, in the gutter. Consequently it is to be expected that he takes a natural interest in this poor creature' (p. 725). Dickens's description of Phil's tending of Jo during his all too brief sojourn at the shooting-gallery-cum-hospital offers a particularly explicit juxtaposition of the harming with the healing: 'Phil Squod with his smoky gunpowder visage, at once acts as a nurse and works as armourer at his little table in a corner' (p. 732). A similar conjunction of the military and the medical characterizes the scenes at the end of the novel, where George cares for the debilitated Sir Leicester Dedlock. As George becomes indispensable at the baronet's bedside, taking him in his arms to position him more comfortably, Sir Leicester remembers their more active times together as young men around the estate:

'Thank you, George. You are another self to me. You have often carried my spare gun at Chesney Wold, George. You are familiar to me in these strange circumstances, very familiar.'
He has put Sir Leicester's sounder arm over his shoulder in lifting him up, and Sir Leicester is slow in drawing it away again, as he says these words (p. 894).

Languages of familiarity are typical of these moments of emotional and physical reliance. Phil is repeatedly described as George's 'Familiar' (p. 417), a supernatural reference that perhaps refers both to Phil's uncanny twisted and stunted body and to his loyalty to and inseparability from the man variously referred to as his master, commander and friend. This language also points to the familial familiarity of these relationships. As Bailin has argued with reference to the alternative

---

[8] Paul Schliche, '*Bleak House*', *Companion*, p. 50.

family groupings that both Florence Nightingale and Harriet Martineau were able to assemble around their sickbeds, various nursing narratives of the nineteenth century allow a reformation and reconstitution of family in elective sickroom communities: 'Often [. . .] illness summons a society suited to one's own specifications and substitutes for the coercions of blood and marriage a physical tie as voluntary as friendship and as essential as survival.'[9] In *Bleak House* these physically caring relationships, particularly the harmonious domestic unit of George and Phil, are infinitely preferable to the novel's many abusive, neglectful, and fragmented biological families. Male healing and the bachelor adoptions discussed in the first chapter are forms of tender masculinities that catalyse a positive re-organization of domesticity and kinship.

George's previously unrecognized aptitude for bodily care has significant effects across the social spectrum of the novel's diverse cast of characters, and is central to the main plot. His friendship with his army superior (who calls himself Nemo while lodging with Krook and turns out to be Esther's father) has also been that of the sickroom.[10] As well as tending to his captain, George cares for Jo the child street urchin; for Phil, the entirely unconnected orphan who has grown into a damaged adult; the reduced gentleman, Gridley; and the baronet, Sir Leicester. This democratic model of care-giving has a female equivalent in the novel, which also uses the central incident of Esther's debilitating illness to dramatize emotional and erotic bonds.

The assortment of (would-be) attendants that cluster at Esther's sick-bed call attention to the diversely classed inter-female relationships explored in the novel. These range from the mutual healing of Esther and the young servant Charley (an orphan left destitute after her debt-collecting father's death), to the highly eroticized genteel reunion of the novel's socially privileged female orphans, Esther and Ada, after Esther's convalescence.[11]

[9] Bailin, p. 17.

[10] Tulkinghorn's effort to exploit George's private knowledge of his captain draws upon a shared understanding of the particular intimacy of sickroom relations: 'You served under Captain Hawdon at one time, and were his attendant in illness, and rendered him many little services, and were rather in his confidence, I am told' (p. 434).

[11] For more on the untrained, but life-preserving nursing of Esther and Charley see Laura Fasick, *Professional Men and Domesticity in the Mid-Victorian Novel* (New York: Edwin Mellen Press, 2003), pp. 107–8.

Esther's illness functions finally to break down physical boundaries between herself and Ada. Similarly when the somewhat precariously middle-class Caddy Turveydrop (née Jellyby) becomes seriously unwell, having exhausted herself assisting her dancing-master husband, her illness allows her to enjoy a physical intimacy with Esther, which she has craved to relive throughout the novel. On their first meeting Esther cushions Caddy as she sleeps – 'I contrived to raise her head so that it should rest on my lap' (p. 63) – beginning a passion in Caddy for her 'best friend', whom (she feels) 'nobody can respect and love [. . .] too much' (p. 374). Indeed Caddy's admiration is so intense that Esther considers herself as a rival to Caddy's husband: 'Caddy, who had not seen me since her wedding day was so glad and so affectionate that I was half inclined to fear I should make her husband jealous' (p. 609). Before her own illness, Caddy had been another eager aspirant to Esther's sickroom, denied admittance despite her 'coming and going early and late' (p. 559). When Caddy sickens Esther intuits that her particular presence is Caddy's best medicine, and goes daily 'to sit with her' (p. 769) for 'eight or nine' weeks, often 'remain[ing] to nurse her' at night (p. 771):

Caddy had a superstition about me, which had been strengthening in her mind ever since that night long ago, when she had lain asleep with her head in my lap. She almost – I think I must say quite – believed that I did her good whenever I was near her. Now, although this was such a fancy of the affectionate girl's, that I am almost ashamed to mention it, still it might have all the force of a fact when she was really ill (p. 769).

Happily Caddy recovers, benefiting both from the healthful presence as well as the assiduous care of the woman that she admires and adores beyond her own husband.

These socially mobile models of benevolence are of particular value in a text centrally concerned with the social and physical dis-ease resulting from a culpable neglect and marginalization of the poor, most strikingly manifested by the horrors of the slum, Tom-all-Alone's. Through Trooper George's significantly tactile encounters with variously classed male bodies Dickens refines a definition of the gentleman primarily based on social status. Though George insistently calls himself 'one of the Roughs' (p. 393, p. 427), Esther, a reliable mouthpiece for moral value in this novel, appreciates the 'gentleness which went so well with his bluff bearing' (p. 796). I've argued elsewhere that novels of this period centrally concerned with the social category of the gentleman often distance this consideration from questions of class and status, preferring an intensely tactile meritocracy, in which masculine social worth is often expressed and formed through acts of male nursing.[12] This is the case in Criak's *John Halifax Gentleman*, in which the eponymous hero is transformed from penniless street orphan to mill-owning industrialist and pillar of the community. This transformation is centrally dramatized through his gentle physical care for his ever ailing friend, Phineas Fletcher, whose father takes Halifax in as a boy after he has wheeled his ill son home. As they grow up Phineas and John are inseparable and cohabit through adulthood, even after John's marriage. In another instance of tactile care forming new familial bonds Phineas is described as an uncle to John's children. A similar narrative is played out in a very different social setting in Yonge's *The Heir of Redclyffe*. Yonge's hero, Sir Guy, proves his worth and rehabilitates a morally corrupt aristocratic line through repeated acts of tactile care that eventually demand the sacrifice of his life.

Dickens's novel most concerned with the question of what makes a gentleman, *Great Expectations*, draws upon this wider cultural recognition of healing as a means of circumventing, and redefining, social barriers. In this novel, Pip's ever ailing body is administered to by a range of male carers. As detailed in the previous chapter, Pip's excitement at being nursed by Herbert Pocket draws a further sexual resonance from the cultural eroticization of nursing in this period. While Dickens's novels often contribute a same-sex dynamic to wider discussions about the erotics of nursing, the proliferation of restorative male touching in *Bleak House* and *Great Expectations* allow these novels to further extend such treatment. As well as the sexual, these novels more fully address the interrelationship between tactility and social boundaries that *Nickleby* and *Chuzzlewit* began to explore. They are also dedicated to a critique of masculine violence, celebrating the gentle

---

[12] Holly Furneaux, 'Negotiating the Gentle-Man: Male Nursing and Class Conflict in the High Victorian Period' forthcoming in *Victorian Literary Cultures in Conflict*, ed. Dinah Birch and Mark Llewellyn (Basingstoke: Palgrave, forthcoming).

possibilities of even the most militaristic male, and demonstrating the unexpected compatibility of physical strength and tenderness.

'GREAT GOOD HANDS': JOE GARGERY AS HEALING BLACKSMITH

The principal carers of *Great Expectations* are Herbert Pocket, who is referred to as a 'gentleman' throughout, and Joe Gargery, the blacksmith who nurses Pip over a prolonged period of delirium and convalescence. After this intimate care Pip, who, like Martin Chuzzlewit, experiences a moral as well as physical rehabilitation, can finally recognize the classless 'wealth of [Joe's] great nature', describing him as 'dear, good noble Joe' and 'this gentle Christian man' (pp. 467, 479, 463). Joe's ability to restore goes beyond the bodily, as the supplanting of social relations with those of nurse and patient work to heal, albeit temporarily, the class rift between himself and Pip. The cessation of the discomforts of class difference between Joe and Pip is skilfully coincident with Joe's literal healing of the wounds of class violence that Orlick has inscribed on Pip's body.

Joe's nursing atones for Pip's suffering at the hands of the other members of the forge household. It comprises belated reparation for the child Pip's abuse by Mrs Joe that Joe had felt powerless to prevent, as well as presenting a rewriting of Orlick's story of the brutal blacksmith. Pip is completely debilitated at the hands of Orlick, in what the novel clearly specifies as a class-fuelled attack. Orlick's animosity is explicitly provoked by the difference in treatment that he and Pip have received at the forge, and more widely in society: 'You was favoured and [. . . Orlick] was bullied and beat' (p. 426). Where Pip has previously noted his murderous attacker's 'great strength' (p. 471), under Joe's tender care this descriptor becomes redefined as a measure of moral as well as physical power as the recovering Pip observes Joe's 'great good hands' (p. 471). While 'gentleman' Herbert provided first aid at the lime-kiln scene, Joe's intensive care of Pip over a prolonged period takes this treatment to new therapeutic levels. The various stages of Pip's cure rely on practitioners from very different class positions. This social dispersal of gentleness is in line with Dickens's inter-related determination to de-couple aggression from class. While Orlick's disenfranchised brutality suggests the violent rage of the 'lower' orders, his brutishness is echoed by his ostensibly well-to-do counterpart, wife-beater Bentley Drummle.[13]

The moving reunion of Joe and Pip begins to heal the wounds of childhood trauma and class antagonism. Social and erotic reconciliation are inextricable here, as they become literal bedfellows in Pip's sickbed: 'Joe had actually laid his head down on the pillow at my side and put his arm round my neck, in his joy that I knew him' (p. 463).[14] Pip and Joe's relationship encompasses a variety of Dickens's strategies for more positive representations of same-sex desire. They are legal brothers-in-law – indeed, Joe emphasizes his interest in caring for the infant Pip in his marriage proposal to Georgiana Pirrip (p. 48) – who attain physical connection through the socially eroticized medium of nursing. Beyond the erotic frisson of such intimate physical scenes however, Joe's touch is most queer, in Dinshaw's terms, in the way that it provokes a reassessment of what passes as natural in the division of class and gender categories. At the same time as he challenges class-based definitions of what constitutes the gentle man, Dickens complicates the constituents of masculine and feminine value.

Throughout Pip's fever Joe maintains a quiet, well ordered and ventilated sickroom, judiciously providing his patient with 'a little nourishment at stated frequent times' (p. 464). Pip describes the arrangements thus:

My bedstead, divested of its curtains, had been removed, with me upon it, into the sitting-room, as the airiest and largest, and the carpet had been taken away, and the room kept always fresh and wholesome night and day [...] He did everything for me except the household work, for which he engaged a very decent woman (pp. 464, 467).

---

[13] In an important early reading of the significance gentlemanliness in *Great Expectations*, Robin Gilmour observes the doubling of Orlick and Drummle, which 'remind[s] us that violence and brutality are not confined to life on the marshes, that they also exist in the supposedly refined society of London'. *The Idea of the Gentleman in the Victorian Novel* (London: Allen and Unwin, 1981), p. 139.

[14] J. M. Léger moves towards an unusually celebratory reading of this scene as a moment 'which threatens violence as a means of establishing homocentric and encoding homoerotic connection' (p. 200). His commitment to flagellation as the most legible erotic code of the period leads him to argue that the eroticism of a gentler touching between Pip and Joe is *only* observable on the back of their earlier experience as 'fellow sufferers' of abuse at the hands of Mrs Joe.

This is absolutely by the book of Nightingale's *Notes on Nursing*, which is concerned with such practical management of the domestic sickroom, with chapters advising on 'ventilation', 'taking food', 'bed and bedding', 'cleanliness of rooms'. Indeed, in the working notes for *Great Expectations* Dickens describes Joe as a 'Ministering Angel', a phrase typically used to refer to nursing women and often applied to Nightingale.[15] Joe's exemplary nursing, however, powerfully resists Nightingale's gendered and classed assumptions: 'On women', implicitly middle-class women, who have been the imagined audience throughout, 'we must depend, first and last, for personal and household hygiene' (p. 79). Indeed, Joe's provision echoes and goes beyond the more conventionally gendered domestic care that Esther offers Caddy in *Bleak House*: 'I took the supreme direction of her apartment, trimmed it up, and pushed her couch and all, into a lighter and more airy and more cheerful corner than she had yet occupied' (p. 771).

Bashford has pointed to the crucial coincidence of the reconfiguring of the new nurse as a 'middle class figure of efficiency, neatness and whiteness' with the movement for sanitary reform.[16] She examines the inextricability of ideals of the purifying domestic woman and the cleanly new nurse, citing an 1869 letter written to Nightingale from an Australian hospital (at this time colonial hospitals were mainly staffed by male nurses) in which men are firmly excluded from discourses of hygiene:

[Their wards are] grimed and insect infested . . . dirty corners, where all kinds of filth and rubbish was stowed away [. . . which] sufficiently attested to what their ideas of order and cleanliness were [. . .] I hope they will never again resume their work where women have been introduced.[17]

That Pip can depend on Joe, whose body fits neither the gendered or classed ideal of purifying angel, suggests that critical understandings of Victorian gender, especially the male domestic role, still need some considerable revision.

Trooper George can similarly be seen to offer suitably sanitary care. He wants Joe to be bathed and cleanly clothed (p. 725), showing a

[15] Quoted by Malcolm Andrews, *Dickens and the Grown Up Child* (Basingstoke: Macmillan, 1994) p. 95.
[16] Bashford, p. 21.
[17] Haldane Turiff to Florence Nightingale, 29 January 1869, quoted by Bashford, p. 33.

Nightingale-esque belief in the correlation of personal hygiene and health. When George attends Sir Leicester at the end of *Bleak House*, the baronet responds with; 'Thank you. You have your mother's gentleness [. . .] and your own strength' (p. 893), again exposing the difficulty with nomenclature experienced even by those authors (including Mary Seacole and Louisa Alcott, as discussed in the previous chapter) most aware of the insufficiency of the default understanding of gentleness as feminine. Pip observes a similar amalgamation in Joe: 'Joe laid his hand upon my shoulder with the touch of a woman. I have often thought him since, like the steam-hammer, that can crush a man or pat an eggshell, in his combination of strength with gentleness' (p. 141).

While George is 'touched home' by theatrical sentiment, Joe is moved to tears by the domestic drama of losing Pip:

O *dear good* Joe, whom I was so ready to leave and so unthankful to, I see you again, with your muscular blacksmith's arm before your eyes, and your broad chest heaving, and your voice dying away. O *dear good faithful tender* Joe, I feel the loving tremble of your hand upon my arm, as solemnly this day as if it had been the rustle of an angel's wing! (emphasis added, p. 141).

Pip's, and Dickens's, wrangling with layered adjectives in an effort to describe the tender virtues of Joe again points to the lack of a suitably gendered emotional and tactile language. As nursing blacksmith, combining force with great delicacy, a 'muscular blacksmith's arm' with the trembling touch of an 'angel's wing', Joe presents a similar gender conundrum to that embodied by General George. They tax existing taxonomies which provide no adequate terminology for such masculine nurture.

Joe Gargery embodies a similar dichotomy to that which Tim Barringer has explored in relation to James Sharples, mid-Victorian blacksmith and artist. Sharples's famous steel engraving, 'The Forge', was completed and widely reviewed in 1859, the year before Dickens began work on *Great Expectations*. As Barringer puts it, 'to confront the historical figure of a blacksmith who was an artist by night – an artist who was a blacksmith by day – is to enter an uncomfortable territory in which traditional ideas of class and status are overturned'. Similarly discomforting in terms of gender, and suggestive of the overhauling of traditional connections of masculinity and force, is the combination of power and physical care that is materialized in Sharples's work: 'Each line, incised with both force and delicacy, is a visible trace of the work of a man, who, with mighty blows of the hammer, also fashioned the components of steam-engines.'[18] The powerful combination of 'force and delicacy' embodied by both Trooper George, with his stiff upper lip and gentle touch and his shooting gallery/makeshift hospital, and Joe Gargery, as nursing blacksmith, demonstrate the need for more subtle understandings of Victorian manliness. In these figures Dickens celebrates a masculinity that could encompass a much more tender muscularity and in which nurture does not signal effeminacy but ideal manly virtue.

BENEVOLENT BATTERIES: WEMMICK'S CASTLE AND THE AMERICAN SERIALIZATION OF *GREAT EXPECTATIONS*

In challenging pre-conceptions of Victorian gender divisions, these narratives most importantly complicate dominant aggressive and military models of manliness. Just as Dickens uses eccentric architectures as settings for queer families, he explores gentle strength both through characters and spaces. In *Great Expectations* the shooting gallery hospital has its more developed equivalent in the brilliantly bizarre design of Wemmick's suburban castle: 'Wemmick's house was a little wooden cottage in the midst of plots of garden, and the top of it was cut out and painted like a battery mounted with guns' (p. 206). The restorative powers of this Walworth edifice are made manifest in two very different

---

[18] Tim Barringer, *Men at Work: Art and Labour in Victorian Britain* (New Haven and London: Yale University Press, 2005), pp. 136, p. 135. Barringer's exploration of the sometimes anxious contemporary fascination with Sharples's physical and creative combination of strength and delicacy resonates with a wider interest in the mixture of these qualities. George Sala, for example, in an 1860 essay, which was the first in a biographical series on William Hogarth (another nurturing male as we saw in Chapter 1's discussion of his connection with the Foundling Hospital and efforts as an adoptive parent), attributes the skills required by engravers such as Hogarth and Sharples to the good biographer, who must similarly combine 'strength and delicacy, vigour and finish'. Using the same steam hammer image applied to Joe, Sala sets up his ideal writer as a 'man with a mind like a Nasmyth's steam hammer, that can roll out huge bars of iron, and anon knock a tin-tack into a deal board with gentle accurate taps'. 'William Hogarth: Painter, Engraver and Philosopher: Essays on the Work and the Time. 1 – Little Boy Hogarth', *Cornhill Magazine* 1 (1860), 177–93, p. 179.

contexts. For British readers, receiving the serial in Dickens's journal *All the Year Round*, this incongruous structure would perhaps be seen to build primarily upon contemporary debates about the relationship between art, work, and masculinity, to which the Wemmick plot explicitly contributes. For American readers, however, who read the instalments of *Great Expectations* in New York periodical *Harper's Weekly*, the benevolence of Wemmick's fort life emerged in the context of the unfolding violence and destruction of the Civil War.

Wemmick's ingenious contrivances of moat, drawbridge and battery complete with firing gun, are chiefly for the delight of his father, 'the Aged parent.' Here the apparatus of inherently violent militarism is appropriated into the benevolent service of male nurturing, a reversal of intent neatly dramatized by the Aged's joyous response to Wemmick's ritual sounding of the Stinger: 'He's fired! I heerd him!' (p. 209). For the Aged, whose acute deafness otherwise cuts him off from social interaction, the nightly firing of the gun is a significant, ritual moment of emotional bonding with his son. This 'great nightly ceremony' (p. 208) resounds with Dickens's wider attention to tender male acts throughout this novel.

Wemmick, clerk to the ruthless lawyer Jaggers, famously leads a double life split between the office and the Castle. As part of the legal machinery that frequently exacts incarceration or the death penalty (as his macabre collection of mourning rings and other final bequests so vividly registers) Wemmick at work is an instrument of physical punishment, a role that contrasts sharply with his home life as domestic carer. His private life, with the softening influence of his dependent father and unconventional home, redeems him from the self-protective hardness and dryness that he exhibits in the city. Wemmick's gothic conversion of cottage to castle is situated within specific contemporary debates about masculinity and work, operating in dialogue with John Ruskin's essay, 'On the Nature of Gothic Architecture and Herein of the Functions of the Workman in Art', which appeared in the second volume of *Stones of Venice* in 1853. Approaching the property Pip describes it as 'the smallest house I ever saw; with the queerest gothic windows (by far the greater part of them sham) and a gothic door almost too small to get in at' (p. 206). The next morning Pip looks out of a 'gothic window' in his 'turret bedroom' (p. 209). Though an isolated rather than a collective act of architectural craftsmanship, as in Ruskin's ideal, the Castle does redeem Wemmick from a work life in which, to use Ruskin's terminology, he is made into another man's 'tool'.[19] In 'The Nature of Gothic' Ruskin celebrates roughness and imperfection of finish in preference to the artificial regularities made possible by mechanized production, delighting in the 'magnificent enthusiasm, which feels as it never could do enough to reach the fullness of its ideal.'[20] In the time, physical and creative effort invested in the Walworth Castle, which has taken Wemmick as engineer, carpenter, plumber, and gardener, 'a good many years to bring the property up to its present pitch of perfection' (p. 208), and in the gap between the imagined perfection and the realities of dry rot and the proximity of livestock (pp. 207–9), the Castle could certainly qualify for Ruskinian admiration. Most importantly, in Ruskin's system of evaluation, there is no division between the processes of invention and realization as Wemmick has made all the contrivances 'with his own hands out of his own head' (p. 295). While Ruskin would prefer that men have ennobling day jobs, Wemmick's unusual domestic retreat 'brushes the Newgate cobwebs away and pleases the Aged' (p. 207), redeeming the fatigued and exploited worker. The dispersal of such shades of the prison house takes place through a strictly benevolent appropriation of the otherwise violent framework of the battery. The Walworth Castle as a site of particular domestic happiness stands as a memorable monument to the many unconventional households with which this book has been concerned.

As he wrote in an 1867 letter, Ruskin found Dickens's novels one of his life's 'chief comforts and restoratives'.[21] For a particular community of Dickens's first readers, the restorative properties of the Castle as benevolent battery were particularly pronounced. The American serialization of *Great Expectations* was published roughly concurrently with the thirty-six *All the Year Round* instalments, appearing in illustrated family magazine, *Harper's Weekly: A Journal of Civilization*, from 24 November 1860 to 3 August 1861.[22] The experience of the 120,000 or

[19] John Ruskin, *On the Nature of Gothic Architecture and Herein the Functions of the Workman in Art* (London: Smith, Elder and Co., 1854), p. 8.

[20] Ruskin, p. 34.

[21] Philip Collins, 'Ruskin', *Companion*, p. 513.

[22] For detailed schedules of the British and American serialization see Edgar Rosenberg, 'Launching *Great Expectations*' in the Norton critical edition of *Great Expectations*, ed. Edgar Rosenberg (New York: Norton, 1999), pp. 389–437.

so *Harper's Weekly* readers was bound up with the inception and early escalation of the American Civil War.[23] Fighting commenced on 12 April 1861, when the serialization of *Great Expectations* was at about its midpoint. As John Winterich has pointed out, at this time 'readers of *Harper's Weekly* had other things to worry about than what happened to Pip and Estella'.[24] The magazine famously devoted the majority of its column space to the war, moving from some vacillation before the conflict to a committed Unionist position throughout the war. Its articles and detailed illustrations of forts and battles, and diagrams of weapons provide a valuable archive for military historians.

There is evidence for the impact of the war on the presentation of Dickens's serial. For instance, as Phillip Allingham has suggested, the three instalments from 11 May 1861 were not illustrated because the publication was devoting the majority of its space to extensive pictorial coverage of the war.[25] If *Great Expectations* was physically squeezed by the war coverage, its imaginative and affective impact was, perhaps, expanded in particular ways as a result of the juxtaposition of this material. Imagine the effect for these readers of the instalment in the 27 April issue, which prints Abraham Lincoln's proclamation of war as the leading editorial and opens with the headline: 'The Bombardment of Fort Sumter. We devote most of our space this week to illustrations of this memorable event.' Dickens's serial in this issue begins with Pip's Sunday visit to the Castle to take Wemmick's Walworth sentiments: 'On arriving before the battlements, I found the Union Jack flying and the drawbridge up; but undeterred by this show of defiance and resistance, I rang at the gate, and was admitted in a most pacific manner by the Aged' (p. 292). This incident is liberally surrounded by descriptions

---

[23] *All the Year Round* had similar circulation figures, selling more than 100,000 copies a week (Rosenberg, p. 392). See also *Dickens's Journalism*, vol. IV: *The Uncommercial Traveller and Other Papers*, ed. Michael Slater and John Drew (London: Dent, 2000), p. xii. Frank Luther Mott gives detailed circulation figures of *Harper's Weekly* over the Civil War period in *A History of American Magazines*, vol. 2 (Cambridge: Harvard University Press, 1938), pp. 473–6. For further detail on this part of the Harper brothers' enterprise see also chapter 15 of J. Henry Harper, *The House of Harper: A Century of Publishing in Franklin Square* (New York and London: Harper and Brothers, 1912).

[24] Quoted by Rosenberg, p. 399.

[25] Phillip Allingham, 'Introduction to John McLenan's *Harper's Weekly* illustrations to *Great Expectations*', http://www.victorianweb.org/art/illustration/mclenan/intro.html.

and illustrations of less benevolent fort life. The issue's centrefold comprises a dramatic picture of the event which inaugurated the Civil War, 'The Bombardment of Fort Sumter by the Batteries of the Confederate States, April 13, 1861', in which a drummer lies dead in the foreground, and confederate troops display a mixture of experience and panic in their responses to the return of fire. Surely the gentle paradox of Dickens's suburban pleasure castle, with its exclusively friendly fire, would have been particularly apparent in this context.

In a similar juxtaposition of tender and violent content one of the period's rare visual representations of a male/male sickbed scene, in which Pip holds Magwitch's hand, sits alongside the multiple depictions of weaponry and battlefields. John McLenan – a household name as the American 'Phiz', whose illustrations were trumpeted as 'splendid' in *Harper's* marketing of *Great Expectations* – provided a plate for the 27 July 1861 instalment depicting Pip seated at Magwitch's prison bedside, holding his dying benefactor's emaciated hand, with a table containing food and medicines to his side.[26] This haunting, tender scene is the only image of the issue that is not directly connected with the violence and destruction of the war. Such juxtapositions suggest that the many gentle male acts in *Great Expectations* could exert a curative power beyond the novel itself. In the context of *Harper's Weekly* the proliferation of male tenderness in Dickens's novel, most powerfully symbolized by Wemmick's benign fort as locale of masculine care, acted as a relief to the otherwise unrelenting visual and verbal depictions of war violence. Dickens's gentle men provided an urgent alternative to the multiplied models of men as instruments of aggression, inflicting or suffering death and injury that filled the other pages of *Harper's Weekly*.

Dickens's close friend, Wilkie Collins, was later to achieve a similar effect in his serialized novel, *The Law and the Lady* (1875). In another reworking of the conventional plotting of nursing romances (as also seen with reference to Collins's *Hide and Seek* in the previous chapter), the hero flees complex love problems at home to join the Spanish

---

[26] The novel uses Pip's visits to Magwitch in the prison infirmary to comment on the use of prisoners as sick nurses – 'malefactors, but not incapable of kindness, God be thanked!' (p. 459) – and to offer an explicit reference to the manner in which illness could facilitate otherwise prohibited intimacy: 'This gave me opportunities of being with him that I could not otherwise have had' (p. 455).

battlefields as a Red Cross Nurse. As Jenny Bourne Taylor points out in her edition of the novel, *The Law and the Lady* was originally serialized in *The Graphic* alongside a series of highly detailed illustrations of the ongoing war in Spain.[27] Commentators such as Andrew Mangham have observed that 'the serialization of nineteenth-century fiction also allowed novelists like Collins to respond to important contemporary events'.[28] As noted in the discussion of the interplay of Dickens's serial fiction with Collins's bachelor journalism in Chapter 2, the proximity and juxtaposition of very different pieces of periodical content could mutually influence journal readers' interpretations. In making his hero, Eustace, a Spanish War nurse, Collins not only adds contemporary piquancy – of a rather more benevolent kind than the exploitation of current murder cases most often attributed to sensation authors – to his novel, he also uses this current event to reveal the hero's moral worth. While Eustace's mother offers a scathing account of her son's conduct, the novel completely undermines her opinion of male nursing as weakness: 'His whole conduct [. . .] has been (I say again) the conduct of an essentially weak man. What do you think he has done now by way of climax? He has joined a charitable brotherhood; and is off to the war in Spain with a red cross on his arm.'[29] Far from exhibiting his weakness Eustace's actions in this conflict, including his daring rescue of a wounded lad in which he is injured, lead to his moral recovery. The topicality of Collins's serialized novel provides, like *Great Expectations* within the Civil War issues of *Harper's Weekly*, an alternative narrative of masculinity to that conveyed by the journal content focused upon the campaigns of the conflict.

In *Poor Miss Finch* (1872) Collins had similarly used an incident of military nursing as the occasion for characters' revaluation of the hero, and for a discussion of the constituents of true manliness. Here, Oscar the hero, disappointed in love, leaves Britain to become a 'hospital man nurse' in Alessandria, 'acting under the surgeons as attendant on the badly-wounded men who had survived the famous campaign of France and Italy against Austria'.[30] Again, Collins uses this narrative to give the serial a certain

---

[27] Jenny Bourne Taylor, ed. note to Wilkie Collins, *The Law and the Lady* (Oxford: Oxford University Press, 1999), note to p. 196.

[28] Andrew Mangham, Introduction to *Wilkie Collins: Interdisciplinary Essays*, ed. Mangham (Newcastle: Cambridge Scholars Publishing, 2007), p. 2.

[29] Collins, *The Law and the Lady*, p. 196.

[30] Wilkie Collins, *Poor Miss Finch* (Oxford: Oxford University Press, 1995), p. 380.

topicality: 'Bear in mind, if you please, that I am writing of the year 1859, and that the peace of Villafranca was only signed in the July of that year' (p. 380). As in *The Law and the Lady* the hero's account of his experience forces others to reassess him:

'I made myself some use (under the regular surgeons and dressers) in nursing the poor mutilated, crippled men; and I have helped a little afterwards, from my own resources, in starting them comfortably in new ways of life.' In these manly and simple words, he told me his story. Once more, I felt what I had felt already, that there were hidden resources of strength in the character of this innocent young fellow, which had utterly escaped my superficial observation of him. In choosing his vocation, he was, no doubt, only following the conventional modern course in such cases. Despair has its fashions, as well as dress. Ancient despair (especially of Oscar's sort) used to turn soldier, or go into a monastery. Modern despair turns nurse; binds up wounds, gives physic, and gets cured or not in that useful but nasty way (p. 386).

Collins's rather flippant account of the manifestation of modern despair in acts of male nursing that can cure both patient and nurse offers a more serious reflection on the mid-Victorian rise of a new sort of hero, the male healer. *Bleak House*'s Trooper George, as an unconventional rendering of the military nurse, and Collins's direct portrayals of battlefield nursing, work to expose the often less visible dynamics of wartime masculinity.

Such widespread celebratory attention to more gentle manliness, especially in the context of war, points to the insufficiency of ongoing assumptions about the innate connection of militarism and masculine aggression. As Das has noted, various recent commentators have re-articulated a belief given authority by Sigmund Freud in his essays 'Thoughts for the Times on War and Death' (1915), in which he equates 'primal man' brought out by war to 'a gang of murderers', and 'Beyond the Pleasure Principle' (1920): 'The tendency to aggression is an innate, independent instinctual disposition in man.'[31] Martin van Creveld, for example, asserts that 'however unpalatable the fact, the real reason we have wars is that men like fighting, and women like men who are prepared to fight on their behalf'.[32] In what is otherwise a

[31] Freud, quoted by Das, p. 101 and by Niall Ferguson, *The Pity of War* (London: Penguin, 1998), p. 358.
[32] Martin van Creveld, *Transformation of War* (New York: The Free Press, 1991), p. 221.

nuanced investigation into the overstatement of the contribution of militaristic politics and culture in the escalation of the First World War, Niall Ferguson includes a controversial section on the 'Joy of War' that similarly speculates that 'men kept fighting because they wanted to', and that 'men may have fought simply because fighting was fun'.[33] The proliferation of mid-nineteenth century military nursing narratives gives Victorian battlefield suffering in particular, and masculinity in general, a more positive angle by featuring the restorative, healing hero.

'SUSTAINER OF SPIRIT AND BODY . . . IN TIME OF NEED': TOUCH AND MAGNETIC PRESENCE IN WALT WHITMAN AND DICKENS

The American Civil War was, of course, the arena for the nineteenth-century's only famous actual male nurse, Walt Whitman, who was himself an enthusiastic and attentive reader of Dickens's work. Whitman recorded his experiences in the field and in the Washington hospitals in his poetry, his published memoirs and his private correspondence. Whitman's ethos of healing, with its egalitarian emphasis and explicitly homoerotic dynamic, parallels the key elements of Dickens's depictions of restorative male touching. Further, Whitman's acts in the hospitals and his writings on the war in various genres have a similar curative effect to that potentially exerted by *Great Expectations* in *Harper's Weekly*, as acts of male intimacy and tenderness are privileged over those of aggression.

In *Specimen Days* (1882–3), reminiscences drawn from the notebooks he jotted during his time in military hospitals, Whitman estimates that he made over six-hundred visits during 'those three years in hospital, camp or field', describing himself 'as sustainer of spirit and body in some degree, in time of need'.[34] As a volunteer carer, unfettered by official professional duties, Whitman was free to expend time on patients in particular need, responding to 'mark'd cases needing special and sympathetic nourishment'. Like Dickens's unprofessional male

---

[33] Ferguson, pp. 357, 360.
[34] Walt Whitman, *Specimen Days and Collect* (Philadelphia: Ross Welsh, 1882–3), p. 78.

healers, Whitman utilizes his unofficial status to provide a unique, highly emotional, and personal brand of care:

There I sit down and either talk to, or silently cheer them up. They always like it hugely (and so do I). Each case has its peculiarities, and needs some new adaptation. I have [...] learnt a good deal of hospital wisdom. Some of the poor young chaps, away from home for the first time in their lives, hunger and thirst for affection; this is sometimes the only thing that will reach their condition.[35]

This avowal of personal pleasure – 'and so do I' – is typical of Whitman's frank acknowledgement of the reciprocity of his emotional and physical engagement with patients.

Throughout *Specimen Days* Whitman records his bodily admiration for patients, describing how he 'took a fancy to one patient', found another 'a fine specimen of youthful physical manliness', and sympathized with another 'poor youth, so handsome athletic, with profuse beautiful shining hair'.[36] As nursing historian Colin Macduff has observed, 'one of the most striking aspects of Whitman's approach was his openness as a man about what he was getting out of the experience personally'.[37] Whitman records instances of mutually beneficial physical contact, such as that shared with Oscar Wilber – 'He behaved very manly and affectionate. The kiss I gave him as I was about leaving he return'd fourfold' – and with a rebel soldier: 'I loved him much, always kiss'd him and he did me.'[38] In his letters, reminiscences and poetry Whitman employs suggestive, sexual language in his tribute to the intense emotional, and perhaps erotic, fulfilment of nursing. In a letter to his brother Jeff he details his response to the wounded with typical frankness: 'I never had my feelings so thoroughly and (so far) permanently absorbed, to the very roots, as by these huge swarms of dear, wounded, sick, dying boys – I get very much attached to some of them, and many of them have come to depend on seeing me.'[39] At the end of *Specimen Days* Whitman describes his time in the

[35] Whitman, *Specimen Days*, p. 51.
[36] Whitman, *Specimen Days*, p. 32, p. 36, p. 37.
[37] Macduff, p. 38.
[38] Whitman, *Specimen Days*, p. 41, p. 74.
[39] Quoted by B. Knapp, *Walt Whitman* (New York: Continuum, 1993), p. 51.

hospitals as 'the greatest privilege and satisfaction [. . .] It arous'd and brought out and decided undream'd of depths of emotion'.[40]

In a war characterized by the ability of new technologies to inflict such widespread and disfiguring damage, irrespective of a body's integral strength, 'youth' or 'athleticism', such a personal treatment of the wounded became an urgent response to the alienations of mass, modern warfare. Katherine Kinney juxtaposes Whitman's highly personal treatments with the detachment characteristic of the government response to war. Such official de-personalization of the casualties was vividly recorded in the displays of the Army Medical Museum, which opened in 1867 exhibiting such so-called 'pathological specimens' as 'A Withered Arm' of a unionist soldier dismembered by cannon fire: 'The withering of flesh and the objective display of the museum mark precisely this loss of sensuality – a loss countered by the "bodily excess" of Whitman's war prose in which injury and his response to it, including writing, remain "sensuous human activity"'.[41] In Whitman's prose and poetry of the Civil War a tender, often homoerotic, response to the casualties is the mode through which the unflinching recognition of the wounds inflicted is made personal and recuperative.

Whitman's poetry provides another explicit exploration of the combined emotional and physical pleasures of nursing, on which the 'Drum-Taps' section of *Leaves of Grass* (first ed. 1865) focuses: 'Bearing the bandages, water and sponge, / Straight and swift to my wounded I go.'[42] Section three of 'The Wound Dresser' offers a detailed cataloguing of injuries which take in the entire body: 'the crush'd head', the cavalryman's

[40] Whitman, *Specimen Days*, p. 78.

[41] Katherine Kinney, 'Making Capital: War, Labour, and Whitman in Washington D.C.' in *Breaking Bounds: Whitman and American Cultural Studies* ed. Betsy Erkkila and Jay Grossman (New York and Oxford: Oxford University Press, 1996), pp. 174–92, p. 182.

[42] Walt Whitman, 'The Wound Dresser', *Leaves of Grass and Other Writings*, ed. Michael Moon (New York and London: Norton, 2002), pp. 259–61, lines 25–6. Robert Leigh Davis proposes that Civil War nursing was a particularly liminal occupation, which placed practitioners at the fault line of 'a culture deeply divided by race, gender, class and regional loyalty'. He compellingly argues that Whitman and Alcott (as well as Emma Edmonds who cross-dressed in terms of race, gender, class, and military loyalty to survive as a field nurse) experienced Civil War nursing as a way of rendering 'normally self-evident boundaries fluid and unstable' and as a means of '"mov[ing]" between" the fixed lines of established order'. *Whitman and the Romance of Medicine* (Berkeley and London: University of California Press, 1997), p. 45.

bullet perforated neck, 'the stump of the arm, the amputated hand', 'the wound in the side, deep, deep', 'the perforated shoulder, the foot with the bullet wound', 'the fractur'd thigh, the knee, the wound in the abdomen'.[43] Whitman's physical response recoups such fragments from the status of the pathological specimen – '(Yet deep in my breast, a fire, a burning flame)' (line 58). Michael Moon observes the way in which this section 'revises the catalogues of the parts of the human body that Whitman had previously carried out in poems like "I Sing the Body Electric"'. Moon also suggests that this poem effects a transformation from Whitman's earlier jingoistic representation of the Pennant of War into the 'revisionary form of "bandages", "clotted rags", "the clotted lint"'.[44] This revision suggests Whitman's increasingly conflicted sense of the value of this war as its human cost rose beyond all expectation.

Throughout the 'Drum-taps' section Whitman repeatedly emphasizes the professional and emotional status of nursing through a focus on damaged and vulnerable bodies that desperately require such care.[45] Leslie Fiedler suggests that 'most people [. . .] remembering images of nurses in literature do not recall this poem, in part because Whitman was of the wrong gender, a male pretender to a role which mythologically we associate with the female of the species'.[46] Fiedler further argues

[43] Whitman, 'The Wound Dresser', from lines 40–57.

[44] Michael Moon, *Disseminating Whitman: Revision and Corporeality in* Leaves of Grass (Cambridge, Massachusetts and London: Harvard University Press, 1991), p. 196.

[45] See, for example, the range of fragile, damaged and vilified bodies with which 'The Sleepers' is concerned. The dreamer immediately encounters 'the wretched features of ennuyés, the white features of corpses, the livid faces of drunkards, the sick-grey faces of onanists / The gashed bodies on battle-fields, the insane in their strong-doored rooms [...]'. 'The Sleepers', *Leaves of Grass*, pp. 356–64, lines 8–9.

[46] Fiedler, p. 108. Whitman did not choose the label 'nurse' to describe his own role, preferring the terms 'hospital missionary' and 'sustainer of spirit and body.' However, as Macduff discerns, his language in *Specimen Days* does destabilize the conventional gendering of nursing: 'In a reversal of the current situation, where *male* is often used to prefix the term *nurse* when discriminating a non-female occupant of the role, Whitman often distinguishes *female* or *lady nurses*' (p. 38). He also provides testimony to the much needed care provided by other men recording, for example, the account of a soldier who, having been left wounded on the field for fifty hours, received kind treatment from a 'good secesh': 'One middle aged man, however, who seemed to be moving around the field, among the dead and wounded for benevolent purposes, came to him in a way he will never forget; treated our soldier kindly, bound up his wounds, cheer'd him, gave him a couple of biscuits and a drink of whiskey and water, asked him if he could eat some beef' (*Specimen Days*, p. 29).

that there is a critical discomfort with Whitman's 'vision of the eros of nursing', with the 'hints of lubricity and sado-masochism' that colour his poetic scrutiny and celebration of maimed male bodies.[47] Macduff suggests that these elements of his writing combined with speculation about Whitman's own homosexuality 'may explain nursing's reluctance to recognize Whitman, in that there is conflict with the popular image of the nurse as "sexless secular saint"'.[48]

The subtle shifts from the clinical to the admiring gaze, from the methodical exterior to the emotional interior, provide a rare description of the professional skill, personal reaction, and erotic response that can come together in the activity of nursing. The dresser's sense that he 'could not refuse this moment to die' to save a young patient and the physicality of the final two lines, point suggestively to the spiritually and sexually transcendent extent of the patient/nurse relations that develop in this heightened atmosphere:

(Many a soldier's loving arms about this neck have cross'd and rested, Many a soldier's kiss dwells on these bearded lips.)[49]

While historians of nursing and, to some extent, literary critics have been unwilling to acknowledge the erotic dynamic of male nursing, articulated so powerfully in Whitman's work, writers in other media have been less reluctant. Philip Dacey's poem 'Walt Whitman Falls Asleep Over Florence Nightingale's *Notes on Nursing*' positions Whitman and Nightingale

---

[47] Fiedler, p. 108.
[48] Macduff, p. 41. Macduff has observed how rarely Whitman, though an important trail blazer for male nurses who still experience a dearth of historical role models (which, as Chad O' Lynn has argued is a major impediment to current recruitment of male nurses), is acknowledged in histories of nursing. Macduff speculates that this is due to discomfort with seeming to bear out the unhelpful association of male nursing with homosexuality.
[49] Whitman, 'The Wound Dresser', lines 37–8, 64–5. Through an identification of the resonances of 'Drum Taps' with Whitman's wider work, Michael Moon has thoroughly debunked the popular, but homophobic, biographical stance that the suspension of 'normal' social mores in the civil war hospitals provided the only setting for a thorough expression Whitman's homoerotic desires. *Disseminating*, pp. 210–11. See also Michael Moon, 'Memorial Rags: Emerson, Whitman, AIDS and Mourning' in *Professions of Desire: Lesbian and Gay Studies in Literature*, ed. George Haggerty and Bonnie Zimmerman (New York: Modern Language Association, 1995), pp. 233–40. However, even this allegedly exceptional hospital homoeros has been subject to a large degree of disavowal and containment (as pathological/ necrophillic/ or plain unpleasant) by various academic disciplines.

side-by-side as icons of care: 'Call us nursing's perfect, if strangest pair.'[50] In a queer vision of this couple in joint charge of a ward Dacey plays with the erotic connotations of nursing, describing Nightingale's as 'the face that launched a dozen suitor's dreams', to suggest the similar romantic response of male patients to both Nightingale and Whitman:

[. . .] Wherever her silhouette
ripples across a pillow as we move,
lips curse-heavy press with a touch as light
as a girl's against coarse cloth, imprinting a love
I do not envy, having known it too.[51]

As well as a frank record of his emotional response to patients, Whitman offers a fascinating record of his belief in healthful 'emanation', feeling that his simple presence exhales a healing 'magnetism' that is found to be more beneficial than the 'routine assistance' of doctors or medicine. In an 1863 letter to his close friend Hugo Fritsch, Whitman describes his life in Washington:

Dear comrade, I still live here as a hospital missionary after my own style, and on my own hook – I go every day or night without fail to some of the great government hospitals – O the sad scenes I witness – scenes of death, anguish, the fevers, amputations, friendlessness, hungering and thirsting young hearts, for some loving presence – such noble young men as some of these wounded are – such endurance, such native decorum, such candour – I will confess to you dear Hugo that in some respects I find myself in my element amid these scenes – shall I not say to you that I find I supply often to some of these dear suffering boys in my presence and magnetism that which nor doctors, nor medicines, nor skill, nor any routine assistance can give.[52]

He recapitulates this in the public register of *Specimen Days*: 'In my visits to the hospitals I found it was in the simple matter of personal presence, and emanating ordinary cheer and magnetism, that I succeeded and helped more than by medical nursing, or delicacies, or gifts of money, or anything else.'[53] In a startlingly direct way, *Bleak House's* trooper George anticipates

[50] Philip Dacey, 'Walt Whitman Falls Asleep Over Florence Nightingale's *Notes on Nursing*', *Shenandoah* 45.2 (1995), 36–9, p. 37.
[51] Dacey, p. 37.
[52] Walt Whitman, *Civil War Poetry and Prose*, ed. Candace Ward (New York: Dover, 1995), p. 69.
[53] Walt Whitman, *Specimen Days*, p. 38.

these descriptions in the galvanizing effect that his physical presence has on those he cares for. For Phil, as we have already seen, it is a tonic to watch George washing: 'the superfluous health his master throws off' is felt to be 'sufficient renovation for one day' (p. 418). George has a similar, albeit temporary, effect on Jo at whose bedside he is 'a frequent visitor, filling the doorway with his athletic figure, and, from his superfluity of life and strength, seeming to shed down temporary vigour upon Jo, who never fails to speak more robustly in answer to his cheerful words' (p. 732). George's ability to restore the voices, and indeed the agency, of the very sick is particularly poignant in relation to Sir Leicester Dedlock. George's presence allows the baronet to gather his energies sufficiently to make his significant declaration of his unchanged feeling for Lady Dedlock.

Such recuperative powers of physical presence have traditionally been attributed to women. Indeed, Dickens also offers a conventionally gendered rendering of this in *Bleak House* when Caddy benefits from the healthful emanations of Esther: 'She almost – I think I must say quite – believed that I did her good whenever I was near her' (p. 769). As Bashford has demonstrated, in the nineteenth century, a widespread attitude that gentlewomen were curative by their simple attendance in hospitals and houses led to practices of middle-class women visiting working class homes, as well as to medical reform.[54] Dickens most memorably represents the supposedly benevolent and beneficial practice of home visiting in the formidable figure of Mrs Pardiggle, who arrives at the brick-makers' cottage in *Bleak House* wielding 'a good book as if it were a staff, and [...] as if she were an inexorable moral Policeman' (p. 132). Mrs Pardiggle's emanations are anything but renovating, indeed she seems to work as a physical blight, as the brick-makers' baby dies during her sermonizing (p. 134). While Dickens challenges the simple equation of femininity and restoring moral goodness, he demonstrates the transmissibility, as noted in the previous chapter, of tender affect between men. Just as Dickens and Whitman believed in their own curative powers, Dickens invests his most heroic male figures with an ability to heal, that positively infects their patients. Martin Chuzzlewit and Pip, for example, acquire a new repertoire of tenderness from those who minister to them, so that Pip, having benefited from the physical care provided by Joe and Herbert is finally able to nurse Magwitch in prison.

[54] Bashford, pp. 33–4.

Whitman, as M. Wynn Thomas suggests, experienced the value of an ability to soothe and heal as 'a different "currency" [that] circulated in the hospitals – a currency of love and affection symbolised [. . .] both by the little gifts he brought the men and the caresses he exchanged with them'.[55] As Whitman put it, 'while cash is not amiss to bring up the rear, tact and magnetic sympathy and unction are, and ever will be, sovereign still'.[56] This alternative currency is very similar to Mark Tapley's eccentric definition of 'credit' through his ministry of tender care in *Martin Chuzzlewit*. Similarly Whitman's valuation of 'magnetic sympathy' resonates with the various renovating experiences of being close to *Bleak House*'s General George, or indeed, to Dickens himself as mesmeric operator. In their representations of male healing, Whitman and Dickens displace conventional markers of worth, attributing the greatest value to the ability to heal. Both Whitman and Dickens, then, present physical and emotional ministration as a means of circumventing class boundaries and the sterile cash nexus.

In his early career as a journalist Whitman wrote a number of pieces on Dickens, displaying an intimate knowledge of the novels and an enthusiasm for the author that extended into a sense of personal fellowship. In an 1842 piece Whitman energetically defends Dickens from charges of recommending crime and being fascinated with vice and degradation:

As I think my humble lance, wielded in defence of Mr Dickens, may meet the sight of the gentleman himself, I cannot lose the opportunity of saying how much I love and esteem him for what he has taught me through his writings – and for the genial influence that these writings spread around them wherever they go. Never having seen Boz in the body, we have yet had many a *tête-à-tête*. And I cannot tamely hear one whom I have long considered a personal friend, and a friend to his species, thus falsely and uncharitably and groundlessly attacked.[57]

Given the evidence for Whitman's attentive reading of Dickens and his particular appreciation of Dickens's socially curative, reformist

[55] M. Wynn Thomas, 'Fratricide and Brotherly Love: Whitman and the Civil War', in *The Cambridge Companion to Walt Whitman*, ed. Ezra Greenspan (Cambridge: Cambridge University Press, 1995), pp. 27–44, p. 43.
[56] Whitman, *Specimen Days*, p. 57.
[57] Walt Whitman, 'Boz and Democracy', *Brother Jonathan*, 26 February 1842, repr. in *The Collected Writings of Walt Whitman: The Journalism*, ed. Herbert Bergman, vol. 1 (New York: Peter Lang, 1998), pp. 35–8, p. 38. He was to continue championing Dickens, albeit in a more qualified form, during the widespread outrage at *American Notes*.

agenda – 'the rich cannot taste the distresses of want from their own experience, it is something if they are made to do so through the power of the pen'[58] – it is just possible that Trooper George had an effect on how Whitman conceived of his own intimate, informal care of those most in need. Less speculatively, it is clear that the loneliness and alienation of many in 1850s London created a similar sense of desolate isolation to that experienced by many of the young soldiers who Whitman encounters, men who are away from home for the first time. In both situations there is desperate need for those able to provide emotional succour that can heal across class lines and other social boundaries.

Whitman is particularly explicit about his refusal to recognize distinctions of allegiance, rank and race in his egalitarian provision of care: 'I can say that in my ministerings I comprehended all, whoever came in my way, northern or southern, and slighted none' (*Specimen Days*, p. 78). As various commentators have observed, the Civil War made a particular contribution to Whitman's vision of a democratic, unified national future. Nicholas Everett, for example, suggests that the wide range of soldiers, in terms of occupation, class, race and allegiance, in 'this first modern war fought by conscripted civilians', with whom Whitman came into contact put him '*in touch* with the scope and character of the country as he had never been before. Visiting them, he became a version of the representative persona he had invented' (emphasis added).[59] Both Whitman and Dickens, then, place the figure of the democratically ministering male at the centre of their idealistic visions of a healthier body politic in which class ruptures are healed.

In Whitman's and Dickens's accounts of restorative touch, homoeroticism comes together with other important valuations of masculine tactility in a redefining of the gentle man that posits a hands-on model of cross-class contact as the heart of social reform. The highly positive intimacy of same-sex bodywork presented in Dickens's fiction anticipates Whitman's explicit celebration of the physical pleasures of nursing men. Once again Dickens's fictional strategies both cohere with actual homoerotic experiences and anticipate the later techniques employed by

---

[58] 'Boz and Democracy', p. 38.
[59] Nicholas Everett, 'Autobiography as Prophecy: Walt Whitman's "Specimen Days"' in *Mortal Pages: Literary Lives, Studies in Nineteenth Century Autobiography*, ed. Vincent Newey and Phillip Shaw (Aldershot: Scolar, 1996), pp. 217–34, p. 220.

those writers who strove for more explicit articulations of homosexuality. Beyond the erotic, the hands of trooper George and Joe Gargery extend a queer touch, showing the limitations of existing terminologies and challenging pre-conceptions of class, gender, and the association of masculinity with violence. In our own hyperbolically militaristic twenty-first century it is vital to denaturalize the pervasive cultural association of manliness and aggression by acknowledging the physical gentleness inherent in a central historical model of ideal masculinity, the Victorian gentle man.

Postscript
Doing Dickens: The Queer
Politics of Adaptation

Dickens's legacy continues to be reshaped by the multiple and diverse rewritings of a prolific adaptation industry, which in its various media captures and redirects the energies with which those Dickens readers who were also authors – including, as we have seen, Mary Braddon, Evelyn Waugh, and Walt Whitman – imaginatively responded to his writing in their own work. The late-twentieth century onwards has been a particularly fruitful time for new insights into Victorian culture from outside academia. Neo-Victorian novels, particularly those by Sarah Waters and Wesley Stace, have offered queer narratives of nineteenth-century sexuality, gender and family.[1] As Sarah Waters says in an interview about her nineteenth-century literary 'pastiche', *Fingersmith* (2002), which was itself adapted for the BBC in 2005, 'lesbian desires [. . . are] sort of there as a subtext to lots of Victorian fiction. But what I've been able to do, writing with our literary mores today, is to tease them right out and put them at the centre of the story rather than kind of at the edges.'[2] Neo-Victorian work of this kind takes a similar debunking message to that expressed in the work of Sweet and Mason to a different and broader audience.[3]

---

[1] See especially Sarah Waters, *Tipping the Velvet* (London: Virago, 1998), *Affinity* (London: Virago, 1999), *Fingersmith* (London: Virago, 2002), and Wesley Stace, *Misfortune* (London: Jonathan Cape, 2004).

[2] Sarah Waters's comments are taken from, 'Behind the Scenes of Fingersmith' DVD feature, *Fingersmith*, dir. Aisling Walsh, Sally Head Productions, 2005.

[3] Cora Kaplan discusses Waters's and other neo-Victorian work in *Victoriana: Histories, Fiction, Criticism* (Edinburgh: Edinburgh University Press, 2007), examining the extent to which such material is in dialogue with academic revisions of the Victorians.

New interpretations of Dickens are offered in numerous adaptations, which, in turn, have an enormous impact on the way in which we encounter his own written work. Given the almost overwhelming plenitude of Dickens adaptation, this postscript focuses on a handful of film and television versions that demonstrate the persisting contestation of Dickens's queer content. Adaptors continue to imbue Dickens's characters with new lives of their own, a project, as we saw in Chapter 2's attention to Dickens's resurrection of Pickwick, that Dickens himself was involved in.

Such reinvention has continued to thrive since those late 1830s stage adaptations that so frustrated Dickens by proffering an ending to his, as yet, incomplete novels. This constant process of reinvention clearly renders obsolete any effort to identify an authentic original. Dickens, unlike the endlessly re-animated Jacob Marley, was never dead, even to begin with. Adaptors clearly respond to a variety of existing stage and screen productions (Dickensian and otherwise) as well as to Dickens's texts – their visual as well as verbal content – which were themselves indebted to a tissue of textual and stage influences and were subject to continuing authorial revision throughout Dickens's lifetime.

This postscript, then, follows a move in adaptation studies away from a fascination with always chimerical faithfulness, examining instead the effects of Dickens's various afterlives.[4] In his collection *Dickens on Screen*, John Glavin suggests that 'the Dickens film now shapes Dickens's fiction'; 'It's these adaptations, for the big screen and the small, that generate whatever possibilities remain for reading the fiction.'[5] Contributors Gerhard Joseph and Robert Polhemous expand this claim with reference to Freud's idea of 'screen memory', as viewing experiences are projected as back-formations into reading, simultaneously obscuring and illuminating aspects of Dickens's work.[6] As Andrew Davies, prolific screen adaptor of Victorian and neo-Victorian

[4] In *Rethinking the Novel/Film Debate* (Cambridge: Cambridge University Press, 2003), Kamilla Elliot discusses the range of influences – literary, filmic, from across the visual arts, theatrical – as well as the credited 'source' text, on film adaptations, and explores the dead-end in adaptation studies of fascination with faithfulness to the 'original'.
[5] John Glavin, 'Introduction' to *Dickens on Screen*, ed. John Glavin (Cambridge: Cambridge University Press, 2003), pp. 1–10, pp. 3, 5.
[6] Gerhard Joseph, 'Dickens, Psychoanalysis and Film: A Roundtable', in *Dickens on Screen*, pp. 11–26 and Robert Polhemus, 'Screen Memories in Dickens and Woody Allen', in *Dickens on Screen*, pp. 72–85.

novels, says: 'the author doesn't necessarily completely own the book. It's an interaction between them and readers at a different time.'[7] Screen versions create both new possibilities of interpretation and new audiences of Dickens readers – as the BBC serialization of Andrew Davies's *Bleak House* (2005) rose to fourth position in UK TV viewing figures, Amazon.co.uk reported a 290% increase in sales of the novel. These audiences bring new expectations and ways of reading to Dickens's work, showing how, even when encountering literary texts directly, we read authors through the prism of their cultural afterlife. My students, even after a close-reading of the novel, tend to remember Brownlow as Oliver Twist's grandfather, or perhaps uncle, demonstrating the impact of this wider cultural bio'logical' reworking of *Oliver Twist*.

As suggested by the range examples of *Twist* adaptation briefly referenced in Chapter 1, which cover conservative tea-time viewing to sexually explicit rent-boy movies, Dickens's work can be variously consumed, interpreted, and reworked. The interest in Donsky's and Tierney's films with sexual trade picks up on both an academic line of interpretation (advanced, for example, by Larry Wolff in his memorable piece on Dickens's knowledge of boy prostitution), and a historic component of *Twist* adaptation, in motion since Lean's buttock shot sexually commodified the screen Oliver. The long, culturally diverse, history of the physical consumption and appropriation of Oliver is strategically dissipated by those films, which as we have seen, use a flawed concept of the biological family as the only place of safety for the child. The schism between, say, Giedroyc's 2007 BBC serial in which Oliver is cosily incorporated into his grandfather's family and Tierney's and Donsky's brutal visions of Oliver as a sexual commodity who can never be accommodated within any family or fulfilled in an emotional relationship, demonstrates the current spectrum of thinking about Dickens. On the one hand he is still a figurehead for a nostalgic vision of the security of Victorian hearth and home, while, on the other, his work presents possibilities for the expression of queer theory's most bruising anti-social thesis.

Susan Zieger has argued that a similarly wide divide is apparent between clearly queer screen versions of Dickens, examining those that present the anti-social thesis – most associated, as we have seen,

---

[7] Andrew Davies, interviewed by Cole Moreton, *Independent*, 26 October 2008.

with the theoretical writing of Bersani, Edelman, and Halberstam – and those that work counter to that thesis in more optimistic readings, associated with the work of Sharon Marcus, Eve Sedgwick (in her most recent writing), and, I hope, this book. Zieger argues that Douglas McGrath's 2002 film of *Nicholas Nickleby* (and I add here Andrew Davies's 2005 screenplay of *Bleak House*, directed by Justin Chadwick and Susanna White) present a different interpretative lens to that of Tierney's and Donsky's films: 'Whereas [Tierney's] *Twist* demonstrates and refines Edelman's main point, that reproductive futurism makes queer lives expendable, McGrath's *Nickleby* suggests possibilities for queer assimilation into the bourgeois family, a move that aligns it with a different critical trend in queer theory and literary studies.'[8] Alternative interpretations less preoccupied with the (im)possibility of queer sociality are offered by the rise of Dickensian burlesque and cabaret, such as Gila Sand's irreverent 2006 musical 'Twist' featuring whipping – and the repeated request 'please, sir, can I have some more?' –, shoe fetishism and camp ballet under the strap-line 'Music, Dickens, Bondage', and Joe Godfrey's 1999 stage-show *A Queer Carol*, in which the ghost of Christmas Past becomes the spirit of Marilyn Monroe.[9] Less campily Tierney's *Twist* and Donsky's *Twisted* confirm the anti-social thesis of an impassable distance between outcast queer life and more inhabitable domestic spaces, which is perhaps most fully elaborated in Dickens's work around the itinerant Miss Wade, while McGrath's and Davies's projects pick up Dickens's non-biological definition of family and his fascination with eccentric, nurturing households.

McGrath's *Nickleby* emphasizes the nurturing romance of Nicholas and Smike and the formation of families of choice. In the director's overview, McGrath speaks of his interpretation of Nicholas and Smike's

[8] Susan Zieger, 'Dickens's Queer Children'; *Nicholas Nickleby*, dir. Douglas McGrath, United Artists, 2002; *Bleak House*, dir. Justin Chadwick and Susanna White, screenplay by Andrew Davies, BBC, 2005.
[9] Twist the musical premiered at the Philadelphia Fringe Festival in September 2006, transferring to the Kraine Theatre, New York for the winter season. For further production details and responses see http://themusicaltwist.com. See Adrienne Onofri's review of the 2001 Manhattan premiere of *A Queer Carol*, directed by Mark Cannistraro at the Duplex Theatre, 'Glitter and Be Gay', www.curtainup.com/gayxmas. Recent restagings include David Clay's 2006 production at the New Conservatory Theatre Centre, San Francisco and Davyn Ryall's at the Mainline Theatre, Montreal (2007).

relationship as the central theme of the novel and 'the heart of the movie', outlining his production decision to film scenes between them in two-shot, rather than in separate close-ups, to 'show the bond, the unity between them'.[10] McGrath identifies Smike's declaration to Nicholas, 'You are my home' (in chapter 13 of Dickens's novel), as 'the most important line in the entire script'. He suggests that Dickens's definition of kinship 'is something quite unique – it isn't what you think it is, that family stands for family that blood stands by blood, it's much more about the people that you care about and the people that you'd give your blood for'. In support of this vision of families of affinity, the script adds extra dialogue to that provided in Dickens's chapter 35, when Smike meets Kate. In the film, Kate offers a new toast, 'Our extended family', to the assorted company, which encompasses the poor and eccentric Newman Noggs and Miss La Creevy. Smike responds with predictable enthusiasm: 'Our family'.

This scene is central to the film's tacit commitment to, at least in part, an optimistic queer rendering of Dickens. At the centre of what must surely be seen as a deliberate casting strategy the film features Charlie Hunnam (famous for his preceding starring role in British TV series *Queer as Folk*) as Nicholas alongside a Smike played by Jamie Bell (best known as ballet dancing Billy Elliot, 2002), with Alan Cumming and Nathan Lane in supporting roles.[11] Australian actor Barry Humphries – best known for comic drag performances as mock-posh matron Dame Edna Everage – appears as Mrs Crummles. This contribution is billed, in a truly Butlerian critique of the authenticity of gender performances, as 'Barry Humphries as Dame Edna Everage as Mrs. Crummles.'[12] Humphries also cameos in a small male role. Dickens's own particular appreciation of role-play through his fascination with commercial and amateur theatricals is acknowledged by the opening credits of the film; here the cast are transformed into the cardboard characters of a Victorian toy theatre, similar to that which Dickens built and played with, with

---

[10] McGrath's comments are taken from 'Audio Commentary with director Douglas McGrath' and 'The Making of *Nicholas Nickleby* Documentary', *Nicholas Nickleby* (2002, collector's edition DVD, 2004).

[11] Showtime's US series *Queer as Folk* was modelled on the UK version.

[12] This billing embodies Butler's classic theory of drag performances as 'imitations which effectively displace the meaning of the original, they imitate the myth of originality itself' (*Gender Trouble*, p. 76).

his children. Humphries's drag and the artistically manipulated cardboard figures of McGrath's credits recall Mrs Jarley's experiments, as
discussed in Chapter 4, with the (gendered) interchangeability of wax-
work characters in *The Old Curiosity Shop*. McGrath's production
continues its confusion of identities, and of gender roles in particular,
through a focus on the suggestive physical similarity of the Nickleby
siblings, casting relatively unknown actress Romola Garai as Kate,
primarily because of her striking resemblance to Charlie Hunnam's
Nicholas. Just as the novel repeatedly emphasizes the importance of
familial body-doubling, the film draws additional attention to this
through the careful casting and costuming of the Cheeryble brothers,
whose bodies and environments are almost indistinguishable even down
to their identically decorated and equipped offices, and twin pet cats.
On Nicholas's first meeting with the twins, carefully composed sym-
metrical frames give the impression of a lateral mirror image, which is
alternated with close-ups of Nicholas's perplexed expression as he encounters this physical doubling.

As a review of McGrath's film entitled 'Putting the Dick back in
Dickens', recognizes: 'Everyone here either is queer, has played queer,
portrayed a queer's mother or father, or once met Madonna.'[13] The actors'
own sexualities and histories as provocative homosexual and gender-
ambivalent characters are re-energized by the film's lingering physical
scenes of Nicholas's bodily care for Smike, and moving representation of
the abused young man's absolute dedication to his handsome rescuer.
McGrath selects Charlie Hunnam's performance of Nicholas's anguish at
Smike's increasing illness as his most 'lovely and tender' scene: 'The person
he's come to love the most, or to feel the very closest to, is in peril, and that
puts his whole composure and his whole happiness in peril.' This film's
prioritizing of this relationship over the attachment between Nicholas and
Madeline parallels Dickens's text. McGrath does add a proposal scene,
notably absent in Dickens's novel, and endeavours to shore up this rather
thin courtship plot with newly scripted, but somewhat trite, conventional
romantic dialogue. He is clearly aware of the heterosexual insufficiencies of
Dickens's work, defending his additions by explaining that 'we could not

---

[13] Planetout.com. Quoted by Zieger, 'Children, Class and Sexuality'. Zieger went on
to examine diverse US press responses to McGrath's film, which succeeded in appealing
to both the gay community and the Christian right.

have the movie without a proper love scene between these two people we've come to care so much about'. However, true to the film's more persistent erotic energies, the wooden 'proper love scene' between Nicholas and Madeline does nothing to dissipate the haunting intensity of those scenes between Nicholas and Smike.

McGrath's emphasis on the terminal romance of Nicholas and Smike both references Dickens's text and draws upon key examples from the buddy film genre, most notably John Schlesinger's *Midnight Cowboy* (1969).[14] Jamie Bell's ragged, poorly-shod, limping performances write Smike's history of neglect and physical abuse onto his body, in the same way that Dustin Hoffman's Rizzo physically records a life of inadequate housing and no healthcare. Both shivering, sweat-sheened bodies also somatically register the disease that Dickens's novel and Schlesinger's film refuse to specify (in McGrath's film Smike is seen by a doctor who diagnoses consumption, Rizzo's coughing and wasting illness is also like TB), but that, from the beginning, anticipates the terminal ending so firmly associated with the plot of male romantic friendship. Smike and Rizzo's first experience of companionship, physical solicitude and, finally, tender treatment arrives in the physically imposing, healthful, tall and blond-haired form of the suited-and-booted outsider (Hunnam/Jon Voight as Joe Buck), who maintains an almost incredible optimism despite penury and desperate living conditions. Both films linger over scenes of the physically diverse pair striding/hobbling though the landscape, the physically stronger holding-up the weaker, and sitting together framed by the broken windows and bare walls of derelict buildings that provide some, if insufficient, respite and refuge.

The projects are also comparable in their weaving of gay identified actors (some associated with controversial previous projects) into a male romance made palatable to a Hollywood audience. Alongside its A-List actors, *Midnight Cowboy*, as Ara Osterweil has documented, cast Viva, Ultra Violet, and Paul Morrisey, stars of Andy Warhol's radical *Lonesome Cowboys* (1967). This earlier film, a partial source for Schlesinger alongside James Leo Herlihy's 1965 novel, contained explicit homo- and heterosexual sex scenes, led to Warhol's investigation by the FBI,

---

[14] *Midnight Cowboy*, dir. John Schlesinger, Metro-Goldwyn-Mayer, 1969. I am thankful to my MA students Sue Boettcher and Jenny Bloodworth for pointing me towards this connection.

provoked moral outrage and achieved commercial cinema success.[15]
McGrath's comparable queer casting in *Nickleby* participates in a
thriving tradition in Dickens adaptation, through which actor's wider
associations, professional and personal affiliations, continue to operate
to propose alternative lines of interpretation, a tradition perhaps inaugurated by Dirk Bogarde's eye-wateringly tight-trousered Sydney Carton in Ralph Thomas's *A Tale of Two Cities* (1958).[16] Bogarde went on,
two years later, to star as the gay hero of Basil Deardon's *Victim* (1961),
directly contributing, as he pointed out in interviews, to that film's
groundbreaking endeavour to advocate tolerance for homosexuals:
'It was the first film in which a man said 'I love you' to another man.
I wrote that scene in. I said, 'there's no point in half-measures. We either
make a film about queers or we don't'.[17]

Warhol was unimpressed by Schlesinger's Oscar winning and carefully physically inexplicit portrayal of male romance in *Midnight Cowboy*, and critics since have noted how Rizzo's fatal end, terminating (and
perhaps punishing) the same-sex intimacy makes this a narrative
that is all too acceptable to mainstream tastes.[18] I find both *Midnight
Cowboy* and McGrath's similarly structured *Nickleby*, with their initially
hopeful relocations which can only finally be journeys to death and loss,
deeply moving films, particularly in the visual space they make available
for a narrative of (always ineffective) male nursing: Voight's/Buck's
belated purchase of medicine, his dressing of Rizzo on the bus and care
for his corpse, Hunnam/Nickleby's carrying of his debilitated friend, his

---

[15] Osterweil, 'Ang Lee's Lonesome Cowboys'.

[16] *A Tale of Two Cities*, dir. Ralph Thomas, Rank, 1958.

[17] Dirk Bogarde, quoted by Russo, *Celluloid Closet*, p. 126. He later played Aschen-
bach in Luchino Visconti's *Death in Venice* (1971). A similar audience effect may be
produced by Simon Callow's current status as the popular face of Dickens in Britain
(Callow even portrayed Dickens in prime-time 2005 BBC series 'Doctor Who'). Callow
performed in the one-man stage show 'The Mystery of Charles Dickens', written by
Peter Ackroyd, first performed in 2000 and much televised in the UK since, which
Kaplan describes as 'camp' and 'tragicomic' (*Victoriana*, p. 10). His performances in this
role surely have a particularly queer resonance for those who witnessed Callow as Oscar
Wilde in a very similarly formatted single-performer production, 'The Importance of
Being Oscar', written by Michael MacLiammor and performed in 1997, and for those
who remember Callow as the nation's Oscar (his institutional status in this alternative
incarnation was reflected in his reading of *De Profundis* at the Wilde Centenary at
Westminster Abbey in 2000).

[18] See Russo, *Celluloid Closet*, quoted on this in my introduction, and Osterweil.

placing of Smike in his own childhood bed, his physical presence at the bedside as he holds Smike's hand as he dies. The more temporally intense experience of McGrath's 127-minute film, distils the wide range of affects produced by Dickens's long serial novel, emotionally eclipsing the potential for queer family held out by the middle of McGrath's production.[19] The interpretative possibilities for reading the novel presented by this film privilege the combined ending of fatal male/male love and predictably bland conventional marriage, an ending which, in this media particularly, can exert a disproportional expunging of the queer family forms that McGrath embraces.

Perhaps expectedly given its more encompassing form, Davies's TV serial *Bleak House* holds out more inhabitable queer possibilities, expanding the fascinations in Dickens's novel with non-biological forms of family, unusual nurturing architectures and male body work. In its soap-opera format of two tantalizingly brief thirty minute weekly episodes (rolled into a one hour weekend omnibus, in a rescheduling move typical of soap-opera, and reminiscent of the various possibilities for re-release utilized by producers of Victorian serial content), the production attempts to recreate the exciting, affectively distinct experience of receiving regular parts. As Producer Nigel Stafford-Clark told *The Mirror*: 'Dickens wrote *Bleak House* as a monthly serial for popular consumption, complete with multiple storylines and cliff-hanger endings. A twice-weekly half-hour television serial felt like returning it to its natural state.' Andrew Davies voiced the popular connection between Dickens and soap opera: 'If Dickens was alive today, he'd be writing for *EastEnders*', and, pointing to the significance of scale, suggested that 'because it totals eight hours, which compared with most serials is a really long one, *Bleak House* is really going to give the flavour of reading a big, long novel.'[20]

The TV serial, like the periodical (as fully discussed in Chapter 2), has multiple opportunities for intertextual implications, as the surrounding televisual content inevitably impinges upon and shapes interpretation. Most poignant for me was the effect of scheduling that

---

[19] Glavin points to the distinctly different rhythms of film watching and novel reading as a reminder that these forms do not neatly map onto one another, *Dickens on Screen*, p. 4.

[20] http://www.digitalspy.co.uk/tv/a19033/bbcs-bleak-house-cast-revealed.html; www.bbc.co.uk/drama/bleakhouse.

allowed Esther's additionally scripted pleas that she might find her mother, to be directly followed by Channel 4's adoption/fostering series *Wanted: New Mum and Dad*, which aired immediately after the Thursday night episodes of *Bleak House*. I enjoyed the serendipitous overlap between the docudrama's effort to prepare one boy for re-homing with 'two dads', and my anticipation of the ending of a possible end to Davies's serial, which could, working closely with Dickens's novel, see the infant Richard ensconced at a remodelled Bleak House with his 'two mamas' (*Bleak House*, p. 988). This is a line of interpretation only partly supported by Davies's serial, which closes with scenes of wedding-day country-dancing in the gardens of the new Bleak House (complete with Ada whirling with baby Richard in her arms), highly reminiscent of the close of McGrath's Nickleby and of many of Davies's earlier adaptation projects, including *Pride and Prejudice* (1995, BBC One).

Though Davies has contributed to enshrining the nuptial pastoral as a set-piece ending for many period adaptations that belies the more complex content of their plots, his *Bleak House*, also, particularly through its rendering of Sergeant George (Hugo Speer), mobilizes and holds open a number of more queer possibilities. The presentation of George – Davies has Miss Flite introduce General George to a desperate Gridley as someone with 'accommodation of a rough sort and a heart of gold' – and his nuanced relationship with Phil, sensitively voices some of the unspoken implications of Dickens's novel. Playing with the possibilities shared by the Victorian prose serial and the modern medium of soap-opera, Davies makes George the hero of two key episodes that explore his commitment to Phil (Michael Smiley), the lame man he cares for, but who, thankfully, does not die! As Hayward has argued, in both these forms 'serial fiction structurally encourages a large cast of characters and multiple story lines and [. . .]subverts the conventional narrative focus on a single hero or heroine'.[21] Episode six of Davies's serial begins with George's visit to Tulkinghorn, in which the trooper refuses to profit by giving information about another man he has cared for, Nemo. On his return to the shooting gallery, George and Phil share an entirely newly written dialogue, in which George renews his promise to Phil to keep him off the street. Davies identifies

[21] Hayward, *Consuming Pleasures*, p. 34.

the mutual intensity of this relationship, and outlines their to-the-death fidelity. In these moments, like those between Nicholas and Smike in McGrath's *Nickleby*, the production is able to visualize and somatically render a type of male tenderness, of both touch and affect, for which there is no obvious verbal equivalent.

Davies's screen play is particularly effective in drawing attention to the combined, apparently antithetical uses of the shooting gallery as a military training school, business, hospital, and domain of male intimacy. Various scenes dramatize the delicious paradox of George as fighting expert and practised carer, enacting the apparent oxymoron of the gentle swordsman. Scenes that capture Phil's delight at watching George spar with Richard are extended when the trooper goes through his military paces as a birthday treat for the eagerly gazing Phil. These subtly erotic scenes of Phil's physical scrutiny of George in action resonate with Dickens's novel's attention to Phil's routine delight in watching George wash. The astute Mr Bucket's interpretation of this performance as 'savage amusements', perhaps does not do full justice to the benevolence of George's militarism here. I see Davies's celebration of George as the previously unsung gentle hero of *Bleak House* as a parallel to what I have tried to achieve in this book.

As these chapters and postscript have shown, Dickens is tirelessly reworked in and outside the academy. Given the intense cultural investments in this figure in Europe and North America, I propose that an appreciation of Dickens's fascination with queer desires, families and lives can make a political intervention into the way we live now. It is my hope that a broader field of queer interpretation and enquiry will be part of our continuing reinvention of the Victorians, a reinvention that fills in the blind-spots of existing histories of sexuality, extending our appreciation of erotic vitality that exceeds those categories that we now find it difficult to think outside of, and that will help to reclaim the family from its conservative appropriators as a historically valid space of queer possibility. At the same time I want *Queer Dickens* to provoke some rethinking in queer theory as it is currently constituted, and to provide an alternative, optimistic line of genealogy for queer parents and children, the determinedly unmarried, gentle men, and would-be lighthouse keepers today.

Bibliography

BOOKS, ARTICLES, PAPERS

Ackroyd, Peter, *Dickens* (London: Sinclair Stevenson, 1990).

Adrian, Arthur, *Dickens and the Parent-Child Relationship* (Ohio: Ohio University Press, 1984).

Ahmed, Sara, *Queer Phenomenology: Orientations, Objects, Others* (Durham: Duke University Press, 2006).

Alcott, Louisa M., *Hospital Sketches* (Massachusetts: Harvard University Press, 1960).

Aldrich, Robert, *Colonialism and Homosexuality* (London and New York: Routledge, 2003).

——, *The Seduction of the Mediterranean* (London and New York: Routledge, 1993).

Ali, Muhsin Jassim, *Scheherazade in England* (Washington DC: Three Continents Press, 1981).

Allingham, Phillip, 'Introduction to John McLenan's *Harper's Weekly* illustrations to *Great Expectations*', http://www.victorianweb.org/art/illustration/mclenan/intro.html.

Altick, Richard, *The Presence of the Present: Topics of the Day in the Victorian Novel* (Columbus: Ohio State University Press, 1991).

Andrews, Malcolm, *Charles Dickens and His Performing Selves: Dickens and the Public Readings* (Oxford: Oxford University Press, 2006).

——, *Dickens and the Grown Up Child* (Basingstoke: Macmillan, 1994).

Archibald, Diana, *Domesticity, Imperialism and Emigration in The Victorian Novel* (Missouri: University of Missouri Press, 2002).

Armstrong, Mary, 'Pursuing Perfection: Dombey and Son, Female Homoerotic Desire, and the Sentimental Heroine', *Studies in the Novel* 28.3 (1996), 281–302.

——, ' "What Can You Two Be Together?": Charles Dickens, Female Homoerotic Desire and the Work of Heterosexual Recovery' (Doctoral thesis, Duke University, 1995).

Arnett, James, 'Striking Abjection, Evacuating Horror'. Paper given at the British Association for Victorian Studies conference, University of Leicester, 3 September 2008.

Bachelard, Gaston, *The Poetics of Space*, trans. Maria Jolas (Boston: Beacon, 1992).

Bailin, Miriam, *The Sickroom in Victorian Fiction* (Cambridge: Cambridge University Press, 1994).

Ball, Roy, 'The Development of Smike', *Dickensian*, 62 (1966), 125–8.

Barickman, Richard, Susan MacDonald, and Myra Stark, *Corrupt Relations: Dickens, Thackeray, Trollope, Collins and the Victorian Sexual System* (New York: Columbia University Press, 1982).

Barringer, Tim, *Men at Work: Art and Labour in Victorian Britain* (New Haven and London: Yale University Press, 2005).

Bartlett, Neil, *Who Was That Man? A Present for Mr Oscar Wilde* (London: Serpent's Tail, 1988).

Bashford, Alison, *Purity and Pollution: Gender Embodiment and Victorian Medicine* (Basingstoke: Macmillan, 1998).

Beer, Gillian, *George Eliot* (Sussex: Harvester, 1996).

Behlmer, George, 'What's Love Got to Do With It? Adoption in Victorian and Edwardian England', in *Adoption in America: Historical Perspectives*, ed. Wayne Carp (Michigan: University of Michigan Press, 2002), pp. 82–100.

——, *Friends of the Family: The English Home and its Guardians, 1850–1940* (Stanford: Stanford University Press, 1998).

Bell, David, and Gill Valentine (eds.), *Mapping Desire: Geographies of Sexualities* (London: Routledge, 1995).

Bentham, Jeremy, *The works of Jeremy Bentham*, ed. John Bowring, 11 vols. (New York: Russell and Russell, 1962).

Bentley, Nicholas, Michael Slater, and Nina Burgis (eds.), *The Dickens Index* (Oxford: Oxford University Press, 1988).

Berebitsky, Julie, *Like Our Very Own: Adoption and the Changing Culture of Motherhood* (Kansas: University Press of Kansas, 2000).

Berlant, Lauren, *The Queen of America Goes to Washington City: Essays on Sex and Citizenship* (Durham and London: Duke University Press, 1997).

Bernstein, Mary, and Renate Reimann (eds), *Queer Families, Queer Politics* (New York: Columbia University Press, 2001).

Bersani, Leo, *Homos* (Cambridge, MA: Harvard University Press, 1995).

Blackman, Lisa, 'Is Happiness Contagious?' *New Formations* 63 (2008), 15–32.

Bleys, Rudi, *The Geography of Perversion* (New York and London: Cassell, 1996).

——, 'Homosexual Exile: The Textuality of the Imaginary Paradise, 1800–1980' in *Gay Studies from the French Cultures*, ed. Rommel Mendès-Leite and Pierre-Olivier de Busscher (New York: Haworth Press, 1993), pp. 165–82.

Bodenheimer, Rosemarie, *Knowing Dickens* (Ithaca and London: Cornell University Press, 2007).

Boone, Joseph, 'Rubbing Aladdin's Lamp', in *Negotiating Lesbian and Gay Subjects*, ed. Monika Dorenkamp and Richard Henke (New York and London: Routledge, 1995), pp. 149–77.

——, 'Vacation Cruises: or the Homoerotics of Orientalism', *PMLA* 110.1 (1995), 89–107.

——, *Tradition Counter Tradition: Love and the Form of Fiction* (Chicago and London: University of Chicago Press, 1987).

Boone, Joseph, and Deborah Nord, 'Brother and Sister: The Seductions of Siblinghood in Dickens, Eliot and Brontë, ' *Western Humanities Review* 46.2 (1992), 164–88.

Bourne Taylor, Jenny, ' "Received, a Blank Child": John Brownlow, Charles Dickens and the London Foundling Hospital – Archives and Fictions', *Nineteenth Century Literature* 56.3 (2001), 293–363.

——, 'Representing Illegitimacy in Victorian Culture', in *Victorian Identities, Social and Cultural Formations in Nineteenth Century Literature*, ed. Ruth Robbins and Julian Wolfreys (Basingstoke: Macmillan, 1996), pp. 119–142.

Bowen, John, *Other Dickens: Pickwick to Chuzzlewit* (Oxford: Oxford University Press, 2000).

——, 'Bebelle and "His Boots": Dickens, Ellen Ternan and the *Christmas Stories*', *The Dickensian* 96.3 (2000), 197–208.

Bowning, Frank, *A Queer Geography: Journeys Toward a Sexual Self* (New York: Crown, 1996).

Bradbury, Nicola, 'Dickens and James: "Watching with my Eyes Closed": The Dream Abroad', *Dickens Quarterly* 17.2 (2000), 77–87.

Braddon, Mary Elizabeth, *Lady Audley's Secret* (London: Penguin, 1998).

Brake, Laurel, *Print in Transition, 1850–1910: Studies in Media and Book History* (Basingstoke: Palgrave, 2001).

Brennan, Teresa, *The Transmission of Affect* (Ithaca: Cornell University Press, 2004).

Brontë, Charlotte, *The Letters of Charlotte Brontë*, ed. Margaret Smith, 3 vols. (Oxford: Clarendon Press, 1995–2004).

Brooks, Peter, *Reading for the Plot: Design and Intention in Narrative* (1984, repr. Harvard: Harvard University Press, 2002).

Brownlow, John, *Hans Sloane: A Tale Illustrating the History of the Foundling Hospital in London* (London: F Warr, 1831).

——, 'Observations on the Education and General Treatment of the Children of the Foundling Hospital', unpublished pamphlet (1827), London Metropolitan Archives, A/FH/MOI/067.

Buckton, Oliver S., ' "The Reader Whom I Love": Homoerotic Secrets in *David Copperfield*,' *ELH* 64.1 (1997), 189–222.

Bullough, Vern, 'Men in Nursing', *Journal of Professional Nursing* 10.5 (1995), 267.

——, 'Men, Women, and Nursing History', *Journal of Professional Nursing* 10.3 (1994), 127.

Bulwer Lytton, Edward, *Pelham, or Adventures of a Gentleman* (London: Routledge, 1848).

Butler, Judith, *Undoing Gender* (New York: Routledge, 2004).

——, 'Is Kinship Always Already Heterosexual?', *differences* 13.1 (2002), 14–44.

——, *Bodies that Matter: On the Discursive Limits of Sex* (New York and London: Routledge, 1993).

——, *Gender Trouble: Feminism and the Subversion of Identity* (London: Routledge, 1990).

Byron, George Gordon, *Byron's Letters and Journals*, ed. Leslie Marchand, 12 vols. (Cambridge: Harvard University Press, 1973–82).

——, *Byron: A Self Portrait: Letters and Dairies*, ed. Peter Quennell, 2 vols. (London: Murray, 1950).

Carlton, W. J., 'The Third Man at Newgate', *Review of English Studies* 8 (1957), 402–407.

Carnell, Jennifer, *The Literary Lives of Mary Elizabeth Braddon* (Hastings: The Sensation Press, 2000).

Carsten, Janet, *After Kinship?* (Cambridge: Cambridge University Press, 2004).

Caserio, Robert, Lee Edelman, Judith Halberstam, Jose Esteban Munoz, and Tim Dean, 'The Antisocial Thesis in Queer Theory', *PMLA* 121.3 (2006), 819–27.

Castle, Terry, *The Apparitional Lesbian: Female Homosexuality and Modern Culture* (New York: Columbia University Press, 1993).

Chambers, Diane, 'Triangular Desire and the Sororal Bond: The Deceased Wife's Sister Bill' *Mosaic* 29.1 (1996), 19–36.

Chase, Karen, and Michael Levenson, *The Spectacle of Intimacy: A Public Life for the Victorian Family* (Princeton: Princeton University Press, 2000).

Christ, Carol, 'Victorian Masculinity and the Angel in the House' in *A Widening Sphere: Changing Roles of Victorian Women*, ed. Martha Vicinus (1977, repr. London: Methuen, 1980), pp. 146–62.

Chudacoff, Howard, *The Age of the Bachelor: Creating an American Subculture* (Princeton: Princeton University Press, 1999).

Clarke, Edward, *Jaspar Tristram*, (London: Heinemann, 1899).

Classen, Constance (ed.) *The Book of Touch*, 'Fingerprints: Writing about Touch' (Oxford and New York: Berg, 2005), pp. 1–9.

Clover, Joshua, and Christopher Nealon, 'Don't Ask, Don't Tell', *Film Quarterly* 60.3 (2007), 62–7.

Clutterbuck, Lady Maria (alias Catherine Dickens), *What Shall We Have for Dinner?* (London: Bradbury and Evans, 1852).

Cocks, H. G., *Nameless Offences: Homosexual Desire in the Nineteenth Century* (London and New York: Tauris, 2003).

Cody, John, *After Great Pain: The Inner Life of Emily Dickinson* (Massachusetts: Belknap Press, 1971).

Cohen, William, *Sex Scandal: The Private Parts of Victorian Fiction* (Durham: Duke University Press, 1996).

Colby, Robert, *Fiction with a Purpose* (Bloomington: Indiana University Press, 1967).

Colligan, Colette, ' "A Race of Born Pederasts": Sir Richard Burton, Homosexuality, and the Arabs', *Nineteenth Century Contexts* 25 (2003), 1–20.

——, 'Raising the House Tops: Sexual Surveillance in Charles Dickens's *Dombey and Son* (1846–8)', *Dickens Studies Annual* 29 (2000), 99–123.

Collins, Philip, 'Dickens's Reading', *Dickensian* 60 (1964), 136–51.

Collins. Phillip (ed.), *Dickens: The Critical Heritage* (London: Routledge and Keegan Paul, 1971).

Collins, Wilkie, *Hide and Seek* (Oxford: Oxford University Press, 1999).

——, *The Law and the Lady* (Oxford: Oxford University Press, 1999).

——, *Poor Miss Finch* (Oxford: Oxford University Press, 1995).

Coppock, A. J., 'Smike, ' *Dickensian* 35 (1939), 162–3.

Coward, Rosalind, *Patriarchal Precedents: Sexuality and Social Relations* (London: Routledge, 1983).

Craik, Dinah, *John Halifax, Gentleman* (Gloucestershire: Nonsuch, 2005).

Cregan-Reid, Vybarr, 'Bodies, Boundaries and Queer Waters: Drowning and Prosopopœia in Later Dickens', *Critical Survey* 17.2 (2005), 20–33.

——, 'Drowning in Early Dickens', *Textual Practice* 19.1 (2005), 71–91.

Creveld, Martin van, *Transformation of War* (New York: The Free Press, 1991).

Crompton, Louis, *Byron and Greek Love: Homophobia in Nineteenth Century England* (Berkeley: University of California Press, 1985).

Cruikshank, George, *The Bachelor's Own Book* (Glasgow: David Bryce, 1888).

Cruse, Amy, *The Victorians and Their Books* (London: George Allen and Unwin, 1935).

Cvetkovich, Ann, *Mixed Feelings: Feminism, Mass Culture and Victorian Sensationalism* (New Brunswick: Rutgers University Press, 1992).

Dacey, Philip, 'Walt Whitman Falls Asleep Over Florence Nightingale's *Notes on Nursing*', *Shenandoah* 45.2 (1995), 36–9.

Dalziel, Margaret, *Popular Fiction 100 Years Ago* (Philadelphia: Dufour, 1958).

Das, Santanu, 'The Dying Kiss: Intimacy and Gender in the Trenches of the First World War', in *The Book of Touch*, ed. Constance Classen (Oxford and New York: Berg, 2005), pp. 188–197.

——, *Touch and Intimacy in First World War Literature* (Cambridge: Cambridge University Press, 2005).

Davidoff, Leonore, *Worlds Between: Historical Perspectives on Gender and Class* (Oxford: Blackwell, 1995).

Davidoff, Leonore, and Catherine Hall, *Family Fortunes: Men and Women of the English Middle Class 1790–1850* (London: Hutchinson, 1987).

Davidoff, Leonore, Megan Doolittle, Janet Fink, Katherine Holden, *The Family Story: Blood, Contract and Intimacy 1830–1860* (London and New York: Longman, 1999).

Davis, Robert Leigh, *Whitman and the Romance of Medicine* (Berkeley and London: University of California Press, 1997).

Dawson, Gowan, *Darwin, Literature and Victorian Respectability* (Cambridge: Cambridge University Press, 2007).

Defoe, Daniel, 'The True Born Englishman', *The Novels and Miscellaneous Works of Daniel De Foe*, ed. Walter Scott, 6 vols. (London: Bohn, 1854–1856), V (1855), pp. 434–63.

Dellamora, Richard, *Friendship's Bonds: Democracy and the Novel in Victorian England* (Philadelphia: University of Pennsylvania Press, 2004).

Dickens, Charles, *A Christmas Carol and Other Christmas Writings* (London: Penguin, 2003).

——, *A Tale of Two Cities* (London: Penguin, 2003).

——, *American Notes and Pictures from Italy* (London: Oxford University Press, 1957).

——, *Bleak House* (London: Penguin, 1996).

——, *David Copperfield* (London: Penguin, 1996).

——, *Dombey and Son* (London: Penguin, 2002).

——, *Great Expectations* (London: Penguin, 2003).

——, *Hard Times* (London: Penguin, 2003).

——, *Little Dorrit* (London: Penguin, 1998).

——, *Martin Chuzzlewit* (London: Penguin, 1999).

——, *Master Humphrey's Clock*, 3 volumes (London: Chapman and Hall, 1840).

——, *Nicholas Nickleby* (London: Penguin, 1999).

——, *Oliver Twist* (London, Penguin, 2003).

——, *Our Mutual Friend* (London: Penguin, 1997).

——, *Sketches by Boz* (London: Penguin, 1995).

——, *The Battle of Life* (London: Penguin, 1985).

——, *The Christmas Stories*, ed. Ruth Glancy (London: Everyman, 1996).

Dickens, Charles, *The Letters of Charles Dickens*, vol. I: 1820–1839. Pilgrim Edition, ed. Madeline House and Graham Storey (Oxford: Clarendon Press, 1965).

——, *The Letters of Charles Dickens*, vol. III: 1842–1843, Pilgrim Edition, ed. Madeline House, Graham Storey and Kathleen Tillotson (Oxford: Clarendon Press, 1974).

——, *The Letters of Charles Dickens*, vol. VII: 1853–1855, Pilgrim edition, ed. Graham Storey, Kathleen Tillotson and Angus Easson (Oxford: Clarendon Press, 1993).

——, *The Mystery of Edwin Drood* (London: Penguin, 2002).

——, *The Old Curiosity Shop* (London: Penguin, 2000).

——, *The Pickwick Papers* (London: Penguin, 2003).

Dickens, Mamie, *My Father as I Recall Him* (1897).

Dilke, Charles, *Greater Britain: Charles Dilke Visits Her New Lands 1866 and 1867*, ed. G. Blainey (Sydney: Methuen Haynes, 1985).

Dinshaw, Carolyn, 'Got Medieval?', *Journal of the History of Sexuality* 10.2 (2001), 202–12.

——, *Getting Medieval: Sexualities and Communities, Pre and Post Modern* (Durham and London: Duke University Press, 1999).

——, 'Chaucer's Queer Touches/ A Queer Touches Chaucer', *Exemplaria* 7.1 (1995), 75–92.

Doan, Laura, 'Queer Trouble: On the Limits of Lesbian History'. Paper presented to the Queer at King's London Seminar, January 2007.

Doan, Laura, and Chris Waters, 'Homosexualities', in *Sexology Uncensored: The Documents of Sexual Science*, ed. Lucy Bland and Laura Doan (Cambridge: Polity Press, 1998).

Dolin, Tim, 'Race and the Social Plot in *The Mystery of Edwin Drood*' in *The Victorians and Race*, ed. Shearer West (Aldershot: Scolar Press, 1996), pp. 84–101.

Dollimore, Jonathan, *Sexual Dissidence: Augustine to Wilde, Freud to Foucault* (Oxford: Clarendon, 1991).

Dorre, Gina Marlene, 'Handling the "Iron Horse": Dickens, Travel and Derailed Masculinity in *The Pickwick Papers*', *Nineteenth Century Studies* 16 (2002), 1–19.

Dossey, B. M., *Florence Nightingale: Mystic, Visionary, Healer* (Springhouse PA: Springhouse, 1996).

Dreher, Nan, 'Redundancy and Emigration: The 'Woman Question' in Mid-Victorian Britain', *Victorian Periodicals Review* 26.1 (1993), 4–8.

Drew, John, 'Voyages Extraordinaires: Dickens's "Travelling Essays" and *The Uncommercial Traveller*', *Dickens Quarterly* 13.2 (1996), 76–96.

Drew, John, and Anthony Chennells, 'Savages and Settlers in Dickens: Reading Multiple Centres', in *Dickens and the Children of Empire*, ed. Wendy Jacobson (Basingstoke: Palgrave, 2000), pp. 153–72.

Bibliography 261

Duggan, Lisa, *The Twilight of Equality? Neoliberalism, Cultural Politics and the Attack on Democracy* (Boston: Beacon Press, 2003).

Duncan, Nancy, 'Renegotiating Gender and Sexuality in Public and Private Spaces', in *Body Space: Destabilising Geographies of Gender and Sexuality*, ed. Nancy Duncan (London: Routledge, 1996), pp. 127–45.

Edelman, Lee, *No Future: Queer Theory and the Death Drive* (Durham and London: Duke University Press, 2004).

Edgecombe, R. S., 'Topographic Disaffection in Dickens's *American Notes* and *Martin Chuzzlewit*', *Journal of English and Germanic Philology* 93 (1994), 35–54.

Edgeworth, Maria, *Belinda* (London and New York: Pandora, 1987).

Elfenbein, Andrew, *Byron and the Victorians* (Cambridge: Cambridge University Press, 1995).

Eli Adams, James, *Dandies and Desert Saints: Styles of Victorian Manhood* (Ithaca and London: Cornell University Press, 1995).

Eliot, George, *Felix Holt: The Radical* (London: Penguin, 1995).

——, *Silas Marner* (Oxford: Oxford University Press, 1998).

Elliot, Kamilla, *Rethinking the Novel/Film Debate* (Cambridge: Cambridge University Press, 2003).

Eng, David, 'Transnational Adoption and Queer Diasporas', *Social Text* 21.3 (2003), 1–37.

Eng, David, with Judith Halberstam and José Muñoz, 'What's Queer about Queer Studies Now', *Social Text* 23 (2005), 1–18.

Evans, John, 'Men in Nursing: Issues of Gender Segregation and Hidden Advantage', *Journal of Advanced Nursing* 26.2 (1997), 226–31.

Everett, Nicholas, 'Autobiography as Prophecy: Walt Whitman's "Specimen Days"', in *Mortal Pages: Literary Lives, Studies in Nineteenth Century Autobiography*, ed. Vincent Newey and Phillip Shaw (Aldershot: Scolar Press, 1996), 217–34.

Faderman, Lillian, 'Emily Dickinson's Letters to Sue Gilbert', *Massachusetts Review*, 18.2 (1977), 197–225.

Fagin, Claire, and Donna Diers, 'Nursing as Metaphor', *New England Journal of Nursing* 309 (1983), 116–17.

Fasick, Laura, *Professional Men and Domesticity in the Mid-Victorian Novel* (New York: Edwin Mellen Press, 2003).

Faulkner, David, 'The Confidence Man: Empire and the Deconstruction of Muscular Christianity in *The Mystery of Edwin Drood*' in *Muscular Christianity: Embodying the Victorian Age*, ed. Donald Hall (Cambridge: Cambridge University Press, 1994), pp. 175–93.

Fein, Mara, 'The Politics of Family in *The Pickwick Papers*', *ELH* 61 (1994), 363–79.

Feltes, Norman, *Modes of Production of Victorian Novels* (Chicago: University of Chicago Press, 1986).

Ferguson, Niall, *The Pity of War* (London: Penguin, 1998).

Fiedler, Leslie, 'Images of the Nurse in Fiction and Popular Culture', in *Images of Nurses: Perspectives from History, Art and Literature*, ed. Anne Hudson Jones (Philadelphia: University of Pennsylvania Press, 1988), pp. 100–12.

Field, Katherine, *Hogarth's Children*, exhibition catalogue (London: The Foundling Museum, 2007).

Fone Byrne, R. S., 'This Other Eden: Arcadia and the Homosexual Imagination', in *Literary Visions of Homosexuality*, ed. Stuart Kellog, pp. 13–34.

Forster, E. M., *Maurice* (London: Penguin, 2005).

——, *Maurice* (London: Edward Arnold, 1971).

Forster, John, *The Life of Charles Dickens*, 3 vols., (London: Chapman and Hall, 1872–74).

Foster, Jeanette, *Sex Variant Women in Literature* (London: Frederick Muller, 1958).

Foucault, Michel, *The History of Sexuality: Volume 1*, trans. Robert Hurley (1976, repr. London: Penguin, 1998).

——, 'Nietzsche, Genealogy, History' (1971) repr. in *The Foucault Reader*, ed. Paul Rabinow (London: Penguin, 1991), pp. 76–100.

——, *Of Other Spaces: Heterotopias* (1967), trans. Jay Miskowiec, http://www.foucault.info/documents/heteroTopia/foucault.heteroTopia.en.html.

Franklin, Sarah, and Helena Ragone (eds), *Reproducing Reproduction: Kinship, Power and Technological Innovation* (Philadelphia: University of Pennsylvania Press, 1998).

Franklin, Sarah, and Susan Mckinnon, *Relative Values: Reconfiguring Kinship Studies* (Durham and London: Duke University Press, 2001).

Fraser, Rebecca, *Charlotte Brontë* (London: Methuen, 1988).

Freer, Scott, 'The Abandoned Child: The Dickensian Influences in Chaplin's *The Kid*' (forthcoming).

Frost, Ginger, *Promises Broken: Courtship, Class and Gender in Victorian England* (Charlottesville and London: University Press of Virginia, 1995).

Furneaux, Holly, 'Negotiating the Gentle-Man: Male Nursing and Class Conflict in the High Victorian Period', forthcoming in *Victorian Literary Cultures in Conflict*, ed. Dinah Birch and Mark Llewellyn (Basingstoke, Palgrave, forthcoming).

——, 'Homoeroticism in the novels of Charles Dickens' (doctoral thesis, University of London, 2005).

Gillis, John, *A World of their own Making: Myth, Ritual and the Quest for Family Values* (New York: Harper Collins, 1996).

Gilmour, Robin, *The Idea of the Gentleman in the Victorian Novel* (London: Allen and Unwin, 1981).

——, 'Dickens, Tennyson and the Past', *Dickensian* 75 (1979), 131–42.

Girouard, Mark, *The Return to Camelot: Chivalry and the English Gentleman* (New Haven and London: Yale University Press, 1981).

Glavin, John, 'Pickwick on the Wrong Side of the Door', *Dickens Studies Annual* 22 (1993), 1–20.

—— (ed.), *Dickens on Screen* (Cambridge: Cambridge University Press, 2003), 1–10.

Gopinath, Gayatri, *Impossible Desires: Queer Diasporas and South Asian Public Cultures* (Durham and London: Duke University Press, 2005).

Gray, Beryl, 'Nobody's Daughters: Dickens's Tattycoram and George Eliot's Caterina Sarti', *George Eliot Review* 32 (2001), 51–62.

Gruner, Elisabeth Rose, 'Born and Made: Sisters, Brothers and the Deceased Wife's Sister Bill', *Signs* 24.2 (1999), 423–47.

Hack, E., and W. Armytage, *Thomas Hughes: The Life of the Author of Tom Brown's Schooldays* (London: Ernest Benn, 1952).

Hager, Kelly, 'Estranging David Copperfield: Reading the Novel of Divorce', *ELH* 63.4 (1996), 989–1019.

——, 'Plotting Marriage: Dickens, Divorce and the Failed-Marriage Plot' (Doctoral thesis, University of California, 1992).

Haggerty, George, 'Love and Loss: An Elegy', *GLQ* 10.3 (2004), 385–405.

——, 'Desire and Mourning: The Ideology of the Elegy', in *Ideology and Form in Eighteenth Century Literature*, ed. David Richter (Texas: Texas Tech University Press, 1999), pp. 385–405.

Halberstam, Judith, *In a Queer Time and Place: Transgender Bodies, Subcultural Lives* (New York: New York University Press, 2005).

——, *Female Masculinity* (Durham and London: Duke University Press, 1998).

Halperin, David, 'Forgetting Foucault: Acts, Identities and the History of Sexuality', *Representations* 63 (1998), 93–120.

Hanson, Ellis, 'Undead', in *Inside/Out Lesbian Theories, Gay Theories*, ed. Diana Fuss (New York and London: Routledge, 1991), pp. 324–40.

Harper, J. Henry, *The House of Harper: A Century of Publishing in Franklin Square* (New York and London: Harper and Brothers, 1912).

Hartley, Jenny, *Dickens and the House of Fallen Women* (London: Methuen, 2008).

Hawksley, Lucinda, *Katey: The Life and Loves of Dickens's Artist Daughter* (London: Random House, 2006).

Hayes, Jarrod, *Queer Nations: Marginal Sexualities in the Maghreb* (Chicago and London: University of Chicago Press, 2000).

Hayward, Jennifer, *Consuming Pleasures: Active Audiences and Serial Fictions from Dickens to Soap Opera* (Kentucky: University Press of Kentucky, 1997).

Himmelfarb, Gertrude, *The Demoralisation of Society: From Victorian Values to Modern Values* (London: Institute of Economic Affairs, 1995).

Hinsliff, Gaby, 'Bring Back Victorian Values, says Key Tory', *Observer*, 10 December 2006.

Hollingsworth, Keith, *The Newgate Novel: 1830–1847* (Michigan: Wayne State University Press, 1963).

Houston, Gail Turley, *Consuming Fictions: Gender, Class and Hunger in Dickens's Novels* (Carbondale and Edwardsville: Southern Illinois University Press, 1994).

Hughes, Linda and Michael Lund, *The Victorian Serial* (Charlottesville and London: University Press of Virginia, 1991).

Hughes, Thomas, *Tom Brown's Schooldays* (Oxford: Oxford University Press, 1999).

Hunt, John (ed.), *In Memoriam: A Casebook* (Basingstoke: Macmillan, 1970).

Hyde, H. Montgomery, *The Other Love: A Historical and Contemporary Survey of Homosexuality in Britain* (London: Mayflower, 1972).

Ireland, Mrs Alexander (ed.), Selections from the Letters of Geraldine Endsor Jewsbury to Jane Welsh Carlyle (London: Longmans, 1892).

Jagose, Annamarie, 'Remembering Miss Wade: *Little Dorrit* and the Historicizing of Female Perversity', *GLQ* 4.3 (1998), 423–51.

James, Louis, 'The Trouble with Betsy: Periodicals and the Common Reader in Mid-Nineteenth Century England', in *The Victorian Periodical Press: Samplings and Soundings*, ed. Joanne Shattock and Michael Wolff (Toronto: Leicester University Press and University of Toronto Press, 1982), pp. 349–66.

——, *Fiction for the Working Man 1830–50: A Study of the Literature Produced for the Working Classes in Early Victorian Urban England* (Oxford: Oxford University Press, 1963).

Jones, Garrett, *Alfred and Arthur, an Historic Friendship* (Hertford: Authors Online, 2001).

Jones, Lloyd, *Mister Pip* (London: John Murray, 2007).

Joseph, Gerhard, 'Dickens, Psychoanalysis and Film: A Roundtable', in *Dickens on Screen*, ed. John Glavin (Cambridge: Cambridge University Press, 2003), pp. 11–26.

Judd, Catherine, *Bedside Seductions: Nursing and the Victorian Imagination, 1830–1880* (Basingstoke: Macmillan, 1998).

Jump, John (ed.), *Tennyson: The Critical Heritage* (London: Routledge, 1967).

Kane, Penny, *Victorian Families in Fact and Fiction* (Basingstoke: Macmillan, 1995).

Kaplan, Cora, *Victoriana: Histories, Fiction, Criticism* (Edinburgh: Edinburgh University Press, 2007).

Bibliography 265

Kaplan, Fred, *Dickens* (Baltimore and London: John Hopkins University Press, 1988).

——, *Dickens and Mesmerism: The Hidden Springs of Fiction* (Princeton: Princeton University Press, 1975).

Katz, Jonathan Ned, *Love Stories: Sex Between Men Before Homosexuality* (Chicago and London: University of Chicago Press, 2001).

Kellog, Stuart (ed.), 'The Uses of Homosexuality in Literature', in *Literary Visions of Homosexuality* (Philadelphia: Haworth Press, 1983), pp. 1–12.

Kestner, Joseph, *Masculinities in Victorian Painting* (Aldershot: Scolar, 1995).

Kincaid, James, 'Fattening Up on Pickwick', *Novel* 25 (1992), 235–44.

——, *Child-Loving: The Erotic Child and Victorian Culture* (New York: Routledge, 1992).

Kinney, Katherine, 'Making Capital: War, Labour, and Whitman in Washington D.C.', in *Breaking Bounds: Whitman and American Cultural Studies*, ed. Betsy Erkkila and Jay Grossman (New York and Oxford: Oxford University Press, 1996), pp. 174–92.

Knapp, B., *Walt Whitman* (New York: Continuum, 1993).

Kolb, Jack, 'Hallam, Tennyson, Homosexuality and the Critics', *Philological Quarterly* 79.3 (2000), 365–96.

—— (ed.), *The Letters of Arthur Henry Hallam* (Columbus: Ohio State University Press, 1981).

Kosky, Jules, *Mutual Friends: Charles Dickens and the Great Ormond Street Children's Hospital* (London: Weidenfeld and Nicholson, 1989).

Lane, Margaret, 'Dickens on the Hearth' in *Dickens 1970: Centenary Essays*, ed. Michael Slater (London: Chapman and Hall, 1970), pp. 153–72.

Ledger, Sally, *Dickens and the Popular Radical Imagination* (Cambridge: Cambridge University Press, 2007).

——, 'From Queen Caroline to Lady Dedlock: Dickens and the Popular Radical Imagination', *Victorian Literature and Culture* 32.2 (2004), 575–600.

Lefebvre, Henri, *The Production of Space* (1974), trans. Donald Nicholson-Smith (Oxford: Blackwell, 1991).

Léger, J. M., 'The Scrooge in the Closet: Homoerotic Tropes in the Novels of Charles Dickens' (Doctoral thesis, University of Notre Dame, 1991).

Levi, Peter, *Tennyson* (Basingstoke: Macmillan, 1993).

Levi-Strauss, Claude, *The Elementary Structures of Kinship*, trans. James Hare Bell, John von Sturmer and Rodney Needham (Boston: Beacon, 1969).

Lewandosi, Ken, 'A New Transportation for the Penitentiary Era: Some *Household Words* on Free Emigration', *Victorian Periodicals Review* 26.1 (1993), 8–18.

Littlewood, Ian, *Sultry Climates: Travel and Sex* (London: Murray, 2001).

Litvack, Leon, 'What Books Did Dickens Buy and Read? Evidence from the Book Accounts with his Publishers', *Dickensian* 94.2 (1998), 85–130.

Lochrie, Karma, *Heterosynchrasies: Female Sexuality When Normal Wasn't* (Minneapolis: University of Minnesota Press, 2005).

Lougy, Robert, 'Nationalism and Violence: America in Dickens's *Martin Chuzzlewit*', in *Dickens and the Children of Empire*, ed. Wendy Jacobson (Basingstoke: Palgrave, 2000), pp. 105–15.

——, 'Repressive and Expressive Forms: The Bodies of Comedy and Desire in *Martin Chuzzlewit*,' *Dickens Studies Annual* 21 (1992), 37–61.

Love, Heather, 'Compulsory Happiness and Queer Existence', *New Formations* 63 (2008), 52–64.

——, *Feeling Backward: Loss & the Politics of Queer History* (Massachusetts: Harvard University Press, 2007).

Lubitz, Rita, *Marital Power in Dickens's Fiction* (New York: Peter Lang, 1996).

Lucey, Michael, *The Misfit of the Family: Balzac and the Social Forms of Sexuality* (Durham and London: Duke University Press, 2003).

Macduff, Colin, 'Meeting the Mother Man: Rediscovering Walt Whitman, Writer and Nurse', *International History of Nursing Journal* 3.2 (1997–8), 32–44.

Mackintosh, Carolyn, 'A Historical Study of Men in Nursing', *Journal of Advanced Nursing* 26.2 (1997), 232–6.

Maine, Henry Summer, *Ancient Law* (New Brunswick: Transaction, 2002).

Mangham, Andrew (ed.), *Wilkie Collins: Interdisciplinary Essays*, (Newcastle: Cambridge Scholars Publishing, 2007).

Marcus, Sharon, *Between Women: Friendship, Desire, and Marriage in Victorian England* (Princeton: Princeton University Press, 2007).

Marcus, Steven, *The Other Victorians: A Study of Sexuality and Pornography in Mid-Nineteenth-Century England* (London: Weidenfield and Nicolson, 1966).

——, 'Who is Fagin', in *Oliver Twist* (1965, repr. New York: Norton, 1993).

Markwick, Margaret, 'Hands-on Fatherhood in Trollope's Novels', in *Gender and Fatherhood in the Nineteenth Century*, ed. Trev Lynn Broughton and Helen Rogers (Basingstoke: Palgrave, 2007), pp. 85–95.

Marsh, Joss Lutz, 'Good Mrs Brown's Connections: Sexuality and Story Telling in *Dealings with the Firm of Dombey and Son*', *ELH* 58 (1991), 405–26.

Martin, Robert Bernard, *Tennyson: The Unquiet Heart* (Oxford: Faber, 1980).

Marvel, I. K., *Reveries of a Bachelor: Or a Book of the Heart* (London: David Bogue, 1852).

Mason, Michael, *The Making of Victorian Sexuality* (Oxford and New York: Oxford University Press, 1994).

May, Leila Silvana, *Disorderly Sisters: Sibling Relations and Sororal Resistance in Nineteenth Century British Culture* (Lewisburg: Bucknell University Press, 2001).

Mayne, Xavier, *The Intersexes* (privately printed, 1908).

McCuskey, Brian, '"Your Love-Sick Pickwick": The Erotics of Service', *Dickens Studies Annual* 25 (1996), 245–66.

Mendes, Peter, *Clandestine Erotic Fiction in English, 1800–1930: A Bibliographic Study* (Aldershot, Scolar Press, 1993).

Metz, Nancy Aycock, '"Fevered with Anxiety for Home": Nostalgia and the New Emigrant in *Martin Chuzzlewit*', *Dickens Quarterly* 18.2 (2001), 49–62.

Michie, Elsie, *Outside the Pale: Cultural Exclusion, Gender Difference and the Victorian Woman Writer* (Ithaca: Cornell University Press, 1993).

Michie, Helena, 'From Blood to Law: The Embarrassments of Family in Dickens', in *Palgrave Advances in Charles Dickens Studies*, ed. John Bowen and Robert Pattern (Basingstoke: Palgrave, 2005), pp. 131–55.

——, *Flesh Made Word: Female Figures and Women's Bodies* (Oxford and New York: Oxford University Press, 1987).

Miller, D. A., 'On the Universality of Brokeback Mountain', *Film Quarterly* 60.3 (2007), 50–60.

——, *Narrative and Its Discontents* (Princeton: Princeton University Press, 1981).

Miller, Karl, *Doubles: Studies in Literary History* (Oxford: Oxford University Press, 1985).

Moon, Michael, 'Memorial Rags: Emerson, Whitman, AIDS and Mourning' in *Professions of Desire: Lesbian and Gay Studies in Literature*, ed. George Haggerty and Bonnie Zimmerman (New York: Modern Language Association, 1995), pp. 233–40.

——, *Disseminating Whitman: Revision and Corporeality in* Leaves of Grass (Cambridge, Massachusetts and London: Harvard University Press, 1991).

Moore, Grace, 'Reappraising Dickens's "Noble Savage"', *Dickensian* 98.3 (2002), 236–44.

——, *Dickens and Empire: Discourses of Class Race and Colonialism in the Works of Charles Dickens* (Aldershot: Ashgate, 2004).

Mott, Frank Luther, *A History of American Magazines*, 5 vols. (Cambridge: Harvard University Press, 1938).

Moussa-Mahmoud, Fatma, 'English Travellers and the *Arabian Nights*', in *The Arabian Nights in English Literature*, ed. Peter Caracciolo (Basingstoke: Macmillan, 1988), pp. 95–110.

Murayama, Toshikatsu, 'A Professional Contest Over the Body: Quackery and Respectable Medicine in *Martin Chuzzlewit*', *Victorian Literature and Culture* 30.2 (2002), 403–20.

Murdoch, Iris, *The Bell* (London: Chatto and Windus, 1961).

Nelson, Claudia, *Family Ties in Victorian England* (Connecticut: Praeger, 2007).

——, *Little Strangers: Portrayals of Adoption and Foster Care in America, 1850–1929* (Bloomington and Indianapolis: Indiana University Press, 2003).

Nemesvari, Richard, 'Robert Audley's Secret: Male Homosocial Desire in *Lady Audley's Secret*', *Studies in the Novel* 27.4 (1995), 515–28.

Nightingale, Florence, *Notes on Nursing: What it is and What it is Not* (London: Duckworth, 1970).

Novy, Marianne, *Reading Adoption: Family and Difference in Fiction and Drama* (Michigan: University of Michigan Press, 2005).

——, 'Adoption in *Silas Marner* and *Daniel Deronda*', in *Imagining Adoption: Essays on Literature and Culture*, ed. Marianne Novy (Michigan: University of Michigan Press, 2001), pp. 35–56.

Nunokawa, Jeff, 'All the Sad Young Men: AIDS and the Work of Mourning', in *Inside/Out: Lesbian Theories, Gay Theories*, ed. Diana Fuss (New York and London: Routledge, 1991), pp. 311–23.

——, '*In Memoriam* and the Extinction of the Homosexual', *ELH* 58, (1991), 427–38.

O'Toole, Tess, 'Adoption and the "Improvement of the Estate" in Trollope and in Craik', in *Imagining Adoption: Essays on Literature and Culture*, ed. Marianne Novy (Michigan: University of Michigan Press, 2001), pp. 11–34.

O'Lynn, Chad, 'Men Working as Rural Nurses: Land of Opportunity', in *Rural Nursing: Concepts, Theory and Practice*, ed. Helen Lee and Charlene Winters (New York: Springer, 2006), pp. 232–47.

O'Lynn, Chad, and Russell E. Tranbarger (eds.), *Men in Nursing: History Challenges and Opportunities* (New York: Springer, 2007).

Osterweil, Ara, 'Ang Lee's Lonesome Cowboys', *Film Quarterly* 60.3 (2007), 38–42.

Park, Hyangji, ' "Going to Wake Up Egypt": Exhibiting Empire in *Edwin Drood*', *Victorian Literature and Culture*, 30.2 (2002), 529–50.

Paroissien, David, *The Companion to Oliver Twist* (Edinburgh: Edinburgh University Press, 1992).

Patten, Robert, 'Publishing in Parts', in *Palgrave Advances in Charles Dickens Studies*, ed. John Bowen and Robert Patten (Basingstoke: Palgrave, 2006), pp. 11–47.

Pearlman, E., 'David Copperfield Dreams of Drowning', *American Imago* 28 (1971), pp. 391–403.

Peebles, Robert Lawson, 'Dickens Goes West', in *Views of American Landscapes*, ed. Mark Gridley and Robert Lawson Peebles (Cambridge: Cambridge University Press, 1989), pp. 111–25.

Pevera, Suvendrini, *Reaches of Empire: The English Novel from Edgeworth to Dickens* (New York: Columbia University Press, 1991).

Plummer, Patricia, 'From Agnes Fleming to Helena Landless: Dickens, Women and (Post-) Colonialism', in *Dickens, Europe and the New Worlds*, ed. Anny Sadrin (Basingstoke: Macmillan, 1999), pp. 267–82.

Polhemus, Robert, 'Screen Memories in Dickens and Woody Allen', in *Dickens on Screen*, ed. John Glavin (Cambridge: Cambridge University Press, 2003), pp. 72–85.

Poovey, Mary, *Uneven Developments: The Ideological Work of Gender in Mid-Victorian England* (Chicago and London: University of Chicago Press, 1988).

Prime-Stevenson, Edward, 'Out of the Sun', in *Her Enemy, Some Friends and Other Personages: Stories and Studies of Human Hearts* (Florence: Obsner, 1913). Repr. in *Pages Passed from Hand to Hand: The Hidden Tradition of Homosexual Literature in English from 1748–1914*, ed. Mark Mitchell and David Leavitt (London: Chatto, 1998), pp. 394–403.

Reade, Charles, *The Cloister and the Hearth* (Sherborne: Traviata, 2005).

Retseck, Janet, 'Sexing Miss Wade', *Dickens Quarterly* 15 (1998), 216–25.

Reverby, Susan, *Ordered to Care: The Dilemma of American Nursing, 1850–1945* (New York: Cambridge University Press, 1987).

Ricks, Christopher, *Tennyson* (Basingstoke: Macmillan, 1989).

Ritchie, Anne Thackeray, 'Charles Dickens as I Remember Him', *Pall Mall Magazine* 49, March 1912. Collected in *From the Porch* (New York: Charles Scribner's Sons, 1914).

Robb, Graham, *Strangers: Homosexual Love in the Nineteenth Century* (London: Picador, 2003).

Robson, Catherine, *Men in Wonderland: The Lost Girlhood of the Victorian Gentleman* (Princeton: Princeton University Press, 2001).

Roof, Judith, *Come as You Are: Sexuality and Narrative* (New York: Columbia University Press, 1996).

Rosenberg, Edgar, 'Launching *Great Expectations*', in the Norton critical edition of *Great Expectations*, ed. Edgar Rosenberg (New York: Norton, 1999), pp. 389–437.

Rossetti, William Michael, *Some Reminiscences*, 2 vols. (London: 1906).

Rossi-Wilcox, Susan M., *Dinner for Dickens: The Culinary History of Mrs Charles Dickens's Menu Books* (Totnes: Prospect, 2005).

Rubin, Gayle, 'Notes on the 'Political Economy' of Sex', in *Toward an Anthropology of Women*, ed. Rayna Reiter (New York: Monthly Review Press, 1975), pp. 157–210.

Ruskin, John, *On the Nature of Gothic Architecture and Herein the Functions of the Workman in Art* (London: Smith, Elder and Co., 1854).

Russell, Shannon, 'Recycling the Poor and the Fallen: Emigration Politics and the Narrative Resolutions of *Mary Barton* and *David Copperfield*', in *Imperial Objects: Essays on Victorian Women's Emigration and the Unauthorised Imperial Experience*, ed. Rita Krandis (New York: Twayne, 1998), pp. 43–63.

Russo, Vito, *The Celluloid Closet: Homosexuality in the Movies* (New York: Harper and Row, 1981).

Sabin, Linda, 'Unheralded Nurses: Male Care Givers in the Nineteenth Century South', *Nursing History Review* 5 (1997), 131–48.

Sadrin, Anny, 'Why D.I.J.O.N? Crossing Forbidden Boundaries in *Dombey and Son*', in *Dickens, Europe and the New Worlds*, ed. Anny Sadrin (Basingstoke: Macmillan, 1999), pp. 14–21.

Said, Edward, *Culture and Imperialism*, 4th edn (London: Vintage, 1994).

Sala, George, 'William Hogarth: Painter, Engraver and Philosopher: Essays on the Work and the Time. 1 – Little Boy Hogarth', *Cornhill Magazine* 1 (1860), pp. 177–93.

Sanders, Andrew, 'The Dickens World' in *Creditable Warriors 1850–1876*, ed. Michael Cotsell (London: Ashfield, 1990), pp. 131–42.

Sanders, Valerie, *The Brother-Sister Culture in Nineteenth-Century Literature* (Basingstoke: Palgrave, 2002).

Schad, John (ed.), *Dickens Refigured: Bodies, Desires and Other Histories*, (Manchester and New York: Manchester University Press, 1996).

Schattschneider, Laura, 'Mr Brownlow's Interest in *Oliver Twist*', *JVC* 6.1 (2001), pp. 46–60.

Schlicke, Paul, ed., *Oxford Reader's Companion to Dickens* (Oxford: Oxford University Press, 1999).

Schneider, Jeffrey, 'Secret Sins of the Orient: Creating a (Homo)Textual Context for Reading Byron's *The Giaour*', *College English* 65.1 (2002), 81–95.

Seacole, Mary, *The Wonderful Adventures of Mrs Seacole in Many Lands* (London: Penguin, 2005).

Sebatos, Terri, 'Father as Mother: The Image of the Widower with Children in Victorian Art', in *Gender and Fatherhood in the Nineteenth Century*, ed. Trev Lynn Broughton and Helen Rogers (Basingstoke: Palgrave, 2007), pp. 71–84.

Sedgwick, Eve Kosofsky, *Touching Feeling: Affect, Pedagogy, Performativity* (Durham: Duke University Press, 2003).

——, *Tendencies* (Durham: Duke University Press, 1993).

——, *Epistemology of the Closet* (Berkely: University of California Press, 1990).

——, 'The Beast in the Closet: James and the Writing of Homosexual Panic', in *Sex, Politics and Science in the Nineteenth Century Novel*, ed. Ruth Bernard Yeazell (Baltimore and London: Johns Hopkins University Press, 1986), pp. 148–86.

——, *Between Men: English Literature and Male Homosocial Desire* (New York: Columbia UP, 1985).

Sharrad, Paul, 'Speaking the Unspeakable: London, Cambridge and the Caribbean', in *De-scribing Empire: Post Colonialism and Textuality*, ed. Chris Tiffin and Alan Lawson (London and New York: Routledge, 1994), pp. 201–17.

Shell, Marc, *Children of the Earth: Literature, Politics and Nationhood* (Oxford: Oxford University Press, 1993).

Showalter, Elaine, *Sexual Anarchy: Gender and Culture at the Fin de Siècle* (London: Bloomsbury, 1991).

Slater Michael, 'Dickens in Wonderland', in *The Arabian Nights in English Literature*, ed. Peter Caracciolo (Basingstoke: Macmillan, 1988), pp. 130–42.

——, *An Intelligent Person's Guide to Dickens* (London: Duckworth, London, 1999).

——, *Dickens and Women* (London: Dent, 1983).

Slater, Michael, ed., *Dickens's Journalism*, vol. I: *Sketches by Boz and Other Early Papers, 1833–39* (London: Dent, 1994).

———, ed., *Dickens's Journalism*, vol. III: '*Gone Astray' and Other Papers from Household Words, 1851–59* (London: Dent, 1998).

Slater, Michael and John Drew (eds.), *Dickens's Journalism*, vol. IV: *The Uncommerical Traveller and Other Papers, 1859–70* (London: Dent, 2000).

Smith, Grahame, 'Suppressing Narratives: Childhood and Empire in *The Uncommercial Traveller* and *Great Expectations*', in *Dickens and the Children of Empire*, ed. Wendy Jacobson (Basingstoke: Palgrave, 2000), pp. 43–53.

Smollett, Tobias, *The Adventures of Peregrine Pickle* (Oxford: Oxford University Press, 1969).

———, *The Adventures of Roderick Random* (Oxford: Oxford University Press, 1979).

Snediker, Michael, 'Queer Optimism', *Postmodern Culture* 16.3 (2006), pp. 1–48.

Snyder, Katherine, *Bachelors, Manhood and the Novel 1850–1925* (Cambridge: Cambridge University Press, 1999).

Sprawson, Charles, *Haunts of the Black Masseur: The Swimmer as Hero* (London: Vintage, 2002).

Stace, Wesley, *Misfortune* (London: Jonathan Cape, 2004).

Stearns, Peter, *Be a Man: Males in Modern Society* (New York: Holmes and Meier, 1979, repr. 1990).

Steig, Michael, 'The Intentional Phallus: Determining Verbal Meaning in Literature', *Journal of Aesthetics and Art Criticism* 36 (1977), 51–61.

Sterne, Laurence, *The Life and Opinions of Tristram Shandy, Gentleman* (London: Penguin, 2003).

Stickney Ellis, Sarah, *The Women of England: Their Social Duties and Domestic Habits* (London: Fisher and Son, 1839).

Stockinger, Jacob, 'Homotextuality: A Proposal', in *The Gay Academic*, ed. Louie Crew (Palm Springs: ETC, 1978), pp. 135–51.

Stonehouse, J. H. (ed.), *Catalogue of the Library of Charles Dickens from Gad's Hill* (London: 1935).

Summers, Anne, *Angels and Citizens: British Women as Military Nurses, 1854–1914* (London: Routledge, 1988).

Sweet, Matthew, *Inventing the Victorians* (London: Faber, 2001).

Swenson, Kristine, *Medical Women and Victorian Fiction* (University of Missouri Press: Columbia and London, 2005).

Tennyson, Alfred, *In Memoriam A. H. H.* (New York: Norton, 1973).

Thomas, M. Wynn, 'Fratricide and Brotherly Love: Whitman and the Civil War', in *The Cambridge Companion to Walt Whitman*, ed. Ezra Greenspan (Cambridge: Cambridge University Press, 1995), pp. 27–44.

Tomalin, Claire, *The Invisible Woman: The Story of Nelly Ternan and Charles Dickens*, 2nd edn (London: Penguin, 1991).

Tooley, Sarah, *The History of Nursing in The British Empire* (London: Bousfield, 1906).

Torgovnick, Marianna, *Closure in the Novel* (Princeton: Princeton University Press, 1981).

Tosh, John, *A Man's Place: Masculinity and the Middle-Class Home in Victorian England* (New Haven and London: Yale University Press, 1999).

——, 'Domesticity and Manliness in the Victorian Middle Class: The Family of Edward Benson White', in *Manful Assertions: Masculinities in Britain since 1800*, ed. Michael Roper and John Tosh (London: Routledge, 1991), pp. 44–73.

Trollope, Anthony, *Doctor Thorne* (London: Penguin, 1991).

Turner, Mark, *Backward Glances: Cruising the Queer Streets of New York and London* (London: Reaktion, 2003).

——, *Trollope and the Magazines: Gendered Issues in Mid-Victorian Britain* (Basingstoke: Macmillan, 2000).

Vicinus, Martha, *Intimate Friends: Women who Loved Women, 1778–1928* (Chicago: University of Chicago Press, 2004).

——, *Independent Women: Work and Community for Single Women, 1850–1920* (London: Virago, 1985).

Waller, Jane, *Two Sisters Loving One Man: the Victorians and the Sisterly Ideal* (MA dissertation, Birkbeck College, University of London, 2003).

Ware, Michele S., '"True Legitimacy": The Myth of the Foundling in *Bleak House*', *Studies in the Novel* 22 (1990), 1–9.

Waters, Catherine, *Dickens and the Politics of the Family* (Cambridge: Cambridge University Press, 1997).

Waters, Sarah, *Fingersmith* (London: Virago, 2002).

——, *Affinity* (London: Virago, 1999).

——, *Tipping the Velvet* (London: Virago, 1998).

Watkins, Mary, 'Adoption and Identity: Nomadic Possibilities for Reconceiving the Self', in *Adoptive Families in a Diverse Society*, ed. Katrina Wegar (New Brunswick: Rutgers, 2006), pp. 259–74.

Waugh, Evelyn, *Brideshead Revisited* (London: Penguin, 1970).

Wedd, Kit, *The Foundling Museum Guidebook*, (London: The Foundling Museum, 2004).

Weeks, Jeffrey, *Coming Out: Homosexual Politics in Britain from the Nineteenth Century to the Present* (London: Quartet, 1977).

Weeks, Jeffrey, Brian Heaphy, and Catherine Donvan, *Families of Choice and Other Life Experiments* (London and New York: Yale University Press, 2001).

Wegar, Katrina (ed.), *Adoptive Families in a Diverse Society* (New Brunswick: Rutgers, 2006).

Weiss, Barbara, 'The Dilemma of Happily Ever After: Marriage and the Victorian Novel', in *Portraits of Marriage in Literature*, ed. Anne Hargrave and Maurine Magliocco (Illinois: Western Illinois University Press, 1984), pp. 67–86.

Welsh, Alexander, *The City of Dickens* (Oxford: Clarendon, 1971).

Weston, Kath, *Families We Choose: Lesbians, Gays, Kinship* (New York and Oxford: Columbia University Press, 1991).

White, Chris (ed.), *Nineteenth-Century Writings on Homosexuality: A Sourcebook* (London: Routledge, 1999).

Whitman, Walt, 'The Wound Dresser', *Leaves of Grass and Other Writings*, ed. Michael Moon (New York and London: Norton, 2002).

——, *The Collected Writings of Walt Whitman: The Journalism*, ed. Herbert Bergman, (New York: Peter Lang, 1998).

——, *Civil War Poetry and Prose*, ed. Candace Ward (New York: Dover, 1995).

——, *Specimen Days and Collect* (Philadelphia: Ross Welsh, 1882–3).

Wills, Gary, 'The Loves of *Oliver Twist*' in *Oliver Twist* (1989, repr. New York: Norton, 1993).

Wilson, Anna, 'On History, Case History, and Deviance: Miss Wade's Symptoms and Their Interpretation', *Dickens Studies Annual* 26 (1998), 187–201.

Wiltshire, John, *Jane Austen and the Body* (Cambridge: Cambridge University Press, 1992).

Winter, Alison, *Mesmerized: Powers of Mind in Victorian Britain* (Chicago: University of Chicago Press, 1998).

Winterson, Jeanette, *Lighthousekeeping* (London: HarperCollins, 2005).

Wise, Sarah, *The Italian Boy: Murder and Grave-Robbery in 1830s London* (London: Jonathan Cape, 2004).

Wolfram, Sybil, *Inlaws and Outlaws: Kinship and Marriage in England* (London and Sydney: Croom Helm, 1987).

Wolff, Larry, ' "The Boys are Pickpockets and the Girl is a Prostitute": Gender and Juvenile Criminality in Early Victorian England from *Oliver Twist* to *London Labour*', *New Literary History* 27.2 (1996), 227–49.

Woods, Gregory, 'Fantasy Islands: Popular Topographies of Marooned Masculinity', in *Mapping Desire: Geographies of Sexualities*, ed. David Bell and Gill Valentine (New York and London: Routledge, 1995), pp. 126–148.

Wright, David, 'The Dregs of Society? Occupational Patterns of Male Asylum Attendants in Victorian England', *International History of Nursing Journal* 1.4 (1996), 5–20.

Zieger, Susan, 'Dickens's Queer Children', *LIT* (forthcoming).

——, 'Children, Class and Sexuality in Dickens's and McGrath's *Nicholas Nickleby*'. Paper given at Dickens Universe, UC Santa Cruz, August 2006.

FILMS AND TELEVISION SERIES

A Tale of Two Cities, dir. Ralph Thomas, Rank, 1958.
Bleak House, dir. Justin Chadwick and Susanna White, screenplay by Andrew
    Davies, BBC, 2005.
Boy Called Twist, dir. Tim Greene, Monkey Films and Twisted Pictures, 2004.
Fingersmith, dir. Aisling Walsh, Sally Head Productions, 2005.
Midnight Cowboy, dir. John Schlesinger, Metro-Goldwyn-Mayer, 1969.
Nicholas Nickleby, dir. Douglas McGrath, United Artists, 2002.
Oliver Twist, dir. Coky Giedroyc, BBC, 2007.
Oliver Twist, dir. David Lean, Independent Productions, 1948.
Oliver Twist, dir. Roman Polanski, Pathé, 2005.
Oliver!, dir. Carol Reed, Columbia Pictures, 1968.
Twist, dir. Jacob Tierney, Strand Releasing 2004.
Twisted, dir. Seth Michael Donsky, Miravista, 1996.

ONLINE RESOURCES

http://news.bbc.co.uk
www.curtainup.com
www.digitalspy.co.uk
www.Planetout.com
www.themusicaltwist.com
www.victorianresearch.org
www.victorianweb.org

PERIODICALS AND NEWSPAPERS

All The Year Round
Blackwood's Magazine
Fraser's Magazine
Household Words
Independent
North British Review
Observer
Once a Week
Telegraph Review
The Times

Index